Walter T. Wilson

The Sentences of Pseudo-Phocylides

Commentaries on
Early Jewish Literature
(CEJL)

Edited by
Loren T. Stuckenbruck
and
Pieter W. van der Horst · Hermann Lichtenberger
Doron Mendels · James R. Mueller

Walter de Gruyter · Berlin · New York

Walter T. Wilson

The Sentences of Pseudo-Phocylides

Walter de Gruyter · Berlin · New York

© Printed on acid-free paper which falls within guidelines
on the ANSI to ensure permanence and durability

Library of Congress – Cataloging-in-Publication Data

Wilson, Walter T.
  The sentences of Pseudo-Phocylides / Walter T. Wilson
    p. cm - (Commentaries on early Jewish literature)
  Text of poem in Greek with English translation; commentary in
English.
  Includes bibliographical references and indexes.
  ISBN 3-11-018241-6 (cloth: alk. paper)
  1. Pseudo-Phocylides. Admonitions. 2. Jewish religious poetry
  – History and criticism. 3. Jewish ethics in literature.   I.
Pseudo-
  Phocylides. Admonitions. English & Greek. II. Title. III. Series.
  PA4273.P4A61539 2005
  229'. 306–dc22
  2005022076

ISBN-13: 978-3-11-018241-5
ISBN-10: 3-11-018241-6

Bibliographic information published by Die Deutsche Bibliothek

Die Deutsche Bibliothek lists this publication in the Deutsche Nationalbibliografie;
detailed bibliographic data is available in the Internet at <http://dnb.ddb.de>

Printed in Germany
Cover Design: Christopher Schneider, Berlin
Typesetting: medionet AG, Berlin
Printing and binding: Hubert & Co. GmbH & Co. KG, Göttingen

For Beth

diligat illa senem quondam, sed et ipsa marito
tum quoque, cum fuerit, non videatur anus.

Martial, *Epigrammata* 4.13.9–10

Acknowledgments

This work owes much to the generous support of more than a few friends and colleagues. I am grateful above all to Emily L. Hayden, who not only assisted with the research but also read the entire manuscript and offered many helpful suggestions. Mention should also be made of the following: Joyce M. Anderson, Michael J. Brown, James H. Charlesworth, John J. Collins, Susan A. Cullen, Antipas Harris, Carl R. Holladay, Luke Timothy Johnson, Elizabeth H. Kruse, Gail R. O'Day, Vernon K. Robbins, Loren T. Stuckenbruck, Pieter van der Horst, John B. Weaver, Cami Koepke Werner, J. Benton White, Carl M. Williams, and at Walter de Gruyter press: Albrecht Döhnert, Klaus Otterburig, Claus-Jürgen Thornton, and Andreas Vollmer. To one and all my sincere thanks.

Walter T. Wilson

Contents

INTRODUCTION

COMMENTARY

APPENDIX

Abbreviations

The following lists consist of abbreviations used in this volume. In the book these usually follow *The SBL Handbook of Style* (ed. by Patrick H. Alexander et al.; Peabody: Hendrickson, 1999). For reasons of space, however, the abbreviations used for biblical and other ancient sources, as well as technical abbreviations, are generally not included in this list. Ancient sources not mentioned in the *Handbook* are given abbreviations in an analogous form. Only a few additional abbreviations or abbreviations differing from the suggestions of the *Handbook* are listed below. In any case, the full titles of all ancient writings are provided in the Index of References.

1. Sources

Anec. Gr.	*Anecdota Graeca*
Anth. Gr.	*Anthologia Graeca*
ARN A	*'Abot de Rabbi Nathan* (Text A)
Carm. aur.	*Carmen aureum*
Dict. Cat.	*Dicta Catonis*
Gnom. Democr.	*Gnomologium Democrateum*
Gnom. Vat.	*Gnomologium Vaticanum*
Instr. Amenem.	*Instruction of Amenemope*
Instr. Ankh.	*Instruction of Ankhsheshonqy*
Instr. Any	*Instruction of Any*
Orph. hymn.	*Orphei hymni*
Paroem. Gr.	*Paroemiographi Graeci*
P.Ins.	Papyrus Insinger

2. Journals, Periodicals, and Series

AB	Anchor Bible
ABD	*Anchor Bible Dictionary*
AnBib	Analecta biblica
ANRW	*Aufstieg und Niedergang der römischen Welt*
APA	American Philological Association
ASP	American Studies in Papyrology

BBB	Bonner Biblische Beiträge
BDAG	Bauer, W., F. Danker, W. Arndt, and F. Gingrich. *Greek-English Lexicon of the New Testament*
BEATAJ	Beiträge zur Erforschung des Alten Testaments und des antiken Judentums
BETL	Bibliotheca ephemeridum theologicarum lovaniensium
BGBE	Beiträge zur Geschichte der biblischen Exegese
BJS	Brown Judaic Studies
BT	Bibliotheca Teubneriana
BZNW	Beihefte zur Zeitschrift für die neutestamentliche Wissenschaft
CBET	Contributions to Biblical Exegesis and Theology
CEJL	Commentaries on Early Jewish Literature
CJ	*Classical Journal*
ConBNT	Coniectanea biblica: New Testament Series
CQ	*Classical Quarterly*
CRINT	Compendia rerum iudaicarum ad Novum Testamentum
DDD	*Dictionary of Deities and Demons in the Bible*
ETL	*Ephemerides theologicae lovanienses*
FRLANT	Forschungen zur Religion und Literatur des Alten und Neuen Testaments
GR	*Greece and Rome*
HTR	*Harvard Theological Review*
HUCM	Monographs of the Hebrew Union College
HUT	Hermeneutische Untersuchungen zur Theologie
JBL	*Journal of Biblical Literature*
JHS	*Journal of Hellenic Studies*
JJS	*Journal of Jewish Studies*
JR	*Journal of Religion*
JRS	*Journal of Roman Studies*
JSHRZ	Jüdische Schriften aus hellenistisch-römischer Zeit
JSJ	*Journal for the Study of Judaism in the Persian, Hellenistic, and Roman Periods*
JSJSup	Journal for the Study of Judaism in the Persian, Hellenistic, and Roman Periods: Supplement Series
JSNTSup	Journal for the Study of the New Testament: Supplement Series
JSOT	*Journal for the Study of the Old Testament*
JSOTSup	Journal for the Study of the Old Testament: Supplement Series
JSP	*Journal for the Study of the Pseudepigrapha*
JSQ	*Jewish Studies Quarterly*
LCL	Loeb Classical Library

LEC	Library of Early Christianity
LSJ	Liddell, H., R. Scott, and H. Jones. *A Greek-English Lexicon*
NIDNTT	*New International Dictionary of New Testament Theology*
NIGTC	New International Greek Testament Commentary
NovT	*Novum Testamentum*
NovTSup	Novum Testamentum Supplements
NTOA	Novum Testamentum et Orbis Antiquus
OBO	Orbis biblicus et orientalis
OTL	Old Testament Library
OTP	*Old Testament Pseudepigrapha*
Phil	*Philologus*
PW	Pauly, A. and G. Wissowa. *Paulys Realencyclopädie der classischen Altertumswissenschaft*
RAC	*Reallexikon für Antike und Christentum*
RGRW	Religions in the Graeco-Roman World
RHPR	*Revue d'histoire et de philosophie religieuses*
SAC	Studies in Antiquity and Christianity
SBLBMI	Society of Biblical Literature. The Bible and Its Modern Interpreters
SBLDS	Society of Biblical Literature Dissertation Series
SBLMS	Society of Biblical Literature Monograph Series
SBLRBS	Society of Biblical Literature Resources for Biblical Study
SBLSP	*Society of Biblical Literature Seminar Papers*
SBLTT	Society of Biblical Literature Texts and Translations
SCHNT	Studia ad corpus hellenisticum Novi Testamenti
SJLA	Studies in Judaism in Late Antiquity
SNTSMS	Society for New Testament Studies Monograph Series
SO	*Symbolae osloenses*
SPhA	*Studia Philonica Annual. Studies in Hellenistic Judaism*
SPhilo	*Studia philonica*
STDJ	Studies on the Texts of the Desert of Judah
SUNT	Studien zur Umwelt des Neuen Testaments
SVTP	Studia in Veteris Testamenti pseudepigraphica
TAPA	*Transactions of the American Philological Association*
TDNT	*Theological Dictionary of the New Testament*
ThQ	*Theologische Quartalschrift*
TRE	*Theologische Realenzyklopädie*
TSAJ	Texte und Studien zum antiken Judentum
TTZ	*Trierer theologische Zeitschrift*
TU	Texte und Untersuchungen zur altchristlichen Literatur
VCSup	Vigiliae christianae Supplements

WMANT	Wissenschaftliche Monographien zum Alten und Neuen Testament
WUNT	Wissenschaftliche Untersuchungen zum Neuen Testament
YCS	Yale Classical Studies
ZNW	*Zeitschrift für die neutestamentliche Wissenschaft und die Kunde der älteren Kirche*
ZRGG	*Zeitschrift für Religions- und Geistesgeschichte*

INTRODUCTION

I. The *Sentences* as Pseudonymous Jewish-Greek Poetry[1]

"Pedagogy is a question of impersonation." [2]

Since its beginnings, varieties of poetic composition have been essential to the expression and dissemination of Greek culture.[3] It comes as no surprise, then, that Jewish thinkers of the Hellenistic era both studied and composed Greek poetry. Philo, for example, deeming them "educators through all our days," regularly cites poets like Homer, Hesiod, and Euripides,[4] while others, such as Theodotus and Ezekiel, employed the forms and language of Greek poetics in producing their own creations.[5] Not content with merely following Hellenic precedents, some Jewish authors set out, in essence, to rewrite the history of Greek poetry, modifying or even forging verses of its founding figures.[6] If for nothing else, the corpus generated by such labors is noteworthy for its pseudonymic scope. A veritable who's who of Greek bards — Orpheus, Homer, Hesiod, Aeschylus, Sophocles, Euripides, Menander, and so on — is made to express sentiments amenable to Judaism. And

---

[1]   *Bibliography:* Attridge, "Fragments of Pseudo-Greek Poets," 821–30; Droge, *Homer*, 1–48; Speyer, *Fälschung*, 111–49; Walter, *Poetische Schriften*, 191–93, 217–76; West and Woodman, *Creative Imitation*; Whitmarsh, *Greek Literature*, 41–89.

[2]   Whitmarsh, *Greek Literature*, 94, referring to Gallop, *Pedagogy*.

[3]   See, e.g., Jaeger, *Paideia*, 34–54 and s.v. poetry.

[4]   Quote from Philo, *Prob.* 143, cf. *Leg. all.* 1.7, 3.202, *Ebr.* 150, *Conf.* 4, 170, *Migr.* 156, 195, *Her.* 5, 189. Some of his treatises cite such sources extensively, e.g., *Prob.* 19, 22, 25, 99, 101–103, 116, 122, 125, 134, 141, 143, 152, *Aet.* 5, 17, 30, 37, 49, 121, 132. For his method, see Dawson, *Allegorical Readers*, 109: "Philo appropriates the prestige of Homer, [Hesiod,] the pre-Socratic Heraclitus, and Plato through direct quotation while undercutting their authority by forcing them to confirm and endorse meanings already firmly tied to scriptural expressions."

[5]   Attridge, "Philo the Epic Poet," 781–84; Fallon, "Theodotus," 785–93; Robertson, "Ezekiel the Tragedian," 803–19; Holladay, *Fragments*.

[6]   It is likely that these verses were compiled (together with authentic quotations) in two or more *florilegia*; see Attridge, "Fragments of Pseudo-Greek Poets," 821–30; Schürer, *History*, 3.1:656–71; Walter, *Poetische Schriften*, 244–76. For the Pseudo-Orphica, see Lafargue, "Orphica," 795–801; Walter, *Poetische Schriften*, 217–43. For the pseudonymous gnomologium known as the *Sentences* of Syriac Menander (probably translated from a Greek original), see Baarda, "Syriac Menander," 583–606; Küchler, *Weisheitstraditionen*, 303–18.

even in their effort to reanimate poetic authorities of the hallowed past by pseude-pigraphical means, the contributors to this corpus would have been following an established Greek practice.[7] Among the epigrams of the *Anthologia Graeca*, for example, one finds offerings from such literary luminaries as Aeschylus, Sophocles, Euripides, and Phocylides—all of them spurious.[8]

The Jewish appropriation of pagan aliases and modes of communication should not of itself lead to the conclusion that the principal audience for such poetry was also pagan. Instead, the impetus for the production of these verses is best understood in relation to certain interpretations being propagated within Hellenistic Jewish circles regarding the history of culture.[9] While these interpretations vary in form and focus, a recurring argument concerned the positive contribution of Judaism to the origins of classical poetry. Illustrative in this regard is Aristobulus, who recasts the early days of Hebraic-Hellenic encounter so that famous Greek poets esteem the wisdom of Moses to such an extent that they acquire from him "significant seeds of inspiration, so that they too are admired." Even Homer and Hesiod, he says, "took their information from our books."[10] The Greeks refrained from explicitly acknowledging their biblical sources, explains Pseudo-Hecataeus, simply out of respect for their "holy and reverent" character.[11] In the course of his sweeping presentation of Moses as *Kultur-bringer*, Artapanus presents us with a similar boast, identifying him as the teacher of Orpheus, one of the traditional precursors of Greek poetics.[12] In the spirit of such claims, the invention of "quotations" from classical poets (note that both Aristobulus and Pseudo-Hecataeus make use of such texts) would have helped to establish the priority and preeminence of Mosaic traditions in Greek literary history, so that Jews would properly see themselves, not only as participants in Greek poetics, but as its forerunners. Demonstrating the indebtedness of the founders of Greek culture to Mosaic wisdom in this way would have facilitated for Jews the task of reconciling their pride in Judaism with their engagement in Hellenistic civilization. They would have recognized in this poetry not only the compatibility of Jewish and Greek cultures but also the significance of their own cultural legacy and identity.[13]

---

[7] We have, e.g., major quantities of spurious verses attributed to Orpheus, Homer, and Menander; see West, *Orphic Poems*, 1–38; West, *Homeric Hymns*; Jaekel, *Menandri Sententiae*. Further, Speyer, *Fälschung*, 111–49; Rosenmeyer, *Ancient Epistolary Fictions*, 193–233; Derron, *Sentences*, xxxii–li.

[8] Page, *Further Greek Epigrams*, 117–308; Gow and Page, *Greek Anthology*, 516–20.

[9] Droge, *Homer*, 1–48; on p. 4 he notes that in the eastern Mediterranean world elaborate theories concerning the origin of Greek culture "became a distinguishing characteristic of the native historical works of the Hellenistic and Roman periods." Cf. Pilhofer, *Presbyteron Kreitton*, 143–220; Niehoff, *Philo*, 139–42.

[10] Aristobulus, frg. 2.4, 5.13.

[11] *Let. Arist.* 31; cf. Josephus, *Ant.* 12.38.

[12] Artapanus, frg. 3.4; cf. Gruen, *Heritage and Hellenism*, 248.

[13] Schürer, *History*, 3.1:690.

In evaluating the nature and purpose of such poetry, it is important to bear in mind that the impulse informing these manipulations of the literary tradition would hardly have seemed irregular within the broader context of Hellenistic cultural trends. In fact, the work of Pseudo-Homer et al. emerged in an age whose aesthetic was shaped by a prevailing "classicizing" mood, in which literary composition generally was supposed to be guided by the acknowledgement and appropriation of great texts from the classical past.[14] Most pivotal in the practical elaboration of this *Zeitgeist* was μίμησις, or *imitatio*, a complex concept embracing both the imitation and revitalization of widely recognized literary models.[15] Participation in the reigning aesthetic entailed molding both one's literary *poiēsis* and one's literary persona through a studied engagement with such models. As a result, the "impersonation of figures from the classical past was ubiquitous" in Greek literature during this era.[16] In order to appreciate the artistic aspirations undergirding these trends, however, it should be noted that there was more to *imitatio* than just writing in archaic dialects or alluding to well-known predecessors. Rather, this concept involves an orientation to the classical tradition premised not upon nostalgic repetition but upon creative transformation, according to which what Tim Whitmarsh calls a "mutually constitutive" relationship between past and present is established.[17] Hellenistic compositions are judged in terms of their filiation with revered literary ancestors, while the classical heritage itself is under constant negotiation, subject to reinvention. In this climate dynamic modalities of literary reception thrived; innovation, even deviation or competition, vis-à-vis the tradition was widely tolerated.[18] Consequently, the tradition's significance for Hellenistic literati was not taken to be stable or self-evident, but necessarily had to be elucidated according to the exigencies of the artistic situation.[19]

An appreciation for the currency of such cultural sensibilities provides a helpful starting point for investigating the *Sentences*, a Hellenistic Jewish text of 219 lines[20]

---

[14] Dihle, *Greek and Latin Literature*, 49-61; Russell, "De Imitatione," 1–16.

[15] For typical examples, see West and Woodman, *Creative Imitation*.

[16] Whitmarsh, *Greek Literature*, 27.

[17] Whitmarsh, *Greek Literature*, 28.

[18] Whitmarsh (*Greek Literature*, 41-89) reviews a variety of writers and writings evidencing this tendency: Plutarch's educative essays; Ps.-Longinus, *On the Sublime*; Dionysius of Halicarnassus, *On Imitation*; Lucian; the Greek novelists. Cf. Bing, *The Well-Read Muse*, 50–90.

[19] In the same vein, mention may be made of *contaminatio*, in which an author utilizes an older work as a model and source, but adulterates it by incorporating it into a new context and/or adding alien material; Pucci (*The Full-Knowing Reader*, 95-99) presents Terence as practitioner and defender of the concept.

[20] The poem's traditional enumeration extends to 230 verses (plus v. 69B), but twelve of these (vv. 31, 36, 37, 87, 116, 117, 129, 144, 145, 146, 155, 218) are not original to the poem; for details, see the textual notes on these verses.

ostensibly penned by Phocylides of Miletus, a famous Greek poet of the sixth century B.C.E.[21] Much like his co-religionist pseudepigraphers, the author of this text
not only appropriates the name of a classical figure, he also strives to "speak in character"—to craft his work according to standards associated with his literary model.
Thus the *Sentences* is couched in old Ionic (the dialect of Phocylides, as well as
Homer and Hesiod),[22] dactylic hexameters (the preferred meter of Phocylides, and
traditionally associated with epic and didactic poetry), and gnomic forms (utilized
to varying degrees by many classical poets, but for which Phocylides was especially
renowned).

A concern for credible imitation would have guided the author in matters of content as well; sentiments familiar from scripture had to be communicated in terms
that could be plausibly attributed to an ancient Greek. In this regard the poem is
notable for the assiduousness with which it has camouflaged its Jewish sources. References to tenets or practices that would have been considered distinctive to Judaism are practically absent.[23] Instead, the author's principle of selection evidences a
preference for elements of his tradition compatible with Greek norms, presented in
Greek dress.[24] This dovetails with a proclivity for generalizing that governs the text's
basic orientation towards its material. Once articulated by "Phocylides," teachings
that in their original context spoke to specifically Jewish concerns now take on
cross-cultural form and application.[25] In the same vein, the *Sentences* also freely
incorporates material of non-Jewish pedigree, again with a preference for ideas that
would have won broad approval in an international setting.[26]

While the evidence is hardly extensive, it appears that our author was sophisti-
cated enough in attending to such matters that the work's original readers did not
detect the forgery. The fact that it survives at all would seem to suggest as much. In
addition, Stobaeus (fifth century C.E.) cites two passages from our *Sentences* as the
handiwork of the original Phocylides, while an interpolator of the second *Sibylline
Oracle* (working no earlier than the second century C.E.) pilfers over sixty of its lines,
a curious move if our text had been exposed as counterfeit.[27] It was widely read and

---

[21] On the pseudonym, see below, Introduction III.

[22] For particulars, see Buck, *Greek Dialects*, 142–43.

[23] Perhaps most distinctively Jewish is the poem's affirmation of physical resurrection in vv. 103–104,
though it is significant that these lines are juxtaposed by some characteristically Greek conceptions of
the afterlife in vv. 105–108.

[24] In Ps.-Phoc. 183, e.g., the prohibition of sex with one's sister-in-law from Lev 18:16 is expressed in
language familiar from a comparable admonition in Hesiod, *Op.* 328–329.

[25] In Ps.-Phoc. 83, e.g., the ban in Exod 22:24 on charging interest on loans to fellow Israelites who are
poor is reformulated as a plea not to be a harsh creditor to anyone who is poor.

[26] E.g., Ps.-Phoc. 195–197 quotes (with noteworthy modifications) Homer's famous lines on the desirability of harmony in marriage (*Od.* 6.182–184).

[27] On the Sibylline interpolation, see below, Introduction VI.

copied, especially as a schoolbook, throughout the late medieval and Renaissance eras and well into the sixteenth century before any doubts were raised concerning its authenticity.[28]

Nevertheless, the poem's attribution to Phocylides of Miletus is untenable for a number of reasons, above all its extensive use of the Septuagint, including LXX Proverbs (second century B.C.E.), a decisive fact for determining the author's religious as well as historical location.[29] He also appears to have employed a now lost compendium of Jewish precepts (known also to Philo and Josephus), which itself probably utilized the Septuagint.[30] In addition, strewn among the text's archaizing lines are over thirty post-classical words or word forms,[31] including eight or nine words whose earliest external attestation is either the first century B.C.E. or the first century C.E.[32] The evidence, all told, indicates a likely floruit for Pseudo-Phocylides of between 100 B.C.E. and 100 C.E.[33]

Our poem, then, despite its pretensions, is an example of classicizing, not classical, literature, entailing as such the transformative impersonation of a great author from the classical past. In its basic profile, the *Sentences* is consistent with other Jewish reimaginings of this past, in which Greek poets find their inspiration in Jewish sources. Pseudo-Phocylides "placed these sentences in the mouth of a Greek thinker who lived centuries earlier in order to show that already in ancient times the wisdom of the Greeks was influenced by the spirit of Moses, with the result that Jewish Torah and Greek ethics were thoroughly in agreement."[34] The "mutually constitutive" relationship that Pseudo-Phocylides establishes with his literary paradigm, then, involves an attempt to constitute the nature of Jewish-Greek relations in the Hellenistic present by reconstituting the nature of those relations in the classical past. In reconfiguring the etiology and ethos of a Greek cultural authority, a work like this would have had the effect of reinforcing for Jewish readers a sense of their own history and place in the Greek world, as well as the possibility of reconciling

---

[28] For the history of research, see van der Horst, *Sentences*, 3–54.

[29] Cf. Cook, "The Dating of Septuagint Proverbs," 383–99.

[30] For discussion of the poem's sources, see below, Introduction III.

[31] van der Horst, *Sentences*, 55–58; Derron, *Sentences*, lxxiii–lxxvi.

[32] πετροφυής (v. 49), ὕψωμα (v. 73), κλόπιμος (vv. 135, 154), νεοτριβής (v. 167), μοιχικός (v. 178), ἄθεσμος (v. 190), ἀκάθεκτος (v. 193), δυστήρητος (v. 217), and possibly γειαρότης (v. 201). Also noteworthy is the *hapax* γαμοκλοπέω (v. 3), whose related forms (γαμοκλόπος, γαμοκλοπίη) are unattested before the first century C.E.

[33] This is the consensus among modern interpreters: van der Horst, "Pseudo-Phocylides Revisited," 15. Derron (*Sentences*, lxvi–lxxii) reviews a host of other matters relating to the poem's grammar and style that prove its post-classical provenance, e.g., its preponderance of "masculine" caesura (after the first syllable of the third foot) over "feminine" caesura (after the second syllable of a dactyl in the third foot), the reverse of what we find in the hexameters of Homer and Hesiod; cf. West, *Greek Metre*, 36, 177.

[34] Lohse, *Theological Ethics*, 22–23.

their traditions with those of the host culture.[35] Such a transfiguration would have presented Jewish readers also with a positive assertion regarding the merit of identifying with the literary and moral legacy of classical Greece. "Phocylides" emerges more vigorously now as an authoritative interpreter of traditions that can edify and empower Jewish readers within Hellenistic society (see below, Introduction V.).

At the same time, there is nothing in its manner of self-presentation that would have prevented Gentiles interested in Phocylidean poetry from reading the *Sentences* as well. Remember that Stobaeus at least appreciated some of its lines well enough to quote them. If the poem circulated in non-Jewish circles, it would have had the effect of encouraging respect, not for Judaism as such (since the text presents the reader with nothing specifically Jewish in form or content), but for something much vaguer, a sort of generally relevant morality as it would have been understood from a Jewish perspective.[36]

---

[35] Similarly, Walter, *Poetische Schriften*, 191–93; Niebuhr, *Gesetz und Paränese*, 66–72. The opposite view appears to be endorsed by Barclay, *Mediterranean Diaspora*, 337: the poem "reflects the perspective of a Hellenized Judaism proud of its Scriptures ... but unafraid ... to attribute its inspiration to a famous dispenser of wisdom from Greek antiquity."

[36] Cf. Crouch, *Colossian Haustafel*, 91–99; Thomas, *Der jüdische Phokylides*, 1–12, 228–35, 352–59. Such interpretations often emphasize (partial) parallels between the *Sentences* and the so-called Noachian laws; cf. van der Horst, "Pseudo-Phocylides," 568–69; van der Horst, *Sentences*, 73–76; and below, p. 76.

II. The *Sentences* as Hellenistic Gnomic Poetry [37]

"Within (my book) are maxims wise; obey them,
and you will be a cleverer and better man for all events.
You need no lengthy speech, only one of these sayings;
bring round to your subject whichever of them is apt." [38]

As we have seen, expressing the material of the *Sentences* in cross-cultural terms was a priority for its author in fashioning a credible pseudepigraphon. In this regard he would have been like other Hellenistic Jewish poetic forgerers. The demands of this particular project, however, would have dictated the use of literary forms for conveying this material which would have both amplified the text's universalizing proclivities and oriented its construction towards some universally practiced literary conventions. In keeping with the work of Phocylides himself, the *Sentences* incorporates many gnomes (γνῶμαι or *sententiae*), short sayings that articulate widely applicable insights regarding the morality of everyday life. [39] As a means of communicating and preserving time-tested wisdom relevant to a broad range of practical issues and situations, such sayings played a crucial role in ancient moral instruction and decision-making. They are among the most elemental forms of ancient discourse, and evidence of their extended literary use can be found in Jewish (e.g., Ben Sira), Egyptian (e.g., the *Instruction of Amenemope*), Greek (e.g., Theognis), Roman (e.g., the *Dicta Catonis*), and Christian (e.g., the *Sentences* of Sextus) sources. By definition, such materials are shaped by a pluralistic tradition of shared cultural perspectives about human experience, evidencing significant commonalties and borrowings across time and place.

Even as they strive to convey the aura of the traditional and the commonplace, however, most gnomic texts (including all of those just mentioned) are attributed to specific authors, who in their self-presentations make special claims for the readers' trust and respect, in the process often thematizing wisdom itself. Theognis,

---

[37] *Bibliography:* Barns, "Gnomologium," 132–37, 5–8; Kloppenborg, *Formation of Q*, 264–306, 329–41; Küchler, *Weisheitstraditionen*, 237–61; Marrou, *History of Education*, 150–75, 234–35; Morgan, *Literate Education*; Wilson, *Mysteries of Righteousness*, 9–41.

[38] Epicharmus, frg. (c) 6–9; cf. Wilson, *Love Without Pretense*, 78.

[39] Wilson, *Love Without Pretense*, 9–24.

for one, introduces himself as "a skilled and wise poet … famous among men."[40] Pseudo-Phocylides displays similar affectation in the prologue of his poem: as the "wisest of men" (v. 2) he would presumably be the ideal teacher for anyone who desires wisdom, that which is "better" for all human institutions and endeavors (vv. 130–131).

Given their compactness and utility, it is not surprising that gnomic sayings could accommodate themselves to a host of different literary genres. As for our text, it is probably most accurate to refer to the *Sentences* as a *gnomic poem*, a designation that offers certain advantages over other recent proposals for its genre.[41] The label *wisdom poem*, to begin with, is appropriate for the work insofar as it properly relates our text to the corpus of ancient, including especially Jewish, wisdom literature and the nonparticularistic approach to ethics it customarily embodies. This term, however, can be used to describe materials that manifest considerable variation in literary form and rhetorical bearing, including pieces that—like Prov 8:1–36 or Bar 3:9–4:4—are more hymnic than gnomic in nature.[42] By contrast, Pseudo-Phocylides' work consists almost entirely of gnomes, supplemented in a few places by illustrative descriptions (e.g., vv. 71–74, 164–174).

Similarly, describing our text as a *didactic poem* helpfully draws attention to its pedagogical orientation, though doing so also brings the *Sentences* into the same comparative ambit as poems that address, not general topics of practical morality, but specific, technical subjects of different kinds, such as farming or astronomy.[43]

Given his probable location in Alexandria (see below), the possibility that Pseudo-Phocylides was familiar with the traditions of *wisdom instruction*, a genre that was especially popular in Egypt, deserves attention.[44] To be sure, a text like Papyrus Insinger resembles our poem in its topical organization, projected educational setting, and extended use of monostichic sayings. By the same token, the maxims in most instructional texts are not in verse, and non-gnomic forms, even extended narratives (e.g., *Instr. Ankh.* 1.7–4.21), frequently supplement them.

Comparison may finally be made with ancient *gnomologia*,[45] for example, the collection of Greek sentences attributed to Menander, which is also replete with monostichic, versified gnomes. Such texts, however, are by definition anthological in

---

[40] Theognis, *El.* 19, 23; cf. Prov 1:1–6; Qoh 12:9–11; Sir 50:27–29; *Instr. Amenem.* 27.7–28.1; Epicharmus, frg. (c) 1–9.

[41] See van der Horst, *Sentences,* 77–78; van der Horst, "Pseudo-Phocylides Revisited," 15.

[42] Cf. Charlesworth, "Jewish Hymns," 411–36; Flusser, "Psalms, Hymns and Prayers," 551–77.

[43] Cf. Toohey, *Epic Lessons;* Volk, *Poetics of Latin Didactic.*

[44] Cf. Kitchen, "Basic Literary Forms," 235–82; Brunner, *Altägyptische Weisheit;* Lichtheim, *Late Egyptian Wisdom Literature;* Kloppenborg, *Formation of Q,* 264–89, 329–36; Wilson, *Mysteries of Righteousness,* 33–41.

[45] Cf. Küchler, *Weisheitstraditionen,* 237–61; Kloppenborg, *Formation of Q,* 289–306, 337–41; Derron, *Sentences,* vii–xxxi; Wilson, *Mysteries of Righteousness,* 25–33.

their mode of composition. In contrast to gnomic poems like Hesiod's *Opera et dies*, the *Carmen aureum*,[46] and (quite possibly) the work of the original Phocylides,[47] they exhibit little thematic connection between lines or overall argumentative structure. With Pseudo-Phocylides, however, it is both obvious that many of his precepts have been incorporated into topical units and likely that the topics of these units have been chosen and organized according to conventional designs for conveying moral instruction (see below, Introduction IV).

The emphasis placed by authors working in these genres on the timeless and the traditional makes determining the *Sitz im Leben* of any particular gnomic work difficult, especially in the case of a text like the *Sentences*, which offers no explicit indication as to its intended readership. As we have seen, a number of the gnomic genres project for themselves an educational setting of some kind, and, in this vein, it has been suggested that our poem may have originally functioned as a schoolbook.[48] This would fit with what is known about the role maxims played in encyclical education in the Greco-Roman world, where gnomic primers or copybooks, frequently in verse, aided instruction in orthography, spelling, and grammar, all the while exposing students to material of literary and moral merit.[49] Indeed, as Teresa Morgan has determined, among the schoolbook papyri of Greco-Roman Egypt gnomic texts survive in greater quantities than any other kind of literature. Furthermore, it appears that such texts figured prominently at every stage of the curriculum, from elementary lessons in reading and writing to more advanced rhetorical exercises.[50] Many of the gnomes selected for these texts were culled from the works of famous Greek poets, so that their study would have facilitated also the students' immersion in literature from the esteemed classical past, which we can safely assume represented a pedagogical priority.[51]

Besides their brevity, gnomic sayings were valuable for encyclical instruction on account of their traditional nature, which lent them an air of authority, as well as their thematic range, which offered students perspectives on various issues relevant

---

[46] See below, Introduction IV.

[47] See below, Introduction III.

[48] van der Horst, *Sentences*, 72–73; Derron, *Sentences*, xlvii–li; Collins, *Jewish Wisdom*, 175–77. On Jewish participation in Greco-Roman *paideia*, see Hengel, *Judaism and Hellenism*, 65–83; Collins, *Jewish Wisdom*, 150–53; cf. Mendelson, *Secular Education*. This would fit, too, with the function the book served during the medieval and Renaissance periods: van der Horst, *Sentences*, 3–4.

[49] Marrou, *History of Education*, 150–59, 234–35; Barns, "Gnomologium," 132–37, 5–8; Bonner, *Education in Ancient Rome*, 172–76; Cribiore, *Writing, Teachers, and Students*, 44–46.

[50] Morgan, *Literate Education*, 69–72, 122, cf. 279–81, 312–13.

[51] Morgan, *Literate Education*, 70–73, 94–100, and passim; cf. Marrou, *History of Education*, 160–75; Whitmarsh, *Greek Literature*, 6: "Across the multiplicity of forms and modes of Roman Greek education, one feature remained common: the attempt to root all forms of status and identity in the prestigious past."

to their general education. Morgan's inventory of the most prominent topics in the gnomic schooltexts provides a point of comparison for assessing the content of the *Sentences* and gives a good sense of the material scope that ancient gnomic literature displays generally.[52] She observes throughout this instruction a concentration on cultivating personal qualities and relationships, especially as they concern the following subjects: wealth, virtue, speech, wisdom, self-control, women, marriage, parents, friends, fate, and death. Meanwhile, issues relating to religious, political, and military matters receive comparatively little attention. The overall ethos, she concludes, places a premium on "self-preservation and respect for what is more powerful than oneself."[53]

In both what it does and does not include, the teaching of the *Sentences* is comparable with this inventory, strengthening the case that Hellenistic readers would have recognized its suitability for use in pedagogical settings. In this regard the thematic breadth of our text is noteworthy: while he does so to varying degrees, all the major topics of the schoolbook papyri are raised also by Pseudo-Phocylides.[54] At the same time, the poem's reticence on cultic and national issues, much noted by contemporary scholars, would have been entirely in keeping with general expectations for these kinds of texts. The most distinctive feature of the *Sentences* that emerges from a comparison with this material is evident not in what it excludes, but in its inclusion of those who are less powerful as objects of the readers' moral obligation, especially the poor, children, slaves, and animals (vv. 10, 19, 22–30, 83–85, 139–140, 150, 207–217, 223–227). While attention to such referents is not unparalleled among pagan moralists, our author's emphasis in this regard is best explained by examining his indebtedness to Jewish moral traditions (see below, Introduction III.).

Given their general lack of historical or geographical specifics, determining the place of composition for gnomic writings often proves to be challenging. Most commentators posit for the *Sentences* an Alexandrian provenance, taking v. 102 as a reference to human dissection, a medical practice apparently unique to that city.[55] However, given the poem's generalizing outlook, and taken together with vv. 100–101, it is likely that v. 102 rejects not the dissection of corpses, but their disinterment and desecration. Even if the line does refer to autopsies, given the paucity of evidence,

---

[52] Morgan, *Literate Education*, 125–44.

[53] Morgan, *Literate Education*, 149.

[54] E.g., wealth (vv. 5–6, 42–47, 62, 109–110), virtue (vv. 67, 163), speech (vv. 7, 20, 48–50, 69, 78, 122–124), wisdom (vv. 53–54, 86–90, 130–131), self-control (vv. 55–69B, 76), women (vv. 179–185, 192, 198), marriage (vv. 175–178, 186, 189, 193, 195–197, 199–205), parents (v. 8), friends (vv. 70, 91–94, 142), fate (vv. 27, 118–121), death (vv. 99–115).

[55] E.g., van der Horst, *Sentences*, 82–83; van der Horst, "Pseudo-Phocylides Revisited," 15.

we cannot rule out the possibility that such procedures were carried out elsewhere, or that moralists in other places would have had occasion to condemn them.[56]

John Collins has made the additional suggestion that the plea in vv. 39–41 ("Let foreigners be held in equal honor among citizens. For we all experience the poverty that comes from roaming widely, and a tract of land has nothing certain for people.") may constitute in part "an *apologia* for the Jews as foreign settlers in Alexandria" and their struggle for civil rights under the Roman prefect Flaccus.[57] However, Jews in other Hellenistic cities faced similar problems,[58] and, as we have seen, there is nothing in the content or form of the *Sentences* that could properly be called Jewish apologetic. Rather than reflecting a specific political situation, these lines (note the emphasis on poverty and economic uncertainty in vv. 40–41) are best taken with a number of precepts in the same paragraph offering general encouragement to extend mercy to the poor and the vulnerable (cf. vv. 22–30) and expressive of a basic sentiment congruous with classical Greek poetry (cf. Homer, *Od.* 15.343–345).

In conclusion, given Alexandria's importance as an intellectual center for Hellenistic Judaism (not to mention the numerous parallels between the *Sentences* and the *corpus Philonicum*), it is a probable locale for the composition of our poem, but no more than that.

---

[56] Schürer, *History*, 3.1:690. Derron (*Sentences*, lxiii–lxv) entertains the possibility of Syrian provenance.

[57] Collins, *Jewish Wisdom*, 164.

[58] See, e.g., Schürer, *History*, 3.1:126–37; Kasher, *Jews*, 289–309; Trebilco, *Jewish Communities*, 167–72.

III. The Sources of the *Sentences*[59]

"While still a child one should learn noble deeds."[60]

Like any gnomic document, our poem configures itself in relation to a broad fund of traditions expressing the cumulative wisdom of ancient people about the moral life. Beyond this, it is possible to speak more concretely about Pseudo-Phocylides' appropriation of specific texts and groups of texts, which inform the constitution of the *Sentences* on various levels. In the dynamics of its textual interactions, the poem evidences what may be called a principle of dual referentiality, integrating elements from two distinct referential fields, the literature of Hellenistic Jewish morality and the literature of classical Greek poetics.[61] These referential fields, however, do not function analogously in the poem's construction. While the former establishes the work's general moral bearing, the latter, in keeping with the author's pseudepigraphical aspirations, establishes the text's means of articulation, doing so in such a way that the presence of the former is left almost entirely tacit. Linguistically, then, the text shares the argot of classical authors like Homer, Hesiod, Theognis, and Phocylides. Explicit verbal echoes of biblical writings are infrequent, even though, more often than not, the poem's subject matter has been determined by these very writings. Only a "knowing reader" can recognize such covert allusions and the manner in which these sources have been re-expressed.

Greek Sources

Most often, Pseudo-Phocylides' utilization of the classical vernacular does not evoke specific passages or works. Instead, terms derived from Homer, Hesiod, etc. tend to be dispersed indiscriminately throughout, so as to lend the text an elevated, classicizing tone, reminiscent of the "non-allusive epicism" Peter Bing detects in certain pagan Hellenistic poems.[62] In Ps.-Phoc. 220–222, for example, we encounter a very high density of individual Homeric words, though their cumulative effect does not

---

[59] *Bibliography:* Carras, "Philo's *Hypothetica*," 431–50; Crouch, *Colossian Haustafel*, 84–88; Niebuhr, *Gesetz und Paränese*; Sterling, "Universalizing the Particular," 64–80; West, "Phocylides," 164–67.

[60] Phocylides, frg. 15.

[61] Cf. Pucci, *The Full-Knowing Reader*, 17–19, 34–36.

[62] Bing, *The Well-Read Muse*, 55.

draw the reader's attention to any specific Homeric passage. Rather, this language has been summoned up as a way of classicizing Lev 19:32, coloring it in the way one would expect of an ancient Greek poet.

On a number of occasions Pseudo-Phocylides employs not just terms but expressions familiar from the Homeric epics, such as "immortal god" (v. 17) and the "threshold of old age" (v. 230).[63] In still other cases, there are sufficient textual markers for us to postulate actual allusions to specific classical texts, the most likely candidates being Ps.-Phoc. 5 (cf. Theognis, *El.* 145–146), 7 (cf. Hesiod, *Op.* 788–789), 48 (cf. Homer, *Il.* 9.312–313), 49 (cf. Theognis, *El.* 213–218), 92 (cf. Theognis, *El.* 115–116), 138 (cf. Hesiod, *Op.* 368–369), 142–143 (cf. Theognis, *El.* 1133–1134), 152 (cf. Theognis, *El.* 105–106), 183 (cf. Hesiod, *Op.* 328–329), 195–197 (cf. Homer, *Od.* 6.182–184), 201–204 (cf. Theognis, *El.* 183–188). This suggests that our author was inspired especially by Hesiod's *Opera et dies* and Book 1 of the *Theognidea*, hardly surprising given their manifest gnomic qualities. Recognizing such allusions becomes particularly important in those cases where it appears Pseudo-Phocylides is establishing a position that departs in some manner from his source text (e.g., vv. 49, 138), essentially engaging in a critical moral conversation with the classical tradition.

As its alleged author, it is worth considering to what extent Phocylides of Miletus himself constitutes a "source" for the *Sentences*. Like most pseudepigraphers, our poet chose to write in the name of a figure whose fame and reputation would lend his message credibility. We get a sense of this reputation from Dio Chrysostom, for example, who praises Phocylides as "one of the highly renowned poets," while Isocrates ranks him alongside Hesiod and Theognis as "the best advisors for human life."[64] By the same token, as he went about creating a credible forgery, our author would have had to take into account the likely familiarity of his audience with his namesake's oeuvre. Unfortunately, just fifteen or sixteen fragments of this work survive, leaving us with only a partial picture of the sorts of expectations ancient readers would have had for Phocylidean composition.[65] It is significant, though, that in almost all of these fragments we can detect at least minor elements that are present also in the *Sentences*. For example:

- frg. 1–6 open with the *sphragis* καὶ τόδε Φωκυλίδεω; Pseudo-Phocylides opens with his own "seal" in vv. 1–2: ταῦτα … Φωκυλίδης.[66]

---

[63] Cf. the commentary on vv. 2, 7, 38, 115, 123, 160; additional locutions are identified in the textual notes.

[64] Dio Chrysostom, *Borysth.* 11 (cf. *2 Regn.* 5); Isocrates, *Ad Nic.* 43; cf. Athenaeus, *Deipn.* 428B, 620C, 632D; *Suda* 4.754.19.

[65] Text and translation: Gerber, *Greek Elegiac Poetry*, 388–403.

[66] On such "seals" see the commentary on these verses.

- frg. 2 gives recommendations on securing a happy marriage; cf. Ps.-Phoc. 195–205.
- frg. 3 asserts the desirability of χάρις ("goodwill") in one's speech; cf. Ps.-Phoc. 123.
- frg. 4 and 11 make reference to κόσμος ("order") as a moral principle, to which we can compare the presentation of ὁμόνοια ("harmony") in Ps.-Phoc. 70–75.[67]
- frg. 5 discusses the mutual obligations of friends (ἑταῖροι); cf. Ps.-Phoc. 70, 91–92.
- frg. 6 includes two terms, χρήστης and παρὰ καιρόν, found also in Ps.-Phoc. 82–83, though they are used differently.
- frg. 7 advises farming for those who want to prosper; cf. Ps.-Phoc. 161.
- frg. 8–10 mention ἀρετή, as do Ps.-Phoc. 67 and 163.
- frg. 9 urges the reader to seek a living (βιοτή); cf. Ps.-Phoc. 153 (with βιοτεύω) and 165 (with βίοτος).
- frg. 10: justice, commended by Phocylides as the sum of every virtue, represents a priority for Pseudo-Phocylides as well, for example, vv. 9, 12, 14, 229.
- frg. 12 agrees with Ps.-Phoc. 69B and 98 in identifying the middle or moderate way as best (ἄριστος).
- frg. 13 commends the pursuit of that which is ἐσθλός (cf. frg. 2, 8); cf. Ps.-Phoc. 65–66, 90.
- frg. 14 counsels decorum in wine drinking; cf. Ps.-Phoc. 69.
- frg. 15 encourages children to learn what is noble; cf. Ps.-Phoc. 89–90, with its disparaging words about those who lack learning.
- frg. 16: the formulation of these lines shows some interesting similarities with Ps.-Phoc. 119–120. The former speaks of different spirits which attend upon men at different times, some "to grant release from coming evil" (ἐπερχομένου κακοῦ ... ἐκλύσασθαι); the latter observes that often in life to the distressed a sudden "release from evil comes" (κακοῦ λύσις ἤλυθεν).

Nothing here suggests that our author was engaged in filching or "quoting" lines directly from his literary model. However, beyond the adoption of generally Phocylidean features like Ionic hexameters and gnomic forms, the *Sentences* does include specific concepts and priorities consistent with the ancient Milesian's work. Furthermore, if we are right in agreeing with M. L. West that originally the maxims of Phocylides "stood together in one book ... intended as a coherent composition," then our author would have also been following Phocylides' example in writing a

---

[67] van der Horst (*Sentences*, 63) conjectures that the choice of pseudonym was based also on the negative statement in frg. 4 about Nineveh, "which may have been (mis)understood as a Biblical allusion." But cf. Korenjak and Rollinger, "ΚΑΙ ΤΟΔΕ ΦΩΚΥΛΙΔΕΩ?" 195–202.

unified poem consisting of many gnomic sayings.[68] If West is also correct (referring especially to frg. 15) in assuming that Phocylides' poetry was used for pedagogical purposes, then this would supply an additional clue as to the original function of Pseudo-Phocylides' poem (see above, Introduction II.).

Jewish Sources

Pseudo-Phocylides' debt to biblical traditions is unquestionable, though the poem's interaction with biblical texts is such that usually we must speak only of implicit influence. It is likely, too, that this influence was at least partly indirect, some biblical teachings being mediated to our author through a now lost compendium of Jewish moral precepts (see below). All this, together with the poem's generalizing tendencies, renders any attempt to tabulate specific biblical "parallels" somewhat tentative, though the following chart gives a sense of the extent and nature of our author's reception of these traditions:[69]

Ps.-Phoc.	LXX		
1–2		21	Tob 4:5
3	Exod 20:13; Lev 18:22; Deut 5:17	22–23	Prov 3:27–28
		24	Isa 42:16, 58:7
4	Exod 20:15; Deut 5:18	25–27	
5	Prov 11:28; Job 20:15; etc.	28	Prov 3:27–28
6	Exod 20:14, 17; Lev 19:11, 13; Deut 5:19, 21	29–30	
		32	Exod 20:15; Deut 5:18
7	Exod 20:16; Deut 5:20	33–34	
8	Exod 20:3, 12; Deut 5:7, 16	35	Exod 22:4; Deut 23:25–26
		38	Deut 20:19
9–10	Exod 23:6–8; Deut 16:18–20	39–41	Lev 19:34, 24:22; etc.
		42	
11	Prov 14:31; Job 13:10–11	43–45	Sir 8:2, 31:5–8; etc.
12	Exod 20:16; Deut 5:20	46–50	
13	Exod 22:6–12; Lev 5:20–26	51–52	Exod 21:13–14; Num 15:27–31
14–15	Lev 19:35–36	53	Jer 9:22
16–17	Exod 20:17; Zech 8:17	54	Deut 6:4
18		55–60	
19	Deut 24:14–15	61	Sir 37:29
20	Sir 1:24, 21:26; etc.	62	Prov 16:19; Sir 21:4

---

[68] West, "Phocylides," 164.

[69] Cf. Derron, *Sentences*, 35–54; Niebuhr, *Gesetz und Paränese*, 7–15.

63–64		140	Exod 23:5
65	Prov 3:31	141	Prov 9:7-8
66–67		142-143	Sir 6:1; etc.
68	Prov 12:11; Sir 18:31	147-148	Exod 22:30
69–69B	Sir 31:12–32:13	149	Exod 22:17;
70	Sir 11:31, 33, 18:15		Deut 18:10; etc.
71–76		150	
77	Lev 19:18	151	Sir 28:8
78		152	Sir 12:1–7
79	Sir 6:7	153	Prov 16:26; etc.
80	Sir 3:31	154	Prov 6:30, 13:4; etc.
81–82	Prov 15:17; Sir 29:22	156–157	Sir 40:28–30
83	Exod 22:24; Lev 25:35–37	158–163	
84–85	Deut 22:6–7	164–174	Prov 6:6–8
86, 88–90	Sir 38:24–39:11	175–176	Gen 1:28, 2:24; Sir 11:28
91–94		177–178	Lev 19:29; Sir 23:22–27
95–96	Sir 16:6, 26:5	179–180	Lev 18:8, 20:11;
97–98	Sir 38:16–23		Deut 23:1, 27:20
99–102		181	Gen 35:22, 49:4
103–104	Dan 12:2–3	182–183	Lev 18:9, 16; Deut 27:22
105		184–186	Exod 21:22–23
106	Gen 1:26-27, 6:3	187	Deut 23:2
107-108	Gen 3:19; Qoh 3:20	188	Exod 22:18; Lev 18:23;
109-110	Ps 48:18; Sir 14:3, 11-16		Deut 27:21
111-113	Job 3:13-19	189	Lev 18:19
114	Job 10:20	190–191	Lev 18:22
115, 118		192–194	
119-120	Qoh 9:11-12	195–197	Sir 25:1, 26:1–2
121-122		198	Exod 22:15;
123	Prov 16:23; Sir 4:24; etc.		Deut 22:28–29
124	Prov 14:7; etc.	199–207	
125-128		208–209	Deut 21:18–21
130	Prov 24:5; Qoh 9:16	210–214	
131	Prov 8:15-16; Wis 8:1, 14;	215–216	Sir 42:9–11
	Sir 24:6	217, 219	
132-133	Deut 13:6, etc.;	220–222	Lev 19:32
	Prov 4:14-15; Sir 12:1-7	223–224	
134	Num 16:26	225	Lev 19:28
135-136	Exod 22:6-12; Prov 29:24	226	Prov 30:10
137-138		227–230	
139	Prov 12:10		

This overview shows that a large majority of the poem's lines accord with biblical teachings and that biblical influence is evident throughout the work. Of course, what constitutes a "parallel" here varies from case to case. In many instances (e.g., the parallels with Ben Sira), the evidence simply suggests our author's participation in a moral tradition shared with other Jewish writers. The nature and density of biblical parallels in a passage like Ps.-Phoc. 3–8, by contrast, make it clear that the author here renders a particular "text," in this case the Decalogue. Of special interest are roughly a dozen passages in which we detect not only similarities in thought but also textual markers sufficient enough to suggest that our author interacts with a specific passage of the Septuagint. Commentators agree, for instance, that Ps.-Phoc. 147–148a is derived from Exod 22:30:

"Eat no meat torn by wild beasts (θηρόβορον … κρέας), but to swiftfooted dogs (κυσίν) leave the remains."

"You shall not consume meat taken from wild beasts (κρέας θηριάλωτον); to the dog (τῷ κυνὶ) you shall throw it."

In typical fashion, though, Pseudo-Phocylides formulates his version of the command using a pair of Homeric locutions, "to eat meat" (cf. *Od.* 9.162) and "swiftfooted dogs" (cf. *Il.* 24.211). For additional examples, see Ps.-Phoc. 12, 19, 22–23, 24, 53, 54, 84–85, 140, 147–148, 164–174, 198, 220–222.

As one would expect, many of Pseudo-Phocylides' verses resemble maxims from Proverbs and Ben Sira. This is particularly true of vv. 55–174, an expansive section that addresses some stock gnomic themes, including self-control, fate, speech, and work. A number of the author's precepts also appear to be drawn from the Pentateuch, especially from three sources: the so-called Covenant Code (Exodus 20–23), chapters 18–20 of the so-called Holiness Code (Leviticus 17–26), and the moral provisions of Deuteronomy, chiefly chapters 5, 20–24, and 27. Predictably, these parallels are concentrated in the sections of the poem that deal with justice and mercy (vv. 3–54) and with sexual mores and familial responsibilities (vv. 175–227). Pseudo-Phocylides' patterns of dependence are significant inasmuch as these same three pentateuchal complexes (similarly augmented by both biblical and non-biblical materials) functioned as basic sources for the construction of other Hellenistic Jewish moral summaries, such as we find, for example, in the *Testament of Issachar* and Book 3 of the *Sibylline Oracles*.[70]

Evidence for such summarizing activity can be found also in the last source for the *Sentences* to be considered, a source which is unfortunately no longer extant. Scholars have long recognized agreements in content between the *Sentences* and two

---

[70] Niebuhr (*Gesetz und Paränese*) surveys these and related texts; cf. Johnson, "The Use of Leviticus 19," 391–401; Weber, *Gesetz*, 283–88.

first century C.E. texts that offer summaries of the Jewish law, Philo, *Hypothetica*
7.1–9 and Josephus, *Contra Apionem* 2.190–219.[71] The most significant of these
agreements can be tabulated as follows:[72]

Ps.-Phoc.	*C. Ap.*	*Hypoth.*
3 (adultery, homosexuality)	2.199, 215	7.1
5–6 (theft)	2.208, 216	7.2, 6
8 (honor God, parents)	2.206	
9 (bribery)	2.207	
13, 135–136 (deposits)	2.208, 216	
14–15 (fair scales)	2.216	7.8
22–23, 29 (almsgiving)	2.211	7.6
34 (impurity of murder)	2.205	
38 (spare trees)	2.212	
39 (non-citizens)	2.209–210	
54 (blessedness of God)	2.190	
80 (benefactors)		7.2
83 (no interest)	2.208	
84–85 (mother bird)	2.213	7.9
99 (bury the dead)	2.211	7.7
100–101 (tomb violation)		7.7
103–104 (afterlife)	2.218	
150 (violence to a child)		7.1
175–176 (marriage, procreation)	2.199	
184 (abortion)	2.202	7.7
185 (exposure)	2.202	
187 (castration)		7.7
190–191 (homosexuality)	2.199	7.1
198 (rape)	2.200, 201, 215	7.1
199–200 (dowry)	2.200	
207–209 (parental care of children)		7.3
213–214 (pederasty)		7.1
220–222 (elders)	2.206	
223–227 (slaves)	2.215	7.2
228 (purifications)	2.198, 203	
230 (better life)	2.218	

---

[71] Cf. Crouch, *Colossian Haustafel*, 84–88; Küchler, *Weisheitstraditionen*, 207–35; Niebuhr, *Gesetz und Paränese*, 31–72; Sterling, "Universalizing the Particular," 64–80.

[72] A more generous approach might yield additional parallels; e.g., see the commentary on Ps.-Phoc. 18, 139, 177, 189.

The number and nature of similarities point to the existence of some sort of literary relationship among these texts. It is striking, for instance, that all three mention the relatively minor command about leaving the mother bird behind when taking her young (cf. Deut 22:6–7). Also noteworthy are several occasions where there is agreement in joining particular rules, for example, the prohibitions of adultery and homosexuality (Ps.-Phoc. 3; *Hypoth.* 7.1; *C. Ap.* 2.199, 215); cf. the commands to honor God and parents (Ps.-Phoc. 8; *C. Ap.* 2.206), the regulations on balances and deposits (Ps.-Phoc. 13–15; *C. Ap.* 2.216), the directives to bury the dead and leave graves undisturbed (Ps.-Phoc. 99–101; *Hypoth.* 7.7), the commands to observe "nature" (φύσις) by marrying and having children (Ps.-Phoc. 175–176; *C. Ap.* 2.199), the condemnations of abortion and exposure (Ps.-Phoc. 184–185; *C. Ap.* 2.202), and the commands not to rape a woman or pay heed to the dowry when choosing a wife (Ps.-Phoc. 198–200; *C. Ap.* 2.200).

Despite their number and specificity, however, the parallels outlined above are probably not best explained by theories of direct literary dependence. Instead, most scholars, pointing to significant differences among the three texts in the overall expression and ordering of material, have concluded that each author independently copied from a common source, a Jewish compendium consisting mainly of moral precepts.[73] This now lost document may conveniently be referred to as a *Gesetzesepitome*,[74] though we should bear in mind that the understanding of obligation it delineated was evidently expansive enough to embrace rules of extra-biblical origin, for example, to bury the dead, to respect one's benefactors, and to ignore the dowry when choosing a wife.

In the hands of Philo and Josephus, this compendium was pressed into the service of Jewish apologetics, especially as part of their response to pagan criticisms that the Mosaic law encouraged a way of life that was lax and misanthropic.[75] Presumably, they found this document amenable to their needs inasmuch as it highlighted both the magnanimity exhibited by Jews who obey the law (e.g., *C. Ap.* 2.211–214) as well as the severity of punishment awaiting those who do not (e.g., *C. Ap.* 2.215–217). For his part, Pseudo-Phocylides used the source selectively, for example, omitting rules it apparently contained on the mistreatment of animals (cf. *Hypoth.* 7.7,

---

[73] It is also significant that in their summaries both Philo and Josephus make statements regarding the applicability of the death penalty that exceed not only biblical injunctions but what both authors themselves say elsewhere; see Crouch, *Colossian Haustafel*, 88; van der Horst, "Pseudo-Phocylides and the New Testament," 197; Carras, "Philo's *Hypothetica*," 449–50; Barclay, *Mediterranean Diaspora*, 339–40; Collins, *Jewish Wisdom*, 173–75.

[74] Cf. Küchler, *Weisheitstraditionen*, 207–35; Niebuhr, *Gesetz und Paränese*, 32–44. This classification would accord with ancient descriptions of these summaries; in *Praep. ev.* 8.6.10, e.g., Eusebius introduces the *Hypothetica* by observing how Philo "made an epitome (ἐπιτέμνεται) of the civic life established for the nation of the Jews from the laws of Moses."

[75] Sterling, "Philo and the Logic of Apologetics," 424–26.

9; *C. Ap.* 2.213), on furnishing fire and water to those who need them (cf. *Hypoth.* 7.6; *C. Ap.* 2.211), and on not divulging a friend's secrets (cf. *Hypoth.* 7.8; *C. Ap.* 2.207). More importantly, he frames its contents as a gnomic poem penned by a Greek author, so that any distinctively apologetic elements are obscured. In doing so, it seems that he discounts the compendium's emphasis on stringent punishments while amplifying its humanitarian dimensions. Verse 9 of the *Sentences*, for example, agrees with *C. Ap.* 2.207 in denouncing judges who accept bribes, though rather than prescribing the death penalty as Josephus does, Pseudo-Phocylides expands the thought with a command in v. 10 to judge the poor with equity.

Our author's extensive reliance on this epitome (as well as other collections of basic moral precepts such as we find in the Covenant and Holiness Codes) provides an important clue as to the principles of inclusion that he followed for the poem's contents. The text presents us with a classical Greek poet whose maxims accord, not with this or that particular biblical teaching, but with the full range of the Hellenistic Jewish moral tradition.

IV. The Literary Structure of the *Sentences*[76]

"... self-control and prudence, justice and courage—
nothing in life is more profitable for mortals than these."[77]

While there may be disagreement as to the details, commentators have long recognized that the maxims of Pseudo-Phocylides are not simply presented *seriatim*,
but have been grouped into a number of topical paragraphs. These include sections on the Decalogue (vv. 3–8), justice (vv. 9–21), mercy (vv. 22–41), wealth (vv.
42–47), moderation (vv. 59–69B), envy (vv. 70–75), death and the afterlife (vv.
97–115), fortune (vv. 118–121), speech and wisdom (vv. 122–131), and work (vv.
153–174).[78] There is also a consensus that the poem concludes in vv. 175–227 with
exhortation whose structure reflects that found in the so-called codes of household
duties (dealing successively with responsibilities the reader has to his wife, children,
and slaves), and that the body of the poem (vv. 3–227) is framed by a coordinated
prologue (vv. 1–2) and epilogue (vv. 228–230). We have also seen that the *Sentences*
both draws on a certain *Gesetzesepitome* and that in its appropriation of this and
other sources it resembles moral summaries compiled by contemporaneous Hellenistic Jewish authors. Inasmuch as the contents of the *Sentences* itself presents its
readers with a compendium or epitome of Jewish moral traditions,[79] it encompasses
a rather broad range of themes, a point that was reinforced when the poem's gnomic
topics were compared with those of the schoolbook papyri (see above, Introduction
II.). Moreover, we have also seen how materials of non-Jewish as well as Jewish origin contribute to these topics, with everything being shaped according to moral and

---

[76] *Bibliography:* North, *Sophrosyne*, 213–31, 323–28; North, "Cardinal Virtues," 165–83; Thom, *Golden
Verses*, 60–61, 125–46; van den Hoek, *Clement of Alexandria*, 111–12; Wilson, *Mysteries of Righteousness*.

[77] Wis 8:7.

[78] For a review of different outlines proposed for the text, see Wilson, *Mysteries of Righteousness*, 9–11;
cf. Thomas, *Der jüdische Phokylides*, 319–27.

[79] van der Horst ("Pseudo-Phocylides Revisited," 16): recent studies "have made abundantly clear that
the characteristics of our poem, such as pseudonymity, the omission of anything exclusively Jewish
(circumcision, shabbath, kashrut, etc.), and the incorporation of originally non-biblical commandments, can all be explained on the assumption that the author wrote a kind of compendium of *misvot*
for daily life which could help Jews in a thoroughly Hellenistic environment to live as Jews without
having to abandon their interest in Greek culture."

literary conventions appropriate to the text's classicizing self-presentation. The question thus arises whether the poem's topical paragraphs have been chosen and organized according to some sort of overall design, and to what extent the compositional principles informing this design might be consistent with the specific configuration of epitomizing, cross-cultural, and pseudepigraphical features we encounter in this text.

To be sure, gnomic writings, like moral writings generally, vary considerably as to literary structure. At the same time, we do encounter in these sources a number of recurring literary configurations and traditional techniques for organizing the diverse themes that often make their way into a gnomic composition. Detecting such techniques in a work is significant for interpretation insofar as their presence may signal the author's interaction with certain broader conversations taking place about human flourishing. Prominent among these conventions is the so-called canon of cardinal virtues, used by a host of Greco-Roman moralists, both on an explicit level, in philosophical debates about the nature of virtue, and on an implicit level, as a criterion for shaping exhortation to pursue virtue. While texts employing the canon differ in form and substance, they all proceed, at least basically, from a two-fold recognition: that the human excellences exist in a multiplicity and that there is a need to conduct discernment about those excellences in an inclusive and coordinated way. As we will see, many of these texts betray educational objectives of some kind, with the canon providing a means of identifying and organizing priorities for the moral development of their readers, often including the specific sorts of moral duties they need to observe.

While a shifting alignment of four or five primary virtues can be detected in the works of classical poets like Pindar and Aeschylus,[80] it was Plato who exercised the most influence in defining the canon, particularly in Book 4 of the *Republic*, which focuses on wisdom (σοφία), justice (δικαιοσύνη), moderation (σωφροσύνη), and courage (ἀνδρεία).[81] The descriptions here derive from Plato's analysis of the tripartite structure of the human self, according to which each faculty of the soul is said to possess its own virtue: wisdom in the rational faculty, courage in the spirited aspect, and moderation in the appetitive part. Additionally, both moderation and justice work simultaneously to maintain harmony among the three faculties. These same virtues are then linked, mutatis mutandis, to the class structure of Plato's ideal community. The canon, then, signifies the various forms of moral excellence as they may be manifested both in the human personality and in the interactions of human society.

In its subsequent reception, the "Platonic" tetrad was subject to various alterations and interpretations. Substitutions in the precise terms employed for one or

---

[80] Pindar, *Isthm.* 8.24–28; Aeschylus, *Sept.* 610; cf. Euripides, frg. 282.23–28; Aeschines, *Ctes.* 168.

[81] Irwin, *Plato's Ethics*, 31–51, 223–43.

more elements, for example, were quite common. Thus self-control (ἐγκράτεια) could stand in place of moderation, for instance, or fortitude (καρτερία) in place of courage.[82] Consistency was not always observed with respect to the number of virtues either. Authors frequently added piety (εὐσέβεια or ὁσιότης) as a fifth element; it could also supplant one of the usual four.[83] Disagreement also arose over the hierarchy of the virtues within the canon. Plato, for one, tended to view wisdom as the foremost of the virtues, encompassing the other three (e.g., *Leg.* 631C). In the *Nicocles*, by comparison, Isocrates, probably representing the more popular opinion, describes justice and moderation as the most beneficial. We also discover a propensity in some circles to divide individual virtues into a number of more specific subvirtues. The different species of δικαιοσύνη, for example, were identified as εὐσέβεια ("piety"), χρηστότης ("honesty"), εὐκοινωνησία ("sociability"), and εὐσυναλλαξία ("affability").[84]

Although not ignored by other philosophical schools, it was the Stoics who made the most extensive use of the canon during the Hellenistic era, though here again we encounter numerous variations.[85] Book 1 of Cicero's *De officiis*, however, which relies on the work of Panaetius of Rhodes, is typical, not least of all in its educative orientation.[86] The body of the treatise, which the author presents as a contribution to his son's moral progress, discusses the latter's duties in terms of the cardinal virtues, with 1.15 providing the rationale:

> All that is morally right rises from some one of four sources: it is concerned either (1) with the full perception and intelligent development of the true; or (2) with the conservation of organized society, with rendering to every man his due, and with the faithful discharge of obligations assumed; or (3) with the greatness and strength of a noble and invincible spirit; or (4) with the orderliness and moderation of everything that is said and done, wherein consist temperance and self-control. Although these four are connected and interwoven, still it is in each one considered singly that certain definite kinds of moral duties have their origin.

---

82 E.g., Plato, *Leg.* 631C–D; Isocrates, *Nic.* 44, *Panath.* 197; Xenophon, *Cyr.* 3.1.16, *Mem.* 1.5.4, 3.9.1–5, 4.8.11; Aristotle, *Eth. nic.* 7.2, 8; Diogenes Laertius, *Vit. phil.* 3.80.

83 E.g., Pindar, *Isthm.* 8.24–28; Aeschylus, *Sept.* 610; Plato, *Lach.* 199D, *Prot.* 349B, *Gorg.* 507C; Xenophon, *Mem.* 4.6.1–12, 4.8.11, *Ages.* 3.1–5; Isocrates, *De pace* 63; Philo, *Det.* 18, *Mut.* 197, *Mos.* 2.216, *Praem.* 160.

84 *SVF* 3:264.24–25, cf. 3:264.40–43; Cicero, *Inv.* 2.159–165; Plutarch, *Stoic. rep.* 1034C–D; Diogenes Laertius, *Vit. phil.* 7.92–93, 126.

85 E.g., *SVF* 3:95, 255–256, 262–266, 275, 280. Cf. North, *Sophrosyne*, 213–31; idem, "Cardinal Virtues," 174–78.

86 On this text, see Dyck, *De Officiis*.

The book proceeds to show how attending to each virtue generates different kinds of responsibilities that one must learn to carry out, beginning with wisdom (18–19), then justice (20–60), fortitude (61–92), and temperance (93–151). In this it is clearly not Cicero's intention to review every possible situation or course of action. Rather, the canon provides general direction as to what sort of "habit" those who prize honorable and beneficial conduct "should practice, so that we can become good calculators of our duties" (59). In part this involves recognizing the different sorts of responsibilities one has to different sorts of referents, for example, familial relations, business associates, compatriots, and fellow human beings (53, cf. 54–58, 122–125). The book's closing remarks take up the question of hierarchy, arguing that one's obligations to observe justice outweigh those pertaining to the other virtues, except in certain extreme cases (152–161). Here and throughout, Cicero promotes a perspective on moral responsibility that orients the recognition of the individual's moral potential towards the necessities of the social good. In asking what is the appropriate relationship of each virtue to the other virtues and to the fundamental appropriation of virtue per se, Cicero perceives also the need for a harmonious arrangement for the various dimensions of the moral life.

The canon also served as a compositional device in more plainly exhortatory texts dealing with moral duties, such as the Hellenistic treatises on kingship (περὶ βασιλείας), which outline the responsibilities of a person in authority.[87] Typically these would be enumerated in "systematically arranged lists of virtues," furnishing a basic blueprint for successful leadership.[88] One illustration of this genre, the *Ad Nicoclem* of Isocrates, is of special interest insofar as it represents "a kind of gnomic oratory" that conveys advice organized according to the canon, first wisdom (10–14), then a major section on justice (15–29a), followed by counsel relating to moderation (29b–35a) and courage (35b–39).[89] This employment of the tetrad coheres with the oration's stated purpose, namely, to enable the reader "to turn to virtue" in such a way that benefits both those who rule and those who are ruled (8). It is important to note that Isocrates does not always identify the individual virtues by name (no doubt the canon was familiar enough to his intended audience) and the fashion in which he depicts each of the virtues is highly selective. Typically his treatment includes the formulation of basic principles for conduct accompanied by advice on specific types of issues or referents offered by way of illustration. The section on justice, for instance, opens by identifying humanity (φιλανθρωπία) as a priority for the responsible ruler (15), and then later encourages its actualization in dealing with foreigners, wrongdoers, and enemies (22b–24b; cf. Ps.-Phoc. 32–41).

---

[87] See below, Introduction V.

[88] van Geytenbeek, *Musonius Rufus*, 126.

[89] Kennedy, *Art of Persuasion*, 190. The body of the treatise is flanked by a coordinated introduction (1–9) and conclusion (40–54); cf. Wilson, *Mysteries of Righteousness*, 49–50.

Another gnomic example comes from the *Carmen aureum*, a Hellenistic poem written as instruction for the moral and spiritual development of students in a Pythagorean community. As Johan Thom has demonstrated, the first part of the poem (vv. 1–49) focuses on the cultivation of virtue, beginning with a summary treatment of the cardinal virtues, addressing first moderation (vv. 10–12), then justice (v. 13), prudence (vv. 14–16), and lastly courage (vv. 17–20).[90] Like the *Ad Nicoclem*, most of the virtues are left unnamed, and the nature of the exhortation is condensed and paradigmatic. Also typical of the gnomic style is the way that individual sections balance encouraging and discouraging forms of instruction. In vv. 10–12, for instance, positive commands to master one's appetites and anger are countered with a negative precept to avoid shameful deeds (cf. Ps.-Phoc. 55–58, 63–64, 67–69B, 76–78). Also noteworthy is the manner in which the author divides the presentation of a virtue into ancillary sub-sections that deal with some of its more specific characteristics. Again we can see this most clearly in the section on moderation, which includes precepts on self-control (vv. 10–11a) and shame (vv. 11b–12).

In light of the discussion so far, it comes as no surprise that the canon also worked its way into the literature of Hellenistic Judaism. The author of the Wisdom of Solomon, for instance, cites the Platonic tetrad with approval in 8:7. The canon enjoys a place of importance for the author of 4 Maccabees as well, who refers to it in his prologue as a means of establishing the text's philosophical presuppositions in cross-cultural terms (1:1–6, cf. 1:18, 5:22–24, 15:10). The canon also appears to function in the design of Ben Sira 36:23–38:23, where the gnomic instruction relates first to justice (36:23–37:15), then to the topics of wisdom (37:16–26), moderation (37:27–31), and finally courage (38:1–23).

Of particular interest in this regard is Philo. The impetus for his use of the canon originates in an attempt to relate the Mosaic law to the so-called ideal law in accordance with nature as articulated by various Greco-Roman philosophical schools.[91] In conjunction with this, he seeks on a number of occasions to demonstrate how the Torah aims to regulate life in accordance with virtue, which constituted one of the primary objectives of this ideal law. On a more concrete level, Philo also explains how the law's individual injunctions were established with a view to inculcating virtue in those who obeyed them. This pertains especially to the commandments of the second table of the Decalogue, and then to the particular laws subordinate to them. The injunctions regarding jurisprudence and commerce, for instance, were designed to promote justice, whereas those concerning marriage and diet foster moderation.

---

[90] Thom, *Golden Verses*, 60–61, 125–46; his analysis is corroborated by observations made in some of the ancient commentaries, e.g., Hierocles of Alexandria, *In aur. pythag. carm. comm.* 10.1.

[91] See Wolfson, *Philo*, 2:200–25; cf. North, *Sophrosyne*, 323–28; Sandmel, "Virtue and Reward in Philo," 215–23; Mott, "Greek Ethics," 25–30; Najman, "The Law of Nature," 55–73.

Although Philo's corpus conveys no single scheme for classifying the commandments and the virtues,[92] the analysis beginning in *De Specialibus Legibus* and continuing in *De Virtutibus* is noteworthy.[93] The former treatise consists largely of an examination of the specific laws arranged under the headings of the ten commandments as presented in *De Decalogo*. Beginning at 4.132, however, the presentation moves in a different direction. After noting that he has adequately treated the ten commandments and the injunctions dependent upon them, Philo states that they additionally correspond with "the virtues of universal value," and that these virtues are exemplified in the various laws. Both individually and as a group the commandments exhort the obedient to follow the company of virtues, which includes piety, wisdom, and temperance (which he claims to have already discussed sufficiently), as well as justice (discussed in *Spec.* 4.136–238), courage (discussed in *Virt.* 1–50), and humanity (discussed in *Virt.* 51–174). These discussions of the individual virtues, in turn, indicate some of the specific obligations associated with each of them, including in many instances illustrations from the Torah.

As Annewies van den Hoek has pointed out, Philo's presentation here, taken as a whole, represents an attempt to give the Mosaic law "a respected position within the thought of his time and environment."[94] Specifically, Philo articulates a "doctrine of virtues," according to which the law offers "a primary training" in virtue: "The prescriptions of the law represent the virtues and not visa versa; the virtues are attributes of the law, labels that make the qualities of the law recognizable in broader terms."[95] The canon is a means for making the law more intelligible to a Hellenized audience, showing how its provisions relate to prevailing moral aspirations of the host culture. Indeed, as Philo sees things, the obligations and priorities of the Jewish tradition are not only communicable in terms of the Greco-Roman virtues, they actually embody the means by which people can achieve these virtues.

Given both its ubiquity and flexibility, it stands to reason that Pseudo-Phocylides would have found the scheme of cardinal virtues useful as a means of organizing a thematically disparate body of moral material in terms that would be appropriate to the classicizing, summarizing, and gnomic character of his work. In fact, it appears that the first major section of the *Sentences* has been structured according to the canon, containing precepts relating first to justice (vv. 9–54), then moderation (vv. 55–96), courage (vv. 97–121), and finally wisdom (vv. 122–131). This is followed by the poem's second major section (vv. 132–227) whose exhortation is

---

[92]   For some other examples of Philo's use of the canon, cf. *Opif.* 73, *Leg. all.* 1.63–65, *Cher.* 5, *Sacr.* 84, *Post.* 128–129, *Agr.* 18, *Ebr.* 23, *Abr.* 219, *Mos.* 2.185, 216, *Spec.* 2.62, *Prob.* 67, 70, *Quaest. Gen.* 1.12; cf. Jastram, "Generic Virtue," 323–47.

[93]   Cf. Hecht, "Preliminary Issues," 1–55.

[94]   van den Hoek, *Clement of Alexandria*, 112; cf. Classen, "Der platonisch-stoische Kanon," 68–88; N. G. Cohen, *Philo Judaeus*, 86–105.

[95]   van den Hoek, *Clement of Alexandria*, 111.

organized according to different kinds of social relationships or referents. Here, too, the arrangement evidences a traditional design, as each paragraph, beginning at the periphery of social existence and moving towards the center, addresses a more specific and more familiar area of moral conduct: how to deal with various types of social "outsiders" (vv. 132–152), the nature and importance of work (vv. 153–174), and obligations within the household (vv. 175–227).[96] Introducing these two major blocks of material is a rendition of the Decalogue in vv. 3–8, which establishes the poem's moral presuppositions. Framing all of this is a coordinated prologue and epilogue identifying the author and indicating the nature of the poem's sources, message, mode of communication, and purpose (vv. 1–2, 228–230).

In its manner of composition, the *Sentences* exhibits a number of features familiar from the literary trends identified in the foregoing survey. For example, like other exhortatory texts that employ the canon as a compositional device, in vv. 9–131 not all of the virtues are explicitly named.[97] In the same vein, Pseudo-Phocylides does not present anything like an exhaustive or systematic exposition of the virtues. Rather, each of the four units includes a variety of basic or representative precepts. In keeping with this, we see that within a specific section the material presented may relate not to the cardinal virtue per se, but to one of its typical facets or sub-virtues. The section on justice, for example, includes a paragraph of maxims (vv. 22–41) encouraging humanity (φιλανθρωπία). Meanwhile, the section on courage does not address that theme in its usual sense at all, but contains precepts that relate to facing death and fate with fortitude. In the course of these exhortations we find a fair balance of positive and negative instruction,[98] as well as a balance of sayings that identify moral principles and counsel on specific situations.[99] Also, the ordering of the paragraphs within the section on the virtues seems to be purposeful, especially the positioning of justice first; quite a few other ancient moralists, including Phocylides himself, assigned a special place to this topic.[100] Finally, we should note that combining exhortation organized according to the virtues with exhortation organized according to the responsibilities one has in dealing with different situations and referents also represents a conventional procedure, as we saw in the discussion of Isocrates' *Ad Nicoclem* and Cicero's *De officiis*. Of particular interest in this regard, though, is *C. Ap.* 2.190–219, where Josephus utilizes a similar combination

---

[96] See below, pp. 164–68.

[97] Though see σωφροσύνη in v. 76 and σοφία in v. 131; we also find numerous terms with the δικ-stem in the section on justice: vv. 9, 11, 12, 14, cf. vv. 1, 229.

[98] E.g., in vv. 48–50 commands against duplicity and capriciousness are coupled with an appeal for sincerity.

[99] E.g., v. 69B's identification of *metron* as "best" is coupled with appeals in v. 69 to observe that principle in matters of eating, drinking, and speaking.

[100] Phocylides, frg. 10, and see the discussion of Isocrates and Cicero above; cf. Wilson, *Mysteries of Righteousness*, 171–72.

in summarizing the Mosaic law for a Hellenized audience; see the discussion in the commentary below (pp. 166–68).[101]

To sum up: not only are the principles informing the literary composition of the *Sentences* traditional in nature, they are familiar from the traditions of both Jewish and Greco-Roman moral exhortation, in keeping with the work's general impulse towards cultural confluence. The canon of cardinal virtues in particular would have facilitated the task of communicating instruction which summarized the traditions of Jewish morality in a Hellenized setting, doing so in terms of the sorts of aspirations and categories one would expect a classical author like Phocylides to endorse.

---

[101] In *C. Ap.* 2.170, he associates the law with the virtues of piety, justice, moderation, fortitude, and harmony.

V. The Moral Outlook of the *Sentences*[102]

> *"The fascination with the past ... was above all*
> *a way for all Greeks, and especially members of the elite, to invoke the*
> *dictum 'know thyself'. Constant rewriting of the classical*
> *period was their way of defining and asserting a group identity."*[103]

Given the miscellaneous nature of its contents, it is neither practical nor particularly helpful to attempt an accounting of every theme or motif present in the *Sentences*. Instead, what follows is a sketch of the poem's basic outlook, by which I mean both the way the text organizes social space and how it encourages its readers to construe themselves as moral agents within that space.

As we have seen, the *Sentences* represents an example of intensive Jewish interaction with the traditions of Greek culture and education, in other words, with Greek *paideia*. Specifically, Pseudo-Phocylides has fashioned a text that his Hellenized contemporaries would have recognized as suitable for the purposes of encyclical education by recreating the gnomic voice of a classical poet, an orientation that is determinative for the text's formal and linguistic profile. At the same time, it is important to bear in mind that the classicism in which our author participated was not a literary or cultural phenomenon only. Rather, the possession and interpretation of paideutic traditions was, as Simon Swain puts it, "how a man showed his integration into the higher levels of society."[104] Access to the sort of literate education represented by the *Sentences* was not open to all, but was the prerogative of elites, who justified the authority they wielded in society in part by appealing to their filiation with the authority of the classical past, expressed in terms of their knowledge of classical literature and their emulation of classical paradigms.[105] *Paideia*, then, played a critical role in the construction of social identity among both those who ruled in Greco-Roman antiquity, what Swain calls "the male establishment class,"

---

[102] *Bibliography:* Blumenfeld, *The Political Paul*, 189–274; F. Cairns, *Virgil's Augustan Epic*, 16–23, 85–108; Hadot, "Fürstenspiegel," 568–610; Höistad, *Cynic Hero*, 150–222; Konstan, "Friendship and Monarchy," 124–43; Moles, "Kingship Orations," 297–375; Swain, *Hellenism and Empire*, 1–13, 65–100, 409–22; Whitmarsh, *Greek Literature*, 1–38, 90–130.

[103] Swain, *Hellenism and Empire*, 87.

[104] Swain, *Hellenism and Empire*, 414; among the examples he discusses (on pp. 135ff.) are Plutarch, Dio Chrysostom, Aelius Aristides, and Lucian.

[105] Whitmarsh, *Greek Literature*, 1–38, 90–130; Swain, *Hellenism and Empire*, 1–13, 65–100, 409–22.

and those who aspired to rule, for whom education in the classical heritage would have represented a means of social empowerment and advancement.[106]

In this light, it is not surprising that the paideutic moral agent is constructed differentially, through the recognition of a series of social polarities. To be educated or cultured in this era, as Tim Whitmarsh points out, entails a process of identifying oneself as the superior party "in a series of highly marked oppositions: human and bestial, Greek and barbarian, free and enslaved, ... philosopher and non-philosopher ... elite and sub-elite, and masculine and feminine."[107] The basis of moral self-making here involves the consolidation of multiple, mutually reinforcing forms of power, all grounded in the revered traditions of the classical past.

As noted earlier, however, the meaning of this past for Hellenistic authors was not fixed, but was frequently contested and reimagined.[108] This fluidity in appropriating the tradition was due in no small part to the diversity that characterized Hellenistic society itself, in which various groups vied to identify themselves positively with classical culture and the construals of power through which it was communicated. As Swain puts it, the "search for cultural and political authority involved idealizing the past, and the result of this idealization was that it was always open to negotiation to say what the past actually was ... and to say what authority it conferred on whom." This was particularly true insofar as "non-Greeks could appropriate the Greek past or even suggest that modern Greeks had no real connection with it."[109] For his part, Pseudo-Phocylides endorses for his fellow "non-Greek" readers the same sort of educational program embraced by the elites of Hellenistic society, including the dynamics of moral formation thereby implicated. However, the authoritative past that constitutes the basis of this pedagogy, in this case the teaching of Phocylides of Miletus, has been "idealized" according to the author's specific pseudepigraphical agenda. It is now a past with which Jewish readers have a special "connection" insofar as they can discern how their own moral traditions have played a critical role in shaping its content.[110] This would have had the effect of conferring legitimacy on Jewish aspirations to participate in Hellenistic *paideia* and the opportunities for social empowerment it afforded.

An important ramification of this social orientation for the *Sentences* is that its prospective student/reader must assume a certain status before fully engaging the

---

[106] The members of this class "took care to associate themselves with the traditions ... of the Greek world, ... and by tying themselves to the leaders of classical Greece furthered their own claims to rule in the present." Swain, *Hellenism and Empire*, 65–66; cf. Dawson, *Allegorical Readers*, 115; Morgan, *Literate Education*, 74–89.

[107] Whitmarsh, *Greek Literature*, 91, with reference to the discussion of *paideia* in Iamblichus, *Vit. Pyth.* 8.44.

[108] Cf. above, Introduction I.

[109] Swain, *Hellenism and Empire*, 7.

[110] See above, Introduction III.

poem's cultural and pedagogical exchange. This is immediately apparent on the linguistic level, as the text assumes an audience that is not only Greek-speaking but sufficiently literate to appreciate the poem's archaic, classical argot. Beyond this, it is apparent that Pseudo-Phocylides' social space is constructed with reference to a number of hierarchies, with the readers being invited, in effect, to imagine themselves making moral decisions from the privileged end of each one.[111]

To begin with, the poem's implied reader is male, adult, and married. This is obvious from the very first precept of the body of the poem (v. 3), which prohibits adulterous and homosexual liaisons. This perspective is extended as well throughout the section whose structure parallels that of the so-called *Haustafeln* (vv. 175–227), in which the reader is addressed as husband not wife, parent not child, and slave-owner not slave—in other words, as the head of a patriarchal household. It is significant here that while issues of female conduct are raised on a number of occasions, women are addressed as moral agents only indirectly, presumably being subject to male supervision (see vv. 177, 184–185, 192, 204, 208).

In concert with this, the dichotomy of rich and poor in the text is always seen from the vantage point of the former. The reader is assumed to be an individual who gives rather than receives alms (vv. 22–23, 28–29), pays rather than earns wages (v. 19), owns rather than seeks shelter (v. 24), lends rather than borrows (v. 83). He hosts meals (vv. 81–82),[112] is familiar with luxuries (v. 61), and is likely to attract the attention of flattering parasites (vv. 91–94).

That the poem's educational transaction is implicated in processes of social empowerment is evident perhaps most distinctly in the way that the author has constructed his literary persona as moral preceptor. Specifically, as the wisest (σοφώτατος) of all men (v. 2), "Phocylides" claims the role of consummate guide for anyone who desires the status of a σοφός, who in his education is distinguished from the "untrained" and the "untaught," who in their ignorance of "noble things" are unable to judge important matters or grasp important teachings (vv. 86–90).[113] Indeed, it is (only) those who possess σοφία who can exercise effective political, economic, and social leadership in the world, guiding the course "of lands and states and ships" (vv. 130–131).[114]

Closely associated with σοφία for Pseudo-Phocylides is λόγος ("speech, reason"), a faculty that serves as a means both of protecting oneself (v. 128) and assisting others (v. 123). It is in its possession of this divinely-allotted "weapon" that the

---

[111] Cf. Thomas, *Der jüdische Phokylides*, 352–55.

[112] Food as a motif: Ps.-Phoc. 68–69, 81–82, 92–94, 139, 146–147, 156–157, 164–169, 223, cf. vv. 18, 38, 84–85.

[113] The projected reader is both someone likely to be in a position to judge others, perhaps in an official capacity (vv. 9–11) and to have a say in who will act as judge (v. 86); he is more likely to have to deal with criminals than to be one himself (vv. 132–136, 141–142, 152).

[114] Note also that the encoded reader is a citizen rather than a foreigner: Ps.-Phoc. 39, 68.

superiority of the human over the bestial in creation is most evident, the latter being ἄλογος (vv. 125–128, 188). Consequently, the reader is to refrain from socially
meaningful interaction with animals, like sharing their food (vv. 139, 147–148)
or mating with them (v. 188), even though their activities provide the author with
some convenient, usually positive, moral models.[115] The poem's treatment of wisdom and reason implies also an anthropological hierarchy for the reader's moral self-
constitution, with the optimal configuration of the human personality requiring the
cultivation of these cognitive faculties, while various non-cognitive capacities (anger,
grief, desire, etc.) are characterized as shameful and destructive, and thus in need
of moderation, even "bridling" (vv. 57–59, cf. vv. 63–64, 67–69B, 97–98, 118,
193–194). This perspective reflects a common conceptualization in Greco-Roman
ethics, according to which "self-mastery and the mastery of others were regarded as
having the same form;" the man who would control his social subordinates must
first learn to control his unruly passions and emotions.[116]

Two other forms of hierarchy are important for the organization of social space
in the *Sentences*, though, in contrast to the forms discussed so far, the moral van-
tage-point of the text's encoded reader is not that of the uppermost position. First,
the text asserts a three-tiered generational hierarchy. While the reader superintends
his own children (vv. 207–217), he is at the same time still a son himself, obliged
to honor his parents (v. 8) and their social peers (vv. 179–181, 220–222, cf. also v.
80).

More extensive are the text's references to the supremacy and rulership of the
divine. The reader owes the highest honor to God (v. 8), who is depicted as the final
source and guarantor of the social order projected by the text, including that which
is necessary to live properly within that order. To begin with, Pseudo-Phocylides
indicates that creation itself reveals a divinely established plan, insofar as God has
assigned to each species a distinguishing feature and means of self-preservation (vv.
125–128). In this scheme of things, people occupy a special position since the human spirit/soul has been created after the divine image (v. 106) and participates in
divine immortality after death (vv. 104, 115). Moreover, God is identified as the
true source of the material wealth (v. 29), the σοφία (v. 54), and the λόγος (v. 128)
that enable people to survive and thrive in the world. Indeed, the benefits offered
by the counsel of the poem itself represent "blessed gifts" that originate ultimately
with God (vv. 1–2). Moreover, because it is of divine making, the world's order is

---

[115] Animal imagery: Ps.-Phoc. 49, 84–86, 125–128, 139–140, 147–148, 164–174, 185, 188, 191, 201–
202. In the same vein, the reader is called upon to observe the moral criterion of φύσις; see below, on
vv. 176, 190.

[116] Foucault, *History of Sexuality*, 2:75, cf. p. 86: "moderation implied that the *logos* be placed in a posi-
tion of supremacy in the human being and that it be able to subdue the desires and regulate behavior."
See also C. Williams, *Roman Homosexuality*, 125–59; Stowers, *Romans*, 42–82; and below, on Ps.-
Phoc. 193–194.

maintained by God, who acts in the realm of human affairs as judge (vv. 11, 17, cf. vv. 77, 101). In sum, God takes on the role of supreme king, ruling (βασιλεύει) over all souls, in this world and the next (v. 111).

In this context, a word should be said concerning Pseudo-Phocylides' "interesting laxity in theological terminology."[117] While its means of expression presents a few challenges in this regard, there is a consensus among interpreters that the *Sentences* can be read in its entirety "without embarrassment within the framework of Jewish monotheism."[118] To begin with, remarks about "heavenly" and "blessed" ones in Ps.-Phoc. 71, 75, and 163 are best taken as references to the celestial bodies, which were widely regarded as animate beings in Jewish as well as pagan circles.[119] As with its discourse about God, these references contribute to the poem's depiction of the moral order of the universe, which the reader is called upon to acknowledge and follow. More striking is the use of θεοί in v. 104, though it appears that this simply contributes to an assertion regarding post-mortem immortality, again a common notion in Jewish as well as pagan circles.[120] The reference to εἷς θεός in v. 54, with its allusion to Deut 6:4, is of particular importance in this context, conveying an affirmation of God's uniqueness and supremacy that is foundational for the poem's theological perspective (cf. v. 194).

The discourse of the *Sentences*, then, constructs social space in terms of various conventional hierarchies. Moreover, it encourages its readers to align themselves with the vantage point of those who occupy positions of power and authority within (almost all of) these hierarchies and to discern their moral obligations accordingly. As with so many other features of the poem, its articulation of these obligations reflects a basic orientation that is thoroughly traditional in nature. This is evident, for instance, when it is compared with a popular contemporaneous genre that was designed expressly to instruct persons of authority in their basic moral responsibilities, the discourse on kingship (περὶ βασιλείας).[121] Addressed to representatives of the ruling class *par excellence*, such treatises were in fact relevant for anyone who desired the moral status of those deemed worthy to govern.[122] As Musonius Rufus puts it, the title of "kingly person" belongs to whoever acquires the skill and ability to rule, even if he has only one or two subjects; indeed, "it is enough to rule one's friends

---

[117] Barclay, *Mediterranean Diaspora*, 341.

[118] Barclay, *Mediterranean Diaspora*, 341.

[119] See the commentary on these verses.

[120] See the commentary on v. 104.

[121] Representative of the genre are the four kingship discourses of Dio Chrysostom; Isocrates, *Ad Nicoclem*; Musonius Rufus, frg. 8; *Let. Arist.* 187–294 (294: "essential teaching on kingship"); Blumenfeld (*The Political Paul*, 189–274) surveys the Hellenistic Pythagorean tractates on kingship. Further, Hadot, "Fürstenspiegel," 568–610.

[122] Cf. Fiore, *Personal Example*, 46, 59–60; F. Cairns, *Virgil's Augustan Epic*, 16, 18.

or one's wife and children or, for that matter, only oneself."[123] As a group, these treatises proceed from the conviction that the successful monarch must excel in the moral qualities generally honored by the society he intends to rule. Consequently, the genre's educational program is steeped in traditional forms and categories, such as the canon of cardinal virtues, as we saw in the discussion of Isocrates' *Ad Nicoclem* (see above, Introduction IV.).

While examples are by no means scarce, Dio Chysostom's third oration on kingship is a particularly useful representative for study inasmuch as it includes many of the perspectives and priorities typical of this literature.[124] Dio begins by stressing that the one in authority must evince moral virtues more rigorously than those who depend on him, since his judgments and example influence many others (7–11). What are these virtues? The king must be temperate, brave, and just,[125] his actions marked by sound judgment rather than insolence, anger,[126] desire, or grief (32–34). He does not indulge in pleasures, luxuries, self-glorification, avarice, or idleness (40).[127] Rather, he abides by the law, prefers truth to flattery,[128] and is willing to endure many toils (2, 34, 39, 83–85).[129] Guided by a sense of humanity, φιλανθρωπία (39), he cares constantly for his subjects, since "it is only when he helps others that he thinks he is doing his duty" (55).[130] He takes thought for the safety and welfare of his subjects much like a shepherd tends his flock or a general provides for his troops (41, 66–67).[131] In all this the king imitates the power and humanity of God, who eternally cares for all people (82–83), believing that "his own oversight is advantageous to others just as the rule of the gods is to himself" (52).[132] Among the

---

[123] Musonius Rufus, frg. 8.66.14–16; cf. van Geytenbeek, *Musonius Rufus*, 124–29.

[124] For a similar sketch of the "good king" stereotype, see F. Cairns, *Virgil's Augustan Epic*, 18–21. On this and Dio's other kingship discourses, see Höistad, *Cynic Hero*, 150–222; Konstan, "Friendship and Monarchy," 124–43; Moles, "Kingship Orations," 297–375.

[125] Often in this literature justice and equity emerge as the king's foremost objectives; cf. Isocrates, *Ad Nic.* 16, 18; Musonius Rufus, frg. 8.60.21–62.9; Dio Chrysostom, *1 Regn.* 35; *Let. Arist.* 189, 212, 216, 232, 257, 267; Blumenfeld, *The Political Paul*, 235–38, 248–50.

[126] Cf. Harris, *Restraining Rage*, 233–38.

[127] Cf. Isocrates, *Ad Nic.* 29, 31–32; Musonius Rufus, frg. 8.62.10–23; Dio Chrysostom, *1 Regn.* 21; *Let. Arist.* 209, 211, 222–223, 237, 263, 284, 290; Blumenfeld, *The Political Paul*, 242, 259.

[128] Cf. Isocrates, *Ad Nic.* 22; Dio Chrysostom, *1 Regn.* 26; *Let. Arist.* 206.

[129] Cf. Dio Chrysostom, *1 Regn.* 21, 34, *3 Regn.* 57 (The king "does not deem his lot any the worse simply because he has to face the most tasks and have the most troubles."); Konstan, "Friendship and Monarchy," 131.

[130] Cf. Isocrates, *Ad Nic.* 15; Dio Chrysostom, *1 Regn.* 20, *2 Regn.* 26, 77, *4 Regn.* 24; Musonius Rufus, frg. 8.66.11; *Let. Arist.* 290; Konstan, "Friendship and Monarchy," 124–25.

[131] Cf. Musonius Rufus, frg. 8.60.8–9; Dio Chrysostom, *1 Regn.* 12–13, 17, 21–24, *2 Regn.* 26, 67, 69; *Let. Arist.* 190, 226–227; Blumenfeld, *The Political Paul*, 238.

[132] Cf. Musonius Rufus, frg. 8.64.10–15; Dio Chrysostom, *1 Regn.* 37–46, *2 Regn.* 71–72; *Let. Arist.* 188, 210, 281; Blumenfeld, *The Political Paul*, 195, 221, 252–55; Moles, "Kingship Orations," 312.

most important benefits the king grants his people is the preservation of order and harmony, again following the example of the divine (73–77).[133]

Similar priorities are evident in the sort of comportment advocated by the *Sentences*. The use of one's resources to benefit others, to begin with, is an overriding concern, with attention paid to what the reader ought to provide to a wide range of (usually weaker) referents: justice for the poor (vv. 9–12), pay for laborers (v. 19), alms for beggars (vv. 22–23, 28–29, cf. vv. 109–110), support for the homeless, the lost, and strangers (vv. 24–26, 39–41), benefactions to benefactors (v. 80), meals for guests (vv. 81–82), proper burial for the dead (vv. 99–102), assistance to anyone who falls (v. 26)—even an enemy's beast (v. 140), protection for sons and daughters (vv. 213–217), food for slaves (v. 223). The author stops to spell out the principles undergirding such activity at a number of junctures: just measures ought to be dispensed "in all circumstances" (v. 14), in giving to those in need one follows the example of God (v. 29), all of that which supports "life" ought to be shared (v. 30), one ought to render to all their due, observing impartiality (v. 137). It is assumed that the reader is able to affect others with his words as well (vv. 78, 123–124, 141–143, 226). It is essential, then, to observe integrity and discretion in one's speech (vv. 7, 12, 16–17, 20, 48–50, 69, 122), and above all to practice speech that will benefit "everyone" (v. 123).

Conversely, Pseudo-Phocylides urges the audience to refrain from the sorts of actions that might injure or deprive others, issuing various commands not to harm, take, or even envy what belongs to someone else (vv. 6, 18, 70, 83–85, 139, 153–157, 187)—even indirect participation in such criminality is condemnable (vv. 135–136). Greed warrants special attention as a destructive social force, generating violent enmity between people, even family members (vv. 42–47, cf. v. 206). Indeed, the proper acquisition and use of wealth represents a major concern for the poem, which is explored from various angles.[134] Similarly, we have advice to refrain from anger, since it often leads to unintended and unnecessary violence (vv. 55–58, 63–64). The use of force in dealing with enemies (vv. 32–34, 77–78), children (vv. 150, 207), and women (v. 198), indeed against anyone (v. 4) is condemned. The reader is to refrain also from excessive grief (vv. 97–98, 118), pride (vv. 53–54, 118, 122, cf. v. 62), and desires (vv. 60–62, 68–69B); by and large, excess in any of the emotions is "grievous" (vv. 59, 69B). He is to refrain especially from desire for extramarital sex (vv. 3, 67, 179–183, 190–191), cultivating instead love for his wife and fellow members of the household (vv. 195–197, 219).

To be sure, in many instances the specific kinds of moral referents and situations raised by Pseudo-Phocylides indicate a reliance on Jewish traditions, especially

---

[133] Cf. F. Cairns, *Virgil's Augustan Epic*, 22–23, 85–108.

[134] Besides the lines just mentioned, cf. Ps.-Phoc. 13–15, 62, 109–110, 134–137, 153–174, 177, 199–204. As a rule it is better to be content with what one has than to become rich unjustly (vv. 5–6).

when attention is being paid to the poor and vulnerable in vv. 9–41 and to sexual matters in vv. 175–194. Nevertheless, in its basic ethical orientation the text would not have been out of place within the milieu of traditional Greco-Roman moral education and exhortation, as illustrated by Dio's third kingship oration. Taken in their entirety, the varied demands made by the *Sentences* have the cumulative effect of fostering the reader's self-understanding as an empowered and active moral agent, someone whose abilities and resources afford him opportunities to affect, both positively and negatively, not only his own well-being but that of many others as well. By implication any meaningful plan of moral self-making must take into account one's responsibilities vis-à-vis a wide range of referents, including many who are of lower social status. In this regard, conduct that confers benefit of some kind on others is encouraged, while conduct that might violate others through the misuse of power is discouraged. Learning these priorities entails respect for and emulation of the divine, the supreme model of the moral use of power, evidenced especially in the promotion of justice, humanity, harmony, and productivity (vv. 11, 17, 29, 71–75, 125–128, 163). Another way in which the poem amplifies this orientation is by advancing a perspective on moral action that takes into account the commonality of human experience, a perspective typical of Greek thought though hardly out of keeping with Jewish wisdom.[135] Reminders that poverty, suffering, and reversals of fortune are realities that all people must face (vv. 27, 40–41, 119–120) promote "a stronger sense of human sympathy and solidarity," bolstering the broad compass of moral responsibility expected of the reader.[136] Similarly, one's evaluation of material wealth and social status should take into account the fact that all people are similarly constituted, subject to the same mortality, and ultimately destined for the same place (vv. 103–115). The "leveling effect" of such reflections becomes all the more pronounced when "Phocylides" includes himself among the "we" of humanity (vv. 103–104, 107–108, 114–115, cf. vv. 40–41, 201–203).

In all this the *Sentences* expresses a pragmatic conservatism that is both familiar from the traditional moral exhortation exemplified by the kingship treatises and in keeping with the poem's gnomic style. The conventional hierarchies within which readers constitute themselves as moral agents are always simply assumed in the discourse of the text, never defended or problematized. Harmony and stability are positively assessed, while association of any kind with discord and its sources is rejected (e.g., vv. 70–75, 95–96, 151). The encoded reader, then, is advised regarding his responsibilities to pursue a variety of aims that contribute to this stability: unity with the unfortunate (v. 30), reconciliation with enemies (vv. 140–143, cf. v. 34), personal emotional balance (vv. 59, 69B, 98, 118–121), a harmonious household

---

[135] E.g., Baldry, *The Unity of Mankind*; Wright, "Cicero on Self-Love and Love of Humanity," 171–95; Clements, *Wisdom in Theology*, 40–64.
[136] Collins, *Jewish Wisdom*, 164.

(vv. 195–197, 219), "food for the winter" (v. 169), and so on. These and similar recommendations are intended to identify what is "fitting" (v. 80), "necessary" (v. 133), "good" (vv. 14, 60, 65, 102), "better" (vv. 81, 130, 142, 195), and "best" (vv. 69B, 98, 137) for people. Adherence to the text's agenda brings "blessings" (v. 2) and "a good life" (v. 230) to the reader, who in the end will learn the difference between what is an "advantage" in life (v. 78) and what is not (v. 60). To a significant extent, this involves judging one's comportment against moral criteria inferred from the larger order of things, an order evidenced in the social, natural, and divine realms.[137]

---

[137] On the "Aphoristic Wisdom of Order," see J. G. Williams, *Those Who Ponder Proverbs*, 35–46.

VI. Manuscript Evidence for the *Sentences*[138]

*"Le bilan de la tradition manuscrite se révèle, il faut
bien le dire, assez décourageant. L'histoire du texte
se résume à une lente détérioration, où foisonnent
contaminations, adaptations et corrections diverses."*[139]

Although the *Sentences* has been preserved in a considerable number of manuscripts, only five of these are important as evidence for the original Greek text:[140]

M (Mutinensis): tenth century
B (Baroccianus): tenth century
P (Parisinus): eleventh or twelfth century
L (Laurentianus): thirteenth century
V (Vindobonensis): thirteenth century

Additionly, in the Ψ group of manuscripts for the *Sibylline Oracles* we find inserted between *Sib. Or.* 2.55 and 149 most of Ps.-Phoc. 5–79. The work of this (probably Christian) interpolator must have occurred in antiquity since it is noted by the *Suda* (4.754.19), who observes (incorrectly) that it was "Phocylides" who lifted these lines from the Sibylline books. The evidence proffered by this extract (conventionally designated Σ) for the text of the *Sentences*, however, is of limited value, since the interpolator has substantially modified his source to fit its new context by altering, omitting, and adding significant amounts of material.[141]

The poem's textual tradition evidences a large number of alterations and corruptions, due in part to Pseudo-Phocylides' mixture of archaizing and post-classical words and word forms, his predilection for unusual terminology, and his sometimes deficient grammar and style. Significant variants are identified in the textual notes. The Greek text printed as an appendix (see below, pp. 217–22) is based on Derron's, though on a number of occasions I have preferred an alternative reading, in consul-

---

[138] *Bibliography:* Derron, "Inventaire des Manuscrits du Pseudo-Phocylide," 237–47; Derron, *Sentences,* lxxxiii–cxvi.

[139] Derron, *Sentences,* cviii.

[140] For discussion, see Derron, *Sentences,* lxxxiii–cxvi.

[141] See Collins, "Sibylline Oracles," 346–48; cf. van der Horst, *Sentences,* 84–85.

tation with the critical editions listed in the general bibliography.[142] Helpful treatment of many textual problems can be found also in van der Horst's commentary. The following is a simplified version of Derron's *stemma codicum*:[143]

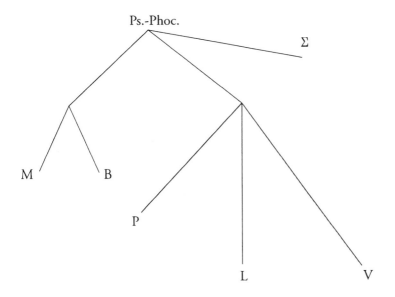

---

[142] See the textual notes on Ps.-Phoc. 6, 10, 14, 23, 61, 82, 98, 127, 150, 157, 179, 204, 208, and 228.

[143] Derron, *Sentences*, cxiii.

VII. General Bibliography

1. Pseudo-Phocylides: Editions, Translations, and Commentaries

Bergk, Theodorus. *Poetae Lyrici Graeci II*. 4th ed. Leipzig: Teubner, 1882.

Bernays, Jacob. *Gesammelte Abhandlungen*. Edited by Hermann Usener. 2 vols. Berlin: Wilhelm Hertz, 1885.

Brunck, Richard F. Ph. *Gnomici Poetae Graeci*. 2nd ed. Leipzig: G. Fleischeri, 1817.

Derron, Pascale. *Pseudo-Phocylide: Sentences*. Budé. Paris: Société d'Edition «Les Belles Lettres», 1986.

Diehl, Ernst, ed. *Anthologia Lyrica Graeca*. 3rd ed. 4 vols. Leipzig: Teubner, 1958.

Farina, Antonio. *Silloge Pseudofocilidea*. Collana di studi greci 37. Naples: Libreria Scientifica Editrice, 1962.

van der Horst, Pieter W. *The Sentences of Pseudo-Phocylides*. SVTP 4. Leiden: E. J. Brill, 1978.

_____. "Pseudo-Phocylides." *OTP* 2 (1985): 565–82.

Walter, Nikolaus. *Poetische Schriften*. JSHRZ 4.3. Gütersloh: Gerd Mohn, 1983.

Young, Douglas, ed. *Theognis*. 2nd ed. BT. Leipzig: Teubner, 1971.

2. Primary Sources

Unless noted otherwise, scriptural references are to the Septuagint. Texts and translations (sometimes with minor changes) for most Greek and Latin authors (including Philo and Josephus) are from the Loeb Classical Library. Also note the following:

'Abot de Rabbi Nathan: Jacob Neusner. *The Fathers According to Rabbi Nathan*. BJS 114. Atlanta: Scholars, 1986.

Anecdota Graeca: J. F. Boissonade, ed. *Anecdota Graeca*. Vol. 1. Hildesheim: Olms, 1962.

Arius Didymus: Arthur J. Pomeroy, ed. *Arius Didymus: Epitome of Stoic Ethics*. SBLTT 44. Atlanta: SBL, 1999.

Carmen aureum: Johan C. Thom. *The Pythagorean Golden Verses*. RGRW 123. Leiden: E. J. Brill, 1995.

Cebetis Tabula: John T. Fitzgerald and L. Michael White, eds. *The Tabula of Cebes*. SBLTT 24. Chico: Scholars, 1983.

Chares: Siegfried Jaekel, ed. *Menandri Sententiae*. BT. Leipzig: Teubner, 1964. Pages 26–30.

Democritus, *Fragments* (from Stobaeus): Hermann Diels and Walter Kranz, eds. *Die Fragmente der Vorsokratiker*. 6th ed. 3 vols. Berlin: Weidmann, 1951–52. Vol. 2, pages 178–207 (B169–297). C. C. W. Taylor. *The Atomists, Leucippus and Democritus: Fragments*. Phoenix Sup. 36. Toronto: University of Toronto Press, 1999.

Derekh Eretz Rabbah: Marcus van Loopik. *The Ways of the Sages and the Way of the World: The Minor Tractates of the Babylonian Talmud*. TSAJ 26. Tübingen: J. C. B. Mohr (Paul Siebeck), 1991. Pages 29–171.

Didache: Kurt Niederwimmer. *The Didache*. Hermeneia. Minneapolis: Fortress, 1998.

Euripides, *Fragments*: Augustus Nauck, ed. *Tragicorum Graecorum Fragmenta*. Hildesheim: Olms, 1964. Pages 361–716.

Ezekiel the Tragedian: R. G. Robertson, ed. "Ezekiel the Tragedian." *OTP* 2 (1985): 803–19.

Gnomologium Democrateum: Hermann Diels and Walter Kranz, eds. *Die Fragmente der Vorsokratiker*. 6th ed. 3 vols. Berlin: Weidmann, 1951–52. Vol. 2, pages 153–65 (B35–115). C. C. W. Taylor. *The Atomists, Leucippus and Democritus: Fragments*. Phoenix Sup. 36. Toronto: University of Toronto Press, 1999. Pages 235–38.

Gnomologium Epictetum: Heinrich Schenkl, ed. *Epicteti Dissertationes ab Arriano Digestae*. 2nd ed. BT. Stuttgart: Teubner, 1916. Reprint, 1965. Pages 476–92.

Gnomologium Vaticanum: Graziano Arrighetti, ed. *Epicuro: Opere*. 2nd ed. Biblioteca di cultura filosofica 41. Torino: Einaudi, 1983. Pages 139–57.

Heraclitus: T. M. Robinson. *Heraclitus: Fragments*. Phoenix Sup. 22. Toronto: University of Toronto Press, 1987.

Hesiod, *Opera et dies*: Martin L. West, ed. *Hesiod: Works and Days*. Oxford: Clarendon, 1978.

Iamblichus, *De Vita Pythagorica*: John Dillon and Jackson Hershbell, eds. *Iamblichus: On the Pythagorean Way of Life*. SBLTT 29. Atlanta: Scholars, 1991.

Instruction of Amenemope: Miriam Lichtheim, ed. *Ancient Egyptian Literature: A Book of Readings*. Vol. II: *The New Kingdom*. Berkeley: University of California Press, 1976. Pages 146–63.

Instruction of Ankhsheshonqy: Miriam Lichtheim. *Late Egyptian Wisdom Literature in the International Context: A Study of Demotic Instructions*. OBO 52. Freiburg: Universitätsverlag; Göttingen: Vandenhoeck & Ruprecht, 1983. Pages 66–92.

Instruction of Any: Miriam Lichtheim, ed. *Ancient Egyptian Literature: A Book of Readings*. Vol. II: *The New Kingdom*. Berkeley: University of California Press, 1976. Pages 135–46.

Maximus of Tyre: M. B. Trapp, ed. *Maximus of Tyre: The Philosophical Orations*. Oxford: Clarendon, 1997.

Menander, *Fragments*: John M. Edmonds, ed. *The Fragments of Attic Comedy*. Vol. III.B. Leiden: E. J. Brill, 1961.

Menander, *Monostichoi*: Siegfried Jaekel, ed. *Menandri Sententiae*. BT. Leipzig: Teubner, 1964.

Menander Rhetor: D. A. Russell and N. G. Wilson, eds. *Menander Rhetor*. Oxford: Oxford University Press, 1981.

Mishnah: Jacob Neusner, ed. *The Mishnah: A New Translation*. New Haven: Yale University Press, 1988.

Musonius Rufus: Cora E. Lutz, ed. *Musonius Rufus: 'The Roman Socrates'*. YCS 10. New York: Yale University Press, 1947.

New Testament: Eberhard Nestle, Erwin Nestle, Kurt Aland et al., eds. *Novum Testamentum Graece*. 27th ed. Stuttgart: Deutsche Bibelgesellschaft, 1993.

Old Testament Pseudepigrapha: James H. Charlesworth, ed. *The Old Testament Pseudepigrapha*. 2 vols. Garden City: Doubleday, 1983, 1985.

Orphic Hymns: Apostolos N. Athanassakis, ed. *The Orphic Hymns*. SBLTT 12. Missoula: Scholars, 1977.

Orphica: M. Lafargue, ed. "Orphica." *OTP* 2 (1985): 795–801.

Papyri Graecae Magicae: Hans Dieter Betz, ed. *The Greek Magical Papyri in Translation*. 2nd ed. Chicago: University of Chicago Press, 1996.

Papyrus Insinger: Miriam Lichtheim. *Late Egyptian Wisdom Literature in the International Context: A Study of Demotic Instructions*. OBO 52. Freiburg: Universitätsverlag; Göttingen: Vandenhoeck & Ruprecht, 1983. Pages 197–234.

Paroemiographi Graeci: Ernst L. Leutsch and F. G. Schneidewin, eds. *Corpus Paroemiographorum Graecorum*. 2 vols. Göttingen: Vandenhoeck & Ruprecht, 1839–51.

Philo the Epic Poet: H. Attridge, ed. "Philo the Epic Poet." *OTP* 2 (1985): 781–84.

Pseudo-Greek Poets: H. Attridge, ed. "Fragments of Pseudo-Greek Poets." *OTP* 2 (1985): 821–30.

Pythagorean Pseudepigrapha: Holger Thesleff, ed. *The Pythagorean Texts of the Hellenistic Period*. Acta Academiae Aboensis A.30.1. Åbo: Åbo Akademi, 1965.

Qumran Library: Florentino García Martínez, ed. *The Dead Sea Scrolls Translated*. 2nd ed. Leiden: E. J. Brill, 1996.

Sallustius: Arthur Darby Nock, ed. *Sallustius: Concerning the Gods and the Universe*. Hildesheim: Olms, 1966.

Secundus: Ben E. Perry, ed. *Secundus the Silent Philosopher*. APA Philological Monographs 22. Ithaca: Cornell University Press, 1964.

Septuagint: Alfred Rahlfs, ed. *Septuaginta*. Stuttgart: Deutsche Bibelgesellschaft, 1935, 1979.

Sextus, *Sententiae*: Richard A. Edwards and Robert A. Wild, eds. *The Sentences of Sextus*. SBLTT 22. Chico: Scholars, 1981.

Sibylline Oracles: J. J. Collins, ed. "Sibylline Oracles." *OTP* 1 (1983): 317–472.

Stobaeus: Curt Wachsmuth and Otto Hense, eds. *Johannis Stobaei Anthologium*. 5 vols. Berlin: Weidmann, 1884–1912. Reprint, 1958.

Syriac Menander, *Sententiae*: T. Baarda, ed. "The Sentences of the Syriac Menander." *OTP* 2 (1985): 583–606.

Teles: Edward N. O'Neil, ed. *Teles, The Cynic Teacher*. SBLTT 11. Missoula: Scholars, 1977.

Theodotus: F. Fallon, ed. "Theodotus." *OTP* 2 (1985): 785–93.

3. Secondary Literature

Adkins, Arthur W. H. *Merit and Responsibility: A Study in Greek Values*. Oxford: Oxford University Press, 1960.

Agrell, Göran. *Work, Toil, and Sustenance*. Verbum: Håkan Ohlssons, 1976.

Allison, Dale C. *Testament of Abraham*. CEJL. Berlin and New York: Walter de Gruyter, 2003.

Amir, Yehoshua. "The Decalogue according to Philo." Pages 121–60 in *The Ten Commandments in History and Tradition*. Edited by Ben-Zion Segal and Gershon Levi. Jerusalem: Magnes, 1990.

Amstutz, Joseph. *ΑΠΛΟΤΗΣ: Eine begriffsgeschichtliche Studie zum jüdisch-christlichen Griechisch*. Theophaneia: Beiträge zur Religions- und Kirchengeschichte des Altertums 19. Bonn: Peter Hanstein, 1968.

Athanassiadi, Polymnia, and Michael Frede, eds. *Pagan Monotheism in Late Antiquity*. Oxford: Clarendon, 1999.

Aune, David C. "Mastery of the Passions: Philo, 4 Maccabees and Earliest Christianity." Pages 125–58 in *Hellenization Revisited*. Edited by Wendy E. Helleman. Lanham: University Press of America, 1994.

Balch, David L. *Let Wives Be Submissive: The Domestic Code in 1 Peter*. SBLMS 26. Chico: Scholars, 1981.

———. "Two Apologetic Encomia: Dionysius on Rome and Josephus on the Jews." *JSJ* 13 (1982): 102–22.

———. "Household Codes." Pages 25–50 in *Greco-Roman Literature and the New Testament*. Edited by David E. Aune. Atlanta: Scholars, 1988.

Baldry, H. C. *The Unity of Mankind in Greek Thought*. Cambridge: Cambridge University Press, 1965.

Barclay, John M. G. *Jews in the Mediterranean Diaspora*. Edinburgh: T. & T. Clark, 1996.

Barns, J. "A New Gnomologium, with Some Remarks on Gnomic Anthologies." *CQ* 44 (1950): 126–37 and 45 (1951): 1–19.

Bauernfeind, Otto. "ἁπλοῦς, κτλ." *TDNT* 1 (1964): 386–87.

Berger, Klaus. *Die Gesetzesauslegung Jesu*. WMANT 40. Neukirchen-Vluyn: Neukirchener Verlag, 1972.

Berquist, Jon L. "Controlling Daughter's Bodies in Sirach." Pages 95–120 in *Parchments of Gender: Deciphering the Bodies of Antiquity*. Edited by Maria Wyke. Oxford: Clarendon, 1998.

Berthelot, Katell. "Philo and Kindness Towards Animals (*De Virtutibus* 125–147)." *SPhA* 14 (2002): 48–65.

_____. *Philanthrōpia Judaica: Le débat autour de la "misanthropie" des lois juives dans l'Antiquité*. JSJSup 76. Leiden: E. J. Brill, 2003.

Bertram, Georg. "ὕβρις, κτλ." *TDNT* 8 (1972): 295–307.

_____. "ὑπερήφανος, κτλ." *TDNT* 8 (1972): 525–29.

Betz, Hans Dieter. "De laude ipsius." Pages 367–93 in Betz, *Plutarch's Ethical Writings*.

_____. "Christianity as Religion: Paul's Attempt at Definition in Romans." *JR* 71 (1991): 315–44.

_____. *The Sermon on the Mount*. Hermeneia. Minneapolis: Fortress, 1995.

Betz, Hans Dieter, ed. *Plutarch's Ethical Writings and Early Christian Literature*. SCHNT 4. Leiden: E. J. Brill, 1978.

Betz, Hans Dieter, and John M. Dillon. "De cohibenda ira." Pages 170–97 in Betz, *Plutarch's Ethical Writings*.

Biale, Rachel. *Women and Jewish Law*. New York: Schocken, 1984.

Billerbeck, Margarethe. "The Ideal Cynic from Epictetus to Julian." Pages 205–21 in *The Cynics: The Cynic Movement in Antiquity and Its Legacy*. Edited by R. Bracht Branham and Marie-Odile Goulet-Cazé. Berkeley: University of California Press, 1996.

Bing, Peter. *The Well-Read Muse: Present and Past in Callimachus and the Hellenistic Poets*. Hypomnemata 90. Göttingen: Vandenhoeck & Ruprecht, 1988.

Blumenfeld, Bruno. *The Political Paul: Justice, Democracy and Kingship in a Hellenistic Framework*. JSNTSup 210. Sheffield: Sheffield Academic Press, 2001.

Bockmuehl, Markus N. A. *Revelation and Mystery in Ancient Judaism and Pauline Christianity*. WUNT 2.36. Tübingen: J. C. B. Mohr (Paul Siebeck), 1990.

Bolkestein, Hendrik. *Wohltätigkeit und Armenpflege im vorchristlichen Altertum*. Utrecht: A. Oosthoeck, 1939.

Bostock, David. *Plato's Phaedo*. Oxford: Clarendon, 1986.

Boswell, John. *Christianity, Social Tolerance, and Homosexuality*. Chicago: University of Chicago Press, 1981.

_____. *The Kindness of Strangers: The Abandonment of Children in Western Europe from Late Antiquity to the Renaissance*. New York: Pantheon, 1988.

Bradley, K. R. *Slaves and Masters in the Roman Empire: A Study in Social Control*. Collection Latomus 185. Bruxelles: Latomus, 1984.

Bréhier, Emile. *Les idées philosophiques et religieuses de Philon d'Alexandrie*. 2nd ed. Etudes de Philosophie Médiévale 8. Paris: J. Vrin, 1925.

Bremmer, Jan N. "Hades." *DDD* (1999): 382–83.

Brooten, Bernadette J. *Love Between Women: Early Christian Responses to Female Homoeroticism.* Chicago: University of Chicago Press, 1996.

Brunner, Helmut. *Altägyptische Weisheit: Lehren für das Leben.* Die Bibliothek der Alten Welt. Zürich: Artemis, 1988.

Büchsel, Friedrich. "ἐλέγχω, κτλ." *TDNT* 2 (1964): 473–76.

Buck, Carl Darling. *The Greek Dialects.* Chicago: University of Chicago Press, 1955.

Bultmann, Rudolf. "ἔλεος, κτλ." *TDNT* 2 (1964): 477–87.

_____. "καυχάομαι, κτλ." *TDNT* 3 (1965): 645–54.

_____. "οἰκτίρω, κτλ." *TDNT* 5 (1967): 159–61.

Burkert, Walter. *Greek Religion.* Cambridge: Harvard University Press, 1985.

Cairns, Douglas L. *Aidōs: The Psychology and Ethics of Honour and Shame in Ancient Greek Literature.* Oxford: Clarendon, 1993.

Cairns, Francis. *Virgil's Augustan Epic.* Cambridge: Cambridge University Press, 1989.

Carras, George P. "Philo's *Hypothetica*, Josephus' *Contra Apionem* and the Question of Sources." Pages 431–50 in *SBLSP* 29. Edited by David J. Lull. Atlanta: Scholars, 1990.

Cavallin, Hans C. C. *Life After Death: Paul's Argument for the Resurrection of the Dead in 1 Corinthians 15. Part 1: An Enquiry into the Jewish Background.* ConBNT 7.1. Lund: Gleerup, 1974.

Charlesworth, James H. "Jewish Hymns, Odes, and Prayers (ca. 167 BCE–135 CE)." Pages 411–36 in *Early Judaism and its Modern Interpreters.* Edited by Robert A. Kraft and George W. E. Nickelsburg. SBLBMI 2. Philadelphia: Fortress, 1986.

Classen, C. J. "Der platonisch-stoische Kanon der Kardinaltugenden bei Philon, Clemens Alexandrinus und Origenes." Pages 68–88 in *Kerygma und Logos: Beiträge zu den geistesgeschichtlichen Beziehungen zwischen Antike und Christentum. Festschrift für Carl Andresen zum 70. Geburtstag.* Edited by Adolf M. Ritter. Göttingen: Vandenhoeck & Ruprecht, 1979.

Clements, Ronald E. *Wisdom in Theology.* Grand Rapids: Eerdmans, 1992.

Cohen, David. *Law, Sexuality, and Society: The Enforcement of Morals in Classical Athens.* Cambridge: Cambridge University Press, 1991.

Cohen, Naomi G. *Philo Judaeus: His Universe of Discourse.* BEATAJ 24. Frankfurt am Main: Peter Lang, 1995.

Cohen, Shaye J. D. *The Beginnings of Jewishness: Boundaries, Varieties, Uncertainties.* Hellenistic Culture and Society 31. Berkeley: University of California Press, 1999.

Cohen, Shaye J. D., ed. *The Jewish Family in Antiquity.* BJS 289. Atlanta: Scholars, 1993.

Collins, John J. *Jewish Wisdom in the Hellenistic Age.* OTL. Louisville: Westminster/John Knox, 1997.

_____. *Between Athens and Jerusalem: Jewish Identity in the Hellenistic Diaspora.* 2ⁿᵈ ed. Grand Rapids: Eerdmans, 2000.

Conzelmann, Hans. "ψεῦδος, κτλ." *TDNT* 9 (1974): 594–603.

Cook, Johann. "The Dating of Septuagint Proverbs." *ETL* 69 (1993): 383–99.

Corley, Jeremy. *Ben Sira's Teaching on Friendship.* Ph.D. dissertation, Catholic University of America, 1996.

Cousin, Jean. *Etudes sur Quintilian.* 2 vols. Paris: Boivin, 1935–36. Reprint, Amsterdam: Schippers, 1967.

Cribiore, Raffaella. *Writing, Teachers, and Students in Graeco-Roman Egypt.* ASP 36. Atlanta: Scholars, 1996.

Crouch, James E. *The Origin and Intention of the Colossian Haustafel.* FRLANT 109. Göttingen: Vandenhoeck & Ruprecht, 1972.

Cullyer, Helen. "Paradoxical Andreia: Socratic Echoes in Stoic 'Manly Courage'." Pages 213–33 in *Andreia: Studies in Manliness and Courage in Classical Antiquity.* Edited by Ralph M. Rosen and Ineke Sluiter. Mnemosyne Sup. 238. Leiden: E. J. Brill, 2003.

Cumont, Franz. *After Life in Roman Paganism.* New York: Dover, 1959.

Damon, Cynthia. *The Mask of the Parasite: A Pathology of Roman Patronage.* Ann Arbor: University of Michigan Press, 1997.

D'Arms, John H. *Commerce and Social Standing in Ancient Rome.* Cambridge: Harvard University Press, 1981.

Dawson, David. *Allegorical Readers and Cultural Revision in Ancient Alexandria.* Berkeley: University of California Press, 1992.

Delling, Gerhard. "Eheleben." *RAC* 4 (1959): 691–707.

_____. "καιρός, κτλ." *TDNT* 3 (1965): 455–64.

_____. "πλεονέκτης, κτλ." *TDNT* 6 (1968): 266–74.

Deming, Will. *Paul on Marriage and Celibacy.* SNTSMS 83. Cambridge: Cambridge University Press, 1995.

den Boer, Willem. *Private Morality in Greece and Rome: Some Historical Aspects.* Mnemosyne Sup. 57. Leiden: E. J. Brill, 1979.

Denniston, John D. *The Greek Particles.* Rev. ed. Oxford: Clarendon, 1978.

Derron, Pascale. "Inventaire des Manuscrits du Pseudo-Phocylide." *Revue d'Histoire des Textes* 10 (1980): 237–47.

Devereux, Daniel. "Courage and Wisdom in Plato's *Laches*." *Journal of the History of Philosophy* 15 (1977): 129–41.

Dickie, Matthew W. *Magic and Magicians in the Greco-Roman World.* London: Routledge, 2001.

Dietrich, Ernst L. "Die Religion Noahs, ihre Herkunft und ihre Bedeutung." *ZRGG* 1 (1948): 301–15.

Dihle, Albrecht. "Gerechtigkeit." *RAC* 10 (1978): 233–360.

_____. *Greek and Latin Literature of the Roman Empire.* London: Routledge, 1994.

Dixon, Suzanne. "The Sentimental Ideal of the Roman Family." Pages 99–113 in Rawson, *Marriage*.

_____. *The Roman Family*. Baltimore: Johns Hopkins University Press, 1992.

Dover, Kenneth J. *Greek Popular Morality in the Time of Plato and Aristotle*. Berkeley: University of California Press, 1974.

Droge, Arthur J. *Homer or Moses? Early Christian Interpretations of the History of Culture*. HUT 26. Tübingen: J. C. B. Mohr (Paul Siebeck), 1989.

Dyck, Andrew R. *A Commentary on Cicero, De Officiis*. Ann Arbor: University of Michigan Press, 1996.

Edwards, Catharine. *The Politics of Immorality in Ancient Rome*. Cambridge: Cambridge University Press, 1993.

Ehrenberg, Victor. *Sophocles and Pericles*. Oxford: Blackwell, 1954.

Elior, Rachel. "Mysticism, Magic, and Angelology: The Perception of Angels in Hekhalot Literature." *JSQ* 1 (1993–94): 3–53.

Engberg-Pedersen, Troels. *Aristotle's Theory of Moral Insight*. Oxford: Clarendon, 1983.

Epstein, Louis. M. *Sex Laws and Customs in Judaism*. New York: KTAV, 1948.

Esser, Hans-Helmut and Colin Brown. "πτωχός." *NIDNTT* 2 (1976): 821–29.

Esteve-Forriol, José. *Die Trauer- und Trostgedichte in der römischen Literatur*. München: A. Schubert, 1962.

Eyben, Emiel. "Family Planning in Graeco-Roman Antiquity." *Ancient Society* 11–12 (1980): 5–82.

Feldman, David M. *Birth Control in Jewish Law: Marital Relations, Contraception and Abortion as Set Forth in the Classic Texts of Jewish Law*. 2nd ed. New York: Schocken, 1974.

Ferguson, Everett. "Spiritual Sacrifice in Early Christianity and its Environment." *ANRW* II.23.2 (1980): 1151–89.

Ferguson, John. *Moral Values in the Ancient World*. London: Methuen, 1958.

Fiedler, Martin. "Δικαιοσύνη in der diaspora-jüdischen und intertestamentarischen Literatur." *JSJ* 1 (1970): 120–43.

Fiedler, Pieter. "Haustafel." *RAC* 13 (1986): 1063–73.

Figueras, Pau. *Decorated Jewish Ossuaries*. Documenta et Monumenta Orientis Antiqui 20. Leiden: E. J. Brill, 1983.

Finegan, Jack. *The Archaeology of the New Testament*. Princeton: Princeton University Press, 1969.

Fiore, Benjamin. *The Function of Personal Example in the Socratic and Pastoral Epistles*. AnBib 105. Rome: Biblical Institute Press, 1986.

_____. "The Theory and Practice of Friendship in Cicero." Pages 59–76 in *Greco-Roman Perspectives on Friendship*. Edited by John T. Fitzgerald. SBLRBS 34. Atlanta: Scholars, 1997.

Fischer, Ulrich. *Eschatologie und Jenseitserwartung im hellenistischen Diasporajudentum*. BZNW 44. Berlin: Walter de Gruyter, 1978.

Fisher, N. R. E. "Hybris and Dishonour." *GR* 23 (1976): 177–93.

_____. *Hybris: A Study in the Values of Honour and Shame in Ancient Greece.* Warminster: Aris & Phillips, 1992.

Fitzer, Gottfried. "τολμάω." *TDNT* 8 (1972): 181–86.

Fitzgerald, John T. "The Problem of Perjury in Greek Context: Prolegomena to an Exegesis of Matthew 5:33, 1 Timothy 1:10, and *Didache* 2.3." Pages 156–77 in *The Social World of the First Christians: Essays in Honor of Wayne A. Meeks.* Edited by L. Michael White and O. Larry Yarbrough. Minneapolis: Fortress, 1995.

Fitzgerald, William. "Labor and Laborer in Latin Poetry: the Case of the *Moretum*." *Arethusa* 29 (1996): 389–418.

_____. *Slavery and the Roman Literary Imagination.* Cambridge: Cambridge University Press, 2000.

Fletcher-Louis, Crispin H. T. *All the Glory of Adam: Liturgical Anthropology in the Dead Sea Scrolls.* STDJ 42. Leiden: E. J. Brill, 2002.

Flusser, David. "Psalms, Hymns and Prayers." Pages 551–77 in *Jewish Writings of the Second Temple Period.* Edited by Michael E. Stone. CRINT 2.2. Philadelphia: Fortress, 1984.

Ford, Andrew L. "The Seal of Theognis: The Politics of Authorship in Archaic Greece." Pages 82–95 in *Theognis of Megara: Poetry and the Polis.* Edited by Thomas J. Figueira and Gregory Nagy. Baltimore: Johns Hopkins University Press, 1985.

Foucault, Michel. *The History of Sexuality.* 3 vols. New York: Pantheon, 1978–86.

Foxhall, Lin. "Foreign Powers: Plutarch and Discourses of Domination in Roman Greece." Pages 138–50 in Pomeroy, *Plutarch's Advice.*

Frank, Karl S. "Habsucht." *RAC* 13 (1986): 226–47.

Freund, Richard A. "The Decalogue in Early Judaism and Christianity." Pages 124–41 in *The Function of Scripture in Early Jewish and Christian Tradition.* Edited by Craig A. Evans and James A. Sanders. JSNTSup 154. Sheffield: Sheffield Academic Press, 1998.

Führer, Rudolf. "Pseudo-Phokylides Vers 127." *Glotta* 70 (1992): 61.

Gallo, Italo, and Emidio Pettine. *Plutarco: Come distinguere l'adulatore dall'amico.* Corpus Plutarchi Moralium 1. Napoli: M. D'Auria, 1988.

Gallop, Jane, ed. *Pedagogy: The Question of Impersonation.* Bloomington: Indiana University Press, 1995.

Gardner, Jane F. *Women in Roman Law and Society.* London: Croom Helm, 1986.

Gardner, Jane F., and Thomas Wiedemann, eds. *The Roman Household: A Sourcebook.* London: Routledge, 1991.

Garlan, Yvon. *Slavery in Ancient Greece.* Rev. ed. Ithaca: Cornell University Press, 1988.

Garland, Robert. *The Greek Way of Death.* Ithaca: Cornell University Press, 1985.

Garnsey, Peter. "Legal Privilege in the Roman Empire." Pages 141–65 in *Studies in Ancient Society.* Edited by M. I. Finley. London: Routledge and Kegan Paul, 1974.

_____. *Famine and Food Supply in the Graeco-Roman World*. Cambridge: Cambridge University Press, 1988.

Gauthier, René-Antonin. *Magnanimité: L'idéal de la grandeur dans la philosophie païenne et dans la théologie chrétienne*. Bibliothèque Thomiste 28. Paris: J. Vrin, 1951.

Gerber, Douglas E., ed. *Greek Elegiac Poetry*. LCL. Cambridge: Harvard University Press, 1999.

Gerhard, Gustav A. *Phoinix von Kolophon*. Leipzig: Teubner, 1909.

Gerstenberger, Erhard S. *Leviticus*. OTL. Louisville: Westminster/John Knox, 1996.

Gertz, Jan C. *Die Gerichtsorganisation Israels im deuteronomischen Gesetz*. FRLANT 165. Göttingen: Vandenhoeck & Ruprecht, 1994.

Gielen, Marlis. *Tradition und Theologie neutestamentlicher Haustafelethik*. BBB 75. Frankfurt am Main: Hain, 1990.

Glad, Clarence E. *Paul and Philodemus: Adaptability in Epicurean and Early Christian Psychagogy*. NovTSup 81. Leiden: E. J. Brill, 1995.

Gooch, P. W. "The Relation Between Wisdom and Virtue in *Phaedo* 69A6–C3." *Journal of the History of Philosophy* 12 (1974): 153–59.

Goodfriend, Elaine A. "Adultery." *ABD* 1 (1992): 82–86.

Gow, A. S. F., and D. L. Page. *The Greek Anthology: Hellenistic Epigrams*. Vol. II. Cambridge: Cambridge University Press, 1965.

Gowers, Emily. *The Loaded Table: Representations of Food in Roman Literature*. Oxford: Clarendon, 1993.

Greene, William C. *Moira: Fate, Good, and Evil in Greek Thought*. Cambridge: Harvard University Press, 1948.

Gruen, Erich S. *Heritage and Hellenism: The Reinvention of Jewish Tradition*. Berkeley: University of California Press, 1998.

Guyot, Peter. *Eunuchen als Sklaven und Freigelassene in der griechisch-römischen Antike*. Stuttgarter Beiträge zur Geschichte und Politik 14. Stuttgart: Klett-Cotta, 1980.

Hadot, Pierre. "Fürstenspiegel." *RAC* 8 (1972): 555–632.

Hallett, Judith P. "Female Homoeroticism and the Denial of Roman Reality in Latin Literature." *Yale Journal of Criticism* 3 (1989): 209–27.

Hands, Arthur R. *Charities and Social Aid in Greece and Rome*. Ithaca: Cornell University Press, 1968.

Harris, William V. "Child-Exposure in the Roman Empire." *JRS* 84 (1994): 1–22.

_____. *Restraining Rage: The Ideology of Anger Control in Classical Antiquity*. Cambridge: Harvard University Press, 2001.

Hauck, Friedrich. "κοινός, κτλ." *TDNT* 3 (1965): 789–809.

_____. "μένω, κτλ." *TDNT* 4 (1967): 574–88.

_____. "μοιχεύω, κτλ." *TDNT* 4 (1967): 729–35.

_____. "πένης, κτλ." *TDNT* 6 (1968): 37–40.

Hauck, Friedrich, and Ernst Bammel. "πτωχός, κτλ." *TDNT* 6 (1968): 885–915.

Havelock, Eric A. *The Greek Concept of Justice.* Cambridge: Harvard University Press, 1978.

Hecht, Richard D. "Preliminary Issues in the Analysis of Philo's *De Specialibus Legibus.*" *SPhilo* 5 (1978): 1–55.

Hengel, Martin. *Judaism and Hellenism.* Minneapolis: Fortress, 1974.

_____. *The Charismatic Leader and his Followers.* New York: Crossroad, 1981.

Herman, Gabriel. *Ritualised Friendship and the Greek City.* Cambridge: Cambridge University Press, 1987.

Hiltbrunner, Otto. "Humanitas." *RAC* 16 (1994): 711–52.

Hine, Harry. "Seneca, Stoicism, and the Problem of Moral Evil." Pages 93–106 in Innes, Hine, and Pelling, *Ethics and Rhetoric.*

Hirzel, Rudlof. *ΑΓΡΑΦΟΣ ΝΟΜΟΣ.* Abhandlungen der (königlichen) sächsischen Gesellschaft der Wissenschaften; Philologisch-historische Klasse 20.1. Leipzig: Teubner, 1900.

Hock, Ronald F. *The Social Context of Paul's Ministry: Tentmaking and Apostleship.* Philadelphia: Fortress, 1980.

Höistad, Ragnar. *Cynic Hero and Cynic King: Studies in the Cynic Conception of Man.* Uppsala: Carl Bloms, 1948.

Holladay, Carl R. *Fragments From Hellenistic Jewish Authors.* Vol. II: *Poets.* SBLTT 30. Atlanta: Scholars, 1989.

Hollander, Harm W., and Marinus de Jonge. *The Testaments of the Twelve Patriarchs.* SVTP 8. Leiden: E. J. Brill, 1985.

Hopfner, Theodor. *Das Sexualleben der Griechen und Römer.* Prague: J. G. Calve, 1938.

Hopkins, Keith. *Conquerors and Slaves.* Sociological Studies in Roman History 1. Cambridge: Cambridge University Press, 1977.

_____. "Brother-Sister Marriage in Roman Egypt." *Society for Comparative Study of Society and History* 22 (1980): 303–54.

Horsley, Richard A. "The Law of Nature in Philo and Cicero." *HTR* 71 (1978): 35–59.

Horst, Johannes. "μακροθυμία, κτλ." *TDNT* 4 (1967): 374–87.

Houtman, Cornelius. *Exodus.* Vol. 3. Historical Commentary on the Old Testament. Leuven: Peeters, 2000.

Ibscher, Gred. *Der Begriff des Sittlichen in der Pflichtenlehre des Panaitios: Ein Beitrag zur Erkenntnis der mittleren Stoa.* München: R. Oldenbourg, 1934.

Ilan, Tal. *Jewish Women in Greco-Roman Palestine.* Peabody: Hendrickson, 1996.

Innes, Doreen, Harry Hine, and Christopher Pelling, eds. *Ethics and Rhetoric: Classical Essays for Donald Russell on his Seventy-fifth Birthday.* Oxford: Clarendon, 1995.

Irwin, Terence. *Plato's Moral Theory: The Early and Middle Dialogues*. Oxford: Clarendon, 1977.

_____. *Plato's Ethics*. New York: Oxford University Press, 1995.

Jackson, Bernard S. *Theft in Early Jewish Law*. Oxford: Clarendon, 1972.

Jaeger, Werner. *Paideia: The Ideals of Greek Culture*. Oxford: Blackwell, 1939.

Jastram, Daniel N. "Philo's Concept of Generic Virtue." Pages 323–47 in *SBLSP* 30. Edited by Eugene H. Lovering. Atlanta: Scholars, 1991.

Jervell, Jacob. *Imago Dei: Gen 1,26f. im Spätjudentum, in der Gnosis und in den paulinischen Briefen*. FRLANT 76. Göttingen: Vandenhoeck & Ruprecht, 1960.

Johnson, Luke T. "The Use of Leviticus 19 in the Letter of James." *JBL* 101 (1982): 391–401.

Jones, Christopher P. *The Roman World of Dio Chrysostom*. Loeb Classical Monographs. Cambridge: Harvard University Press, 1978.

_____. "Stigma: Tattooing and Branding in Greco-Roman Antiquity." *JRS* 77 (1987): 139–55.

Kamlah, Ehrhard. "Frömmigkeit und Tugend: Die Gesetzesapologie des Josephus in c Ap 2, 145–195." Pages 220–32 in *Josephus-Studien: Untersuchungen zu Josephus, dem antiken Judentum und dem Neuen Testament. Otto Michel zum 70. Geburtstag gewidmet*. Edited by Otto Betz, Klaus Haacker, and Martin Hengel. Göttingen: Vandenhoeck & Ruprecht, 1974.

Kasher, Aryeh. *The Jews in Hellenistic and Roman Egypt*. TSAJ 7. Tübingen: J. C. B. Mohr (Paul Siebeck), 1985.

Kassel, Rudolf. *Untersuchungen zur griechischen und römischen Konsolationsliteratur*. Zetemata 18. München: C. H. Beck, 1958.

Kennedy, George A. *The Art of Persuasion in Greece*. History of Rhetoric 1. Princeton: Princeton University Press, 1963.

Kitchen, Kenneth A. "Basic Literary Forms and Formulations of Ancient Instructional Writing in Egypt and Western Asia." Pages 235–82 in *Studien zu altägyptischen Lebenslehren*. Edited by Erik Hornung and Othmar Keel. OBO 28. Freiburg (Schweiz): Universitätsverlag; Göttingen: Vandenhoeck & Ruprecht, 1979.

Kleinknecht, Hermann et al. "ὀργή, κτλ." *TDNT* 5 (1967): 382–447.

Kloppenborg, John S. *The Formation of Q: Trajectories in Ancient Wisdom Collections*. SAC. Philadelphia: Fortress, 1987.

Koep, Leo. "Biene." *RAC* 2 (1954): 274–82.

Koester, Helmut. "ΝΟΜΟΣ ΦΥΣΕΩΣ: The Concept of Natural Law in Greek Thought." Pages 521–41 in *Religions in Antiquity*. Edited by Jacob Neusner. Leiden: E. J. Brill, 1968.

Konstan, David. "Friendship and Monarchy: Dio of Prusa's Third Oration on Kingship." *SO* 72 (1997): 124–43.

Korenjak, Martin, and Robert Rollinger. "ΚΑΙ ΤΟΔΕ ΦΩΚΥΛΙΔΕΩ? 'Phokylides' und der Fall Ninives." *Phil* 145 (2001): 195–202.

Kötting, Bernhard. "Digamus." *RAC* 3 (1957): 1016–24.

Kötting, Bernhard, and Theodor Hopfner. "Bigamie." *RAC* 2 (1954): 282–86.

Kranz, Walther. "Sphragis: Ichform und Namensiegel als Eingangs- und Schlusz-motiv antiker Dichtung." *Rheinisches Museum für Philologie* 104 (1961): 3–46, 97–124.

Krause, Jutta. *ΑΛΛΟΤΕ ΑΛΛΟΣ: Untersuchungen zum Motiv des Schicksalswechsels in der griechischen Dichtung bis Euripides*. Tuduv Studies, Reihe Kulturwissenschaften 4. München: Tuduv-Verlagsgesellschaft, 1976.

Krischer, Tilman. "Die logischen Formen der Priamel." *Grazer Beiträge* 2 (1974): 79–91.

Kröhling, Walter. *Die Priamel (Beispielreihung) als Stilmittel in der griechisch-römischen Dichtung*. Greifswalder Beiträge zur Literatur- und Stilforschung 10. Greifswald: Hans Dallmeyer, 1935.

Küchler, Max. *Frühjüdische Weisheitstraditionen: Zum Fortgang weisheitlichen Denkens im Bereich des frühjüdischen Jahweglaubens*. OBO 26. Freiburg: Universitätsverlag; Göttingen: Vandenhoeck & Ruprecht, 1979.

Kugel, James. "Reuben's Sin with Bilhah in the *Testament of Reuben*." Pages 525–54 in *Pomegranates and Golden Bells: Studies in Biblical, Jewish, and Near Eastern Ritual, Law, and Literature in Honor of Jacob Milgrom*. Edited by David P. Wright, David Noel Freedman, and Avi Hurvitz. Winona Lake: Eisenbrauns, 1995.

Lang, B. "Das Verbot des Meineids im Dekalog." *ThQ* 161 (1981): 97–105.

Lattimore, Richard. *Themes in Greek and Latin Epitaphs*. Urbana: University of Illinois Press, 1962.

Lausberg, Heinrich. *Handbook of Literary Rhetoric: A Foundation for Literary Study*. Leiden: E. J. Brill, 1998.

Licht, Hans. *Sexual Life in Ancient Greece*. New York: Barnes & Noble, 1963.

Lilja, Saara. *Homosexuality in Republican and Augustan Rome*. Helsinki: Societas Scientiarum Fennica, 1983.

Link, Hans-Georg. "ἐλέγχω." *NIDNTT* 2 (1976): 140–42.

Lohse, Eduard. "πρόσωπον, κτλ." *TDNT* 6 (1968): 768–80.

_____. *Theological Ethics of the New Testament*. Minneapolis: Fortress, 1991.

Luck, Ulrich. "σώφρων, κτλ." *TDNT* 7 (1971): 1097–1104.

_____. "φιλανθρωπία, κτλ." *TDNT* 9 (1974): 107–12.

Ludwich, Arthur. "Über das Spruchbuch des falschen Phokylides." Pages 1–26 in *Programm Königsberg*. Königsberg: Universität Königsberg, 1904.

Lumpe, Adolf. "Essen." *RAC* 6 (1966): 612–35.

MacDowell, Douglas M. *Athenian Homicide Law in the Age of the Orators*. Manchester: Manchester University Press, 1963.

_____. "Hybris in Athens." *GR* 23 (1976): 14–31.

Mack, Burton L. *Logos und Sophia: Untersuchungen zur Weisheitstheologie im hellenistischen Judentum*. SUNT 10. Göttingen: Vandenhoeck & Ruprecht, 1973.

Maier, Johann. "Armut IV." *TRE* 4 (1979): 80–85.

Malherbe, Abraham J. *Social Aspects of Early Christianity*. 2nd ed. Philadelphia: Fortress, 1983.

_____. *Moral Exhortation: A Greco-Roman Sourcebook*. LEC 4. Philadelphia: Westminster, 1986.

_____. *Paul and the Popular Philosophers*. Minneapolis: Fortress, 1989.

Marrou, Henri I. *A History of Education in Antiquity*. London: Sheed and Ward, 1956.

Martin, Dale B. *Slavery as Salvation: The Metaphor of Slavery in Pauline Christianity*. New Haven: Yale University Press, 1990.

_____. *The Corinthian Body*. New Haven: Yale University Press, 1995.

_____. "Slavery and the Ancient Jewish Family." Pages 113–29 in Cohen, *Jewish Family*.

Martin, Josef. *Antike Rhetorik: Technik und Methode*. Handbuch der Altertumswissenschaft 2.3. München: C. H. Beck, 1974.

McGinn, Thomas A. J. *Prostitution, Sexuality, and the Law in Ancient Rome*. Oxford: Oxford University Press, 1998.

McKane, William. "Functions of Language and Objectives of Discourse According to Proverbs 10–30." Pages 166–85 in *La Sagesse de l'Ancien Testament*. Edited by Maurice Gilbert. 2nd ed. BETL 51. Leuven: Leuven University Press, 1990.

McKeating, Henry. "Sanctions against Adultery in Ancient Israelite Society." *JSOT* 11 (1979): 57–72.

Meeks, Wayne A. "The Circle of Reference in Pauline Morality." Pages 305–17 in *Greeks, Romans, and Christians: Essays in Honor of Abraham J. Malherbe*. Edited by David L. Balch, Everett Ferguson, and Wayne A. Meeks. Minneapolis: Fortress, 1990.

Mendelson, Alan. *Secular Education in Philo of Alexandria*. HUCM 7. Cincinnati: Hebrew Union College, 1982.

Merki, Hubert. "Ebenbildlichkeit." *RAC* 4 (1959): 459–79.

Meyers, Eric M. *Jewish Ossuaries: Reburial and Rebirth*. Rome: Biblical Institute Press, 1971.

Michel, Diethelm. "Armut II." *TRE* 4 (1979): 72–76.

Milgrom, Jacob. *Leviticus 17–22*. AB 3A. New York: Doubleday, 2000.

Miller, Fred D. "Naturalism." Pages 321–43 in *The Cambridge History of Greek and Roman Political Thought*. Edited by Christopher Rowe and Malcolm Schofield. Cambridge: Cambridge University Press, 2000.

Milobenski, Ernst. *Der Neid in der griechischen Philosophie*. Klassisch-philologische Studien 29. Wiesbaden: Otto Harrassowitz, 1964.

Mitchell, Margaret M. *Paul and the Rhetoric of Reconciliation: An Exegetical Investigation of the Language and Composition of 1 Corinthians*. HUT 28. Tübingen: J. C. B. Mohr (Paul Siebeck), 1991. Reprint, Louisville: Westminster/John Knox, 1992.

Moles, John. "The Kingship Orations of Dio Chrysostom." *Papers of the Leeds International Latin Seminar* 6 (1990): 297–375.

Morgan, Teresa. *Literate Education in the Hellenistic and Roman Worlds.* Cambridge: Cambridge University Press, 1998.

Mott, Stephen C. "Greek Ethics and Christian Conversion: The Philonic Background of Titus 2:10–14 and 3:3–7." *NovT* 20 (1978): 22–48.

Moulinier, Louis. *Le Pur et l'Impur dans la Pensée des Grecs d'Homère à Aristote.* Etudes et Commentaires 12. Paris: Klincksieck, 1950.

Najman, Hindy. "The Law of Nature and the Authority of Mosaic Law." *SPhA* 9 (1999): 55–73.

Nelson, Richard D. *Deuteronomy.* OTL. Louisville: Westminster/John Knox, 2002.

Nesselrath, Heinz-Günther. *Lukians Parasitendialog: Untersuchungen und Kommentar.* Untersuchungen zur antiken Literatur und Geschichte 22. Berlin and New York: Walter de Gruyter, 1985.

Neusner, Jacob. *The Idea of Purity in Ancient Judaism.* SJLA 1. Leiden: E. J. Brill, 1973.

Newman, Robert J. "*Cotidie meditare:* Theory and Practice of the *meditatio* in Imperial Stoicism." *ANRW* II.36.3 (1989): 1473–1517.

Niebuhr, Karl-Wilhelm. *Gesetz und Paränese: Katechismusartige Weisungsreihen in der frühjüdischen Literatur.* WUNT 2.28. Tübingen: J. C. B. Mohr (Paul Siebeck), 1987.

Niehoff, Maren. *Philo on Jewish Identity and Culture.* TSAJ 86. Tübingen: J. C. B. Mohr (Paul Siebeck), 2001.

Nock, Arthur Darby. "Eunuchs in Ancient Religion." Pages 7–15 in *Arthur Darby Nock: Essays on Religion and the Ancient World.* Vol. 1. Edited by Zeph Stewart. Cambridge: Harvard University Press, 1972.

Norden, Eduard. *Agnostos Theos: Untersuchungen zur Formengeschichte religiöser Rede.* Leipzig and Berlin: Teubner, 1913. Reprint, Darmstadt: Wissenschaftliche Buchgesellschaft, 1956.

North, Helen. "Canons and Hierarchies of the Cardinal Virtues in Greek and Latin Literature." Pages 165–83 in *The Classical Tradition: Literary and Historical Studies in Honor of Harry Caplan.* Edited by Luitpold Wallach. Ithaca: Cornell University Press, 1966.

———. *Sophrosyne: Self-Knowledge and Self-Restraint in Greek Literature.* Cornell Studies in Classical Philology 35. Ithaca: Cornell University Press, 1966.

Novak, David. *The Image of the Non-Jew in Judaism: An Historical and Constructive Study of the Noahide Laws.* Toronto Studies in Theology 14. New York: Mellen, 1983.

Nussbaum, Martha C. *The Therapy of Desire: Theory and Practice in Hellenistic Ethics.* Princeton: Princeton University Press, 1994.

———. "Erōs and Ethical Norms: Philosophers Respond to a Cultural Dilemma." Pages 55–94 in Nussbaum and Sihvola, *The Sleep of Reason.*

Nussbaum, Martha C., and Juha Sihvola, eds. *The Sleep of Reason: Erotic Experience and Sexual Ethics in Ancient Greece and Rome*. Chicago: University of Chicago Press, 2002.

_____. "Introduction." Pages 1–20 in Nussbaum and Sihvola, *The Sleep of Reason*.

Page, D. L. *Further Greek Epigrams*. Cambridge: Cambridge University Press, 1981.

Parker, Robert. *Miasma: Pollution and Purification in Early Greek Religion*. Oxford: Clarendon, 1983.

Patterson, Cynthia. "Not Worth the Rearing: The Causes of Infant Exposure in Ancient Greece." *TAPA* 115 (1985): 103–23.

_____. "Plutarch's Advice to the Bride and Groom: Traditional Wisdom Through a Philosophic Lens." Pages 128–37 in Pomeroy, *Plutarch's Advice*.

Pelletier, A. "La philanthropia de tous les jours chez les écrivains juifs hellénisés." Pages 35–44 in *Paganisme, Judaïsme, Christianisme: Influences et affrontements dans le monde antique. Mélanges offerts à Marcel Simon*. Paris: Editions E. de Boccard, 1978.

Percy, William A. *Pederasty and Pedagogy in Archaic Greece*. Urbana: University of Illinois Press, 1996.

Perdue, Leo G. *Wisdom and Cult: A Critical Analysis of the Views of Cult in the Wisdom Literature of Israel and the Ancient Near East*. SBLDS 30. Missoula: Scholars, 1977.

Peterson, Erik. *ΕΙΣ ΘΕΟΣ: Epigraphische, formgeschichtliche und religionsgeschichtliche Untersuchungen*. FRLANT 24. Göttingen: Vandenhoeck & Ruprecht, 1926.

Phillips, Anthony. "Another Look at Adultery." *JSOT* 20 (1981): 3–25.

Pilhofer, Peter. *Presbyteron Kreitton: Der Altersbeweis der jüdischen und christlichen Apologeten und seine Vorgeschichte*. WUNT 2.39. Tübingen: J. C. B. Mohr (Paul Siebeck), 1990.

Plescia, Joseph. *The Oath and Perjury in Ancient Greece*. Tallahassee: Florida State University Press, 1970.

Pohlenz, Max. "Τὸ πρέπον: Ein Beitrag zur Geschichte des griechischen Geistes." Pages 53–92 in *Nachrichten von der Gesellschaft der Wissenschaften zu Göttingen. Philologisch-historische Klasse*. Berlin: Weidmannsche Buchhandlung, 1933.

Pomeroy, Sarah B. *Families in Classical and Hellenistic Greece*. Oxford: Clarendon, 1997.

Pomeroy, Sarah B., ed. *Plutarch's Advice to the Bride and Groom, and A Consolation to His Wife*. New York: Oxford University Press, 1999.

Powell, J. U., and E. A. Barber. *New Chapters in the History of Greek Literature*. Oxford: Clarendon, 1921.

Praechter, Karl. *Hierokles der Stoiker*. Leipzig: Dieterich'sche Verlags-Buchhandlung, 1901.

Preisker, Herbert. "κλέπτω, κτλ." *TDNT* 3 (1965): 754–56.

Preuß, Horst D. "Barmherzigkeit I." *TRE* 5 (1980): 215–24.

Price, A. W. *Love and Friendship in Plato and Aristotle*. Oxford: Clarendon, 1989.

Pucci, Joseph. *The Full-Knowing Reader: Allusion and the Power of the Reader in the Western Literary Tradition*. New Haven: Yale University Press, 1998.

Race, William H. *The Classical Priamel from Homer to Boethius*. Mnemosyne Sup. 74. Leiden: E. J. Brill, 1982.

Ranft, Joseph. "Depositum." *RAC* 3 (1957): 778–84.

Rawson, Beryl, ed. *Marriage, Divorce, and Children in Ancient Rome*. Oxford: Clarendon, 1991.

Rech, Ph. "Ameise." *RAC* 1 (1950): 375–77.

Reicke, Bo. *Die Zehn Worte in Geschichte und Gegenwart*. BGBE 13. Tübingen: J. C. B. Mohr (Paul Siebeck), 1973.

Reinhartz, Adele. "Philo on Infanticide." *SPhA* 4 (1992): 42–58.

Riaud, Jean. "Quelques observations sur les relations parents-enfants dans les *Sentences* du Pseudo-Phocylide." *RHPR* 80 (2000): 79–92.

Richlin, Amy. *The Garden of Priapus: Sexuality and Aggression in Roman Humor*. New Haven: Yale University Press, 1983.

_____. "Not Before Homosexuality: The Materiality of the *Cinaedus* and the Roman Law against Love between Men." *Journal of the History of Sexuality* 3 (1993): 523–73.

Rickert, GailAnn. *EKΩN and AKΩN in Early Greek Thought*. American Classical Studies 20. Atlanta: Scholars, 1989.

Riddle, John M. *Contraception and Abortion from the Ancient World to the Renaissance*. Cambridge: Harvard University Press, 1992.

Riedweg, Christoph. *Mysterienterminologie bei Platon, Philon und Klemens von Alexandrien*. Untersuchungen zur antiken Literatur und Geschichte 26. Berlin and New York: Walter de Gruyter, 1987.

Rist, John M. *Stoic Philosophy*. Cambridge: Cambridge University Press, 1969.

_____. *Human Value: A Study in Ancient Philosophical Ethics*. Philosophia Antiqua 40. Leiden: E. J. Brill, 1982.

Rorty, Amélie O., ed. *Essays on Aristotle's Ethics*. Major Thinkers Series 2. Berkeley: University of California Press, 1980.

Rosenmeyer, Patricia A. *Ancient Epistolary Fictions: The Letter in Greek Literature*. Cambridge: Cambridge University Press, 2001.

Rosivach, Vincent J. "Some Athenian Presuppositions About 'The Poor'." *GR* 38 (1991): 189–98.

Roth, Paul. "The Theme of Corrupted *Xenia* in Aeschylus' *Oresteia*." *Mnemosyne* 46 (1993): 1–17.

Rowe, Christopher J. "Justice and Temperance in *Republic* IV." Pages 336–44 in *Arktouros: Hellenic Studies Presented to Bernard M. W. Knox*. Edited by Glen W. Bowersock, Walter Burkert, and Michael C. J. Putnam. Berlin and New York: Walter de Gruyter, 1979.

Russell, D. A. "De Imitatione." Pages 1–16 in West and Woodman, *Creative Imitation*.

Saller, Richard P. *Personal Patronage under the Early Empire*. Cambridge: Cambridge University Press, 1982.

_____. "Corporal Punishment, Authority, and Obedience in the Roman Household." Pages 144–65 in Rawson, *Marriage*.

Sanders, E. P. *Jewish Law from Jesus to the Mishnah: Five Studies*. London: SCM; Philadelphia: Trinity Press International, 1990.

Sandmel, Samuel. "Virtue and Reward in Philo." Pages 215–23 in *Essays in Old Testament Ethics: J. Philip Hyatt, In Memoriam*. Edited by James L. Crenshaw and John T. Willis. New York: KTAV, 1974.

_____. *Philo of Alexandria: An Introduction*. Oxford: Oxford University Press, 1979.

Scarborough, John. *Roman Medicine*. Ithaca: Cornell University Press, 1969.

Schiffman, Lawrence H. "The Prohibition of Judicial Corruption in the Dead Sea Scrolls, Philo, Josephus and Talmudic Law." Pages 155–78 in *Hesed Ve-Emet: Studies in Honor of Ernest S. Frerichs*. Edited by Jodi Magness and Seymour Gitin. BJS 320. Atlanta: Scholars, 1998.

Schlier, Heinrich. "καθήκω." *TDNT* 3 (1965): 437–40.

Schmid, Ulrich. *Die Priamel der Werte im Griechischen von Homer bis Paulus*. Wiesbaden: Otto Harrassowitz, 1964.

Schmid, Walter T. *On Manly Courage: A Study of Plato's Laches*. Philosophical Explorations. Carbondale: Southern Illinois University Press, 1992.

Schmidt, Leopold. *Die Ethik der alten Griechen*. 2 vols. Berlin: W. Hertz, 1882. Reprint, Stuttgart: Friedrich Frommann, 1964.

Schrenk, Gottlob. "δίκη, κτλ." *TDNT* 2 (1964): 174–225.

Schürer, Emil et al. *The History of the Jewish People in the Age of Jesus Christ*. Vol. 3, Pt. 1. Rev. ed. Edinburgh: T. & T. Clark, 1986.

Schwer, W. "Armenpflege." *RAC* 1 (1950): 689–98.

Scott, Alan. *Origen and the Life of the Stars*. Oxford: Clarendon, 1991.

Scroggs, Robin. *The New Testament and Homosexuality*. Philadelphia: Fortress, 1983.

Sedlmeier, Franz. "Höre, Israel! JHWH: Unser Gott (ist er) … ." *TTZ* 108 (1999): 21–39.

Seland, Torrey. *Establishment Violence in Philo and Luke: A Study of Non-Conformity to the Torah and Jewish Vigilante Reactions*. Biblical Interpretation Series 15. Leiden: E. J. Brill, 1995.

Shaw, Brent, "Debt in Sallust." *Latomus* 34 (1975): 187–96.

Shelton, Jo-Ann. *As the Romans Did: A Sourcebook in Roman Social History*. 2nd ed. Oxford: Oxford University Press, 1998.

Sirinelli, Jean et al. *Plutarque: Œuvres Morales*. Vol. 1, Pt. 2. Budé. Paris: Société d'Edition 'Les Belles Lettres,' 1989.

Skehan, Patrick W., and Alexander A. DiLella. *The Wisdom of Ben Sira*. AB 39. Garden City: Doubleday, 1987.

Sorabji, Richard. "Aristotle on the Role of Intellect in Virtue." Pages 201–19 in Rorty, *Essays*.

Spanneut, Michel. "Geduld." *RAC* 9 (1976): 243–94.

Speyer, Wolfgang. *Die literarische Fälschung im heidnischen und christlichen Altertum*. Handbuch der Altertumswissenschaft 1.2. München: C. H. Beck, 1971.

Spicq, Ceslas. *Theological Lexicon of the New Testament*. 3 vols. Peabody: Hendrickson, 1994.

Stadter, Philip. "Subject to the Erotic: Male Sexual Behaviour in Plutarch." Pages 221–36 in Innes, Hine, and Pelling, *Ethics and Rhetoric*.

Stafford, Emma J. "Plutarch on Persuasion." Pages 162–72 in Pomeroy, *Plutarch's Advice*.

Stählin, Gustav. "ἴσος, κτλ." *TDNT* 3 (1965): 343–55.

―――. "χήρα." *TDNT* 9 (1974): 440–65.

Stanford, William B. *The Ulysses Theme: A Study in the Adaptability of a Traditional Hero*. Oxford: Blackwell, 1954.

Sterling, Gregory E. "Philo and the Logic of Apologetics: An Analysis of the *Hypothetica*." Pages 412–30 in *SBLSP* 29. Edited by David J. Lull. Atlanta: Scholars, 1990.

―――. "Universalizing the Particular: Natural Law in Second Temple Jewish Ethics." *SPhA* 15 (2003): 64–80.

Stommel, Eduard. "Domus aeterna." *RAC* 4 (1959): 109–28.

Stork, Traudel. *Nil Igitur Mors est ad Nos: Der Schlussteil des dritten Lukrezbuchs und sein Verhältnis zur Konsolationsliteratur*. Habelts Dissertationsdrucke, Reihe klassische Philologie 9. Bonn: Rudolf Habelt, 1970.

Stowers, Stanley K. *A Rereading of Romans: Justice, Jews, and Gentiles*. New Haven: Yale University Press, 1994.

Striker, Gisela. *Essays on Hellenistic Epistemology and Ethics*. Cambridge: Cambridge University Press, 1996.

Stumpff, Albrecht. "ζῆλος, κτλ." *TDNT* 2 (1964): 877–88.

Swain, Simon. *Hellenism and Empire: Language, Classicism, and Power in the Greek World AD 50–250*. Oxford: Clarendon, 1996.

―――. "Plutarch's Moral Program." Pages 85–96 in Pomeroy, *Plutarch's Advice*.

Szesnat, Holger. "Philo and Female Homoeroticism." *JSJ* 30 (1999): 140–47.

Taubenschlag, Rafael. *The Law of Greco-Roman Egypt in the Light of the Papyri*. 2nd ed. New York: Herald Square, 1955.

Thiselton, Anthony C. *The First Epistle to the Corinthians*. NIGTC. Grand Rapids: Eerdmans, 2000.

Thomas, Johannes. *Der jüdische Phokylides: Formgeschichtliche Zugänge zu Pseudo-Phokylides und Vergleich mit der neutestamentlichen Paränese*. NTOA 23. Freiburg: Universitätsverlag; Göttingen: Vandenhoeck & Ruprecht, 1992.

Thornton, Bruce S. *Eros: The Myth of Ancient Greek Sexuality*. Boulder: Westview, 1997.

Thraede, Klaus. *Grundzüge griechisch-römischer Brieftopik*. Zetemata 48. München: C. H. Beck, 1970.

Toohey, Peter. *Epic Lessons: An Introduction to Ancient Didactic Poetry*. London: Routledge, 1996.

Tracy, Valerie A. "The Lenomaritus." *CJ* 72 (1976): 62–64.

Trebilco, Paul R. *Jewish Communities in Asia Minor*. SNTSMS 69. Cambridge: Cambridge University Press, 1991.

Treggiari, Susan. *Roman Marriage*. Oxford: Oxford University Press, 1991.

Trenchard, Warren C. *Ben Sira's View of Women*. Chico: Scholars, 1982.

van de Sandt, H. "Didache 3.1–6: A Transformation of an Existing Jewish Hortatory Pattern." *JSJ* 23 (1992): 21–41.

van den Hoek, Annewies. *Clement of Alexandria and his Use of Philo in the Stromateis: An Early Christian Reshaping of a Jewish Model*. VCSup 3. Leiden: E. J. Brill, 1988.

van der Horst, Pieter W. "Pseudo-Phocylides and the New Testament." *ZNW* 69 (1978): 187–202.

_____. "Pseudo-Phocylides Revisited." *JSP* 3 (1988): 3–30.

_____. *Ancient Jewish Epitaphs*. CBET 2. Kampen: Kok Pharos, 1991.

van Geytenbeek, A. C. *Musonius Rufus and Greek Diatribe*. Wijsgerige Teksten en Studies 8. Assen: van Gorcum, 1962.

van Otterlo, W. A. A. "Beiträge zur Kenntnis der griechischen Priamel." *Mnemosyne* 8 (1940): 145–76.

van Straaten, F. T. "Gifts for the Gods." Pages 65–151 in *Faith, Hope and Worship: Aspects of Religious Mentality in the Ancient World*. Edited by H. S. Versnel. Studies in Greek and Roman Religion 2. Leiden: E. J. Brill, 1981.

Vermes, Geza. "Sectarian Matrimonial Halakhah in the Damascus Rule." *JJS* 25 (1974): 197–202.

_____. "A Summary of the Law by Flavius Josephus." *NovT* 24 (1982): 289–303.

Vokes, F. E. "The Ten Commandments in the New Testament and in First Century Judaism." Pages 146–54 in *Studia Evangelica 5*. Edited by F. L. Cross. TU 103. Berlin: Akademie-Verlag, 1968.

Volk, Katharina. *The Poetics of Latin Didactic: Lucretius, Vergil, Ovid, Manilius*. Oxford: Oxford University Press, 2002.

Walcot, Peter. *Envy and the Greeks: A Study of Human Behavior*. Warminster: Aris & Phillips, 1978.

Ward, Roy Bowen. "Why Unnatural? The Tradition behind Romans 1:26–27." *HTR* 90 (1997): 263–84.

Waszink, Jan H. "Aether." *RAC* 1 (1950): 150–58.

Weber, Reinhard. *Das Gesetz im hellenistischen Judentum*. Arbeiten zur Religion und Geschichte des Urchristentums 10. Frankfurt am Main: Peter Lang, 2000.

Wedderburn, A. J. M. *Baptism and Resurrection: Studies in Pauline Theology against its Graeco-Roman Background*. WUNT 44. Tübingen: J. C. B. Mohr (Paul Siebeck), 1987.

West, David, and Tony Woodman, eds. *Creative Imitation and Latin Literature*. Cambridge: Cambridge University Press, 1979.

West, Martin L. "Phocylides." *JHS* 98 (1978): 164–67.

_____. *Greek Metre*. Oxford: Clarendon, 1982.

_____. *The Orphic Poems*. Oxford: Clarendon, 1983.

West, Martin L., ed. *Homeric Hymns, Homeric Apocrypha, Lives of Homer*. LCL. Cambridge: Harvard University Press, 2003.

Westbrook, Raymond. *Property and the Family in Biblical Law*. JSOTSup 113. Sheffield: JSOT, 1991.

White, Stephen A. *Sovereign Virtue: Aristotle on the Relation Between Happiness and Prosperity*. Stanford Series in Philosophy. Stanford: Stanford University Press, 1992.

Whitmarsh, Tim. *Greek Literature and the Roman Empire: The Politics of Imitation*. Oxford: Oxford University Press, 2001.

Wiedemann, Thomas E. J. *Greek and Roman Slavery*. London: Croom Helm, 1981.

_____. *Adults and Children in the Roman Empire*. New Haven: Yale University Press, 1989.

Wilckens, Ulrich, and Georg Fohrer. "σοφία, κτλ." *TDNT* 7 (1971): 465–528.

Wilckens, Ulrich et al. "Heuchelei." *RAC* 14 (1988): 1205–31.

Wilkins, John. *The Boastful Chef: The Discourse of Food in Ancient Greek Comedy*. Oxford: Oxford University Press, 2000.

Williams, Bernard. "Justice as a Virtue." Pages 189–199 in Rorty, *Essays*.

Williams, Craig. *Roman Homosexuality: Ideologies of Masculinity in Classical Antiquity*. New York: Oxford University Press, 1999.

Williams, James G. *Those Who Ponder Proverbs: Aphoristic Thinking and Biblical Literature*. Sheffield: Almond, 1981.

Willis, Timothy M. *The Elders of the City: A Study of the Elders-Laws in Deuteronomy*. SBLMS 55. Atlanta: SBL, 2001.

Wilson, Walter T. *Love Without Pretense: Romans 12:9–21 and Hellenistic-Jewish Wisdom Literature*. WUNT 2.46. Tübingen: J. C. B. Mohr (Paul Siebeck), 1991.

_____. *The Mysteries of Righteousness: The Literary Composition and Genre of the Sentences of Pseudo-Phocylides*. TSAJ 40. Tübingen: J. C. B. Mohr (Paul Siebeck), 1994.

Winkler, John J. *The Constraints of Desire: The Anthropology of Sex and Gender in Ancient Greece*. New York: Routledge, 1990.

Winston, David. *The Wisdom of Solomon*. AB 43. Garden City: Doubleday, 1979.

_____. "Philo's Ethical Theory." *ANRW* II.21.1 (1984): 372–416.

_____. "The Sage as Mystic in the Wisdom of Solomon." Pages 383–97 in *The Sage in Israel and the Ancient Near East.* Edited by John G. Gammie and Leo G. Perdue. Winona Lake: Eisenbrauns, 1990.

Wolfson, Harry A. *Philo.* 2 vols. Cambridge: Harvard University Press, 1947.

Wood, Ellen Meiksins, and Neal Wood. *Class Ideology and Ancient Political Theory.* New York: Oxford University Press, 1978.

Woodbury, L. "The Seal of Theognis." Pages 20–41 in *Studies in Honor of Gilbert Norwood.* Edited by Mary E. White. Phoenix Sup. 1. Toronto: University of Toronto Press, 1952.

Wright, M. R. "Cicero on Self-Love and Love of Humanity in *De Finibus* 3." Pages 171–95 in *Cicero the Philosopher.* Edited by J. G. F. Powell. Oxford: Clarendon, 1995.

Yarbrough, O. Larry. *Not Like the Gentiles: Marriage Rules in the Letters of Paul.* SBLDS 80. Atlanta: Scholars, 1986.

Ziegler, Konrat. "Tyche." PW (1948) II.7A.2:1643–96.

COMMENTARY

I. Prologue (Title + Verses 1–2)
and Epilogue (Verses 228–230)

Bibliography: Bockmuehl, *Revelation and Mystery*, 69–81. Collins, *Between Athens and Jerusalem*, 210–60. E. Ferguson, "Spiritual Sacrifice," 1151–89. Kranz, "Sphragis," 3–46, 97–124. Neusner, *The Idea of Purity*, 32–71. Parker, *Miasma*, 281–307. van Straaten, "Gifts for the Gods," 65–151.

MAXIMS OF PHOCYLIDES

1	These resolutions of God through holy judgments
2	Phocylides, wisest of men, reveals as blessed gifts.
…	…
228	Let there be purity of the soul where there are purifications of the body.
229	These are mysteries of righteousness; living by them
230	you may achieve a good life until the threshold of old age.

TEXTUAL NOTES

Title. In lieu of Φωκυλίδου γνῶμαι (in L, P), B, M have Φωκυλίδου φιλοσόφου ποίησις ὠφέλιμος ("A Beneficial Poem of Phocylides the Philosopher"), apparently amplifying the incipit with conventional designations for the poet (cf. *Suda* 4.754.19) and his poetry (cf. Dio Chrysostom, *Borysth.* 13). V omits. The title ΓΝΩΜΑΙ was attached to various gnomic writings in antiquity: Küchler, *Weisheitstraditionen*, 245–62. Verses 1–2. Despite the prologue's omission from V, most commentators agree that it is original to the poem; see van der Horst, *Sentences*, 59, 109–10; Derron, *Sentences*, xlv–xlvii. Verse 228. Following West's conjecture for the line in *CR* 30 (1980): 137. Cf. Young, *Theognis*, 112: ἁγνείη ψυχῆς, οὐ σώματός εἰσι καθαρμοί (followed by Derron, *Sentences*, 18: "La pureté est une purification de l'âme, non du corps.") and Ludwich, "Spruchbuch," 23: ἁγνείη ψυχῆς, οὐ σώματός εἰσι καθαρμοί (followed by van der Horst, *Sentences*, 103 n. 4, 258: "Purifications are for the purity of the soul, not [for the purity] of the body."). For discussion, see the commentary.

COMMENTARY

The main body of the *Sentences* (vv. 3–227) is framed by a prologue (vv. 1–2) and epilogue (vv. 228–230), the former functioning as the work's σφραγίς, a common device in classical literature. Ordinarily, a "seal" of this kind afforded an author the opportunity to identify himself by name and claim a composition as his own property, though it could reveal key facts about the nature of the work as well.[1] Phocylides of Miletus, for example, introduced some of his compositions simply with "Thus also (spake) Phocylides."[2] The seal of Theognis, by contrast, is more developed, encompassing certain claims apropos of the poem's moral objectives and divine inspiration.[3] Ps.-Phoc. 1–2, together with the title, is comparable in form and function, identifying the author and providing some initial indications as to the derivation, content, and purpose of the *Sentences*.[4] In order to evaluate this information properly, though, it needs to be examined in light of the way in which the prologue has been coordinated with the epilogue, a feature that helps to establish the work's broader material and literary parameters.[5] For this reason, these two elements of the poem are best examined together.

The most obvious sign of coordination between the prologue and epilogue is the verbal affinity of ταῦτα δίκῃσ' at the beginning of the poem's first sentence (vv. 1–2) with ταῦτα δικαιοσύνης at the beginning of its final sentence (vv. 229–230), references that reinforce the emphasis placed by the poet elsewhere on justice, especially in vv. 9–54 (cf. v. 77). The designation of the author's judgments as "holy" in v. 1 both complements the bid for purification in v. 228 and anticipates subsequent lines where he will have recourse to the language and issues of purity (vv. 4, 5, 34, 132, 177, 219). The prologue and epilogue are also mutually supportive in asserting the poem's potential benefits: v. 2 refers to its contents as "blessed gifts,"[6] while vv. 229b–230 promises "a good life" to the obedient "until the threshold of old age," both phrases entailing Homeric allusions.[7] Josephus frames his summary of the law

---

[1] Kranz, "Sphragis," 3–46, 97–124.

[2] See Phocylides, frg. 1–6.

[3] Lines 1–38; see the analysis below, p. 77–78. Further: Woodbury, "The Seal of Theognis," 20–41; Ford, "The Seal of Theognis," 82–95.

[4] For the pseudonym, see above, Introduction III.

[5] Cf. Kranz, "Sphragis," 100.

[6] It is interesting to note that Isocrates also refers to his advice in *Ad Nicoclem* as a gift (δωρεά), and that these references also frame the body of the work (1–2, 54). Such identifications may have been a conventional device in gnomic writings of this type. On the epistle as a gift, see Demetrius, *Eloc.* 224; Thraede, *Brieftopik*, 17, 30.

[7] For the former, cf. Homer, *Od.* 13.41–42; for the latter, cf. Homer, *Il.* 22.60, 24.487, *Od.* 15.246, 348, 23.212; Hesiod, *Op.* 331; Plato, *Resp.* 328E; Philo, *Somn.* 2.148.

in *Contra Apionem* similarly, balancing an affirmation of God's blessedness (2.190) with a promise that God will grant the obedient "a better life" after death (2.218).

Mention should be made lastly of the correlation between divine "resolutions" (v. 1) and "mysteries of righteousness" (v. 229), characterizations for the poem that draw attention to θεός both as a determinative character in its moral universe (cf. vv. 8, 11, 17, 29, 54, 106, 111, 125) and as the ultimate source of its precepts. In addition to their role in establishing the writer's authority, the claims implicit in these appellations accord with the universalizing posture projected by the work itself. While the former, θεοῦ βουλεύματα, could function as an apt label for the Torah, we should bear in mind that Greek authors also used terms like βουλή, βούλευμα, and βούλομαι with reference to the divine will.[8] Similarly, moralists of various backgrounds could depict their counsel as the product of divine inspiration, supernatural knowledge, or participation in sacred mysteries. In its manner of self-description, the *Sentences* in fact belongs to a stream of Jewish thought in which appeal is made to a special or "higher" source of revelation that serves as the basis for communicating biblically informed instruction in a Hellenized milieu.[9] The basis of the moral life in these instances derives not from one's participation in the Jewish community or any of its distinctive practices, but from "the right understanding of wisdom."[10]

In this light we can better appreciate the claim "Phocylides" makes to be ὁ σοφώτατος. According to the logic of ancient exhortatory discourse, authentic insight regarding morality is not simply to be had. Rather, it is to be sought out from individuals gifted with the greatest access to divine knowledge, those who can disclose holy secrets about the path to virtue and its rewards. Given this epistemological orientation, it comes as no surprise that supremacy in wisdom, and the epithet "wisest" in particular, would have been widely coveted.[11] No doubt for the poem's original readers it would have been redolent especially of Solomon, whose legendary quest for wisdom is developed most fully in Wis 6:1–9:18, a passage which, like our *Sentences*, asserts its revelatory character with terminology taken over from the mystery religions.[12] Here Wisdom is likened to an initiate (μύστις) of divine knowledge (8:4–8), while in 6:22–25 the king himself takes on the role of mystagogue:

---

[8] E.g., Josephus, *Ant.* 2.232, 304, 4.42, 9.189; Philo, *Her.* 246, *Mos.* 1.287; Aeschylus, *Prom.* 171, 619; Plato, *Tim.* 41B; Diodorus Siculus, *Bibl.* 17.66.7; Dio Chrysostom, *Def.* 15; further: LSJ s.v. βουλή, βούλησις, βούλομαι; BDAG s.v. βουλή, βούλομαι.

[9] Collins, *Between Athens and Jerusalem*, 210–60.

[10] Collins, *Between Athens and Jerusalem*, 260.

[11] Cf. Dan 1:17–20; Ezek 28:3; Eupolemus, frg. 1; 4Q212 II, 23; Aristophanes, *Nub.* 1378; Xenophon, *Mem.* 1.2.52, *Symp.* 4.6.4; Isocrates, *Big.* 28; Plato, *Apol.* 21A–B, 22C–23B, *Resp.* 390A, 391C; Athenaeus, *Deipn.* 632C.

[12] Cf. Wis 2:21–24; Josephus, *Ant.* 8.24; van der Horst, *Sentences*, 108–109. Further, Winston, "The Sage as Mystic," 383–97.

> What Wisdom is, and how she came into being, I will relate;
> I will conceal no mysteries from you,
> but will track her from her first beginnings
> and bring the knowledge of her into the open ...
> Be instructed then by my words, and you will be profited.

Comparable formulations are expressed by other Jewish authors. Philo, for instance, adopts the language of the mysteries to portray both the promulgation of the law as well as his own inspiration in unfolding its hidden meanings.[13] Such forms of self-description and purpose would have lent the claims made by these authors wide-ranging appeal, especially inasmuch as recourse to the vernacular of the mysteries was something of a literary convention in Greco-Roman philosophical circles.[14]

The various designations in Ps.-Phoc. 1–2 and 228–230 presuppose an appeal to a higher source of revelation in a manner similar to what we find in such universalizing Hellenistic Jewish texts. The wisdom of the *Sentences* is not a matter of ordinary human perspicacity; rather its contents are divine mysteries that the author "reveals" (φαίνει) by virtue of his unsurpassed wisdom.[15] This privileged access to divine judgments serves as a guarantee of the blessings and "good life" promised the obedient. The appeal to this transcendent authority corresponds also with the broad foundations of the moral counsel included in the body of the poem itself.

Of course, religious protocol would have dictated that only the ritually pure are worthy to receive divine revelations. Consequently, before one can be initiated into a sacred mystery and partake of its blessings, certain ablutions are in order.[16] Participation is restricted, says Philo, to μύσται whose ears "have been purified" (κεκαθαρμένοι), so that the mysteries may find reception in their souls (*Cher.* 48). This common understanding probably explains the position of Pseudo-Phocylides' rule on ritual purity. As Derron notes, the language of the mysteries characterizes all three verses of the epilogue, not only "mysteries" itself, but also the references

---

[13] E.g., Philo, *Leg. all.* 3.71, *Cher.* 42, 48–49, *Sacr.* 60, 62, *Gig.* 54, *Fug.* 85, *Quaest. Gen.* 4.8. Cf. Bockmuehl, *Revelation and Mystery*, 69–81; Wolfson, *Philo*, 1:36–55; Riedweg, *Mysterienterminologie*, 71–96.

[14] Wilson, *Mysteries of Righteousness*, 164–67.

[15] Cf. Philo, *Spec.* 3.6: "So behold me daring, not only to read the sacred messages of Moses, but also in my love of knowledge to peer into each of them and unfold and reveal (ἀναφαίνειν) what is not known to the multitude." Also *Leg. all.* 3.169–170, *Cher.* 28–29, *Det.* 159, *Ebr.* 88, *Conf.* 169, *Her.* 96, *Spec.* 1.155, 2.257–258; Sir 1:6, 24:27, 32, 39:6–8.

[16] Parker, *Miasma*, 281–307; Moulinier, *Le Pur et l'Impur*, 116–32; Burkert, *Greek Religion*, 75–84. The steps taken to achieve ritual purity were seen as the means of preparing initiates for their new way of life, which itself was characterized by the ideal of purity, e.g., Plato, *Phaedr.* 244D–E, *Resp.* 364E–365A.

to purity in v. 228.[17] This suggests that we should interpret the line in light of the author's designations of the poem's contents and function in v. 229.

Significantly, v. 228 not only introduces the idea of ritual purification in association with the author's mysteries, but it does so by emphasizing the importance and priority of psychic purity in the performance of such rites. Although Pseudo–Phocylides rarely raises ritual matters, the extent to which he amplifies the moral dimension of religious life at this point is in keeping with his priorities elsewhere and echoes discussions in various ancient moral texts.[18] Among the noteworthy witnesses to this discussion in Jewish traditions is the corpus of wisdom literature,[19] with Sir 34:18–35:10 representing perhaps the most developed treatment of the theme.[20] Passages of this sort critically reformulate the concept of ritual in two closely related ways. On one hand, there is the argument that ritual is ineffectual if not motivated by spiritual conviction and guided by human reason. On the other, while refusing to eliminate ritual life altogether, these texts tend to transpose the idea of ritual from the cultic realm to the realm of moral conduct.

Likewise, while we can detect in v. 228 a certain "moralization" of purificatory rituals and their rationale, it should be emphasized that Pseudo-Phocylides does not abrogate the actual performance of such rites, and he appears to take for granted the validity of their purity rules in the somatic, as well as in the moral, domain. What specific rites he may have had in mind is impossible to say: as Josephus observes in his epitome of the law, ἀγνεῖαι are prescribed for a variety of occasions (C. Ap. 2.198, cf. 203). Regardless of how they manifest themselves, though, the higher objective of the rites should be the purification of the ψυχή (cf. vv. 105, 111, 115), a prerequisite for participating in virtue's mysteries.[21]

---

[17] Derron, *Sentences*, 18 n. 1. Perhaps ἐκτελέω in v. 230 also belongs to the vernacular of the mysteries; see LSJ and BDAG s.v. τέλειος, τελειόω, τελέω. Cf. Plato, *Phaed.* 69C, *Euthyd.* 277D–E; Philo, *Cher.* 42–43, 48–49, *Sacr.* 60, *Gig.* 54, *Abr.* 122, *Spec.* 1.319, *Legat.* 56; *PGM* XXXVI.306: ... ἕως ἐλθοῦσα (ἡ δεῖνα) ἐκτελέσῃ τὸ τῆς Ἀφροδίτης μυστήριον.

[18] Thus it comes as no surprise that a number of other gnomic utterances from antiquity approximate v. 228 in form and content; Derron (*Sentences*, 18 n. 2) notes Ps.-Epicharmus, frg. B26: καθαρὸν ἂν τὸν νοῦν ἔχῃς, ἅπαν τὸ σῶμα καθαρὸς εἶ. Cf. *Let. Arist.* 234 (One best honors God not with sacrifices, "but with purity of heart and of devout disposition."); Sextus, *Sent.* 23: "Recognize that the best purification is to harm no one." Further: van der Horst, *Sentences*, 258–60; Thomas, *Der jüdische Phokylides*, 195–99. Such purity rules are related also to wider discussions regarding the moral requirements of cultic sacrifice, for which see E. Ferguson, "Spiritual Sacrifice," 1151–89; van Straaten, "Gifts for the Gods," 65–151.

[19] Perdue, *Wisdom and Cult*, 345–62 and passim. Some examples: Prov 15:8, 27b, 16:6, 17:1, 21:3, 27; Tob 4:10–11; Wis 18:9; Sir 3:30; Sextus, *Sent.* 46b, 47, 102, 103, 371; P.Ins. 16.11–14; cf. Qoh 5:1–7; Philo, *Plant.* 30; Isocrates, *Nic.* 20.

[20] Cf. Skehan and DiLella, *Ben Sira*, 411–23.

[21] Cf. Plato, *Phaed.* 69C, where the canon of cardinal virtues is characterized as "a kind of purification" (καθαρμός τις) that prepares one for the philosophical mysteries.

By emphasizing the spiritual and moral implications of purification this way, Pseudo-Phocylides participates in a tradition within Hellenistic Judaism that endeavored to demonstrate a link between the observance of ritual prescriptions and the cultivation of righteousness.[22] According to the *Letter of Aristeas*, the Mosaic purity rules were established "for unblemished investigation and amendment of life for the sake of righteousness" (144) and to keep the obedient "pure in body and soul" (139).[23] Similarly, in *Ant.* 18.117–118, Josephus reports on the ritual of John the Baptist, noting his insistence that those who participate in his baptism "must not employ it to gain pardon for whatever sins they committed, but as a consecration of the body implying that the soul was already thoroughly cleansed by right behavior."[24] Philo also contributes to such characterizations. In *Decal.* 45, for example, he remarks that the Jewish people assembled before Mt. Sinai were required to purify themselves before receiving the law. According to *Spec.* 3.208–209, the law's pronouncements regarding purity address not only the body but extend to matters of the soul, since it is the unjust and impious person who is "unclean" in the true sense of the word. As Jacob Neusner observes, all told, Philo's "interpretation of cultic and priestly purity emphasizes the spiritual or philosophical virtue symbolized by purity."[25] Likewise, in v. 228 of the *Sentences*, spiritual purity constitutes a prerequisite for initiation into the mysteries of righteousness as well as a component of the life informed by these mysteries.

---

[22] Neusner, *The Idea of Purity*, 32–71; Sanders, *Jewish Law*, 29–42, 134–51, 258–71.

[23] Cf. *Let. Arist.* 142, 146–148, 151, 162, 168–169.

[24] Cf. H. J. de Jonge in *NedTT* 33 (1979): 247.

[25] Neusner, *The Idea of Purity*, 46. Cf. Philo, *Cher.* 90–96, *Deus immut.* 7–8, *Plant.* 162, *Somn.* 1.209–212, *Spec.* 1.256–266, 269–270; also 1QS III, 8–9, 11–14, V, 13.

II. Summary of the Decalogue (Verses 3–8)

Bibliography: Berger, *Die Gesetzesauslegung Jesu*, 142–68, 258–90. Freund, "The Decalogue," 124–41. Küchler, *Weisheitstraditionen*, 241–45, 303–18. Niebuhr, *Gesetz und Paränese*, 7–20, 25–26, 53–57. Thomas, *Der jüdische Phokylides*, 89–102, 166, 308–309, 404–15, 442.

3	Neither commit adultery nor rouse male passion.
4	Neither contrive deceptions nor defile your hands with blood.
5	Be not unjustly rich but earn a living from licit means.
6	Be satisfied with what you have and refrain from what belongs to others.
7	Do not tell lies, but always say things that are true.
8	First of all honor God, and thereafter your parents.

TEXTUAL NOTES

Verses 3–5. P transposes vv. 3b and 4b; it also inverts the order of vv. 4 and 5. Verse 5b. For βιοτεύειν, cf. Sir pr. 36 (ἐννόμως βιοτεύειν) and below, on v. 153. Verse 6a. Reading παρεοῦσι with Diehl (*Anthologia*, 2:97) and Σ in lieu of παρ᾽ ἑοῖσι in M, V, P², and printed by Young, *Theognis*, 96; Derron, *Sentences*, 2. Bergk (*Poetae Lyrici Graeci*, 81) has παρ᾽ ἑοῖς. P, L: παρεοῖσι; B: παρέουσι. As van der Horst (*Sentences*, 114) notes, "ἀρκεῖσθαι is always followed by a simple dative without παρά." Cf. Walter, *Poetische Schriften*, 197, who translates our reading: "Begnüge dich mit dem, was vorhanden ist." Verse 7. Σ appends to this line: "Do not revere idols to no good purpose but always the imperishable one." Verse 8a. M, B, P, V, Σ: θεὸν; L: θεοὺς.

COMMENTARY

Commentators usually identify this section as a versified rendition or "summary" of the Decalogue (see Exod 20:3–17; Deut 5:7–21), with allusions to its prohibitions of adultery, murder, theft, and false witness, and the commands to honor God and parents.[1] Like comparable summaries from the Second Temple period (see below), this one departs from its source in various ways. The sequence of duties, to begin with, deviates from that of the biblical text, though the treatment of adultery before murder in vv. 3–4 does reflect the Septuagint's order.[2] More importantly, commands regarding distinctively Jewish religious scruples (idolatry, taking the Lord's name in vain, and Sabbath observance) are absent, while ordinances not found in the Decalogue have been included, namely, the censures of homosexuality and unjust wealth.

As for its literary structure, the summary has been divided into two parts depending on the nature of the referents involved, vv. 3–7 focusing on the reader's "horizontal" relationships and v. 8 on his "vertical" relationships. In its basic construction, this arrangement reflects the common procedure in antiquity of categorizing moral responsibilities according to the so-called canon of two virtues. The first of these (often εὐσέβεια or ὁσιότης) pertains to obligations owed to one's superiors, especially the gods, parents, and the dead. The second (usually δικαιοσύνη or φιλανθρωπία) refers to obligations owed to one's peers, especially friends, neighbors, and fellow citizens.[3] Philo also found this scheme appropriate in analyzing the Decalogue, arranging the commandments into two sets (or tables) of five, the first dealing with duties towards God, the second duties towards humanity.[4] In *Decal.* 50–51, for example, he notes that the first set begins with God and ends with parents, drawing together the same referents as Ps.-Phoc. 8. He goes on to observe that the second set contains all the prohibitions, listing adultery before murder, much in the same way as Ps.-Phoc. 3–7.[5] Philo seems to have found such a procedure effective inasmuch as it suggested the full range of civic and religious responsibilities

---

[1] Bernays, *Gesammelte Abhandlungen*, 227–28; van der Horst, *Sentences*, 110–17; Walter, *Poetische Schriften*, 197; Niebuhr, *Gesetz und Paränese*, 7–20, 25–26; Derron, *Sentences*, 19 n. 5; cf. Thomas, *Der jüdische Phokylides*, 89–102, 404–13, 442.

[2] Cf. Luke 18:20; Rom 13:9; Jas 2:11; Niebuhr, *Gesetz und Paränese*, 16; also cf. the citation of Philo, *Decal.* 50–51 below.

[3] Betz, "Christianity as Religion," 339–43; Berger, *Die Gesetzesauslegung Jesu*, 142–68. The preamble for the *Carmen aureum*, vv. 1–8, also demonstrates affinities with the introduction to our *Sentences*, chiefly in its division of primary moral duties according to first "vertical" and then "horizontal" relationships; see Thom, *Golden Verses*, 102–25.

[4] Philo, *Decal.* 50–51 (cited in the next note), *Her.* 167–173; cf. Berger, *Die Gesetzesauslegung Jesu*, 151–52, 156–60; Amir, "The Decalogue," 121–60; Jastram, "Generic Virtue," 332.

[5] "We find that God divided the ten into two sets of five which were engraved on two tables, and the first five obtained the first place, while the other was awarded the second ... The superior set of five treats the following matters: the monarchical principle by which the world is governed; idols of stone and wood and images in general made by human hands; the sin of taking the name of God in vain; the reverent observance of the sacred seventh day as befits its holiness; the duty of honoring parents ... Thus one set of enactments begins with God the Father and Maker of all, and ends with parents who copy God's nature by begetting particular persons. The other set of five contains all the prohibitions, namely adultery, murder, theft, false witness, covetousness or lust."

addressed by the Decalogue (and, by implication, the Mosaic law) in a manner that would have been familiar to a Hellenized audience.[6] Similarly, in availing himself of this organizing principle, our author indicates from the outset something of the nature and scope of his instruction.

As this comparison shows, Pseudo-Phocylides was by no means the only moral writer to summarize the Decalogue. In fact, the creation of such renditions represents a fairly common practice in Hellenistic-Jewish and early Christian circles; compare, for example, *Did.* 2:2–3:[7]

> You shall not murder. You shall not commit adultery. You shall not corrupt boys. You shall not fornicate. You shall not steal. You shall not practice magic. You shall not mix poison. You shall not murder a child, whether by abortion or killing it once it is born. You shall not covet what belongs to your neighbor. You shall not swear falsely. You shall not bear false witness.

The paragraph's structure follows a loose interpretation of the second table of the Decalogue, exhibiting considerable freedom in selection, formulation, and arrangement. The specific injunctions exhibit numerous parallels with Ps.-Phoc. 3–7, including commands against murder, adultery, theft, covetousness, and speaking falsely. Also, in each passage the format of the exhortation is predominantly negative in its orientation, the commands appear to be arranged seriatim, and the gnomic style dominates both the context and the mode of communication (cf. Ps.-Philemon, frg. 1.8–16). It may be significant, too, that both Decalogue summaries occur near the beginning of their respective texts (see below). Like Pseudo-Phocylides, the editor of the *Didache* also omits references to peculiarly Jewish practices, while incorporating prohibitions from outside the Decalogue, which, although they appear to be primarily Jewish in nature, could expect to find a sympathetic hearing with a more general audience.[8]

This last point raises the issue of the extent to which the content and tone of such renditions of the Decalogue, including Pseudo-Phocylides', participate also in conventions familiar from non-biblical sources. To begin with, modern critics have documented how most of the injunctions in vv. 3–8 are analogous to the sorts of

---

6   Cf. Philo, *Abr.* 107–118, 208, *Jos.* 240, *Mos.* 1.198, *Decal.* 110–111, *Spec.* 1.304, 2.62–64, *Virt.* 51, 76, 94–95, 175, *Hypoth.* 6.8; Winston, "Philo's Ethical Theory," 394–96; further also Josephus, *Ant.* 6.265, 8.121, 314, 9.16, 10.50, 14.283; *Let. Arist.* 24, 131; Berger, *Die Gesetzesauslegung Jesu*, 151–65.

7   Cf. Niederwimmer, *Didache*, 88–91. For such summaries, see Vokes, "The Ten Commandments," 146–54; Berger, *Die Gesetzesauslegung Jesu*, 258–77; Niebuhr, *Gesetz und Paränese*, 15–20; Freund, "The Decalogue," 124–41. Of the various New Testament summaries, Luke 18:20 (mentioning adultery, murder, stealing, false witness, and honoring parents) best approximates Ps.-Phoc. 3–8.

8   Some of these are paralleled elsewhere in the *Sentences*, for example, vv. 149, 184–185.

moral obligations enumerated in various popular codes, especially the "unwritten laws." The numerous extant summaries of these ἄγραφοι νόμοι manifest a host of special adaptations as to the number, order, and types of duties listed, though prescriptions to revere the gods, to honor one's parents, to abhor murder, and to abstain from incest and other sex acts appear regularly.[9] A number of these summaries are also employed in gnomic contexts, for example, Isocrates, *Demon.* 16.[10] Other popular Greco-Roman codes comparable in form and substance to such collections include the so-called laws of Buzyges[11] and the *Praecepta Delphica*.[12] In rabbinic Judaism we also encounter the so-called Noachian laws, which were held to be equally valid for Gentiles as well as for Jews. Although their number varies, the seven precepts mentioned most frequently were the prohibitions of idolatry, blasphemy, murder, adultery, robbery, and eating flesh torn from a living animal, and the command to establish systems of justice.[13] It should be emphasized that while a concentration of parallels with these different moral codes appears in Ps.-Phoc. 3–8, similarities can be detected also at various points throughout the poem. This suggests that traditional collections of mores comparable to those described above may have constituted basic sources for our author. By drawing upon these kinds of widely approved materials, Pseudo-Phocylides establishes the traditional and multicultural stance of his instruction.

Besides its role as a summary of the Decalogue, it is also possible to think of vv. 3–8 as providing a summary introduction or preview of the poem itself. In this regard the section corresponds functionally to what Greco-Roman rhetoricians called the πρόθεσις, or *propositio*, a concise statement placed near the beginning of an oration that sets forth the matters to be discussed.[14] In this capacity, the mate-

---

[9]   E.g., Aeschylus, *Suppl.* 701–709; Xenophon, *Mem.* 4.4.18–25; Plato, *Leg.* 838A–839D; Philo, *Hypoth.* 8.7.6–8; Ps.-Plutarch, *Lib. ed.* 7E; cf. Hirzel, *ΑΓΡΑΦΟΣ ΝΟΜΟΣ;* Crouch, *Colossian Haustafel,* 37–46; Küchler, *Weisheitstraditionen,* 244–45; Niebuhr, *Gesetz und Paränese,* 53–57; Thomas, *Der jüdische Phokylides,* 468–69.

[10] Also significant here is the fact that Isocrates links his presentation of some of the unwritten laws with a scheme of virtues (cf. above, Introduction IV): "Consider that no adornment so becomes you as modesty, justice, and self-control; for these are the virtues by which, as all men are agreed, the character of the young is held in restraint. Never hope to conceal any shameful thing which you have done; for even if you do conceal it from others, your own heart will know. Fear the gods, honor your parents, respect your friends, obey the laws."

[11] Schmidt, *Die Ethik der alten Griechen,* 1:88, 2:278–79; Bernays, *Gesammelte Abhandlungen,* 262–82; Bolkestein, *Wohltätigkeit und Armenpflege,* 69–71; Niebuhr, *Gesetz und Paränese,* 55–56.

[12] Derron (*Sentences,* 19–20 nn. 5, 7, 9–11) notes Delphic parallels for vv. 3–8, particularly with the collection attributed to Sosiades preserved in Stobaeus, *Anth.* 3.1.173. Also similar are the so-called "Sayings of the Seven Sages;" cf. Küchler, *Weisheitstraditionen,* 241–44.

[13] Dietrich, "Die Religion Noahs," 301–15; Novak, *Image of the Non-Jew,* Part I.

[14] It was also known as the *partitio* or *divisio;* see Aristotle, *Rhet.* 3.13; Cicero, *Inv.* 1.31–33; Ps.-Cicero, *Rhet. Her.* 1.10.17; Quintilian, *Inst.* 4.4.1–4.5.28, cf. 3.9.2, 5, 3.11.27; Cousin, *Quintilian,* 247–52; Lausberg, *Handbook,* §§ 289, 346; J. Martin, *Antike Rhetorik,* 91–95.

rial in vv. 3–8 not only introduces the poem's underlying moral perspective, it also anticipates a number of specific themes to which it will return, as indicated by the following chart:

Verse 3:   Cf. vv. 67, 177–183, 190–191, 213–214.
Verse 4:   Cf. vv. 32–34, 57–58.
Verse 5:   Cf. vv. 42–47, 61–62.
Verse 6:   Cf. vv. 18, 70–74, 135–136, 154.
Verse 7:   Cf. vv. 12, 16–17, 48–50.
Verse 8:   Cf. vv. 53–54, 106, 111, 179–180, 220–222.

If we carry this analogy one step further, then the bulk of the text (vv. 9–227) may be described as the πίστις, or *probatio*. This is that part of the oration, usually the longest and most complex, that marshals various arguments or proofs in support of the *propositio*.[15] The designation of this part of the poem as the *probatio* is not intended to suggest that the summary of the Decalogue in vv. 3–8 is in need of "proof" in the sense that the author sought validation or confirmation for it. Rather, the heart of the poem strives to develop in the readers an improved understanding about the nature, authority, and value of the *propositio*, as well as the conviction necessary to implement its principles in their own moral decision-making. The proof section thus expands upon and explains the proposition, showing its implications for the audience.

It appears, then, that vv. 3–8, together with the poem's "seal," or σφραγίς, in vv. 1–2 (see the discussion above, on p. 68), functions as the introduction to the *Sentences*. As we have seen, in constructing this opening segment, the author not only draws from the Torah for his material, he also benefits from different popular sources and rhetorical strategies familiar from the moral discourse of the time. It comes as no surprise, then, that we can observe some of these same strategies at work in the introductions designed for other ancient gnomic texts.

The prologue to the *Theognidea*, to begin with, while not employing a summary of the Decalogue like Pseudo-Phocylides' *Sententiae*, exhibits similar features in the context of gnomic exhortation. After an invocation of the gods, indicating the author's divine inspiration (Apollo and Artemis in vv. 1–14, the Muses and Graces in vv. 15–18), we have the σφραγίς proper (vv. 19–26). A preview of the text's basic principles and objectives in outline form follows in vv. 27–38: (1) Theognis will bequeath to the reader wisdom he acquired in his youth from the ἀγαθοί, (2) in conjunction with this, he orders the reader to do nothing dishonorable or unjust, and

---

[15] It was also known as the *confirmatio* or *argumentatio*; see Aristotle, *Rhet.* 3.17; Cicero, *Inv.* 1.34; Ps.-Cicero, *Rhet. Her.* 1.10.18; Quintilian, *Inst.* 5; Cousin, *Quintilian*, 253–307; Lausberg, *Handbook*, §§ 348–49; J. Martin, *Antike Rhetorik*, 95–137.

(3) to consort with the ἀγαθοί while avoiding the κακοί.[16] Like Pseudo-Phocylides, Theognis demonstrates in his introduction some concern to suggest the divine origin as well as the traditional nature of the advice contained in his poetic verses. Both authors also tend to conceptualize their opening appeals antithetically, contrasting two opposing types of conduct.

With respect to its structure and function, the prologue to the *Sentences* of Syriac Menander offers perhaps the most instructive parallel to vv. 1–8 of our poem. Like Pseudo-Phocylides, this work represents a pseudonymous Hellenistic-Jewish document that is predominantly gnomic in character, and, in fact, the two compositions share a number of themes and features.[17] After a σφραγίς identifying the author (v. 1), which forms an *inclusio* with the poem's epilogue (v. 474), the section opens with a programmatic maxim: "Prior to the words of man are all his activities." This is followed by a number of commands in summary form (vv. 3–19), all of which have analogues in vv. 3–8 of Pseudo-Phocylides' *Sentences*. The readers are instructed to (1) beget children (vv. 3–8; cf. Ps.-Phoc. 3), (2) fear God (v. 9; cf. Ps.-Phoc. 8a), (3) honor their parents (vv. 10–14; cf. Ps.-Phoc. 8b), and (4) refrain from murder (vv. 15–19; cf. Ps.-Phoc. 4). Afterwards the author has assembled a lengthy collection of gnomic sayings and other ethical materials arranged by topic, for which vv. 1–19 serve in part as a material and rhetorical foundation. As this brief description suggests, the prologue to *Syriac Menander* displays several features that are akin to those observed in Ps.-Phoc. 1–8 in terms of its content, structure, context, and function. Like Pseudo-Phocylides, the author of this prologue has utilized a σφραγίς followed by a summary of the Decalogue that incorporates some of the "unwritten laws" as an introduction for his gnomic text.[18] The substance and ethical perspective of both texts appear to be primarily Jewish in nature, though both authors benefit significantly from the employment of non-Jewish materials and structures that are consistent with the more universalistic posture that they seek to establish.

Verse 3. In light of the analysis above, v. 3a is most likely based on Exod 20:13 and Deut 5:17, though the biblical condemnation of adultery comes to expression in various ways,[19] and constitutes a *topos* of the wisdom literature.[20] While ancient moralists were generally far more anxious about female infidelity, with this counsel we might compare texts like Isocrates, *Nic.* 36–42 (incorporating criticism of men

---

[16] Also compare Theognis' use of ταῦτα in vv. 31 and 37 with Ps.-Phoc. 1.

[17] See Baarda, "Syriac Menander," 583–606; Küchler, *Weisheitstraditionen*, 303–18.

[18] Cf. the introduction to the *Epitome* of *Syriac Menander*, vv. 1–6.

[19] Cf. Lev 18:20, 20:10; Num 5:11–31; Deut 22:22–29; McKeating, "Adultery," 57–72; Phillips, "Adultery," 3–25.

[20] E.g., Prov 6:32–35, 18:22, 30:20; Sir 9:9, 23:18–26, 25:2. Cf. *Syr. Men.* 240–247, 347–353; *T. Ash.* 2:8; *T. Jos.* 4:6; *3 Bar.* 4:17, 8:5, 13:4; Philo, *Decal.* 121–131, *Spec.* 3.8–11, 52–63.

who are "slaves to the passions whose objects are boys and women") and Plutarch, *Conj. praec.* 144A–D, which view a husband's extramarital affairs as a crime and breach of trust, emphasizing mutual chastity in marriage.[21]

Κύπρις was a moniker of Aphrodite (her cult on Cyprus was well-known), and hence a metonym for passion, popular with Greek poets like Euripides;[22] cf. Ps.-Phoc. 67, 190. The source for v. 3b must be Lev 18:22 ("With a man you shall not lie as with a woman," cf. 20:13), the font of a tradition of Hellenistic-Jewish rhetoric against same-sex couplings, for which see the discussion of Ps.-Phoc. 190–192 below.

With γαμοκλοπέειν our author apparently coined a new term, though the cognate γαμοκλοπίη occurs, together with κύπρις, as part of a description of the messianic age in *Sib. Or.* 5.429–430: "terrible things no longer happen to wretched mortals, no adulteries or illicit passion for boys." The *Sibylline Oracles* elsewhere link adultery with sexual unions between males (3.595–596, 764, 4.33–34, 5.166), as do Philo (*Hypoth.* 7.1) and Josephus (*C. Ap.* 2.199, 215, cf. 201) in their respective summaries of the law,[23] suggesting an interpretive tradition in early Judaism that took the Decalogue's prohibition of adultery to be inclusive of other sexual infractions.[24] Such linkage would have resonated with Greco-Roman moralists as well, especially those who held that unrestrained sexuality, as manifest in both adulterous and homosexual activity, posed a threat to social order. As Catherine Edwards observes, this critique rested in part on the assumption that the same excess associated with the passive role in male-male sex in particular was also a root cause of a man's proclivity to commit adultery. Consequently, men deemed effeminate by Roman standards could be accused of what she calls "bi-sexual promiscuity," a sample of which we find in Curio's famous quip about Julius Caesar: "A man to every woman and a woman to every man."[25] Also representative is Musonius Rufus, frg. 12.86.8–

---

[21]　Cf. *Instr. Ankh.* 21.18–19, 23.6–7; P.Ins. 7.21–22, 8.14; Demosthenes, *Or.* 59.87; Lysias, *Or.* 1.30–31; Euripides, *Andr.* 469–470; Plato, *Leg.* 841C–D; Aristotle, *Eth. eud.* 2.3.17–18; Ps.-Aristotle, *Oec.* 1.4.1; Plutarch, *Amat.* 767E; Cicero, *Sest.* 20, *Mil.* 72; Horace, *Sat.* 1.3.104–106; and see below, on Ps.-Phoc. 177–178.

[22]　E.g., Euripides, *Andr.* 179, 223, 240, 631, *Bacch.* 688, 773, *Hec.* 825, *Hel.* 364, *Iph. aul.* 553, 569, 1301, 1305; cf. Hesiod, *Theog.* 192–199.

[23]　Cf. Philo, *Abr.* 135–136, *Spec.* 2.50; *Did.* 2:2.

[24]　Cf. Goodfriend, "Adultery," 82; also Matt 15:19; Mark 7:21–22; 1 Cor 6:9.

[25]　Edwards, *Politics of Immorality*, 91 (quoting Suetonius, *Jul.* 52.3), cf. 63–97; Richlin, *Garden of Priapus*, 88–92; Plato, *Leg.* 841D; Epictetus, *Diatr.* 2.10.17–18; Cicero, *Cat.* 2.23; Ovid, *Ars* 3.433–438; *SIG* 3.985.27–28 ("corrupt neither boy nor virgin"); *Anth. Gr.* 5.302.7–8; Aristotle, *Pol.* 7.14.12: "As to intercourse with another woman or man, in general it must be dishonorable to be known to take part in it in any circumstances whatever as long as one is a husband." Mention may also be made here of the *lex Iulia de adulteriis* (for which see Edwards, *Politics of Immorality*, 34–62; Treggiari, *Roman Marriage*, 277–98; McGinn, *Prostitution*, 140–247) and the *lex Scantinia*; the latter "could be invoked against men who had willingly been penetrated," though it may have addressed sexual

10: "Of all sexual relations those involving adultery are most unlawful, and no more tolerable are those of men with men, because it is a monstrous thing and contrary to nature." Both crimes, he says, are to be explained by a man's lack of proper self-restraint.[26] Pseudo-Phocylides will also introduce the rhetoric of "nature" in his polemic against same sex couplings; see below, on vv. 190–191.

Verse 4. This line appears to unite the Decalogue's prohibition of murder (Exod 20:15; Deut 5:18) with passages like Exod 21:14, which prohibit killing "by deceit" (δόλῳ); cf. Lev 19:16; Deut 27:24. Its diction, however, is familiar from other sources. The phrase δόλους ῥάπτειν, to begin with, has a Homeric ring; cf. *Od.* 3.118–119: "we were busy contriving (ῥάπτομεν) evils for them with all manner of deceptions (δόλοισι)."[27] Prov 26:24, though, is also comparable, which speaks of the man who "contrives deceptions" (τεκταίνεται δόλους).[28] The precise expression of the second half of the verse is reminiscent especially of Isa 59:3, "their hands (χεῖ ρες) have been stained with blood (αἵματι)."[29] The polluting effect of bloodshed is frequently asserted in the biblical tradition;[30] see also the discussion of v. 34 below. As v. 228 indicates, Pseudo-Phocylides tends to emphasize the moral dimensions of pollution and purification language.

Verses 5–6. In v. 1, ὅσιος characterized God's judgments as "holy." Here, the term's meaning is determined by its opposition to ἀδίκως and so carries the moral connotation of "just" or "sanctioned" (cf. vv. 132, 219).[31] As Arius Didymus describes it, "holiness … is justice with respect to the gods" (*Epit.* 5b12).[32]

    Despite the context, the theme of wealth unfairly acquired belongs principally not to the Decalogue or even the Pentateuch, but the wisdom corpus, for example, Job 20:15; Prov 11:28, 13:11, 22, 28:8, 21–22; Wis 5:8; Sir 5:8, 13:24, 14:9, 21:4, 40:13. The language of v. 5a matches Theognis, *El.* 145–146, which may supply the inspiration for the entire verse: "Prefer to live righteously with a few possessions than to be rich with possessions unjustly gained (ἢ πλουτεῖν ἀδίκως χρήματα

---

    infractions involving women as well as men: C. Williams, *Roman Homosexuality*, 119–24 (quote from p. 122); Lilja, *Homosexuality*, 112–21; Richlin, "Not Before Homosexuality," 554–71.

26   Cf. van Geytenbeek, *Musonius Rufus*, 71–77.

27   Cf. Homer, *Il.* 6.187, *Od.* 16.379, 423; *Sib. Or.* 2.119, 3.38.

28   Cf. Ps 49:19, 51:4; Prov 12:5, 26:26.

29   Cf. Qoh 7:18 v.l. (μὴ μιάνῃς τὴν χεῖρά σου); 5 Ezra 1:26. The blood of murder on one's hands is *miasma*: Aeschylus, *Eum.* 280–281, *Ag.* 206–211.

30   E.g., Num 35:33–34; Deut 19:13, 21:6–9; Jdt 9:3–4; Ps 105:38–39; Ezek 22:3–4, 23:37–38.

31   For the pairing of *hosios* and *dikaios*, cf. Plato, *Gorg.* 507B, *Leg.* 663B; Xenophon, *Hell.* 1.7.19; Isocrates, *Nic.* 13; Polybius, *Hist.* 22.10.8; Luke 1:75; Eph 4:24; 1 Thess 2:10; Titus 1:8.

32   Dover, *Popular Morality*, 248.

πασάμενος)."[33] Both Philo (*Hypoth.* 7.2, 6) and Josephus (*C. Ap.* 2.208, 216) include commands against theft in their respective summaries of the law.

While v. 6 expresses the same thought as biblical injunctions against stealing (Exod 20:14, 21:37–22:3; Lev 19:11, 13; Deut 5:19) and covetousness (Exod 20:17; Deut 5:21),[34] it has been formulated with recourse to a pair of Greek colloquialisms. With v. 6a we may compare ἀρκεῖσθαι τοῖς παροῦσιν, an expression that was proverbial for being content with one's possessions.[35] According to Teles, frg. 4A.84–85, a philosopher neither craves wealth nor bemoans poverty, but lives "satisfied with what he has" (ἀρκούμενος τοῖς παροῦσι). Fostering such a disposition safeguards against the temptation to steal; as Xenophon puts it, "those who are most satisfied with what they have (τὰ παρόντα ἀρκεῖ) are least likely to covet what belongs to others" (*Symp.* 4.42). The biblical sages also counseled contentment as a way of life, for example, Prov 12:11, 13:25, 25:16; Sir 29:23, 40:18. Conversely, the greedy are depicted as constantly dissatisfied with what they have (Qoh 4:8, 5:9, 6:7; Sir 14:9). In *C. Ap.* 2.291, Josephus points out that the law teaches αὐτάρκεια, self-sufficiency, a virtue whose cultivation in many ways represented "the general philosophy of the Greek world."[36]

The second part of the verse is also proverbial in its expression, familiar from various sources, including Plato, *Resp.* 360B (ἀπέχεσθαι τῶν ἀλλοτρίων) and Aristotle, *Eth. nic.* 4.1.39 (ἀπέχονται τῶν ἀλλοτρίων).[37] The verb ἀπέχομαι ("to refrain, abstain, avoid") is a favorite of our author, indicative of his general interest in delimiting the reader's conduct; cf. vv. 31, 35, 76, 145, 149.[38] For the problem of the desire for wealth and possessions in our poem, see also below, on Ps.-Phoc. 42–47.

Verse 7. While the point of departure for this verse may be the Decalogue's injunction against false witness (Exod 20:16; Deut 5:20; cf. Lev 19:11; Deut 19:18–19), its diction is hardly biblical. The first part of the maxim mirrors Hesiod, *Op.* 788–789 (βάζειν ψεύδεα), while the phrasing of the second half is familiar from the

---

[33] Cf. Theognis, *El.* 1155–1156; Solon, frg. 13.7–15; Isocrates, *Demon.* 38; *Gnom. Vat.* 43; *Gnom. Democr.* 78; Democritus, frg. 220–221; Diogenes Laertius, *Vit. phil.* 1.37; Menander, *Mon.* 421; *Sib. Or.* 2.109–110.

[34] Cf. 4 Macc 2:5–6; Prov 6:30–31; Philo, *Decal.* 135–137, 171, *Spec.* 4.1–40; *T. Iss.* 4:2; Jackson, *Theft*, s.v. Robbery; Preisker, "κλέπτω," 754–56.

[35] Xenophon, *Cyr.* 8.4.11, *Symp.* 4.38, *Mem.* 1.6.9; Dio Chrysostom, *Charid.* 33; Cassius Dio, *Hist.* 38.8.3 (cf. 38.38.1); Teles, frg. 2.84; Democritus, frg. 191; Heb 13:5.

[36] J. Ferguson, *Moral Values*, 133–58, quoting from p. 154; cf. Democritus, frg. 246; Aristotle, *Eth. nic.* 1.7.6–8, 10.7.4; Teles, frg. 2; Diogenes Laertius, *Vit. phil.* 7.30, 10.130; Phil 4:11; 1 Tim 6:6–8; Sextus, *Sent.* 98.

[37] See also Xenophon, *Cyr.* 5.1.13; Isocrates, *Nic.* 49; Epictetus, *Diatr.* 3.7.11.

[38] Cf. Spicq, *Lexicon*, 1:166–67.

recurrent Homeric appeal, "And tell me this truly (ἀγόρευσον ἐτήτυμον), that I may know full well."[39] In fact, v. 7 says nothing about the problem of false witness per se (which is raised in v. 12) but addresses the more basic issue of honesty, expressing a sentiment that would have been as prosaic in antiquity as it is today. Condemnations of falsehood[40] and acclamations of truthfulness[41] are commonplace in biblical wisdom. On the Greek side, Solon's similarly structured maxim, "Do not lie, but tell the truth," summarizes an extensive gnomic tradition.[42]

Verse 8. Precedent for joining the Decalogue's first and fifth commands (Exod 20:3, 12; Deut 5:7, 16) can be found in several wisdom texts (Prov 1:7–8; Sir 7:27–31; *Syr. Men.* 9–10), as well as in Josephus' summary of the law: "honoring parents is second only to honoring God" (*C. Ap.* 2.206, cf. 217).[43] Indeed, the combination may have been generally understood as a summary of the first table of the Decalogue, which, as Philo observes, "begins with God the father and creator of all, and ends with parents, who imitate God's nature by begetting particular persons" (*Decal.* 51, cf. 119–120). In 3:1–16 Ben Sira preserves an extended gnomic essay on this theme, which v. 6 sums up by promising that "he who honors his father shall have long life, and he that heeds the Lord shall comfort his mother."[44]

In its Hellenistic context, the maxim in Ps.-Phoc. 8 constitutes a poetic rendering of the foremost *agraphoi nomoi*. Among what he considers divinely authored "unwritten laws" Xenophon first mentions fearing the gods and honoring one's parents (*Mem.* 4.4.19–20).[45] Polybius, *Hist.* 6.4.5 exhibits the same priorities ("it is traditional and customary to reverence the gods, to honor our parents," etc.), as does Aristotle, *Eth. nic.* 9.2.8 ("honor is also due to parents, as it is to the gods.").[46] In

---

[39] Homer, *Od.* 1.174, 4.645, 13.232, 14.186, 24.258, 297, 403, *Hymn.* 3.467. For ἀγορεύω see also below, on vv. 48, 50.

[40] Prov 6:19, 8:7, 12:22, 14:5, 25, 17:7, 19:5, 9, 22, 21:6, 28, 24:2, 28, 25:14, 18, 26:28, 28:6, 30:8–9; Sir 7:12–13, 20:24–26; cf. *Did.* 2:5.

[41] Prov 8:7, 14:22, 20:28, 21:3, 22:21, 26:28, 28:6, 29:14; Sir 4:25, 28; cf. *Ahiqar* 132; *Instr. Ankh.* 13.15; Eph 4:25; Col 3:9; Jas 3:14; Sextus, *Sent.* 158–159, 165a–f.

[42] Stobaeus, *Anth.* 3.1.172; cf. Theognis, *El.* 607–610; Democritus, frg. 225; Menander, *Mon.* 849; see Stobaeus, *Anth.* 3.11–12 for additional examples; also Conzelmann, "ψεῦδος," 594–603; Spicq, *Lexicon*, 1:66–86.

[43] Cf. Lev 19:32; *Syr. Men.*, *Epit.* 2–3; *Sib. Or.* 3.593–594; *Jub.* 7:20; Philo, *Spec.* 2.235.

[44] Cf. Skehan and DiLella, *Ben Sira*, 153–57. Respect for parents: Lev 19:3; Deut 27:16; Prov 19:26, 20:9, 23:22, 30:17.

[45] On the pairing of gods and parents in moral literature, see Schmidt, *Die Ethik der alten Griechen*, 2:141–49; Berger, *Die Gesetzesauslegung Jesu*, 278–90; Niebuhr, *Gesetz und Paränese*, 18–19; Thom, *Golden Verses*, 116–17; Thomas, *Der jüdische Phokylides*, 99–101, 166, 308–309, 413–15.

[46] Cf. Isocrates, *Demon.* 16; Plato, *Leg.* 717B–C; Euripides, frg. 853; *Carm. aur.* 1–4; Menander, *Mon.* 525–526; Diogenes Laertius, *Vit. phil.* 8.23; additional examples: van der Horst, *Sentences*, 116.

this connection θεὸν τιμᾶν appears to have been a slogan of conventional piety.[47] This tradition influenced gnomic authors as well, for example, Menander, *Mon.* 322: "Honor God foremost, and secondly your parents" (θεὸν προτίμα, δεύτερον δὲ τοὺς γονεῖς.).

---

[47] Cf. Josephus, *Ant.* 4.130, 8.208, 9.153, 256, 12.323, 16.174; *Let. Arist.* 234; Aeschines, *Tim.* 28; Euripides, *Bacch.* 1011, *Heracl.* 903; Chares, frg. 1.5; Xenophon, *Mem.* 4.3.17, 4.6.2; Diodorus Siculus, *Bibl.* 6.1.4; Pausanias, *Descr.* 2.35.5; Strabo, *Geogr.* 16.2.35.

III. Justice and Mercy (Verses 9–54)

Bibliography: Amstutz, *ΑΠΛΟΤΗΣ*, 42. Bolkestein, *Wohltätigkeit und Armenpflege*, 200–14, 337–41. Dihle, "Gerechtigkeit," 233–360. Dover, *Popular Morality*, 170–75, 180–84, 193, 249. Fisher, *Hybris.* Frank, "Habsucht," 226–47. Havelock, *Justice*, 155–78, 193–217. Hiltbrunner, "Humanitas," 711–52. Rickert, *ΕΚΩΝ and ΑΚΩΝ*, 44–48, 111–17.

The arrangement of the section in the *Sentences* organized according to the canon of cardinal virtues (vv. 9–131) shows signs of some planning, beginning with the placement of the first and longest part, which consists of instruction relating to the theme of justice (vv. 9–54). This concept played a prominent role in Hellenistic Jewish ethics, especially as it was understood to epitomize the basis and purpose of the Mosaic law.[1] The high regard that Phocylides of Miletus himself had for justice, ranking it above all other virtues, may even offer a clue as to our author's choice of pseudonym, though it should be noted that he was hardly alone in this opinion.[2] Pseudo-Phocylides' teaching on the theme consists of two major subsections. The first (vv. 9–21) is a series of maxims that fall under the heading of justice more-or-less directly, whereas the second (vv. 22–54) conveys exhortation on related topics. The latter in turn has two paragraphs, the first (vv. 22–41) focusing on mercy, the second (vv. 42–54) on sources of injustice.

In vv. 9–21, we find advice on justice in its stricter, particularly legal, sense. Accordingly, the language of the courtroom echoes throughout the passage, and terms containing the δικ- stem run throughout these lines as a thread.[3] Related issues of just dealing in economic matters are also addressed (vv. 13–15). The opening and concluding maxims (vv. 9 and 21) contain broad topical statements, antithetically formulated, that establish the section's material focus, framing the more concrete injunctions of vv. 10–20. The precept in v. 14 conveys an appeal that seems to be especially foundational for the section, particularly in its reference to τὸ μέτρον, or due measure.

---

[1] See Schrenk, "δίκη," 193–98; Spicq, *Lexicon*, 1:318–47; M. Fiedler, "Δικαιοσύνη," 120–43; Dihle, "Gerechtigkeit," 233–306; cf. Niebuhr, *Gesetz und Paränese*, 20–26; Thomas, *Der jüdische Phokylides*, 161–70.

[2] Phocylides, frg. 10; cf. above, p. 16.

[3] δίκαια (v. 9), ἀδίκως (v. 10), δικάσῃς, δικάσσει (v. 11), τὰ δίκαια (v. 12), τὰ δίκαια (v. 14), ἀδικεῖν, ἀδικοῦντα (v. 21); for similar applications of this stem, cf. Hesiod, *Op.* 213–224, 274–285; Theognis, *El.* 731–752; Sextus, *Sent.* 63–66.

Following Derron, the maxims in the next paragraph, vv. 22–41, may be grouped under the title περὶ φιλανθρωπίας. This term, to be sure, does not occur anywhere in the paragraph. It is clear, however, that all of its individual precepts address in one way or another the humane treatment of different sorts of people.[4] As Derron also notes, the instruction here represents an extension of the preceding paragraph (vv. 9–21). The way in which it does so is consistent with the ancient view that justice entails not only compliance with the law and the avoidance of harmful deeds, but also positive actions motivated by a sense of mercy and solidarity. To illustrate: Philo often introduces concepts associated with φιλανθρωπία into his analysis of justice,[5] for example, in *Spec.* 4.136–238, which includes a fair number of injunctions familiar from Ps.-Phoc. 22–41. Rulers, he says, should strive to extend justice to the helpless, strangers, widows, and orphans (176–178). Furthermore, no one should mistreat the deaf or the blind (197–202), and restraint should be demonstrated when confronting enemies (219–225); even crops should be spared from needless destruction (226–229). Not surprisingly, comparable themes turn up when Philo investigates the concept of φιλανθρωπία itself, especially in *Virt.* 51–174. Among those who must be dealt with humanely, he says, are the poor (90–94, 97–98, 121–123), strangers (102–108), and enemies (109–120); similar concern should be shown to the crops of the land, since people depend upon them for their survival (148–160).[6]

Pseudo-Phocylides' paraenesis relating to φιλανθρωπία in vv. 22–41 contains four clusters of sayings, each based upon a different sort of referent: people who are poor or otherwise in need (vv. 22–30), enemies (vv. 32–34), neighbors and their crops (vv. 35, 38), and strangers (vv. 39–41).[7] The first of these is the most developed, beginning with a series of commands to render assistance (vv. 22–26), followed by supporting motivation (vv. 27–30).

The advice of the third and final sub-section (vv. 42–54) also contributes to the theme of justice, though not by exploring its positive implications, but by addressing some of the more common impediments to its fulfillment. Comparison with

---

[4] On φιλανθρωπία: Pelletier, "La Philanthropia," 35–44; J. Ferguson, *Moral Values*, 102–17; Luck, "φιλανθρωπία," 107–12; Spicq, *Lexicon*, 3:440–45; Hiltbrunner, "Humanitas," 711–36.

[5] E.g., Philo, *Mut.* 225, *Mos.* 2.9, *Decal.* 164, *Spec.* 2.63, 72, 96; cf. Berthelot, *Philanthrōpia Judaica*, 233–321.

[6] In *Off.* 1.20ff., Cicero orients his presentation of justice in a similar fashion, linking justice with the goals of *beneficentia*, *benignitas*, and *liberalitas*. He proceeds at some length to demonstrate why and how acts of generosity ought to be considered part of justice, which should be extended not only to fellow citizens, family, and friends (1.53–59), but even to enemies (1.34–40), slaves (1.41), and strangers (1.51–52). Cf. Ibscher, *Der Begriff des Sittlichen*, 19–54; Cicero, *Off.* 2.54–64; Plutarch, *Stoic. rep.* 1040A–1042A.

[7] The reference to poverty in vv. 40–41 recalls the poor man of v. 22, creating a thematic frame for the section.

the analysis of ἀδικία (the opposite of δικαιοσύνη) in Ps.-Aristotle, *Virt. vit.* 7.1–6 sheds some light on the principle at work in the addition of this paragraph and the logic behind its internal construction. Specifically, the author observes that unrighteousness takes three principal forms: impiety (ἀσέβεια), greed (πλεονεξία), and insolence (ὕβρις).[8] Given our author's general reluctance to broach topics relating to religious practice, it comes as no surprise that detailed treatment of the first of these topics is not offered (though see v. 54). He does, however, introduce the topics of greed and insolence, in vv. 42–47 and 48–54 respectively.

In vv. 42–47, Pseudo-Phocylides critiques what was perhaps the most notorious species of greed, the love of money. The initial gnome (v. 42), which has the appearance of a reformulated proverb, stands as a general heading and "text," with vv. 43–47 serving as a more specific elucidation, including an extended apostrophe to Gold. Ancient moralists concurred that the various personal motives associated with greed are among the foremost sources of injustice. In the *Ethica Nicomachea*, for instance, Aristotle generally associates πλεονεξία with ἀδικία.[9] As he argues, if justice demands the fair distribution of goods, honor, and so forth according to what each person is legally entitled, then the πλεονέκτης brings about the unjust disruption of this balance by wanting more than he legally deserves or by wanting what rightfully belongs to someone else (5.1.8–11, 5.2.1–5).

Next, the maxims in vv. 48–54 attack particular types of wrongful behavior (hypocrisy, presumptuousness, and arrogance) all of which contribute to the general theme of insolence.[10] This was an important topic in gnomic sources, with authors beginning at least with Hesiod and Theognis condemning it as the antithesis of justice.[11] The term usually referred both to a disposition characterized by insolence and arrogance, as well as the kinds of insulting behaviors such a disposition might precipitate.[12]

Some of Cicero's remarks in *De officiis* attest to how the sorts of considerations raised in vv. 42–54 could be integrated into exhortation on justice. He maintains, for example, that greed and ambition often cause individuals to lose sight of the responsibilities dictated by justice, adding that in measuring the culpability of an unjust act one must take into account whether the offender committed it willfully or not (1.25–27). He arrives at a similar conclusion regarding those people who are

---

[8] The author goes on to relate unrighteousness to such things as the transgression of agreements, lying, imposture, pretentiousness, and unscrupulousness.

[9] B. Williams, "Justice as a Virtue," 189–99; Engberg-Pedersen, *Aristotle's Theory of Moral Insight*, 53–62. Cf. Theognis, *El.* 465–466.

[10] Cf. Thom, *Golden Verses*, 138.

[11] On ὕβρις as the antithesis of justice, see Hesiod, *Op.* 213–285; Theognis, *El.* 40, 151, 153, 291, 307, 379, 541, 603, 732, 835, 1103, 1174; *SVF* 3:578; Fisher, *Hybris*, s.v. *dikaiosyne*.

[12] Fisher, *Hybris*, 493: "the deliberate infliction of shame and dishonour," including "the impetus to commit such acts." Cf. Bertram, "ὕβρις," 295–307; MacDowell, "Hybris in Athens," 14–31.

absorbed with their own self-interest (1.29–30) and observes how such misdeeds as chicanery, fraud, and false posturing can foment injustice (1.33).[13]

We may also note how literary patterns comparable to those at work in Pseudo-Phocylides' teaching on justice in vv. 9–54 as a whole are visible in other gnomic texts, for example, the 21st Instruction of P.Insinger (entitled, "The teaching not to slight lest you be slighted."), which has justice as its overriding theme.[14] Accordingly, within the instruction we come across a paragraph of injunctions repudiating unjust conduct, particularly in monetary and legal matters (26.18–27.1),[15] among clusters of sayings on ethical issues analogous to those set forth in vv. 22–54 of the *Sentences*, including greed (25.15–19), lying (25.21–23), violence (27.4–9), and arrogance (27.16–21). The unit also contains a series of maxims that advise correct behavior vis-à-vis different sorts of individuals, among them the needy, enemies, and neighbors (26.1–6).

---

[13] Analogous combinations of themes occur in gnomic exhortation as well, e.g., Sir 5:1–6:4, which links prescriptions against arrogance (especially vv. 1–2) and sinning (vv. 4–6) with a condemnation of deceitful wealth (v. 8) and hypocrisy (vv. 9ff.).

[14] Cf. Lichtheim, *Late Egyptian Wisdom*, 223–25.

[15] Cf. P.Ins. 27.11–15.

A. Verses 9–21

9   Always render just decisions, and prolong no judgment for a favor.
10   Do not unjustly oppress a poor man; judge not by his countenance.
11   If you judge evilly, God will afterwards judge you.
12   Shun false testimony; make just decisions.
13   Safeguard a deposit, and protect your integrity in all circumstances.
14   Dispense just measures; it is good to have measure in all circumstances.
15   Tip not a scale to one side, but weigh (both sides) equally.
16   Do not commit perjury, either unknowingly or willingly.
17   Immortal God detests anyone who swears a false oath.
18   Do not steal seeds; cursed is anyone who takes them.
19   Give a worker his wage; oppress not a poor person.
20   Be mindful of your tongue; keep your word hidden in your heart.
21   Do not be willing to do wrong, and therefore do not give leave to a
       wrong-doer.

TEXTUAL NOTES

Verse 9b. Cf. van der Horst, *Sentences*, 117–18 ("stretch not judgement for a favor");
Walter, *Poetische Schriften*, 198 ("verdrehe nach Gunst nicht das Urteil"); Derron,
Sentences, 3 ("ne pas fausser un jugement pour une faveur"). Verse 10a. Following
Bernays (*Gesammelte Abhandlungen*, 216 n. 1), who conjectures θλίψης (cf. v. 19)
instead of ῥίψης ("cast down;" cf. Tob 2:3) in the mss. and printed by Young, *Theognis*, 96; Derron, *Sentences*, 3; cf. van der Horst, *Sentences*, 118. Verse 12b. M, B, P, L:
βραβεύειν; L^{γρ}, V, Σ: ἀγορεύειν (cf. Hesiod, *Op.* 280). Verse 13a. Most editors agree
in replacing παρθενίην ("virginity") in the mss. with παρθεσίην. Verse 14b. Following West (*CR* 30 [1980]: 137), who proposes ἐπὶ μέτρον ἄπασι (cf. ἐπὶ μέτρον
in M, L, V, and ἄπασι in L^{2γρ}, Σ) instead of ἐπίμετρον ἀπάντων in B, which is
printed by Young, *Theognis*, 96; Derron, *Sentences*, 3. Verse 15. Cf. Walter, *Poetische
Schriften*, 198: "Drücke die Waage nicht nach einer Seite." // For σταθμός meaning
"scale," see LSJ s.v. III.1. // For κρούω meaning "to tap," see LSJ s.v. 4. // ἕλκω is
often used of weighing, in the sense of lifting up scales: Homer, *Il.* 8.72, 22.212;
Herodotus, *Hist.* 1.50 (ἕλκων σταθμόν, "to weigh in a scale"); LSJ s.v. A.I.7, A.II.9.
// V appends to this line (cf. vv. 16, 18, 21), "He shall not take everything for himself, either unknowingly or willingly" (ἅπαντα μήτ' ἀγνῶς μήτ' ἐθελοντὶ ἐλεῖται).
Verse 16. For μή … μήτε, see Denniston, *Greek Particles*, 508–509. Verse 17. For
(ψεύδ)ορκος + ὄμνυμι, cf. LSJ s.v. ὅρκος I.2; BDAG s.v. ὅρκος. // For στυγέω in
reference to divine abhorrence, cf. Homer, *Il.* 20.65, *Hymn.* 5.246; Hesiod, *Theog.*

739, 775, 805, 810; Theognis, *El.* 739, 810. // Σ replaces ἄμβροτος ὅστις with ὅττι κεν ἄν τις; after the verse it adds: "Never accept in your hand a gift which derives from unjust deeds." Verse 18. Σ continues with: "to generations of generations, to the scattering of life. Do not practice homosexuality, do not betray information, do not murder." Verse 20. Cf. Walter, *Poetische Schriften*, 199: "ein Wort im Vertrauen behalte fest für dich." // After this verse, Σ adds: "Make provision for orphans and widows and those in need." Verse 21. For μήτ' ... μήτ' οὖν, see Denniston, *Greek Particles*, 419–20.

COMMENTARY

Verses 9–12. Verse 9a introduces the theme for the entire section. The expression δίκαια νέμειν was proverbial in antiquity for the fair administration of justice (radicalized here by πάντα), as articulated in numerous texts, such as Plato, *Pol.* 301D, where we hear that it is a ruler's duty "to dispense justice rightly to all" (τὰ δίκαια ... διανέμειν ὀρθῶς πᾶσι); compare Aristotle, *Eth. nic.* 5.9.15 (νεμόμενα δίκαια) and Josephus, *Ant.* 7.147 (τῷ δικαίῳ νέμουσι).[16] Also see below, on vv. 12b and 14a. The second part of the verse lends some specificity to the content of δίκαια, offering also a clue as to the social location of the poem's intended reader, someone in a position to render judgment over others (cf. vv. 86–90).[17] Whether this pertains to private or public settings is difficult to say, though v. 10 may point toward the latter. The expression ἐς χάριν probably means "for a favor" rather than "to gain favor," and so constitutes a warning against soliciting or accepting bribes.[18] The corruption of justice by such practices is the subject of commentary in biblical sources,[19] with the qualifications articulated in Exod 23:6–8 and Deut 16:18–20 being of special interest for the interpretation of Ps.-Phoc. 9–10. The former issues rules for judges: do not pervert "the sentence of the poor" (κρίμα πένητος), abstain from unjust rulings, do not accept bribes.[20] In the latter, the people are told to appoint for themselves judges who will render their decisions "with righteous judgment" (κρίσιν δικαίαν), neither showing favoritism (οὐκ ἐπιγνώσονται πρόσωπον) nor accepting any bribe.[21] Similarly, Pseudo-Phocylides' ideal judge is neither partial to

---

[16] Cf. Xenophon, *Cyr.* 3.2.20; Aristotle, *Pol.* 7.8.4; *Sib. Or.* 1.272, 295, 2.49.

[17] Homeric νέμω is a favorite verb of the author (vv. 9, 14, 125, 137, 219, 224): the projected reader is someone in a position to "dispense" things to others. Cf. also Garnsey, "Legal Privilege," 141–65.

[18] Cf. Theocritus, *Id.* 5.69; Demosthenes, *Or.* 19.1.

[19] E.g., Deut 10:17; 1 Kgdms 8:3; 2 Chr 19:7; Ps 14:5; Prov 17:23; Job 36:18; Amos 5:11–12; Mic 3:11; Isa 1:23, 5:23; cf. Philo, *Spec.* 4.62–69; Josephus, *Ant.* 4.216–217; 11Q19 LI, 11–18; *m. 'Abot* 1:8–9; Schiffman, "Judicial Corruption," 155–78.

[20] Cf. Houtman, *Exodus*, 246–50.

[21] Cf. Gertz, *Gerichtsorganisation*, 33–41.

those who have the resources (and inclination) to offer bribes nor unfair to those who lack them. In his summary of the law, Josephus also denounces judges who accept bribes (*C. Ap.* 2.207).

In this context, ἕλκειν has the meaning "to drag out," in the sense of unnecessarily prolonging a process or activity,[22] though ordinarily it means "to draw or drag," which is the case in Hesiod, *Op.* 220–221: "There is a noise when justice is being dragged (ἑλκομένης) in the way where those men who devour bribes and give sentence with crooked judgments take her." In both cases, the word graphically conveys how justice can be abused by those in authority.[23]

The next line contains the first of several maxims in this section that address the reader's responsibility to the poor (cf. vv. 19, 22–29, 39–41). Its content is familiar from biblical appeals not to afflict (θλίβειν) the weak[24] or judge the poor unfairly.[25] The language of the second part of the verse seems to be inspired by biblical injunctions to judge impartially, without regard to a person's πρόσωπον ("face, countenance"), that is, his or her personal presence or circumstance.[26]

The motivation for v. 10's charge is provided by v. 11's threat, which is based on the biblical belief that divine judgment awaits those who afflict the weak and pervert the case of the poor, for example, Prov 14:31 ("He that oppresses the poor provokes his Maker.") and Job 13:10–11: "If you should secretly show partiality (πρόσωπα θαυμάσετε), will not terror from (God) fall upon you?"[27] The reality of divine vengeance against human injustice is elemental to Hesiod's worldview as well, for example, *Op.* 249–251 (cf. 248–273): "The immortal gods are near among mortals and mark all those who oppress others with crooked judgments, considering not the gods' anger."[28] Plautus, *Rudens* pr. 17–20 (cf. 13–16) sets forth both the same problem and the same outcome as Ps.-Phoc. 11–12: "When the wicked expect to win their suits by perjury or press false claims before the judge, the case adjudged is judged again by him (sc. Jove). And the fine he fines them far exceeds their gains in courts of law."[29]

---

[22] For which see LSJ s.v. ἕλκω A.II.6; also cf. on Ps.-Phoc. 15 below.

[23] Cf. Theognis, *El.* 43–52; Plato, *Leg.* 955C–D; Demosthenes, *Or.* 19.268; Aeschines, *Tim.* 87–88, *Fals. leg.* 154–155; Menander, *Mon.* 373; Epictetus, *Gnom.* 51; Publilius Syrus, *Sent.* 85; Rosivach, "Athenian Presuppositions," 192.

[24] Exod 23:9; Lev 19:33; Deut 23:17; cf. Lev 25:17; Prov 22:22; Amos 4:1, 8:4; Ezek 22:29.

[25] Exod 23:3, 6; Lev 19:15; Prov 31:8–9; Isa 32:7. On views of the poor in Judaism, cf. Hauck, "πένης," 37–40; Michel, "Armut," 72–76; Maier, "Armut," 80–85.

[26] Lev 19:15; Deut 1:17, 16:19 (discussed above); 1 Esd 4:39; Prov 18:5, 24:23; Sir 4:22, 27, 7:6, 35:13; Mal 2:9; cf. Philo, *Jos.* 72; Matt 22:16; Luke 20:21; Jas 2:1–9; Ps.-Heraclitus, *Ep.* 7.1; Lohse, "πρόσωπον," 779–80.

[27] Cf. Exod 22:20–26; Prov 17:5, 15; Job 36:15–18; Amos 5:10–12; Isa 10:2–3; Ezek 18:12–13.

[28] Cf. West, *Works and Days*, 219–25; Havelock, *Justice*, 193–217.

[29] Cf. Plato, *Leg.* 937B–C; Plautus, *Men.* 839; Babrius, *Fab.* 50.19–20.

In light of the opinions expressed in vv. 97–115, it is possible that our author has retribution in the hereafter, rather than in this life, in view. This is not necessarily the case, however, since nowhere in that paragraph (or elsewhere) does Pseudo-Phocylides actually articulate the idea of post-mortem judgment; see below, pp. 137–40, 145–51. The emphasis would seem to be on the certainty of divine judgment, not its nature or timing. The formulation of the verse, with the repetition of δικάζω, draws attention to the dynamic of reversal and retribution. The gnomic paradox of "the judged judge," the judge liable to the same scrutiny he metes out to others, informs other ancient *sententiae* as well, for example, Matt 7:2 ("With the judgment you make you will be judged."); Epictetus, *Gnom.* 55 ("It is shameful for the judge to be judged by others."); Sextus, *Sent.* 183–184: "The one who judges a person is judged by God. There is greater danger in judging than in being judged."[30] Since justice requires that all are equal before the law, even those who administer justice must be held accountable to it.

No doubt v. 12a stems from the Decalogue's injunction against false witness: οὐ ψευδομαρτυρήσεις ... μαρτυρίαν ψευδῆ (Exod 20:16; Deut 5:20, cf. 19:16–21). Apparently the maxim has been placed here, rather than in the Decalogue summary (vv. 3–8), because of its relevance to the judicial content of vv. 9–11. False witness is emphatically condemned in the book of Proverbs,[31] as well as in numerous early Christian texts.[32] In v. 12, this is a practice from which the readers are instructed to "flee," i.e., they should neither give nor accept it.[33] As Aristotle points out, such misconduct is especially criminal insofar as it is committed in the very place where criminals are supposed to be sentenced (*Rhet.* 1.14.6, cf. 1.15.17, 26). See the discussion below on Ps.-Phoc. 16–17.

The expression τὰ δίκαια βραβεύειν in v. 12b appears to have been proverbial for deciding and/or awarding what is just, for example, Musonius Rufus, frg. 8.60.22–23: It is incumbent upon a king "to arbitrate justice (τὰ δίκαια βραβεύειν) between his subjects," so that each "may receive honor or punishment as he deserves."[34] The appeal functions as a suitable conclusion for the sub-section. Note in particular the frame δίκαια νέμειν and δίκαια βραβεύειν create for vv. 9–12, which, in their entirety, can be compared with *Instr. Amenem.* 20.21–21.6: "Do not confound a man in the law court, in order to brush aside one who is right. Do not incline to the well-dressed man, and rebuff the one in rags. Don't accept the gift of a powerful man,

---

[30] Also Ezek 7:27; Luke 6:37; Rom 2:1; Publilius Syrus, *Sent.* 673. Pronouncements of this type can be understood as applications of the *ius talionis*, for which see Betz, *Sermon*, 275–77.

[31] Prov 12:17, 14:5, 19:5, 9, 21:28, 24:28–29, 25:18; cf. Philo, *Decal.* 138, 172, *Spec.* 4.41–43; Josephus, *Ant.* 4.219; *Instr. Amenem.* 16.1–2, 20.8–19; *Instr. Ankh.* 16.13; *Dict. Cat.* 3.3.

[32] Matt 15:19, 19:18; Mark 10:19; Luke 18:20; Rom 13:9 v.l.; *Did.* 2:3.

[33] For this use of φεύγω, cf. Wis 1:5; Sir 21:2; 1 Cor 10:14; also below, on Ps.-Phoc. 151.

[34] Cf. Philo, *Leg. all.* 1.87, *Ios.* 72, *Spec.* 4.64–66; Josephus, *Ant.* 5.232; *Sib. Or.* 2.45; Demosthenes, *Or.* 3.27; Plutarch, *Cic.* 9.3; Diodorus Siculus, *Bibl.* 14.65.3.

and deprive the weak for his sake. *Maat* is a great gift of god; he gives it to whom he wishes." Respect for the principles of divine judgment ought to determine how one relates to both the weak and the strong in the execution of justice.

Verses 13–15. This cluster of sayings addresses justice in economic matters. In *C. Ap.* 2.216 (cf. 208), Josephus also attaches an injunction against stealing deposits to instruction on the just use of weights and measures, suggesting that Pseudo-Phocylides here follows the source he shares with that author and Philo (cf. *Hypoth.* 7.8).

Biblical literature hands down a number of rules regarding the proper handling of deposits or "pledges" (usually παραθήκη, παρακαταθήκη, or ἐνέχυρον).[35] Plato and Aristotle agree in counting it among the basic responsibilities one has to justice.[36] Philo is of the opinion that this is the most sacred of all transactions between individuals because it is founded on the good faith (πίστις) of the one to whom the deposit is entrusted.[37] For Pseudo-Phocylides, too, safeguarding a deposit is a test of one's πίστις. In this regard, the parallelism of τηρεῖν and φυλάσσειν is notable:[38] protecting the pledge is tantamount to protecting one's integrity, while the expression πίστιν (δια)φυλάσσειν was proverbial for preserving loyalty.[39] Pseudo-Phocylides takes up the problem of accepting stolen deposits in vv. 135–136; see below.

In vv. 69, 69B, and 98, μέτρον has to do with moderation in one's comportment, while in v. 139 it means "ration." Here, taken with vv. 14b–15, μέτρα νέμειν τὰ δίκαια refers to the use of fair measures, which may be taken as a specific instance of τὰ δίκαια βραβεύειν in v. 12b. Lev 19:35–36, then, is the likely source for these lines: "You shall not act unjustly (ἄδικον) in judgment, in measures and balances and scales (ἐν μέτροις καὶ ἐν σταθμίοις καὶ ἐν ζυγοῖς). There shall be for you just scales and just balances (ζυγὰ δίκαια καὶ στάθμια δίκαια)." Similar requirements for commercial transactions are indicated elsewhere in scripture.[40] The pairing of

---

[35] The problem of lost or stolen deposits is the concern of Exod 22:6–12 and Lev 5:20–26; cf. Exod 22:25; Deut 24:6, 10–13; Ezek 18:7, 12, 16, 33:15; 4Q416 2 III, 3–5; Josephus, *Ant.* 4.285–287; Ranft, "Depositum," 778–84.

[36] In Ps.-Aristotle, *Mag. mor.* 1.33.34 (cf. Aristotle, *Eth. nic.* 5.8.4), e.g., confiscating a deposit is included alongside stealing and adultery in a list of typical unjust acts; cf. Democritus, frg. 265; Plato, *Resp.* 331E–332B; Cicero, *Tusc.* 3.17; *Dict. Cat.* pr. 4; Taubenschlag, *Law*, 349–52.

[37] *Spec.* 4.30–40; cf. Isocrates, *Demon.* 22.

[38] Parallel constructions with the two verbs are common, e.g., Prov 2:11, 13:3, 16:17, 19:16, 25:10; Wis 10:5; Dan 9:4; John 17:12; Philo, *Leg. all.* 3.189; Epictetus, *Diatr.* 1.4.20; Dio Chrysostom, *Rhod.* 150.

[39] E.g., 3 Macc 3:3; Josephus, *Vita* 39, 93, *Ant.* 10.230, 12.8, 396; Sophocles, *Oed. col.* 626; Polybius, *Hist.* 18.41.9; *Anth. Gr.* 9.346.3; Marcus Aurelius, *Med.* 9.42.4; Strabo, *Geogr.* 5.2.5.

[40] Deut 25:14–15; Prov 20:10; Mic 6:10–11; Ezek 45:10–12; cf. Philo, *Her.* 162; *Sib. Or.* 3.237; *Instr. Amenem.* 17.18–19.9; Plato, *Leg.* 746D–E, 757B; Thomas, *Der jüdische Phokylides*, 141–59.

στάθμιον and ζυγόν (which must have influenced the choice of ἑτερόζυγος in v. 15) in Lev 19:35–36 was conventional in this kind of discourse.[41]

Verses 16–17. Yet another allusion to the Decalogue is possible here, this time Exod 20:7 (cf. Deut 5:11): "You shall not take the name of the Lord your God in vain; for the Lord will not acquit him that takes his name in vain."[42] Also comparable is Zech 8:17, which specifically names swearing falsely as an object of divine wrath: "'Love not a false oath (ὅρκον ψευδῆ), for all such things I hate,' says the Lord Almighty."

The language and thought of these verses are reminiscent especially of Hesiod, *Theog.* 231–232, a prediction that mortals will be grieved by "divine Oath" if anyone "willingly swears a perjured oath (ἑκὼν ἐπίορκον ὀμόσσῃ)." Hesiod broaches the subject again in *Op.* 282–284: "Whoever gives false testimony willingly, swearing a perjured oath (ὃς δέ κε μαρτυρίῃσι ἑκὼν ἐπίορκον ὀμόσσας ψεύσεται), harming justice and sinning beyond repair, that man's generation is thereafter left obscure."[43] Pseudo-Phocylides agrees, though he goes one step further: even those who perjure themselves out of ignorance are liable to the judgment of "immortal God," invoking a Homeric phrase (see *Il.* 20.358, 22.9, 24.460, *Od.* 24.445).[44]

The condemnation of swearing falsely is found throughout biblical literature, as is the conviction that those guilty of this crime will face divine punishment.[45] The Greek sages were in agreement on this theme, for example, Theognis, *El.* 1195–1196: "Do not swear a perjured oath (ἐπίορκον) by the gods, for to hide from the immortals a debt that is owed is not to be tolerated."[46] On the whole, they decry oath-breaking as an act of impiety, as Joseph Plescia notes: "Perjury as an invocation to the gods to guarantee the truth of a false statement was a personal affront to the gods which carried its own penalty, the curse."[47] The large part that oaths played in

---

[41] Prov 11:1, 16:11, 20:23; Sir 42:4; Amos 8:5; Philo, *Spec.* 4.193–194.

[42] Cf. Lang, "Das Verbot des Meineids," 97–105.

[43] Cf. Homer, *Il.* 3.278–279: the gods take vengeance on "whoever has sworn a false oath" (ὅτις κ' ἐπίορκον ὀμόσσῃ); cf. *Il.* 3.298–301, 19.258–265.

[44] For the problem of ignorant wrongdoing, cf. Aristotle, *Eth. nic.* 5.8.6; Rickert, *ΕΚΩΝ and ΑΚΩΝ,* 111–17; also see the discussion of Ps.-Phoc. 51–52, below.

[45] E.g., Lev 5:22, 19:12; Num 30:3; Ps 23:4; Wis 14:25, 28, 30; Sir 23:9–11, 27:14; Zech 5:3–4; Mal 3:5; Jer 5:2, 7:9; Matt 5:33; 1 Tim 1:10; Jas 5:12; cf. Philo, *Decal.* 82–95, *Spec.* 1.235–236, 2.26–28, 255, 4.40; *3 Bar.* 4:17, 13:4; *Did.* 2:3.

[46] Cf. Isocrates, *Demon.* 13; Menander, *Mon.* 347; Euripides, *El.* 1355–1356, *Med.* 1391–1392; Aristophanes, *Ran.* 150; *Carm. aur.* 2; Demosthenes, *Or.* 48.52; Diogenes Laertius, *Vit. phil.* 8.22; Stobaeus, *Anth.* 3.27–28; *Instr. Ankh.* 16.13.

[47] Plescia, *Perjury,* 88, cf. 83–88; Burkert, *Greek Religion,* 250–54; Betz, *Sermon,* 259–66; J. T. Fitzgerald, "The Problem of Perjury," 156–77.

commercial transactions may help account for the placement of these lines, adjacent to vv. 13–15.[48]

Verse 18. This unusual petition, which has no specific biblical analogue, apparently extends the Decalogue's prohibition of theft (οὐ κλέψεις) to seeds.[49] Perhaps the line should be interpreted together with v. 38, which enjoins the reader not to damage the fruit (καρπός) of the land. In this connection, mention may be made of Lev 27:30, which indicates that σπέρματα are to be included with καρπός in the tithe of the land, which would be some indication of their value. In *Adul. amic.* 56B, Plutarch reproves servants so shameless that they steal not only from a heap of crops but even from the seed (κλέπτουσιν ἀλλ' ἀπὸ τοῦ σπέρματος). Among the "unwritten customs" of the Jewish people, Philo includes an ordinance against filching from a garden, wine-press, threshing-floor, or heap "anything great or small," which presumably would include seeds (*Hypoth.* 7.6).[50]

We can assume that the cursing involved in v. 18b originates with God, and so the motivation for observing this rule is similar to that of vv. 11 and 17. To express this imprecation our author apparently coined a new term, ἐπαράσιμος; cf. Homer, *Il.* 9.456; Euripides, *Orest.* 286; Plato, *Leg.* 684E, 931B.

Verse 19. Biblical writings are unanimous in the opinion that a worker's wage (μισθός) ought to be paid promptly and without fraud.[51] In its consideration for the economic vulnerability of day-laborers, Deut 24:14–15 addresses the concern of this verse: "You shall not unjustly withhold the wage of the poor man (μισθὸν πένητος) … you shall pay him his wage the same day … because he is poor and has his hope in it."[52] In *Virt.* 88, Philo cites this passage as evidence of the law's φιλανθρωπία. Comparison may also be made with Josephus, *Ant.* 4.288: "One must not deprive a poor man of his wages, knowing that this, instead of land and other possessions, is the portion which God has granted him." For his part, Pseudo-Phocylides (given the parallelism of the two halves of the verse) seems to assume that those who work for a wage are by definition poor; failure to pay them is an injustice.

Verse 20. The problem of speech is a major theme for our poem; cf. vv. 7, 12, 16–17, 69, 122–124. The advice here needs to be assessed especially in relation to the counsel about sincerity in vv. 48–50, for which see below. Sins of the tongue were a preoccupation of the biblical sages, who stressed the need for discipline and

---

[48] Dover, *Popular Morality*, 249.

[49] Exod 20:14, cf. 21:17, 21:37–22:3; Lev 19:11; Deut 5:19; Tob 2:13.

[50] Cf. Virgil, *Ecl.* 8.95–100.

[51] Lev 19:13; Tob 4:14; Sir 34:21–22; Mal 3:5; Luke 10:7; 1 Tim 5:18.

[52] Cf. Philo, *Spec.* 4.195–196; *T. Job* 12:1–4; Jas 5:4; *Der. Er. Rab.* 2.27; Menander, *Mon.* 376, 542.

discretion in one's speech. Prov 18:21 indicates the high stakes involved: "Life and death are in the power of the tongue; they that control it shall eat its fruits." Generally speaking, taciturnity, entailing especially a reluctance to discuss confidential matters, was seen as a way of gaining the respect and trust of others. In this context, the imagery of protection could be invoked: the sage will "hide" his words (Sir 1:24) and "guard" his mouth (Prov 13:3).[53] Conversely, rash speech is a sure sign of the fool; his lack of self-control leads to embarrassment and ruin.[54]

This theme has strong roots outside the biblical tradition as well, with Isocrates, *Demon.* 41 providing a good summary: "Always when you are about to say anything, first weigh it in your mind; for with many the tongue outruns the thought. Let there be but two occasions for speech – when the subject is one which you thoroughly know and when it is one on which you are compelled to speak. On these occasions alone is speech better than silence."[55] References in such contexts to the "mind' (i.e., the power of reason; cf. Ps.-Phoc. 48), as well as to the "heart" (i.e., the seat of the passions; cf. Ps.-Phoc. 122), are suggestive of the anthropological dynamic thought to be involved; compare P.Ins. 21.14 ("He who guards his heart and his tongue sleeps without an enemy."), Sextus, *Sent.* 151 ("Let your tongue be obedient to your mind."), or Sir 21:26, memorable for its symmetry: "The heart of fools is in their mouth, the mouth of the wise is in their heart."

Verse 21. This concluding maxim addresses one of the prevailing concerns of ancient wisdom literature, the need to resist ἀδικία ("injustice, wrongdoing") and those associated with it.[56] Exod 23:7 ("From every unjust thing you shall abstain.") may be part of the background here, though Pseudo-Phocylides' focus on unwillingness to do wrong as an impediment to the wrongdoing of others is absent. For v. 21a, Tob 4:5 is a better parallel: "Do not be willing to sin … do not follow the ways of wrongdoing." Our verse seems most at home, however, in the Greek traditions, where unwillingness to do wrong (τὸ μὴ θέλειν ἀδικεῖν) was well-established

---

[53] Cf. Ps 38:2; Prov 10:14, 11:13, 21:23; Sir 22:27, 28:25.

[54] For gnomic observations about wisdom and folly in speech, see Ps 33:14; Prov 10:20, 31–32, 15:1–2, 4, 17:4, 20, 18:18–21, 26:28, 31:25; Qoh 5:1; Sir 4:23–29, 5:13–14, 6:5, 9:18, 17:6, 19:16, 20:7–8, 18–20, 21:7, 23:7–8, 25:8, 28:12–26, 37:18, 40:21; Jas 1:19, 26, 3:1–12; *Syr. Men.* 304–313; Sextus, *Sent.* 151–165g, 171, 253a, 426–427, 430–432.

[55] Further: Hesiod, *Op.* 719–720; Theognis, *El.* 421–424, 815–816, 1163–1164, 1185–1186; Diogenes Laertius, *Vit. phil.* 1.69–70; Menander, *Mon.* 136, 289, 305, 318; Epictetus, *Ench.* 33.1–3; cf. *Ahiqar* 98–99, 109, 141; *Instr. Ankh.* 7.23–24, 10.7, 12.24, 14.12, 15.16; P.Ins. 3.6, 22.20.

[56] E.g., Prov 8:13, 28:16; Wis 1:5; Sir 7:1–3, 10:7–8, 17:26, 27:10, 35:3; Theognis, *El.* 29–30, 947–948; Menander, *Mon.* 8, 66, 119, 632, frg. 774; *Gnom. Vat.* 7; Sextus, *Sent.* 23; Stobaeus, *Anth.* 3.10. Also cf. Ps.-Phoc. 5, 10, 51–52, 135.

as a standard of justice.[57] The topic of one's intention or disposition in the face of temptations to do wrong could also be cast in gnomic form, for example, Menander, *Mon.* 37–38: "A just man is not one who does no wrong, but whoever is unwilling to do wrong even when he can." The form of *Gnom. Democr.* 62 is particularly close to that of our verse: "It is good not to do no wrong, but not to wish to" (ἀγαθὸν οὐ τὸ μὴ ἀδικεῖν, ἀλλὰ τὸ μηδὲ ἐθέλειν.).

For v. 21b, we can turn again to the *Gnomologium Democrateum*, this time line 38: "It is a fine thing to prevent someone from doing wrong – but if not, to have no part in the wrongdoing." Compare also Aelius Aristides, *Or.* 2.270: "Not only will the orator himself do no wrong (οὐκ ἀδικήσει), he will not even permit (οὐδ' ἐάσει) another to do so."[58] In *De officiis*, Cicero argues for the need to recognize that injustice can take not one but two forms: the first attaches to those who actually inflict wrong, while the other concerns "those who, although they can, do not shield from wrong those upon whom it is being inflicted." The latter are likened to those found guilty of deserting their family, friends, or country (1.23). Like these parallels, our verse extends the sphere of responsibility for justice to include not only one's actions but also one's intentions, as well as the actions of others (cf. vv. 132–134).

---

[57] E.g., Xenophon, *Mem.* 4.4.12, *Cyr.* 5.2.9–10; Euripides, *El.* 1354; Plato, *Resp.* 344A; *Anec. Gr.* 1.153.

[58] Cf. Democritus, frg. 261.

B. Verses 22–41

22	To a beggar give at once, and do not tell him to come tomorrow.
23	You shall fill your hand; give alms to one in need.
24	Receive a homeless person into your house, and guide a blind man.
25	Pity a shipwrecked person, since sailing is uncertain.
26	To one who falls lend a hand, and save an unprotected man.
27	Common to all is suffering; life's a wheel; unstable is happiness.
28	Having wealth extend your hand to the poor.
29	From what God has given you provide for those in need.
30	Let all of life be in common and all things united.
32	Gird on your sword not for murder but for defense.
33	But may you need it not at all, unlawfully or justly;
34	for if you slay a foe, you stain your hand.
35	Keep away from a neighbor's field, and so do not trespass.
38	Harm not any fruit growing in a field.
39	Let foreigners be held in equal honor among citizens.
40	For we all experience the poverty that comes from roaming widely,
41	and a tract of land has nothing certain for people.

TEXTUAL NOTES

Verse 22a. Σ replaces πτωχῷ with πτωχοῖς. // εὐθύ is rarely used of time, though see the examples in LSJ s.v. εὐθύς B.I.3. Verse 23. Following Young's (*Theognis*, 97) text, πληρώσει σέο, in M, B, L, V; cf. Ps.-Phoc. 28: "Extend your hand to the poor." Derron (*Sentences*, 4, cf. 21 n. 2) prints πληρώσεις ἕο χεῖρ' ("You shall fill his hand."); cf. van der Horst, *Sentences*, 128–29. // Σ has: "With perspiring hand give a portion of corn to one who is in need." It continues with: "Whoever gives alms knows that he is lending to God. Mercy saves from death when judgment comes. God wants not sacrifice but mercy instead of sacrifice. Therefore clothe the naked; give the hungry a share of your bread." Verse 28. For χεῖρα ... ὄρεξον, cf. Homer, *Il.* 15.371, 23.99, 24.506, 743, *Od.* 9.527, 12.257, 17.366. Verse 30. Σ has: "The life of every human is common, but falls out unequally." It continues with: "When you see a poor man, never mock him with words, and do not verbally abuse a person who is at fault. Life is assessed in death. Whether one acted lawlessly or righteously will be distinguished when one comes to judgment. Do not damage your mind with wine or drink to excess." [Verse 31.] "Consume no blood; abstain from food offered to idols." (αἷμα δὲ μὴ φαγέειν, εἰδωλοθύτων ἀπέχεσθαι.) A spurious line (only in Σ); see van der Horst, *Sentences*, 135–36. Verse 32. For this use of ἀμφιβάλλω, cf. Homer, *Od.* 22.103. // Σ replaces φόνον with φίλον. Verse 35b. For this use of ὑπερβαίνω, cf. Job 24:2; also see below, on Ps.-Phoc. 64. [Verse 36.] = Ps.-Phoc. 69B (for which see below); a spurious verse, missing from L, P, and V; Σ has: "Every boundary is just, but trespass is grievous." See van der Horst, *Sentences*, 137–38. [Verse 37.]: "Acquisition of honest things is useful, of unjust things, wicked." (κτῆσις ὀνήσιμός ἐσθ' ὁσίων, ἀδίκων δὲ πονηρά.) A spurious verse (only in Σ); see van der Horst, *Sentences*, 138. Verse 40. Or perhaps, "For we all have experience of wide-ranging poverty." // For πολύπλαγκτος, cf. Homer, *Il.* 11.308, *Od.* 17.425, 511, 20.195; Aeschylus, *Suppl.* 572; Sophocles, *Ant.* 615; *Sib. Or.* 3.387. // Σ expands the line: "For all will experience exile of many hardships as guests of each other. But no one will be a stranger among you since you are all mortals of one blood." Verse 41. Cf. van der Horst, *Sentences*, 140–42 ("and the land has nothing constant for men."); Walter, *Poetische Schriften*, 201 ("und nirgends gibt es einen sicheren Platz auf Erden für die Menschen."); Derron, *Sentences*, 5 ("et la terre n'a point de lieu sûr pour les hommes."). // For χώρης πέδον (both words are Homeric), cf. Aeschylus, *Prom.* 1; Aristophanes, *Nub.* 573.

COMMENTARY

Verses 22–26. These lines open a unit on the reader's relationship with the economically poor and vulnerable, concentrating on the need to give assistance; note δίδου framing the unit in vv. 22a and 26a.[59] In its perspective on the subject, our poem may be said to promote a certain socio-economic agenda, inasmuch as it makes the case that the realities of poverty ought to matter to the reader and recommends concrete acts that would ease the plight of the poor. Verse 19 focused on the working poor; here attention turns to the beggarly poor, those who would have suffered the most severe economic deprivation. Their association with other types of destitute people as objects of moral responsibility would have been natural. Of the Stoic sage, for example, Seneca maintains that "to the shipwrecked he will give a hand, to the exile shelter, to the needy alms ... he will give as a man to his fellow-man out of the common store" (*Clem.* 2.6.2).

In his summary of the law, Philo mentions the obligation to offer food to beggars as an "unwritten custom" of the Jews (*Hypoth.* 7.6; cf. Josephus, *C. Ap.* 2.211).[60] Pseudo-Phocylides' point of departure for these lines may have been the legal source he shares with Philo and Josephus, though vv. 22–23a at least appear to be a paraphrase of Prov 3:27–28: "Do not abstain from doing good to the needy, whenever your hand (ἡ χείρ σου) can help. Do not say (μὴ εἴπῃς), 'Come back another time; tomorrow I will give (αὔριον δώσω)'." Although no specific mention is made here

---

[59] Cf. above, p. 85.
[60] Cf. Philo, *Virt.* 82–87, 90–94, 97–98, 121–123.

of the πτωχός, acknowledgement of his needs is made elsewhere in Proverbs, for example, 14:21, 31, 17:5, 19:7, 17, 22:9, 28:27.[61] Opening one's "hand" was a biblical idiom for giving alms to the poor; besides Prov 3:27, see Deut 15:7–11; Prov 31:20; Sir 7:32; and below, on v. 26. The practice of almsgiving figures prominently especially in two Hellenistic Jewish texts, Tobit and Ben Sira, texts which not coincidentally also extol the virtue of mercy, ἐλεημοσύνη.[62] Pseudo-Phocylides similarly associates mercy with the practice of almsgiving through the use of ἔλεον in v. 23b. Inherent in this concept was the obligation to offer unilateral assistance to one's social subordinates, without any prospect of reciprocation or self-benefit.[63]

The emphasis on aiding the destitute betrays something of our poem's Jewish proclivities, though in this area (like many others) the prevailing Hellenistic ethos would have been shaped to no small degree by the Homeric epics, where the practice of aiding a πτωχός is taken for granted (*Od.* 6.207–208, 14.57–59, 17.10–12) and failure to give alms to indigent strangers is characterized as shameful (17.500–504).[64] For the element of promptness we may compare Publilius Syrus, *Sent.* 274: "To do a kindness to the needy at once is to give twice."

Verse 24, which continues the topic of mercy to the needy and vulnerable, may be a conflation of Isa 58:7 and 42:16 (cf. 43:8):

πτωχοὺς ἀστέγους εἴσαγε εἰς τὸν οἶκόν σου. "Lead homeless beggars into your house."[65]
ἄξω τυφλοὺς ἐν ὁδῷ. "I will lead the blind on the way."[66]

The reference to πτωχοί in Isa 58:7 might help to explain the proximity of v. 24 to vv. 22–23, which also deal with beggars, while the reference to ὁδός in Isa 42:16 may have had something to do with the selection of ὁδήγει in v. 24b. With δέξαι in v. 24a (cf. Isaiah's εἴσαγε), Pseudo-Phocylides introduces into his discourse the

---

[61] Cf. Sir 4:1–8, 10:23; *T. Iss.* 7:5; *T. Job* 10:7, 11:5, 9, 12:1, 15:5; *Jos. Asen.* 10:12; Hauck and Bammel, "πτωχός," 885–915; Esser and Brown, "πτωχός," 821–29.

[62] Tob 1:3, 16, 2:14, 3:2, 4:7–11, 16, 12:8–9, 14:2, 7, 9–11; Sir 3:30, 7:10, 12:3–7, 16:14, 17:22, 29:8, 12–13, 31:11, 35:2, 40:17, 24; cf. *Instr. Any* 8.4–5; *T. Job* 9:8, 10:3; *Sib. Or.* 2.79–83; *T. Zeb.* 5:1–8:6 (with Hollander and de Jonge, *Testaments*, 253–75); *T. Benj.* 4:4; CD 14.12–14; Matt 6:2–4; Acts 3:2–3, 10, 9:36, 10:2, 4, 24:17; *Did.* 1:5, 4:5–8, 15:4.

[63] Bultmann, "ἔλεος," 485–87; cf. Preuß, "Barmherzigkeit," 215–24.

[64] Cf. Theognis, *El.* 1162; Demosthenes, *Or.* 10.43; Lysias, *Or.* 16.14; Ps.-Diotogenes, *Regn.* 2.72.30–31; Diogenes Laertius, *Vit. phil.* 5.17; Dionysius of Halicarnassus, *Ant. rom.* 5.68.1–2; Seneca, *Ep.* 81.14; Havelock, *Justice,* 161–78; Bolkestein, *Wohltätigkeit und Armenpflege,* 200–14, 337–41; den Boer, *Private Morality,* 162–78; Schwer, "Armenpflege," 689–93.

[65] Cf. *Barn.* 3:3.

[66] Cf. Lev 19:14; Deut 27:18; Rom 2:19; Euripides, *Phoen.* 834–835.

idiom of hospitality, a much-discussed subject in Hellenistic moral literature.[67] In the lore of Second Temple Judaism, Abraham and Job were especially thought to embody this virtue. *T. Abr.* (A) 1:1–2 introduces the former by describing how he welcomed (ἐδέχετο) strangers, the poor, and the helpless into his house.[68] The latter, for his part, was celebrated as "the host of strangers" and "the light of the blind."[69] Homelessness, of course, would have been generally associated with poverty.[70]

Verses 25–26 extend the exhortation on mercy, advocating compassion for those who have met with misadventures of some kind.

In the biblical ambit, to have pity (οἰκτείρω) on the unfortunate, a trait associated with mercy (e.g., Prov 13:11), was a basic characteristic of the righteous, as Ps 36:21 explains.[71] To include the shipwrecked among those especially deserving of such compassion would have surprised no one in antiquity, where the risks associated with seafaring were well-known.[72] As evidence that he is not indifferent to the misfortune of others, Dio Chrysostom explains that "many is the time I have pitied shipwrecked travelers, … taken them into my dwelling, given them food and drink, and helped them however I could" (*Ven.* 52, cf. 53–58; Plutarch, *Mulier. virt.* 246D–E). A sailor by definition lives an uncertain (ἄδηλος) existence, as Secundus notes in *Sent.* 14–15.[73] In its reference to this particular vocation, the supporting statement of v. 25b anticipates more general ruminations about life's vicissitudes in vv. 27 and 40–41. As 3 Macc 4:4 observes, "the uncertain (ἄδηλον) turning of life" is in fact a reality with which all people must contend.[74]

Like the preceding line, v. 26 has no biblical parallels, though the sentiment of Ps 144:14 ("The Lord supports all who fall.") is similar. The meaning of ἀπερίστατον, a post-classical term, is indicated by Epictetus, who uses it of an "isolated" (and therefore vulnerable) man – someone with no family, friends, or country.[75]

---

[67] For this meaning of δέχομαι, see LSJ s.v. II.1; BDAG s.v. 3; Malherbe, *Social Aspects*, 96. Further, see below, on Ps.-Phoc. 39, 81–82.

[68] Cf. Allison, *Testament of Abraham*, 66–72.

[69] *T. Job* 53:3, cf. 10:1–4, 17:3; Job 29:15–16, 31:32; *m. 'Abot* 1:5 ("Let your house be wide open. And seat the poor at your table."); *ARN* A 7.1.1–4.1.

[70] Cf. below, on Ps.-Phoc. 40–41.

[71] Cf. Ps 111:5; Prov 13:9, 21:26; Bultmann, "οἰκτίρω," 159–61.

[72] E.g., Ps 106:23–30; Wis 14:1–5; Sir 43:24; Jonah 1:3–16; Acts 27:9–44; 2 Cor 11:25–26; Philo, *Deus immut.* 98, *Migr.* 217, *Jos.* 138; Hesiod, *Op.* 665–694; Strabo, *Geogr.* 8.6.20; Babrius, *Fab.* 71.

[73] Cf. Athenaeus, *Deipn.* 154F–155A.

[74] The future is ἄδηλον: Philo, *Jos.* 116, *Virt.* 152; Demosthenes, *Or.* 15.21; Ps.-Plutarch, *Cons. Apoll.* 107A.

[75] Epictetus, *Diatr.* 4.1.159; cf. Polybius, *Hist.* 6.44.8.

Verses 27–30. The combination κοινός + πᾶς/ἅπας + ὁ βίος in vv. 27 and 30 both frames this paragraph and betokens its main theme, the solidarity of human experience.

The opening line, unique in the poem for its three-part structure, occupies an important place in the section on justice and mercy inasmuch as it articulates some of the basic principles underwriting its moral advice, encouraging a sense of identification with those who struggle in life, since their plight is that of all people.

The tone of the first maxim is reminiscent of Qoheleth's somber teaching about pain and difficulty as humankind's common lot: all our days are "darkness" (5:16) and "full of suffering" (2:23). The Greek gnomological tradition shared this perspective, for example, Menander, *Mon.* 97 ("It is not easy for a mortal to live without grief."), especially in connection with the treatment of τύχη, or fortune, for example, Isocrates, *Demon.* 29 ("Taunt no one with his calamity, for fortune is common to all and the future is unseen.") and Menander, *Mon.* 514: "Believe that misfortunes are common to all."[76]

In this ideational context the wheel served as a cross-cultural symbol for the twists and turns of life: everyone will eventually encounter some difficulty.[77] This would apply especially of course to the ephemerality of ὄλβος, happiness or prosperity, as Herodotus observes: "Human fortunes are on a wheel, which in its turning suffers not the same one to prosper forever" (*Hist.* 1.207).[78] The unpredictability of success was a gnomic *topos*, evidenced by texts like Isocrates, *Demon.* 42 ("Consider that nothing in human life is stable.") and Theognis, *El.* 318: "Possessions belong now to one among mortals, now to another."

Ancient writers sometimes seized on such observations to induce cautious reflection in their readers, Sir 18:25–26 being representative: "Remember the time of hunger in the time of plenty, poverty and want in the day of wealth. Between morning and evening the measure changes."[79] The author of *Consolatio ad Apollonium* takes issue with people who become arrogant in their prosperity, "not bearing in mind the uncertainty of fortune (τῆς τύχης ἄστατον)." He continues by quoting a proverb: "to try to find any constancy in what is inconstant is a trait of people who do not rightly reason about the circumstances of life; for 'the wheel goes round, and

---

[76] Cf. Democritus, frg. 293; Epicurus, *Ep. Men.* 133; Ps.-Plutarch, *Lib. ed.* 5D, *Cons. Apoll.* 104D; Menander, *Mon.* 10, 570, 577 ("Fortune gives to some and takes away from others."), 625, 652 ("Many who fair ill are set right by fortune."), 745; Seneca, *Ep.* 47.1 ("Fortune has equal rights over slaves and free alike."); Stobaeus, *Anth.* 4.41; Ziegler, "Tyche," 1650–73; Greene, *Moira,* s.v. *Tyche.*

[77] Sophocles, frg. 871.1–2; Philo, *Somn.* 2.44; Plutarch, *Num.* 14.5; *Anacreont.* 30.7; *Paroem. Gr.* 2.87.16; *Anec. Gr.* 1.19, 87; Ps.-Ovid, *Cons. Liv.* 51–52.

[78] Cf. Pindar, *Pyth.* 3.105–106; Euripides, *Phoen.* 558, *Herc. fur.* 511–512; Nonnus, *Dion.* 25.122.

[79] Cf. Qoh 2:18–21, 5:10–14, 6:1–6; Sir 11:18–25, 20:9; *Syr. Men.* 110–112; Philo, *Mos.* 1.30–31, 41.

of the rim now one and now another part is at top.'"[80] In contrast to these authors, Pseudo-Phocylides addresses this theme by focusing on the importance not of being prepared, or of adopting the proper comportment (cf. below, on vv. 118–121), but of identifying with the situation of the unfortunate. Demosthenes adopts a comparable strategy in *Or.* 15.21, arguing that the fortunate should always give consideration to the unfortunate, since the future is ἄδηλον.[81]

Verses 28–29 essentially restate the exhortation of vv. 22–23, though specifying in addition the preconditions under which such charity ought to be practiced. Given the likely influence of Prov 3:27–28 on those verses, our author may have had in mind the circumstances for almsgiving stipulated there: "Do not abstain from doing good to the needy, whenever your hand can help. Do not say, 'Come back another time; tomorrow I will give,' when you are able to do good." Sir 14:13 makes a similar qualification: "According to your ability stretch out (your hand) and give." Tobit also advises that almsgiving be carried out with regard for one's substance (4:7–8, 16), as does Menander in *Mon.* 478: "Remember when you are rich to aid the poor."[82] These sources agree, then, on fixing no absolute standard for when or how much one ought to give to the needy; almsgiving is viewed rather as a general obligation of those with the resources to do so.

Verse 29 presents divine beneficence as the basis and model of human charity, imaging God as a generous provider and the almsgiver as the steward and distributor of divine gifts. This conceptualization is familiar from various Jewish, Christian, and pagan writings, for example, *T. Zeb.* 7:2 ("From what God has provided you, be compassionate and merciful to all without discrimination."), Sextus, *Sent.* 242 ("What you freely receive from God freely give."), and Menander, *Mon.* 198: "Give to the poor as you receive from God the giver."[83] Philo applies this logic in explicating the law, which he claims is replete with injunctions to practice mercy and *philanthrōpia*, encouraging individuals (especially the affluent) to look upon their wealth as something to be shared (κοινά) with the needy; in doing this they imitate God's generosity (*Spec.* 4.72–74, cf. *Virt.* 169). The religious underpinnings

---

[80] Ps.-Plutarch, *Cons. Apoll.* 103E–F.

[81] Cf. Sophocles, *Phil.* 501–503: "Save me, pity me, seeing that for mortals all things are full of fear and of the danger that after good fortune may come evil."

[82] Cf. Sextus, *Sent.* 228, 296 ("Nothing is good that is not shared."), 377 ("Better to have nothing than much without sharing."); Josephus, *C. Ap.* 2.207; *Syr. Men.* 229–239; *T. Iss.* 3:8; 2 Cor 8:3; Cicero, *Off.* 1.44.

[83] Cf. Deut 15:14; 2 Cor 9:8; *Did.* 1:5b; Sextus, *Sent.* 378; P.Ins. 16.3–5. P.Ins. 16.10–15 elaborates on the theme, specifying (in a manner our author characteristically does not) the compensation the merciful can anticipate: "(Giving) food without dislike removes all dislike. The god gives a thousand for one to him who gives it to another. The god lets one acquire wealth on account of doing the good deed of mercy. He who gives food to him who is poor, the god credits it to him for an offering of millions. The giving of food contents the heart of the god <more than> the heart of him who finds it."

of charity are similarly highlighted in his summary of the law: "To the poor or lame begging food one should give as an offering to God" (*Hypoth.* 7.6).

Verse 30 overlaps in meaning with v. 27. It hardly relates to the common life of the Essenes,[84] but rather advocates a perspective that honors sharing and harmony on more basic terms. In passages like 2 Macc 4:5, for example, κοινός refers to the public weal.[85] The importance attached to sharing in relationships of trust and mutual interest is reflected also in the Greek proverb, "Friends have everything in common (κοινά)."[86] In contrast to both of these, v. 30 in its context advances the idea that those with whom the reader ought to seek a common life include individuals in the greatest economic need; aiding them benefits the "common" good. In this regard the argument of vv. 27–30 is comparable to *Did.* 4:5–8, which links almsgiving with the obligation to "hold everything in common with your brother."[87] The promotion of social harmony, then, functions for our author as a criterion for the proper use of wealth.[88] With this we may compare Democritus, frg. 255: "When those who can venture to contribute to those without means and to help and favor them, this shows pity, so that they are not abandoned, and they become comrades and take one another's part and the citizens are in concord."

For v. 30b, which explicates the meaning of this common life, see Theognis, *El.* 81–82: those who are of one mind (ὁμόφρονα) share equally in hardships as well as successes. Strabo suggests something of the affinity associated with such agreement in *Geogr.* 6.3.3: "they were all of one mind, regarding themselves as virtually brothers of one another." Compare 1 Pet 3:8 (πάντες ὁμόφρονες) and Rom 12:16, where "being of the same mind" involves "associating with the lowly."[89] The "common" life, then, entails not only the habit of sharing resources, but the idea that such sharing ought to strengthen unity of purpose, even with those who are most deserving of one's pity. This seems to be the basic attitude that is supposed to motivate the practices outlined in this section of the poem.

---

[84] See van der Horst, *Sentences*, 134, and cf. Josephus, *Ant.* 18.20, *Bell.* 2.122; Philo, *Prob.* 85–86, *Hypoth.* 11.4–5, 11–13. For the common life of the Pythagoreans, see Iamblichus, *Vit. Pyth.* 6.29–30, 18.81, 30.168.

[85] Cf. 2 Macc 9:21; 3 Macc 4:4; 4 Macc 3:21; Prov 15:23; LSJ s.v. κοινός A.II; Hauck, "κοινός," 789–809. Josephus, *C. Ap.* 2.196, 291: the law teaches κοινωνία ("generosity, fellowship"). Philo associates κοινωνία with the law's φιλανθρωπία, e.g., *Virt.* 51, 80, 96, 103, 119.

[86] Diogenes Laertius, *Vit. phil.* 8.10, 10.11; Plato, *Phaedr.* 279C, *Resp.* 424A, 449C, *Leg.* 739C; Aristotle, *Eth. nic.* 8.9.1, 9.8.2; Plutarch, *Quaest. conv.* 743E, *Amat.* 767E; Cicero, *Off.* 1.51; Philo, *Abr.* 235; Dio Chrysostom, *3 Regn.* 110.

[87] Cf. Niederwimmer, *Didache*, 107–109.

[88] As Strabo puts it, to have all things in common means to refrain from greediness and to be "orderly towards one another" (*Geogr.* 7.3.9). Cf. the use of *koinos* in Acts 2:44–45, 4:32; Diodorus Siculus, *Bibl.* 5.9.4, 10.8.2; Arius Didymus, *Epit.* 11b; also *Sib. Or.* 3.241–247.

[89] Cf. Wilson, *Love Without Pretense*, 179–86.

Verses 32–34. In v. 77 ἄμυνα pertains to vengeance; the subject here is defense or protection, in the first place presumably of oneself, though perhaps of others as well.[90] Pseudo-Phocylides' advice constitutes an extension and application of the Decalogue's prohibition of murder (οὐ φονεύσεις), to which v. 4 alluded (cf. vv. 46, 58).[91] Murder, of course, constitutes a crime in a range of biblical texts,[92] here being characterized as "unlawful."[93] Although the Pentateuch does treat cases of accidental death (e.g., Deut 19:5), the problem of killing in defense is not raised as such. In our author's estimation, while resorting to deadly force for protection may be technically lawful, the homicide still has the effect of "staining" the offender (again cf. v. 4).[94]

This judgment can be evaluated within the context of ancient law, which recognized various categories of justifiable homicide. According to Plutarch, for example, homicide for the purpose of defense (ἄμυνα) carries no legal penalty (De esu 998E).[95] At the same time, in determining the consequences of violent death, criteria expressed with the language of ritual purity could also be applied. The image of bloodshed-pollution as a "stain" on the perpetrator's hands was particularly common.[96] In the most general sense, the offender was thought to incur pollution because the destruction of life violates the natural or divinely-instituted order, therefore requiring some manner of expiation that recognizes and restores that order. In Plato's Leges, for instance, killings in cases of self-defense or the defense of a relation, as well as inadvertent homicides, are not punishable by law. Nevertheless, irrespective of intent or circumstances, the perpetrator still incurs a certain defilement that must be cleansed before he can fully rejoin society (865A–B, 868C, cf. 869C–E, 874B–C).[97] Presumably the purificatory rites Pseudo-Phocylides advocates in v. 228 would be meant in part to address such extra-legal consequences. Philo applies similar principles in his interpretation of Num 31:19–24: "though the slaughter of

---

[90] Cf. Esth 6:13; Ps 117:10–12; Isa 59:16.

[91] Exod 20:15; Deut 5:18.

[92] 2 Macc 4:35; Prov 1:18; Wis 14:24–25; Hos 4:2; Isa 59:7 (cf. v.l.); Jer 22:17; Ezek 43:7, 9.

[93] For this use of ἔκνομος, cf. Philo, Flacc. 189; Arrian, Anab. 4.14.2.

[94] Syr. Men. 15–17 provides an interesting parallel (with references to "your hands" and "the sword"), though with no mention of self-defense: "You shall do no murder and your hands shall not do what is hateful, for the sword lies in the midst." Cf. Jos. Asen. 29:1–4; Sextus, Sent. 324.

[95] Demosthenes, Or. 23.601: homicide for the purpose of self-defense is to kill δικαίως (cf. Ps.-Phoc. 33), i.e., the law permits it. Plato, Euthyd. 4B–C: in adjudicating the culpability involved in manslaughter, "the only issue to consider is whether the action of the slayer was justified (ἐν δίκῃ) or not: if so, one ought to leave him alone; but if not, one ought to proceed against him." Cf. Democritus, frg. 257–260; Demosthenes, Or. 20.158, 23.74; Philo, Spec. 4.7–10.

[96] For what follows, see Parker, Miasma, 104–43; also cf. above, on Ps.-Phoc. 4.

[97] Demosthenes, Or. 23.72: the involuntary killer must purify himself. Sophocles, El. 558–560: to kill δικαίως or not, both are shameful. According to Josephus, C. Ap. 2.205, after a funeral the house and relatives of the deceased must be purified, lest anyone guilty of murder consider himself pure.

enemies is lawful (νόμιμοι), the one who kills another, even if he does so justly and in self-defense (δικαίως καὶ ἀμυνόμενος) ... has something to answer for, in view of the primal common kinship of humanity; therefore purification was required of the slayers, to absolve them of what was held to have been a pollution" (*Mos.* 1.314). Pseudo-Phocylides considers the problem of inadvertent homicide in vv. 57–58.

Verses 35, 38. These lines, with their references to fields and crops, are agricultural in scope, though they articulate concepts of potentially wide-ranging application. The first verse functions as a generalization of biblical commands like Exod 22:4 (to keep one's beast off neighbors' fields) and Deut 23:25–26 (to bring neither sickle nor bowl when entering a neighbor's field).[98] But for a simple rule against trespassing a closer parallel is *Instr. Ankh.* 14.21 ("Do not trespass on the territory of another."), which gives some indication of the issue's currency.[99]

If we read the second line with the first, it continues the theme of respecting the property of others. Its most likely source is Deut 20:19, which prohibits the destruction of fruit-bearing trees during a siege, legislation to which Josephus also alludes in his epitome of the law (*C. Ap.* 2.212).[100] As is his wont, Pseudo-Phocylides generalizes the rule, articulating it with recourse to the Homeric expression, "fruit of the field" (καρπὸν ἀρούρης).[101] In *Virt.* 149, Philo does much the same, holding up as a sign of the law's humanity its directive that "in general no fruit is to be destroyed so that people may be well supplied with a rich store of different kinds of food."

Verses 39–41. Given the poem's lack of obvious references to Jewish tenets or practices, it is improbable that ἐπήλυδες in v. 39 refers to proselytes.[102] Taken with vv. 40–41, it is more likely that the line corresponds with various biblical texts urging the fair treatment of foreigners and strangers, for example, Lev 24:22 ("There shall be one judgment for the stranger and the native."); Num 15:15–16; Deut 24:14: "You shall not unjustly withhold the wages of the poor and needy of your brethren, or of the strangers in your cities." As this last example illustrates, strangers were often included among categories of marginalized or weak people deserving merciful treatment, for example, Deut 27:19; Jer 7:6, 22:3.[103] Philo organizes a similar argument around the unique historical experience of the Jewish people (cf. Lev 19:34: "The stranger shall be as the native ... for you were strangers in the land of

---

[98] Cf. Philo, *Spec.* 4.22.

[99] Cf. *T. Iss.* 7:5; Gardner and Wiedemann, *Roman Household*, 38.

[100] Cf. Philo, *Spec.* 4.226–229, *Virt.* 148–160; 4 Macc 2:14; Dionysius of Halicarnassus, *Ant. rom.* 15.2.2.

[101] Homer, *Il.* 3.246, 6.142, 21.465.

[102] Though the term could be used that way, e.g., Philo, *Spec.* 1.52–53, 2.118–119, *Virt.* 102–104.

[103] Cf. Num 15:29; 3 Kgdms 8:41–43; 2 Chr 6:32–33; Ezek 47:22–23; *T. Abr.* (A) 1:1–2; *T. Job* 10:1–4; *T. Zeb.* 6:4–6; *Instr. Amenem.* 26.11.

Egypt.").[104] They were themselves strangers in Egypt, compelled by economic hardship to migrate there and dependent on the mercy of its inhabitants. They ought, therefore, to regard strangers eager to obtain equal rights (ἰσοτιμία; cf. ὁμότιμοι in Ps.-Phoc. 39) as suppliants and friends (*Mos.* 1.34–35).[105] In the same vein, Josephus' summary of the law argues that it promotes fairness (ἐπιείκεια) for foreigners (*C. Ap.* 2.209–210).

Hospitality for the stranger represented a basic norm in Greco-Roman civilization as well. Some of Menander's *Monostichoi* are representative in this regard: 376, 542 ("Do not hurry past a stranger who is poor."), 543, 544, 550, 553 ("To honor a stranger is a special duty for mortals."), 554 ("Welcome strangers, lest you become a stranger."), 558 ("Honor a stranger and you'll earn a good friend."), 559. Welcoming a stranger into one's home could be understood as a demonstration of fairness and humanity; see Diodorus Siculus, *Bibl.* 5.34.1.[106]

Verse 40, notable for its alliteration, articulates most emphatically the section's humanitarian perspective (cf. vv. 27, 119–120) with a comment about the universality of indigence and vagrancy in human experience. Odysseus, of course, could speak with authority on the subject: "Than roaming there is nothing more evil for mortals, yet for their cursed belly's sake men endure evil woes, when wandering and sorrow and pain come upon them" (Homer, *Od.* 15.343–345). Wandering was naturally associated with poverty,[107] while the difficulties of working the land were all too well known.[108] As we hear in Xenophon, *Oec.* 5.18–20, the outcome of the farmer's toil is in the hands of the gods: "For hailstorms and frosts sometimes, and droughts and rains and blight ruin schemes well planned and well carried out."

---

[104] Cf. Exod 23:9; Deut 10:19, 23:8.

[105] Cf. Barclay, *Mediterranean Diaspora*, 344.

[106] Cf. Homer, *Od.* 6.207–208, 9.270–271; Hesiod, *Op.* 225–227; Aeschylus, *Suppl.* 701–703, *Eum.* 269–272; Aristophanes, *Ran.* 147; Plato, *Leg.* 879D; Diodorus Siculus, *Bibl.* 13.83.1; Cicero, *Off.* 1.51–52; Musonius Rufus, frg. 15.96.28; *Dict. Cat.* 2.1; Spicq, *Lexicon*, 3:454–57; Havelock, *Justice*, 155–61 and s.v. *Xenos*.

[107] E.g., Ps 106:39–41, 108:10; Sir 29:17–18; Plato, *Symp.* 203C–D; Demosthenes, *Or.* 19.310; Diogenes Laertius, *Vit. phil.* 6.38; Solon, frg. 36/37.10–12; Tyrtaeus, frg. 10.3–14.

[108] See below, on Ps.-Phoc. 161; also Garnsey, *Famine and Food Supply*, 43–68 and passim; Shelton, *As the Romans Did*, 157–58.

C. Verses 42–54

42   The love of money is the mother of every evil.
43   Gold and silver are always a delusion for people.
44   Gold, you source of evils, life-destroyer, crushing everything,
45   would that you were not to mortals such a desirable disaster!
46   On your account there are fights and robberies and murders,
47   and children are enemies to their parents, and brothers to their kinfolk.
48   Do not hide one intention in your heart while speaking another;
49   and do not vary with the situation like the rock-clinging polyp.
50   In everything be sincere, and speak from the soul.
51   Whoever does wrong willingly is an evil man; but if he does so perforce
52   I will not predict the outcome: it is the intention of each that is called to account.
53   Do not pride yourself on wisdom, might, or wealth.
54   God alone is wise, mighty, and also rich in blessings.

TEXTUAL NOTES

Verse 42. Σ precedes this line with: "Neither wish to be wealthy nor pray for it. But pray for this: to live from modest means, having nothing unjust." It appends the line with: "Have no desire for gold or silver. Also in those there will be a double-edged iron which destroys the spirit." Verse 45. For εἴθε + acc. + inf., cf. LSJ s.v. εἰ A.2.b. Verse 47. For ἀδελφειοί in lieu of the usual ἀδελφεοί, cf. Homer, *Il.* 5.21, 6.61, 7.120, 13.788. Verse 48. Σ precedes this line with: "Do not weave plots, and do not arm your heart against a friend." Verse 51a. M², P, L, V, Σ: ὅστις ... ἀδικεῖ; M, B: ἔστιν ... ἀδικεῖν. Verse 52b. B, P, Lᵃᶜ, Σ: βουλὴ; M, Lᵖᶜ, V: βουλὴν. // Only Σ has εὐθύνεθ᾽, though cf. P (εὐθύνεται), also M, B (εὔθυνες), M², L, V (εὔθυνε). // LSJ s.v. εὐθύνω III: "to examine;" cf. v. 88; Thucydides, *Hist.* 1.95.5 (called to account in a court of law). Verse 53. ἐνί is poetic for ἐν.

COMMENTARY

Verses 42–47. Verse 42, the paragraph's thematic statement, transmits a standard formulation of the Greco-Roman gnomic tradition. From numerous examples mention may be made of an aphorism attributed to Diogenes: "The love of money is the mother-city of all evils."[109] Versions of the saying may be found in Jewish and Christian sources as well, for example, *Sib. Or.* 3.235 ("The love of money, which begets innumerable evils.") and 1 Tim 6:10 ("The love of money is a root of all evils.").[110] Biblical authors routinely counsel on the dangers of wealth[111] and of greed,[112] chastising lovers of money.[113]

The ensuing verses spell out the tragic irony inherent in the love of money: the avaricious are destroyed by the very wealth they pursue. This is the lesson of P.Ins. 15.12–19, which describes how wealth and greed "snare" family members in unending worry, distrust, and strife.[114] Singling out gold and silver as sources of distress has biblical precedents, for example, Sir 8:2 ("Gold has destroyed many.");[115] though for a passage where gold is apostrophized we must turn to Greek sources, for example, the saying of a certain Choricius: "Gold, you cause of evils, terror to the one who possesses you, grief to the one who does not!"[116] Compare Theognis, *El.* 523–524: "Not to purpose, Wealth, do mortals honor you most of all, for you readily put up with evil." Ingredient to such protests are observations that the love of money is destructive of human life,[117] that such destruction extends to all aspects of life, and that its danger resides to no small extent in its deceptiveness. This last point is encapsulated in the paradoxical πῆμα ποθεινόν of v. 45, reminiscent of Secundus, *Sent.* 16, which defines wealth as "a beloved piece of misfortune" and "a much longed-for hardship."

Later in the poem (v. 206), the readers will be counseled to avoid strife with their kinfolk over possessions. In vv. 46–47, such enmity is rooted in the desire for wealth. Catalogues of the treacheries and woes born out of avarice are familiar from Greek moral literature, for example, Plato, *Phaed.* 66C: "The body and its desires are the only cause of wars and factions and battles; for all wars arise for the sake

[109] Diogenes Laertius, *Vit. phil.* 6.50; cf. Stobaeus, *Anth.* 3.10; van der Horst, *Sentences,* 142–43.

[110] Cf. Polycarp, *Phil.* 4.1.

[111] E.g., Ps 61:11; Prov 11:28, 28:22; Qoh 4:8, 5:9–14.

[112] E.g., Ps 118:36; Sir 26:29–27:3; Hab 2:9; Ezek 22:27; cf. *T. Levi* 14:6; *T. Jud.* 17:1, 18:2, 19:1–2, 21:8; *T. Dan* 5:7; *T. Naph.* 3:1; *T. Gad* 2:4; *T. Benj.* 5:1; Philo, *Conf.* 46–48, *Mos.* 2.186, *Spec.* 4.212–218, *Prob.* 78–79; *Did.* 3:5.

[113] E.g., 2 Macc 10:20; 4 Macc 1:26, 2:8; Luke 16:14; 2 Tim 3:2; Heb 13:5; Philo, *Spec.* 1.281, *Prob.* 21. Further: Delling, "πλεονέκτης," 266–74; Spicq, *Lexicon,* 3:117–19; Frank, "Habsucht," 226–47; Dover, *Popular Morality,* 170–75, 180–84, 193.

[114] Cf. Isocrates, *Nic.* 49–50; *T. Jud.* 17:1–19:1.

[115] Prov 26:23; Job 31:24–28; Sir 31:5–8.

[116] *Anec. Gr.* 1.96; cf. Euripides, frg. 324; *Anacreont.* 58.19–36; *Anth. Gr.* 9.394; *Paroem. Gr.* 2.728.41b; Seneca, *Ben.* 7.10.1; other examples in van der Horst, *Sentences,* 144.

[117] For βιοφθόρε in v. 44, cf. Wis 14:12; Jonah 2:7; *Orph. hymn.* 73.7–8; *Anth. Gr.* 11.270.

of gaining money."[118] Catalogues of conflicts and crimes could be used in other contexts as well, for example, Plutarch, *Pyth. orac.* 401C, which is particularly close to the formulation of v. 46 with its list of "murders and battles and robberies."[119] Lists of this sort have the rhetorical effect of intensifying the depths of·violence being described.[120] The love of money is a force so pernicious it corrupts the order of human society, breaking even familial bonds. Compare Ps.-Lucian, *Cyn.* 8: "those many costly provisions for happiness, in which you take such pride, come to you only at the cost of great misery and hardship. Consider, if you will, the gold for which you pray, the silver ... consider how much they cost in trouble, in toil, in danger, or rather in blood, death, and destruction for humankind ... because they are bitterly fought for, and for them you lay plots against one another ... children against fathers, and wives against husbands."[121]

Verses 48–50. These verses form a unit on verbal integrity: note the forms of ἀγορεύω at the end of vv. 48 and 50, framing the section. The preceding lines drew attention to wealth's power to deceive (especially v. 43). Here the same problem is raised with respect to the power of speech; the dilemma of self-deception will be the topic of discussion presently, in vv. 53–54.

The language of v. 48 draws on Homer, *Il.* 9.312–313: hateful is "one who hides one thing in his mind and says another" (ὅς χ᾽ ἕτερον μὲν κεύθῃ ἐνὶ φρεσίν, ἄλλο δὲ εἴπῃ). Duplicity in speech was generally associated with enmity and bad faith. An adversary is, by definition, someone who cannot be trusted to speak his true feelings; he is busy contriving evil deceits in his head, even as his "smooth lips" make all sorts of promises (Prov 26:23–25).[122] Theognis, *El.* 91–92 observes that the person "with one tongue and two minds" is a better foe than friend. Sallust identifies one of the major causes of such insincerity: "Ambition drove many men to become false, to have one thought locked in the breast, another ready on the tongue" (*Bell. Cat.* 10.5). In this context, it stands to reason that integrity of speech, especially when

---

[118] Cf. Plato, *Leg.* 870C; Isaeus, *Men.* 29; Ps.-Lucian, *Cyn.* 15; Ps.-Plutarch, *Cons. Apoll.* 108A; Stobaeus, *Anth.* 4.31.84; Juvenal, *Sat.* 14.173–178.

[119] Cf. Homer, *Od.* 11.612 ("conflicts, fights, murders, and manslaughters"); Sophocles, *Oed. col.* 1232–1233; Aristotle, *Pol.* 2.1.14; *Sib. Or.* 13.87.

[120] For such coordinating accumulation in the interests of amplification, see Lausberg, *Handbook*, §§ 666–75.

[121] Cf. P.Ins. 15.12–14 ("Greed puts strife and combat in a house. Greed removes shame, mercy, and trust from the heart. Greed causes disturbance in a family."); Euripides, *Iph. aul.* 376–377; Isocrates, *Panath.* 184.

[122] Cf. Sir 12:16; Philo, *Virt.* 184; Menander, frg. 767, 821.

offering advice, constitutes a moral priority for gnomic writers, P.Ins. 25.21 being representative: "Do not let your tongue differ from your heart in counsel."[123]

Supplementing this admonition is a warning about inconstancy and capriciousness, one that entails an implicit critique of Theognis, *El.* 213–218 (cf. 1071–1074): "My heart, keep turning a versatile disposition in accordance with all your friends, mingling with it the mood which each one has. Adopt the mood of the cunning polyp, which seems to resemble the rock to which it clings. Now follow along in this direction, now take on a different complexion. Cleverness is in truth superior to inflexibility." These lines, celebrating the polyp as an icon of adaptability,[124] would go on to become the subject of some discussion in antiquity, both pro and con.[125] Of particular interest is *Amic. mult.* 96F–97B, where Plutarch suggests that those interested in cultivating true friendships ought to ignore Theognis' advice about assimilating oneself to many persons and to seek instead "a fixed and steadfast character which does not shift about, but continues in one place and in one intimacy." This sort of critique needs to be assessed against the background of the larger conversation in antiquity regarding the vices of hypocrisy and opportunism.[126] The delicate matter of balancing candor with propriety in one's speech was a topic of special interest in ancient discussions about friendship and education; an effective counselor needed to adapt his manner of discourse to the particular dispositions and circumstances of his friends or students, but without appearing to be obsequious or unprincipled.[127]

Like Plutarch, for Pseudo-Phocylides the polyp is also a negative model of dishonest vacillation. In contrast to those who would conform their words and actions to every situation, the readers are exhorted not to "change." In this, he would have been in agreement with Ben Sira, who decries the fool because he "changes like the moon" (27:11) and "the double-tongued sinner" because he "winnows in every wind and goes in every path" (5:9, cf. 5:10, 33:5). The end for such individuals is spelled out by Prov 17:20: "A man changeful with his tongue will fall into evils."

Including an appeal to ἁπλότης ("singleness, sincerity") would have been typical of an exhortation on honesty, since the term was a conventional way of naming

---

[123] Cf. P.Ins. 25.22 ("A false man does not tell to another what is in his heart."), 26.22 ("What is in the heart of the wise man is what one finds on his tongue.").

[124] E.g., Sophocles, frg. 307; Athenaeus, *Deipn.* 316A–318F; *Paroem. Gr.* 1.184.23, 1.298.73; Pliny, *Nat.* 9.46.85–87. The ancient moral assessment of Odysseus ("the man of many turns") simultaneously praised him for his resourcefulness and criticized him for his unscrupulousness: Stanford, *Ulysses Theme*, 7, 17, 26–27, 118–19, and passim.

[125] E.g., Plutarch, *Quaest. nat.* 916C, *Terrestr. aquat.* 978E; more examples in van der Horst, *Sentences*, 147.

[126] On the ancient critique of hypocrisy, see Spicq, *Lexicon*, 3:406–13; Wilckens, "Heuchelei," 1205–31.

[127] Glad, *Paul and Philodemus*, 15–52; cf. D. B. Martin, *Slavery as Salvation*, 91–100.

comportment undistracted by calculation or deceit. As a virtue, it was an important concept of moral anthropology, specifying the personal integrity that accompanies the correspondence of inner feeling with external expression.[128] Predictably, the "soul" or "heart" was identified as the locus of moral efforts intended to cultivate this trait.[129] It was frequently aligned with truthtelling.[130]

Verses 51–52. This unit, with its trappings of a legal principle, is comparable to pentateuchal legislation in Exod 21:13–14 and Num 15:27–31. The first passage draws a distinction between killing unwillingly (οὐχ ἑκών) and killing with deceit (δόλῳ); only those guilty of the latter are liable to capital punishment. The second distinguishes between one who sins inadvertently (ἀκουσίως) and one who acts "with a presumptuous hand;" again, only the later deserves to die.[131] In each instance, it seems that it is the classification of a misdeed as accidental that warrants special consideration in punishing the offender.[132] In its attention to involuntary acts, vv. 51–52 is similar in scope, though here the focus is on the special case of sinning perforce. For this issue, 4 Macc 5:13 probably represents a broad consensus: transgressions committed "under compulsion" (δι’ ἀνάγκην) are pardonable.[133] Pseudo-Phocylides would appear to agree, indicating that in such cases the *telos* of the case lies beyond the purview of human discernment. This is because the criterion for determining guilt is intentionality (cf. vv. 16, 58). Presumably, then, in v. 52b we have an indirect reference to divine judgment, a concept that figures also in vv. 11, 17, and 18. In this case Pseudo-Phocylides would agree with Heb 4:12: it is God who judges the intentions of the human heart (cf. 1 Cor 4:5).

Verses 53–54. The reader has just heard how everyone will be called to account, not only for their actions but also for their intentions (vv. 51–52). This segues into an

---

[128] Cf. Bauernfeind, "ἁπλοῦς," 386–87; Spicq, *Lexicon*, 1:169–73; Amstutz, *ΑΠΛΟΤΗΣ*, 42 and passim.

[129] E.g., 1 Chr 29:17; Prov 11:25 (cf. 10:9); Wis 1:1; Eph 6:5; Col 3:22; *T. Iss.* 3:8, 4:1, 7:7; *T. Reub.* 4:1; *T. Sim.* 4:5. For the correspondence of speech and the content of one's heart, see also Ps 14:2; Job 33:3; Matt 12:34, 15:18; *T. Naph.* 2:6; *Instr. Amenem.* 13.17.

[130] E.g., Aeschylus, frg. 176: "simple (ἁπλᾶ) are the words of truth;" Euripides, *Phoen.* 469; Aristotle, *Eth. eud.* 3.7.6; Xenophon, *Cyr.* 1.4.3; Polybius, *Hist.* 1.78.8; Plutarch, *Adul. amic.* 62C. Plato, *Hipp. min.* 364E–365B: quotes Homer, *Il.* 9.308–314 (vv. 312–313 cited above) as evidence that the speaker (Achilles) is "true and simple" (ἀληθής τε καὶ ἁπλοῦς).

[131] Cf. Num 35:11, 15–28; Deut 4:42, 19:4; Philo, *Spec.* 1.156, 3.77, 141.

[132] Aristotle (*Rhet.* 1.13.5) takes it as an established opinion that injustice (τὸ ἀδικεῖν) is by definition an injury inflicted voluntarily (ἑκούσιον); cf. Xenophon, *Mem.* 4.2.19–20; Demosthenes, *Or.* 21.43, 23.73, 24.67; Lysias, *Or.* 13.52; Menander, *Mon.* 11: "It is wrong (ἄδικον) to grieve one's friends willingly (ἑκουσίως)."

[133] Cf. 4 Macc 8:14, 22; 1 Pet 5:2; Aristotle, *Rhet.* 1.10.7, *Eth. nic.* 5.8.4, *Eth. eud.* 2.3.18, 2.8.3–4; Rickert, *ΕΚΩΝ and ΑΚΩΝ*, 44–48.

admonition buttressed by reminders about the greatness of the one who carries out such scrutiny.

The diction of the warning against pride in v. 53 draws on Jer 9:22 (μὴ καυχάσθω ... σοφίᾳ ... ἰσχύι ... πλούτῳ), with γαυροῦ substituting for καυχάσθω, and ἀλκῇ (cf. vv. 126, 130) for ἰσχύι. Like the biblical text (cf. 1 Kgdms 2:10), the justification for such humility lies in the recognition of God's manifold greatness. The same logic is at work in Ben Sira's maxim, "In your clothes do not boast, and on the day of glory do not exalt yourself, for wonderful are the works of the Lord" (11:4). Not only do those who exult in their own good fortune fail in their regard for divine power, but they also show themselves to be ignorant of the impermanence of all human possessions and accomplishments (cf. vv. 27, 40, 110–114, 119–120, 122).[134]

In all likelihood εἷς θεός in v. 54 alludes to Deut 6:4 ("The Lord our God is one Lord."),[135] though, taken with the preceding line, εἷς here functions as an adverb rather than as an adjective; hence "Only God," etc.[136] While the specific elements of the list that follows were no doubt chosen to contrast with those of v. 53,[137] we find similar qualities attributed to God elsewhere in Jewish wisdom, for example, Sir 1:8 ("There is one who is wise, greatly to be feared, sitting on his throne.") and Job 9:4: "For (God) is wise in mind, mighty, and great."[138] At the same time, there is little in these lists that is specifically Jewish in character. Even pagan theologians could make comparable affirmations, for example, Heraclitus ("One thing, the only wise thing, is ... Zeus.") and Pythagoras ("No one is wise but God alone.").[139] What Pseudo-Phocylides declares here, together with the poem's other references to God (cf. vv. 1, 8, 11, 17, 29, 106, 111, 125), furnishes the necessary criterion for interpreting the statements in vv. 71, 75, 104, and 163. While the universe may be populated by suprahuman beings of various kinds, the supremacy of θεός in all facets of existence is taken for granted.

---

[134] See for the latter point Philo, *Spec.* 1.311; cf. 3 Macc 3:11; Euripides, frg. 22, 92, 662; Menander, *Mon.* 510 ("Never boast of wealth you have in store.").

[135] Cf. Sedlmeier, "Höre, Israel!" 21–39; N. G. Cohen, *Philo Judaeus*, s.v. *Shema*.

[136] See the discussion in van der Horst, *Sentences*, 151; also cf. BDAG s.v. εἷς 2.b.

[137] For these terms as divine qualities: BDAG s.v. σοφός 2.b and s.v. δυνατός 1.a.α. πολύολβος is an epithet of Athena in *Orph. hymn.* 32.8 (cf. 38.2, 43.2, 66.9, 83.6). Josephus opens his summary of the law proclaiming God to be "perfect and blessed" and "one" (*C. Ap.* 2.190, 193).

[138] Cf. 1 Chr 29:11–12; 2 Macc 1:24–25; Sir 18:1–5; Philo, *Opif.* 171, *Decal.* 65; *Sib. Or.* 3.11–12; *Let. Arist.* 132; Ps.-Orph. 10; further: Peterson, *ΕΙΣ ΘΕΟΣ*.

[139] Heraclitus, frg. 32; Diogenes Laertius, *Vit. phil.* 1.12; cf. Xenophanes, frg. 23; Maximus of Tyre, *Or.* 11.5; Ps.-Aristotle, *Mund.* 7; Norden, *Agnostos Theos*, 244–45; further: Athanassiadi and Frede, *Pagan Monotheism*.

IV. Moderation and Harmony (Verses 55–96)

Bibliography: D. L. Cairns, Aidōs, 54–60, 121–26, 185–88, 305–40. Damon, Mask of the Parasite. J. Ferguson, Moral Values, 118–32. Harris, Restraining Rage, 104–18, 131–53. Milobenski, Der Neid, 116–34. North, Sophrosyne. Nussbaum, Therapy, 13–47, 93–99, 391–438.

The second part of instruction in the *Sentences* structured according to the canon of virtues contains various sayings that contribute to the theme of σωφροσύνη, or moderation. The position of the unit, adjacent to the section on justice, is noteworthy, since moral philosophers sometimes ranked justice and moderation together as the most significant or beneficial of the four major virtues.[1] The two concepts also share something on the ideational level. As Johan Thom observes, Greek thinkers beginning at least with Democritus depicted moderation and justice as moral counterparts, the former being "the internal principle of moral control, with justice as its external social manifestation."[2]

Helen North has chronicled the long and complicated history of moderation in Greek, Roman, Jewish, and Christian thought.[3] As a general observation, this virtue encompasses the objectives of both self-understanding (often being linked with the interpretation of the Delphic maxim γνῶθι σαυτόν) and self-mastery. It comes as no surprise that the latter is more prominent in paraenetic materials, and there survives an extensive body of advice urging moderation especially with respect to personal passions and desires. In this respect σωφροσύνη often overlaps in meaning with the virtue of ἐγκράτεια, or self-control. In turn, both concepts were associated with other ideals, especially harmony (ὁμόνοια) and propriety (πρέπον).[4] These are primary themes for gnomic wisdom as well, particularly in connection with the interpretation of the Delphic maxims μηδὲν ἄγαν and μέτρον ἄριστον. The traditions associated with these sayings urged individuals both to eschew excess and to aim for

---

[1] E.g., Plato, *Phaed.* 82A–B, *Prot.* 323A; Isocrates, *Nic.* 29–30; Philo, *Opif.* 81, *Det.* 143, *Abr.* 103, *Praem.* 15; cf. Rowe, "Justice and Temperance," 336–44.

[2] Thom, *Golden Verses*, 133.

[3] North, *Sophrosyne*.

[4] E.g., Plato, *Resp.* 430D–432A; Ps.-Aristotle, *Virt. vit.* 4.5; *SVF* 3:264; Diogenes Laertius, *Vit. phil.* 7.126; Cicero, *Off.* 1.93–151; cf. Pohlenz, "Τὸ πρέπον," 53–92; North, *Sophrosyne*, s.v. *enkrateia, homonoia, kosmiotēs, prepon*.

the ethical mean, that which is generally considered measured, balanced, and safe.[5] In this light, it makes sense that a number of gnomic exhortations from antiquity resemble Ps.-Phoc. 55–96 formally and materially. We may compare, for example, Isocrates, *Demon.* 21–32, which illustrates the sorts of concrete recommendations the theme of moderation could generate; readers are advised to show discretion in choosing friends (24–25; cf. Ps.-Phoc. 79, 95–96), to surpass their friends in doing kindness (26; cf. Ps.-Phoc. 80), and to avoid envious friends (26; cf. Ps.-Phoc. 70–75). There is also exhortation to be tasteful in one's dress (27; cf. Ps.-Phoc. 61), to be moderate in acquiring wealth (27–28; cf. Ps.-Phoc. 62), not to taunt others in their misfortune (29; cf. Ps.-Phoc. 83–85), to abhor flatterers (30; cf. Ps.-Phoc. 91–94), never to be quarrelsome or angry (31; cf. Ps.-Phoc. 55–58, 75–78), and to avoid drinking parties (32; cf. Ps.-Phoc. 81–82, 92–94).

The maxims in this part of Pseudo-Phocylides' *Sentences* are organized in three paragraphs: vv. 55–69B, on moderating one's emotions and desires, vv. 70–75, on achieving harmony by avoiding envy, and vv. 76–96, on practicing restraint and caution in various (especially interpersonal) situations.

The tone of the first paragraph is set by vv. 59 ("Let emotions be moderate.") and 69B: "Of all things moderation is best." The body of the paragraph is comprised of a series of indicative statements (vv. 60–68) that counsel against excessiveness, especially in one's emotions and desires. Structural considerations may be at work in its organization, with vv. 61–64 being in the form of cause-and-effect statements, vv. 65–67 in the form of contrastive statements.

In the second paragraph, the reader is encouraged to heed the example set by the cosmos, maintaining harmony and eschewing envy. As "Aristotle" notes in the *De virtutibus et vitiis*, the avoidance of envy is essential to training in moderation (4.5). The author of the *Carmen aureum* apparently shares this opinion, incorporating a warning against envy into his teaching on moderation in vv. 32–38.[6] Both envy and the incitement of envy entail actions that exceed common sense and due measure.

An appeal to "practice moderation" (σωφροσύνην ἀσκεῖν) in v. 76a serves as a heading for the third paragraph, which urges circumspection and restraint, especially in interpersonal exchanges. While some attention is paid to the reader's interaction with social peers (e.g., vv. 80–82), the focus of the passage is on dealing with weaker parties (vv. 83–85) and various categories of people who, for one reason or another, are unreliable (vv. 86–96).

---

[5]   Cf. Luck, "σώφρων," 1097–1104; Spicq, *Lexicon*, 3:359–65; Thom, *Golden Verses*, 162–63. For gnomic instruction on the theme, see Stobaeus, *Anth.* 3.5, 21.

[6]   "Practice moderation in drinking, eating, and physical exercises. By moderation I mean that which will not distress you … guard against doing the kind of thing that incurs envy … Moderation is in everything the best."

A. Verses 55–69B

55	Exhaust not your liver over bygone ills;
56	for what's been done can be undone no more.
57	Be not rash with your hands; bridle wild anger;
58	for often with a blow one inadvertently commits murder.
59	Let emotions be moderate, neither great nor excessive.
60	A good that is excessive is for mortals no gain.
61	Great luxuriousness leads to ignoble desires.
62	Great wealth is boastful and fosters insolence.
63	Wrath that steals over one brings on baneful fury.
64	Anger is a longing, but when it goes too far it is rage.
65	Zeal for good things is noble, for bad things, excessive.
66	Boldness is destructive in evil deeds, but greatly profits one toiling for noble ones.
67	Love of virtue is revered, but love of passion earns shame.
68	One who is too pleasant is called senseless among the citizens.
69	Eat in moderation, drink and converse in moderation.
69B	Of all things moderation is best, but excesses are grievous.

TEXTUAL NOTES

Verse 55. For the phrase παροιχομένοισι κακοῖς, cf. Xenophon, *Hell.* 1.4.17. // P, L, V, Σ have ἦτορ ("heart") in lieu of ἧπαρ (M², B), the latter being the *lect. diff.* Verse 56. ἄτυκτος ("undone") is a *hapax.* Verse 57. For χείρ used "of deeds of violence," see LSJ s.v. IV. // In lieu of ὀργήν (in Lʸᵖ, Vʸᵖ, Σ), M, B, P, L, V have ἄρην ("bane, ruin"), which gives little sense. Verse 58. For πλήσσω meaning to strike so as to kill, cf. Exod 22:2; 2 Kgdms 11:15. Verse 59. Cf. Derron, *Sentences*, 7: "Il faut des sentiments normaux: point d'excès ni d'orgueil." // In lieu of ὑπέροπλον (in M, B, P, L, Σ), V has ὑπέροφρυ ("supercilious"), cf. LSJ s.v.; the former is an epic term, with the sense of "excessive, defiant, presumptuous," e.g., Homer, *Il.* 15.185, 17.170; Hesiod, *Theog.* 516; Pindar, *Pyth.* 6.48. Verse 60. Cf. van der Horst, *Sentences*, 153: "Excess, even of good, is never a boon to mortals;" Walter, *Poetische Schriften*, 203: "Denn (selbst) Gutes bringt, (wenn es) im Übermaß (kommt), den Sterblichen kein Heil;" Derron, *Sentences*, 7: "Surabondance de bien ne profite pas aux mortels." Verse 61. Reading ἀσέμνους (cf. Ps.-Phoc. 67a; Plutarch, *Comp. Aem. Tim.* 2.10) with P, L, V, and printed by Bergk (*Poetae Lyrici Graeci*, 90) and Bernays (*Gesammelte Abhandlungen*, 256), against ἀμέτρους ("immoderate") in M, B, Vʸᵖ, Σ, which is printed by Diehl (*Anthologia*, 2.102), Young (*Theognis*, 101), and Derron (*Sentences*, 7); the latter seems to be an effort to bring the gnome into accord with the paragraph's emphasis on observing μέτρον (see especially vv. 69–69B, also vv. 14, 98; cf. Ps.-Plato, *Ep.* 8.354D). Verse 63. M, B: ὑπερχόμενος; variant readings alter the sense only slightly, L: ὑπερχεόμενος ("overflowing"); P: ὑπερεχόμενος ("prevailing"); V: ἐπερχόμενος ("coming upon"); Σ: ὑπαρχόμενος ("accruing"). // ὀλοόφρων ("baneful") is Homeric: *Il.* 2.723, 15.630, 17.21–22 (with θυμός), *Od.* 1.52, 10.137, 11.322. Verse 64. LSJ s.v. ὄρεξις: "appetency, conation, longing." Verse 65. Only M reads ὑπέρογκος. B, P, L²ʸᴾ, V have ὑποεργός ("serviceable") which gives little sense, ruining the antithesis. Vʸᴾ corrects with ἀΐδηλος ("destructive"), which is printed by Bergk (*Poetae Lyrici Graeci*, 90) and Bernays (*Gesammelte Abhandlungen*, 256); cf. v. 194. For different conjectures, see van der Horst, *Sentences*, 157–58. // For the translation of the line, cf. Walter, *Poetische Schriften*, 204: "Eifer um Gutes ist edel, um Schlimmes ist er unerträglich;" Derron, *Sentences*, 7: "L'émulation pour le bien ist noble; pour de vils objets, elle est exagérée." Verse 66. Σ has: "Boldness in evil deeds is destructive, but that of the good brings glory." Verse 68. ἄγαν ἄφρων is the conjecture of Bergk (*Poetae Lyrici Graeci*, 90); M, B, L, Σ have ἀγανόφρων; V: ἀγωνόφρων; P: ἀγαλεόφρων. For the translation, cf. van der Horst, *Sentences*, 159–60 ("A man who is too simple"); Derron, *Sentences*, 7 ("L'homme trop conciliant"); Walter, *Poetische Schriften*, 204: "(Wer sich jedermann) allzu angenehm (macht)." Cf. van der Horst, "Pseudo-Phocylides Revisited," 20–21. Verse 69. μυθολογεύειν: cf. Homer, *Od.* 12.450, 453. Verse 69B. M, Bʸᴾ, P, L, V: ἀλεγειναί (Σ: ἀλεγεινόν); B: ἀλεεῖνον; B¹: ἀλέεινε (cf. Hesiod, *Op.* 828).

COMMENTARY

Verses 55–58. That the past is unalterable was a gnomic and philosophical commonplace, for example, Theognis, *El.* 583–584: "The things that have been done cannot possibly be undone."[7] The observation here supports advice focusing on the reader's liver, an organ that was generally understood to be the seat of strong emotions, especially dismay, fear, and wrath.[8] In light of the lines that immediately follow (vv. 57–58, also vv. 63–64), the locution "to consume one's liver"[9] may refer in the first place to being "consumed" with anger, though there is no reason why a more complex emotional trajectory could not also be in view. In this case we may compare *T. Dan* 4:5–6: "If you suffer a loss, if you undergo the destruction

---

[7] Cf. Simonides, frg. 603 ("For what has once happened will never be undone."); Pindar, *Ol.* 2.15–17; Plato, *Prot.* 324B; Ps.-Plutarch, *Cons. Apoll.* 115A; Sophocles, *Aj.* 377–378: "Why vex thyself over what is past recall? What's done is done and naught can alter it."

[8] LSJ s.v. ἧπαρ I; Aeschylus, *Ag.* 432, 792, *Eum.* 135; Sophocles, *Aj.* 938; Euripides, *Suppl.* 599; Archilochus, frg. 131; *T. Reub.* 3:4; *T. Naph.* 2:8; *T. Gad* 5:9, 11; Juvenal, *Sat.* 1.45.

[9] τρύχω: "to wear out, consume, afflict;" cf. Theognis, *El.* 913; Sophocles, *Oed. tyr.* 666; Wis 11:11, 14:15.

of anything, do not become alarmed … If you lose something, by your own action or otherwise, do not be sorrowful, for grief arouses anger."[10] Passages of this sort recognize that dwelling on misdeeds of the past can engender emotional responses that are not only vain but potentially harmful as well. The logic underlying this sort of argument is mirrored in Horace, *Ep.* 1.2.59–63: "He who curbs not his anger will wish that undone which vexation and wrath prompted, as he made haste with violence to gratify his unsated hatred. Anger is short lived madness. Rule your passion, for unless it obeys, it gives commands. Check it with a bridle – check it, I pray, with chains." Anger in the *Sentences* is similarly presented as a troublesome passion (cf. Ps.-Phoc. 59) that gives way to senseless rage (cf. Ps.-Phoc. 63–64): unless vigorously restrained it incites unintended and regretted actions.

In the same vein, Greek and Jewish sages agreed that rashness, προπέτεια, gives rise to transgressions and catastrophe, sayings like Menander, *Mon.* 631 ("Rashness is for many the source of ills.") and Prov 10:14 ("The mouth of the rash draws near to ruin.") being representative.[11] Verse 57 concentrates on the sort of recklessness associated with violent emotions, specifically anger. The critique of this emotion (cf. v. 64) is a major topic in Proverbs and Ben Sira.[12] It was also much discussed in Stoic circles, in conjunction with their analysis of the passions, which they treated as sick and disruptive conditions of the personality.[13]

Verse 58 supplies the reason for the preceding line by identifying a likely negative consequence of the failure to heed its counsel. In vv. 32–34, Pseudo-Phocylides raised the problem of homicide motivated by defense. Here he identifies another circumstance that often attends such violence, this time focusing not so much on the question of one's intent (cf. vv. 16, 51–52) as on internal forces that can work contrary to it and wreak havoc. Our author would agree with Philo that occasions often arise in which a person commits murder, not with premeditation, but because

---

[10] Cf. *Dict. Cat.* 2.15; Sir 22:21–22: "Even if you drew your sword against a friend, do not despair, for there may be a way back. Even if you opened your mouth against a friend, do not fear, for there may be a reconciliation."

[11] Cf. Prov 13:3, 25:8; Qoh 7:9; Sir 9:18; Acts 19:36; 2 Tim 3:4; Musonius Rufus, frg. 16.104.19–20; Spicq, *Lexicon*, 3:189–90.

[12] Prov 12:16, 15:1, 16:32, 27:3–4, 29:8; Sir 10:18, 16:6, 23:16, 27:30, 28:3, 10; cf. Matt 5:22; Eph 4:26, 31, 6:4; Col 3:8; Jas 1:19–20; Publilius Syrus, *Sent.* 87, 88, 290, 344–345.

[13] See especially Seneca's *De ira* (with Nussbaum, *Therapy*, 391–438) and Plutarch's *De cohibenda ira* (with Betz and Dillon, "De cohibenda ira," 170–97). According to their doctrine, it is in the very nature of a passion like anger that those in its grips act in an uncontrolled and uncalculated manner. Chrysippus, e.g., observes that in anger, "we get so far outside ourselves and are so completely blind in our difficulties that sometimes if we have a sponge or some wool in our hands we raise it up and throw it, as if by doing this we could accomplish some end. If we had happened to have a knife or something else of the sort, we would have used it in the same way." *SVF* 3:478; trans. from Nussbaum, *Therapy*, 397. Further, Kleinknecht, "ὀργή," 382–85; Harris, *Restraining Rage*, 104–18.

he has been "carried away by his anger" (*Spec.* 3.104).[14] The necessity of bridling such passions, much like one would bridle a wild horse, was therefore a traditional image, as we saw in the passage from Horace's *Epistles* above.[15] From the biblical ambit we might compare Isa 37:29 ("Your wrath ... has risen to me; therefore I will put a bridle in your lips."). The *Testament of Dan* is especially instructive for understanding this emotion and its connection with violence and murder. The protagonist blames "the spirit of anger" for persuading him to kill his brother (1:7–8; cf. Wis 10:3), characterizing it as a deceptive force (2:1–5) that dominates the soul and gives the body savage strength, "so that it can accomplish every lawless act" (3:2, cf. 3:1–6).[16] The point is made most plainly in *Did.* 3:2: "Do not be an angry person, for anger leads to murder" (cf. Num 35:21).[17]

Verses 59–62. In v. 27, κοινὰ πάθη referred to "common sufferings." Here the phrase represents a variation on the concept of μετριοπάθεια, which in turn belonged to the Hellenistic argot of emotional self-realization.[18] While exercising discipline over one's passions and appetites was foundational to every philosophical school's definition of the virtuous life, there was substantial disagreement as to how the appropriate regimen was best conceived.[19] The two basic alternatives are summarized by Philo in *Leg. all.* 3.129–137, with Moses embodying the goal of the extirpation of the harmful passions, Aaron the goal of their moderation. While the former may represent the human ideal, it seems that Aaron better exemplifies the objective to which most individuals can realistically aspire.[20] A similar principle is articulated in 4 Maccabees, with its argument that within the human personality "pious reason" ought to control, though not destroy, the emotions.[21]

---

14 For the problem of involuntary homicide, see Plato, *Leg.* 865B–C; Demosthenes, *Or.* 23.53; Aristotle, *Ath. pol.* 57.3; MacDowell, *Homicide Law,* 58–68, 117–26; and above, on Ps.-Phoc. 32–34.

15 Cf. Lucian, *Salt.* 70, *Tyr.* 4; Philo, *Leg. all.* 3.118, 127–128, 222–224, *Sacr.* 45.

16 Cf. Hollander and de Jonge, *Testaments,* 276–94.

17 Cf. Menander, *Mon.* 22, 99, 348, 528.

18 E.g., Plutarch, *Virt. mor.* 443C–D ("Reason does not wish to eradicate passion completely ... but puts upon it some limitation and order and implants ethical virtues, which are not the absence of passion but a due proportion and measure therein."), *Cohib. ira* 458C, *Frat. amor.* 489C; Ps.-Plutarch, *Cons. Apoll.* 102D, 113B; Aristotle, *Eth. nic.* 2.7.1–2.9.9, 3.10.1–3.12.10, 4.5.1–15; Diogenes Laertius, *Vit. phil.* 5.31; Dionysius of Halicarnassus, *Ant. rom.* 8.61.1; Cicero, *Off.* 2.18, *Tusc.* 4.37–46; Seneca, *Ira* 1.7.1, 3.16.2; Nussbaum, *Therapy,* 93–99.

19 Nussbaum, *Therapy,* 13–47 and passim; Braund and Gill, *Passions,* 5–7.

20 Cf. Philo, *Abr.* 257, *Jos.* 26, *Virt.* 195; *Let. Arist.* 256; Heb 5:2; Winston, "Philo's Ethical Theory," 400–405.

21 E.g., 4 Macc 1:6, 28–30, 2:17–18, 3:3–4; cf. Aune, "Mastery of the Passions," 125–58.

As was their wont, the approach gnomic authors adopted toward the problem was motivated by pragmatic self-interest.[22] Like Pseudo-Phocylides (see vv. 61–62, 68–69), they highlight the importance of minding the appetitive passions so that they advance, rather than hinder, one's contentment. Representative in this regard is *Gnom. Democr.* 70–74: "It belongs to a child, not a man, to desire immoderately. Inappropriate pleasures give rise to distress. Violent desires for anything blind the soul to the other things. It is righteous love to desire what is fine without insolence. Do not admit anything pleasant if it is not beneficial." While emotions like desire appear to have an inevitable, even salutary, place in the human personality, the dominant assumption is that they are prone to harmful excesses and therefore must be vigilantly checked. The appropriate course is one of moderation, determined according to the criteria of personal soundness and stability. In what follows, Pseudo-Phocylides will urge moderation with respect to a number of items that were traditionally listed among the πάθη, for example, desire, anger, zeal, boldness, and envy (cf. Aristotle, *Eth. nic.* 2.5.2).

The verb ἔφυ (φύω c. dat.: "to fall to one by nature") is well-suited for gnomic constructions (cf. vv. 130, 217), as in Sophocles, *El.* 860: πᾶσι θνατοῖς ἔφυ μόρος ("Doom is the lot of all mortals.").[23] It is used in v. 60 to express a generally held truth in Hellenistic culture about the human condition. If they wish to thrive, people must respect the "natural" limits imposed on their existence, a thought epitomized by the Delphic precept "nothing overmuch;" cf. Sextus, *Sent.* 140: "Every excess is a mortal's enemy."[24] In v. 60, Pseudo-Phocylides dramatizes this point, claiming that an overabundance even of what is "good" in fact offers one no advantage. The maxim's formulation implies that the dilemma of self-deception is ingredient to the situation: something that appears to be good turns out to be harmful. This gnomic paradox is reminiscent especially of a saying attributed to Menander, that "the chief source of evils among people … is good things in excess (τὰ λίαν ἀγαθά)."[25] That this aphorism circulated in Hellenistic Jewish circles is attested by Philo, who quotes it in a passage that exhibits a number of similarities with Ps.-Phoc. 60–62: "Often luxury, growing to excess (τρυφὴ πλεονάσασα) by lavish supplies of superfluities, has upset the laws; because the mass of people, being unable to bear 'good things

---

[22] E.g., Epictetus, *Gnom.* 5 ("Check your emotions lest you be punished by them."); Menander, *Mon.* 496, 587; Sextus, *Sent.* 75, 204–207, 209; Horace, *Ep.* 1.2.55–56 ("Scorn pleasures. Pleasure bought with pain is harmful. The covetous heart is ever in want. Aim at a fixed limit for your desires."); cf. Thom, *Golden Verses*, 46–47.

[23] LSJ s.v. φύω B.II.4; cf. Euripides, *Iph. aul.* 31–32; Menander, *Mon.* 795.

[24] Theognis, *El.* 335 ("Strive for nothing overmuch: the mean is best of all." μηδὲν ἄγαν σπεύδειν· πάντων μέσ' ἄριστα.), 401; cf. Plato, *Charm.* 165A, *Prot.* 343B; Aristotle, *Rhet.* 2.12.14; Ps.-Plutarch, *Cons. Apoll.* 116C–E; *Paroem. Gr.* 2.80.79.

[25] Quoted in Plutarch, *Comm. not.* 1076C (= frg. 724).

in excess,' becomes surfeited and insolent (ἐξυβριζόντων)."²⁶ In this light, the false "good" of v. 60 may refer in the first place to the kind of wealth and luxury addressed in vv. 61–62, as well as to the violent desires allied with indulgence in such excesses. Compare Democritus, frg. 173: "Evils accrue to people from good things."

Jewish and Christian moralists generally associated τρυφή with unseemly and immoderate behavior. Hence the apprehension expressed in dictums like Sir 37:29 ("Be not insatiable in much luxury.") and Sextus, *Sent.* 73 ("The result of luxury is ruin."). Verse 61 images the vice as a force that acts on the human will, literally "dragging" or "drawing" unsuspecting individuals to desires beyond their control.²⁷ The rejection of luxury was a defining practice for the Cynic's ascetic code,²⁸ though it was also the object of criticism in a wide range of moral and political writings, since it provided occasion for the multiplication of untoward passions.²⁹ Compare Sextus, *Sent.* 240: "As you control your stomach, so you will control your sexual desires."

Earlier in the poem, the delusion and destructiveness of greed were portrayed (vv. 42–47), and the self-importance associated with riches was presented as a failure to recognize one's place in the divine order (vv. 53–54). In v. 62 the idea presented is that wealth, once it becomes great, necessarily leads to arrogance and pride. In the biblical ambit, such vices are understood as predictable consequences of affluence.³⁰ Not surprisingly, wealth is also linked to ὕβρις, or insolence (Prov 16:19; Sir 21:4), a connection made also in Greek literature, for example, Menander, *Mon.* 792: "Wealth begets insolence."³¹ Aristotle gathers some prototypical complaints about the rich in *Rhet.* 2.16.1–4 (cf. 2.2.5–6), which also gives some sense of how their *hubris* was thought to manifest itself:

> The wealthy are insolent and arrogant, being mentally affected by the acquisition of wealth, for they seem to think that they possess all good things ... they are luxurious and swaggerers ... ill-mannered because ... (they) suppose that what they themselves

---

²⁶ Philo, *Mos.* 2.13, cf. *Abr.* 134–135.

²⁷ For this use of ἕλκω, cf. Philo, *Opif.* 157–158, *Agr.* 103, *Mos.* 2.139; *T. Jos.* 3:8; Jas 1:14; Plato, *Phaedr.* 238A; Xenophon, *Cyr.* 8.1.32.

²⁸ E.g., Ps.-Crates, *Ep.* 23, 34.3; Diogenes Laertius, *Vit. phil.* 6.71; Höistad, *Cynic Hero*, s.v. τρυφή.

²⁹ E.g., Prov 19:10, 23:2–3, 6; Sir 18:30–32; *T. Benj.* 6:3; Philo, *Cher.* 12, *Sacr.* 21, *Ebr.* 21, *Somn.* 1.123, *Spec.* 2.240; Luke 7:25; Jas 5:5; 2 Pet 2:13; Sextus, *Sent.* 117; Plato, *Resp.* 590B; Plutarch, *Alc.* 16.1, *Lys.* 19.4, *Sull.* 1.3, *Galb.* 19.2; Ps.-Plutarch, *Lib. ed.* 2E, 6C; *Dict. Cat.* 2.6, 19. Cf. Shaw, "Debt in Sallust," 187–96; Edwards, *Politics of Immorality*, 173–206.

³⁰ E.g., Ps 48:7; Wis 5:8; Sir 11:4; Ezek 16:49–50; 1 Tim 6:17.

³¹ Also Theognis, *El.* 153–154; Diogenes Laertius, *Vit. phil.* 1.59; Philo, *Agr.* 32, cf. *Post.* 98, *Spec.* 2.18–19, *Virt.* 161–162. On the *hubris* of the rich, cf. Thucydides, *Hist.* 3.45.4; Aristotle, *Pol.* 4.9.4; Demosthenes, *Or.* 21.98; Dover, *Popular Morality*, 110–11. Fisher, *Hybris*, 495: "the social and political dangers of *hybris* are seen essentially to lie in the depredations, insults and violence of the rich and powerful."

are emulous of is the object of all other men's emulation … Their unjust acts are not due to malice, but partly to insolence, partly to intemperance, which tends to make them commit assault and battery and adultery.

In *Leg.* 679B–C, Plato intimates a concern about the rich as well, though he presumes another stock theme, namely, the idea that wealth and its *hubris* undermine social harmony: "A community which has no communion with either poverty or wealth is generally the one in which the noblest characters will be formed; for in it there is no place for the growth of insolence and injustice, of rivalries and jealousies."

Verses 63–64. These lines closely parallel one another: wrath (θυμός) and anger (ὀργή) overlap considerably in meaning and are often treated as a pair in moral literature.[32] Verses 57–58 warned that unchecked anger leads to violent, though unintended, crime. Here attention turns to the emotion's internal psychic dynamic. Wrath and anger are not repudiated per se, rather it is the "fury" or "rage" they cause (note the semblance of μανίη and μῆνις).[33] The destructive potential of wrath and anger is asserted in a number of sentential writings. Ben Sira, for instance, can say of the enraged man, "The sway of his wrath is his downfall."[34] Of particular interest are Menander, *Mon.* 326, 339 ("If you have sense, never indulge your wrath."), 348, 355 ("Beware of wrath, for it lacks sanity."), and 503 ("We are all mad, whenever we grow angry."); cf. Seneca, *Ep.* 18.14: "Ungoverned anger begets madness."[35] The same sentiment is expressed in the *Testament of Dan*, which speaks of how "the spirit of wrath" can overcome good sense and corrupt the soul; it ensnares a person "in nets of deceit, blinds the eyes, darkens his understanding by means of a lie" (2:4, cf. 2:1–3:6). The Stoics were perhaps the most fastidious in analyzing and classifying the various emotions associated with ire. Zeno, for example (see Diogenes Laertius, *Vit. phil.* 7.113–114), categorized ὀργή and μῆνις as species of irrational longing (ἄλογος ὄρεξις; cf. Ps.–Phoc. 64), positing the derivation of the latter from the former as follows: "rage is anger which has long rankled and has become malicious, waiting for its opportunity."[36] Anger here is envisioned as a persistent and seditious enemy of reason; left unopposed it will easily ambush its victim.

---

[32] E.g., Prov 27:4; Rom 2:8; Eph 4:31; Col 3:8; *Did.* 3:2; Josephus, *Ant.* 6.304, 7.186; Aristophanes, *Av.* 401–402; Aristotle, *Rhet.* 1.10.16; Menander, *Mon.* 112; cf. BDAG s.v. θυμός 2.

[33] van der Horst (*Sentences*, 156) also notes the supposed etymological connection of the words, referring to *Etym. Magn.* p. 583, 20. On Homeric μῆνις, see Harris, *Restraining Rage*, 131–53.

[34] Sir 1:21, cf. 10:18, 28:8, 48:10; Prov 15:18, 22:24–25, 29:22; Qoh 7:9. Also see 4 Macc 1:33, 35; Sir 18:30, 23:6 (on the need to control ὄρεξις); for μῆνις, cf. Sir 10:6, 27:30, 28:5, 7.

[35] Cf. Publilius Syrus, *Sent.* 241; Cicero, *Tusc.* 4.77; Seneca, *Ira* 1.1.2–4, 2.36.4–6; Apollonius of Tyana, *Ep.* 86: "A quick temper blossoms into madness."

[36] Cf. Cicero, *Tusc.* 4.21; Seneca, *Ira* 1.4.1–3; Arius Didymus, *Epit.* 10b–c; *SVF* 3:395, 397; Herm. *Mand.* 5.2.4: "From bitterness there is wrath, and from wrath anger, and from anger rage."

Verses 65–67. These three antithetically constructed lines form a unit, each showing how the same human passion can render either positive or negative results depending on how it is directed. In and of themselves, then, zeal, boldness, and love are both morally ambiguous and in need of constant supervision.

Biblical authors could use ζῆλος or ζηλόω in a favorable sense, for example, Sir 51:18 ("I had zeal for the good." ἐζήλωσα τὸ ἀγαθόν.) and Gal 4:18: "Good is always to be courted (ζηλοῦσθαι) in a good way."[37] More often the terms have to do with the vices of envy, jealousy, and covetousness. The sages were acutely aware of the dangers involved in desiring the wrong things; in this regard the banal Prov 3:31 ("Neither procure the reproaches of bad men nor covet their ways.") is typical.[38] For the antithesis, compare Isocrates, *Nic.* 59: "Emulate (ζηλοῦτε) not those with the most possessions but those whose hearts know no evil."

Verse 66 communicates a certain ambivalence about the trait of τόλμα, boldness. The blurry line between bravery and foolhardiness is the crux of Menander's wordplay in *Mon.* 226: "Decide to be daring (εὔτολμος), not reckless (τολμηρός)." Gnomic authors characteristically prefer erring on the side of caution, for example, Sir 8:15: "Travel not with a bold man (τολμηροῦ), lest you are destroyed with him."[39] Like others before him, Pseudo-Phocylides draws a distinction depending on the gain or loss that will accrue, for example, Euenus, frg. 4: "With wisdom, daring (τόλμαν) is of great advantage, but without, it is harmful and brings wickedness." Our author goes one step further, however, qualifying the former type of daring as a category of πόνος, toil, a concept that figures prominently later in the poem (see vv. 153–174, especially v. 163). That one profits from "good" work is a point with which Wis 3:15 concurs: "The fruit of good toils (ἀγαθῶν … πόνων) is glorious renown."[40]

Verse 67 also suggests that opposed outcomes can derive from the same inner impulse or drive.[41] In contrast to the LXX, where ἔρως names a base passion, it refers here to indeterminate human desire.[42] That people "love" is taken for granted, but alternatives exist as to the direction of that desire. Presumably, these alternatives are understood in mutually exclusive terms, as we see in Sextus, *Sent.* 141: "If you love what you should not, you will not love what you should." Compare

---

[37] Cf. 4 Macc 13:24; Prov 6:6; Titus 2:14; 1 Pet 3:13; Lucian, *Ind.* 17; Menander, *Mon.* 275. For Philo's use of this terminology (e.g., *Virt.* 15, 175), see Seland, *Establishment Violence*, 126–31.

[38] Cf. Ps 36:1, 72:3; Prov 4:14, 23:17, 24:1, 19; Sir 9:11, 30:24, 48:2; Jas 3:14; Stumpff, "ζῆλος," 877–88.

[39] Further, Sir 19:3; *Jos. Asen.* 28:7; *Sib. Or.* 5.31; Josephus, *Bell.* 2.469; Sophocles, *Trach.* 582–583; Aristophanes, *Thesm.* 702; Menander, *Mon.* 248. But cf. also Pindar, *Nem.* 7.59; Thucydides, *Hist.* 3.56.5; Menander, frg. 792–793; Fitzer, "τολμάω," 181–85.

[40] Cf. Prov 3:9; Wis 10:17; Sir 11:21.

[41] Note ὀφέλλει in both vv. 66b and 67b.

[42] Cf. Prov 7:18, 30:16.

Arius Didymus, *Epit.* 5b9: "the erotic man is … spoken of in two senses; in one sense with regard to virtue as a type of worthwhile person, in the other with regard to vice as a reproach, as in the case of a person mad with erotic love." The logic of Pseudo-Phocylides' gnome involves identifying the consequences that follow from the decision one way or another for an individual's moral reputation. Elsewhere in the poem, he emphasizes the scurrilousness of ἔρως as illicit sexual desire (cf. vv. 61, 193–194, 214). Here the love of sexual passion, κύπρις (cf. vv. 3, 190), brings on shame, αἶσχος.[43] Inasmuch as the latter term would have implicated a public venue of moral assessment (cf. below, on v. 76), the thought of the line anticipates v. 68.

At the same time, ancient moralists could also speak of a love directed toward what is morally good, for example, Aeschines, *Tim.* 151: "There is a love (ἔρως) that leads people to temperance and virtue (ἀρετήν), an envied gift."[44] The latter, by definition, denoted moral excellence;[45] as Isocrates puts it, "Nothing is more revered and enduring" than virtue (*Demon.* 5; cf. Menander, *Mon.* 69).

Verses 68–69B. Verse 68 follows on v. 67, discussing those who revel not in sexual pleasure but in pleasure more generally. The adjective ἡδύς (literally, "sweet") can in the sentential literature describe an individual who is overindulgent in pleasantries, incurring therein public disapprobation, for example, Prov 12:11 and 14:23, the former stating that, "Whoever is pleasant (ἡδύς) in wine banquets will in his strongholds leave dishonor."[46] Similar advice is given elsewhere, for example, Sir 18:31 ("If you allow yourself the satisfaction of desire it will make you a laughingstock among your enemies."), *Syr. Men.* 63–64 ("There is no one who follows his lust and his stomach who will not immediately be dishonored and despised."), and P.Ins. 3.4 ("Do not let yourself be called a fool because of your thoughtless gluttony."); cf. Ps.-Phoc. 61; *Gnom. Democr.* 68, 74. The fool, ἄφρων, a common object of scorn in wisdom texts, is generally subject to all manner of public ridicule and reproof (Prov 1:22, 12:23, etc.).[47] The sort of senselessness connoted here probably refers in the first place to eating and drinking, which is the theme of the following line (note the contrast of ἄγαν and μέτρῳ). Pseudo-Phocylides' precept could in fact function quite well as a summary of Ben Sira's instruction on banqueting (31:12–32:13),

---

[43] Cf. Sir 41:17; Philo, *Mos.* 2.139; Cicero, *Tusc.* 4.69–70; D. L. Cairns, *Aidōs*, 121–26, 185–88, 305–40.

[44] Cf. *Gnom. Democr.* 73 ("It is righteous *erōs* to desire fine things without *hubris*."); Philo, *Agr.* 91 ("love of honor and zeal for virtue"), cf. *Sacr.* 129, *Congr.* 166, *Fug.* 195; Diogenes Laertius, *Vit. phil.* 7.130; *SVF* 3:717.

[45] See above, pp. 16, 24–28.

[46] Cf. Ps.-Phoc. 195; Isocrates, *Demon.* 20; Plutarch, *Adul. amic.* 53E; *Ahiqar* 147–148: "Do not be overly foolish lest […] be extinguished. Do not be too sweet, lest you be [swallowed]." Homer often describes wine as ἡδύς, e.g., *Od.* 9.162, 557, 10.477, 12.30.

[47] Cf. BDAG s.v. ἄφρων.

in which the need for moderation figures prominently.[48] The latter recommends drinking wine in moderation, eating in moderation (so as to sleep well), and keeping one's speech short (cf. Ps.-Phoc. 20, 122–124). The importance of self-restraint in banqueting in fact reflects a wide-ranging gnomic concern,[49] which we see also in P.Ins. 6.8–19:

> The life that controls excess is a life according to the wise man's heart.
> …
> He who sates himself with too much bread becomes ill and suffers.
> He who sates himself with too much wine lies down in a stupor.
> All kinds of illness are in the limbs because of being too sated.
> He who is moderate in his manner of life, his flesh is not disturbed.
> Illness does not burn him who is moderate in food.
> …
> The fool has neither shame nor fidelity because of (his) gluttony.

Such stock descriptions of the overindulgent offer a clue as to the meaning of "grievous" for Pseudo-Phocylides in the following line: excesses are detrimental to one's health and physical well-being, as well as to one's reputation.

Verse 69B both generalizes the thought of v. 69 and serves as a summarizing statement for the entire paragraph in vv. 55 ff. The preeminence of moderation was proverbial, for example, Carm. aur. 38 ("Moderation in all things is best." μέτρον δ᾽ ἐπὶ πᾶσιν ἄριστον.) and Theognis, El. 614: "The noble know how to observe moderation in everything (πάντων μέτρον)."[50] This is combined with a phrase familiar from Homer, Od. 3.206 (ὑπερβασίης ἀλεγεινῆς).[51]

---

[48] Cf. Skehan and DiLella, Ben Sira, 384–92.

[49] E.g., Prov 23:20–21, 29–32; Sir 37:29–30; Syr. Men. 52–66; Sextus, Sent. 108–111, 240, 265–270, 345; Democritus, frg. 235; Theognis, El. 467–502; Carm. aur. 33–34; Epictetus, Gnom. 17–26. Further, Musonius Rufus, frg. 18A–B; Josephus, C. Ap. 2.234; Lumpe, "Essen," 615–17.

[50] Cf. Phocylides, frg. 12 (πολλὰ μέσοισιν ἄριστα); Hesiod, Op. 694; Pindar, Ol. 13.48, Pyth. 2.34, Isthm. 6.71; Theognis, El. 331, 335, 694; Euripides, Med. 125; Macrobius, Sat. 5.16.6; Stobaeus, Anth. 3.1.172. And cf. Ps.-Phoc. 98. For the theme of right measure, cf. P.Ins. 4.13–22.

[51] Cf. Sib. Or. 2.101, 142.

B. Verses 70–75

70   Envy not the goods of friends; do not place blame on them.
71   The heavenly ones are quite without envy even among themselves:
72   the moon does not envy the sun's much stronger rays,
73   nor the earth the heavenly heights though it is below,
74   nor the rivers the seas. Rather they always have harmony.
75   For if strife were among the blessed ones, the firmament would not stand
       firm.

TEXTUAL NOTES

Verse 70. Instead of ἑτάροις (in M², P, V), L has ἑτέροις ("others"). // Σ abridges
vv. 70–75 (with its talk of "heavenly ones") to: "Be not envious or faithless or a
slanderer or of evil mind, or an inordinate deceiver." Verse 72. M, B, P, L: μήνη;
V: σελήνη. // ἡλίου αὐγαῖς is Homeric, cf. Il. 16.188, 17.371–372, Od. 2.181,
11.498, 619, 15.349. Verse 73. ὕψωμα is a late word (since Philo), though the
expression "heavenly heights" is reminiscent of passages like Josh 2:11; 1 Esd 4:34;
Ps 102:11; Prov 25:3; Sir 1:3; Pr. Man. 1:9; Acts 2:19. Verse 74. For the phrase "to
have harmony," cf. 4 Macc 13:23 v.l.; also below, on Ps.-Phoc. 219. Verse 75. LSJ
s.v. πόλος I.3: "celestial sphere, vault of heaven."

COMMENTARY

Envy was a major topic of Jewish and Greco-Roman moral literature.[52] Expressing a
common viewpoint, the Testament of Simeon (subtitled "On Envy") describes how it
foments all manner of wrath, savagery, and bloodshed; it is as potentially harmful to
the one who envies as to the one who is envied.[53] In v. 70, Pseudo-Phocylides aims
his counsel specifically against envying the goods of one's friends (ἑτάροις = ἑται
ροις, cf. vv. 91–92, 142), for which see also Isocrates, Demon. 26: "Admit among
your friends (ἑταίρων) not just those who show distress at your trouble, but those
who show no envy at your successes." The incompatibility of envy and friendship

---

[52] E.g., Tob 4:7, 16; Wis 2:24, 6:23; Sir 14:10; Syr. Men. 422; ARN A 16.2.1; Gnom. Democr. 88; Plato,
Leg. 731A–B; Chares, frg. 3; Menander, Mon. 52; Carm. aur. 36; Dio Chrysostom, Invid. 1–45; Sto-
baeus, Anth. 3.38. Further: Spicq, Lexicon, 3:434–36; Walcott, Envy, 1–21 and passim; Milobenski,
Der Neid, 116–34 and passim.

[53] Cf. Hollander and de Jonge, Testaments, 109–28.

would go on to become a philosophical *topos*.[54] The second half of v. 70 continues the thought with a command not to criticize one's friends out of envy. While the wording is Homeric (cf. *Od.* 2.86; also Nonnus, *Dion.* 12.231, 37.413, 42.225), the sentiment is closer to Ben Sira, for whom placing blame on others is a mark of deceitfulness.[55] Predictably, enviousness often engenders fault-finding; cf. Babrius, *Fab.* 59.17–18: "Let not envy be the judge: Nothing whatsoever is pleasing to the one who blames."

The nature of the recommendations Pseudo-Phocylides makes within the larger context of the section (see vv. 60–62, 69–69B, 81–82) suggests that he has in mind not only the avoidance of envy on the readers' part but also their refraining from the sorts of things that might arouse envy in others. As Cato the Elder observes, since people generally do not envy other people themselves but rather their circumstances, the ability to refrain from excess and ostentation reduces the risk of inciting this vice. Thus, "those who use their good fortune reasonably and moderately are least envied."[56]

In the *Theogony*, Hesiod speaks of the gods as beings whose status is both "heavenly" and "blessed." In vv. 101–113, for instance, the race of "blessed gods" includes the earth, rivers, seas, and stars.[57] In our passage, these epithets likewise refer to both celestial and terrestrial bodies, whose divinity was a basic affirmation of pagan religion.[58] Such beliefs were so pervasive that even a Hellenized Jew like Philo could speak of the sun, moon, planets, and stars as "that mighty host of visible gods whose blessedness from of old has been recognized."[59] The absence of envy in the realm of the divine was a philosophical tenet, for example, Aristotle, *Metaph.* 1.2.13 ("It is impossible for the Deity to be envious."), Plato, *Phaedr.* 247A ("Envy is excluded from the celestial band."), and *Tim.* 29E: "The (Demiurge) was good, and in him that is good no envy ever arises concerning anything; and being devoid of envy he desired that all should be, so far as possible, like himself."[60] As the last of these illustrations suggests, the divine banishment of envy could be understood as establishing a pattern for others to follow. This belief developed into a favorite device of Greco-

[54] E.g., Plato, *Phileb.* 49D, *Lys.* 215D; Ps.-Plato, *Def.* 416A; Demosthenes, *Or.* 23.164; Plutarch, *Frat. amor.* 484B–485E, *Inv. od.* 536F; Xenophon, *Cyr.* 2.4.10, *Mem.* 2.6.20–23, 3.9.8: defines the envious as those "annoyed at their friends' successes."

[55] Sir 11:31 (cf. v.l.), 33, 18:15.

[56] Plutarch, *Reg. imp. apophth.* 199A.

[57] Cf. Homer, *Od.* 10.299; Hesiod, *Theog.* 486, 502, *Op.* 136; Solon, frg. 13.3; Aeschylus, *Suppl.* 1019; Euripides, *Hec.* 146, *El.* 482, 1329.

[58] E.g., Homer, *Il.* 3.277–278; Plato, *Apol.* 26D, *Tim.* 40A–C, *Crat.* 397D, *Leg.* 887E; Plutarch, *Exil.* 601A; Cicero, *Resp.* 6.15, 17; Seneca, *Ben.* 4.23.4; Wis 13:2; Philo, *Conf.* 173, *Decal.* 52–53, *Contempl.* 3.

[59] Philo, *Aet.* 46, cf. *Opif.* 27, *Gig.* 8, *Spec.* 1.13–14, 19, *Aet.* 112, *Quaest. Gen.* 1.42, 4.157.

[60] Cf. Philo, *Spec.* 2.249, *Prob.* 13.

Roman speeches on *homonoia*, which held up the harmony of the cosmos as a model for human imitation.[61] According to Dio Chrysostom, the sun, moon, and stars, as well as the cosmic "elements" exhibit this virtue (*Nicom.* 11, cf. *Borysth.* 55). Similarly, Aelius Aristides reminds his audience that the sun, moon, and stars maintain their unity "because agreement prevails among them and there are no disagreements present" (*Or.* 23.77, cf. 24.42, 27.35). Philo contrasts with humanity's chaos the sun, moon, and heaven, which always move "in harmonious order" (*Jos.* 145).[62] In this regime of concord, envy poses a major threat. Aelius Aristides exhorts his listeners to *homonoia* with the advice, "let each side dispense with its envy and greed – I speak of the envy felt by the poor for the rich, and of the greed of the rich against the poor" (*Or.* 24.32). That envy engenders strife is suggested on several occasions in the Pauline corpus (Rom 1:29; Gal 5:20–21; Phil 1:15; 1 Tim 6:4), reflecting a common theme.[63] All this suggests that in our passage it is only with vv. 74b–75 that we reach the main point: the reader ought to refrain from envy and emulate the cosmic order so as to avoid conflict and cultivate harmony in his life.[64]

---

[61] Though it may also be mentioned that *eris* among the gods is a basic narrative element of the *Iliad*, e.g., 20.66, 134, 21.385, 390, 394; cf. Hesiod, *Theog.* 705; Euripides, *Hel.* 878–879.

[62] Cf. Ep Jer 60; Euripides, *Phoen.* 543–555; Maximus of Tyre, *Or.* 41.3; D. B. Martin, *Corinthian Body*, 38–77; Mitchell, *Rhetoric*, 60–64.

[63] On the association of *phthonos* and conflict: Democritus, frg. 245; Plato, *Lys.* 215C–D; Philo, *Jos.* 5; Epictetus, *Diatr.* 3.22.61; Dio Chrysostom, *Invid.* 17, 29–30.

[64] On *homonoia*: J. Ferguson, *Moral Values*, 118–32; Jones, *Roman World*, 83–94.

C. Verses 76–96

76   Practice moderation, and refrain from shameful deeds.
77   Do not imitate evil, but leave vengeance to justice.
78   For while persuasion is an advantage, strife sows strife in turn.
79   Trust not quickly, before you truly see the end.
80   To outdo one's benefactors with further benefactions is fitting.
81   It is better to entertain guests promptly with simple meals
82   than with many festivities extending beyond due time.
83   Never become a harsh creditor to a poor man.
84   Let no one take all the birds from a nest at the same time,
85   but leave behind the mother so that you may again have her chicks.
86   Never allow untrained men to judge.
88   A wise man manages wisdom, a fellow-craftsman, crafts.
89   An untaught ear does not grasp a great teaching;
90   for surely those who never learned noble things do not comprehend.
91   Make not table-clearing flatterers your friends.
92   For many are friends of drinking and eating,
93   beguiling time whenever they can satisfy themselves,
94   all being annoyed with little and insatiable with much.
95   Trust not the people: the mob is shifty.
96   For people and water and fire are ever uncontrollable.

TEXTUAL NOTES

Verse 77. LSJ s.v. ἄμυνα II: "vengeance;" cf. v. 32; Josh 10:13; Wis 5:17, 11:3. Verse 78. L²ᵞᵖ, Σ have ὄνειαρ, while M, B, P, L, V have instead ὄφελ(λ)ος ("gain"); as van der Horst notes (*Sentences*, 167), the former is the *lect. diff.* Verse 79b. For πρίν + future ind., see Derron, *Sentences*, lxxvii (with n. 3). Verse 80. εὖ ἔρδειν (cf. v. 152) is Homeric: *Il.* 5.650; cf. Theognis, *El.* 105–112, 955–956; Bacchylides, frg. 1.163, 5.36, 14.18. Verses 81–82. For καλὸν ... ἤ, cf. BDAG s.v. ἤ 2.b.β; van der Horst, *Sentences*, 170. Verse 82. Following Brunck (*Gnomici Poetae Graeci*, 159) and van der Horst (*Sentences*, 93 n. 1, 170), who suggest θαλίαισι instead of δολίαισι, which is printed in Young, *Theognis*, 102; Derron, *Sentences*, 8 (with the mss.). With the latter reading we might translate: "than with many contrived (meals) that are long in coming," or "than with many diversions that drag on too long." Verse 86. For ἀδαήμων ("unskilled, ignorant"), cf. Homer, *Il.* 5.634, 13.811, *Od.* 12.208, 17.283. [Verse 87.] "Render no judgment before you hear the word of both sides." (μηδὲ δίκην δικάσῃς, πρὶν <ἂν> ἄμφω μῦθον ἀκούσῃς.) A spurious verse (only in Mᵃ; cf. Aristophanes, *Vesp.* 725–726), disrupting the flow of the comparative argument in vv. 86, 88–90; see van der Horst, *Sentences*, 173–74. Verse 88a. LSJ s.v. εὐθύνω I: "to direct, govern," cf. v. 52; P, L, V replace εὐθύνει (in M, B) with ἴθυνει ("guide"). Verse 89. LSJ s.v. χωρέω III.1: "to be capable of;" cf. BDAG s.v. χωρέω 3.b.β; Josephus, *C. Ap.* 1.225; Matt 19:11–12. // M, B, P, L²ʸᵖ, V: διδαχὴν; L: δὲ δίκην. Verse 90. M, B, Lʸᵖ, V have οὐ γὰρ δὴ νοέουσ'; P, L have instead οὔποτε γὰρ κλύουσ' (κλύω: "hear, perceive"). // οὐ γὰρ δή: cf. Denniston, *Greek Particles*, 243–44. Verse 91. The mss. have τραπεζοφόρους ("bearing a table, table-bearers"), which most editors replace with τραπεζοκόρους. Verse 93. LSJ s.v. θωπεύω: "to flatter, fawn." // For καιρός, cf. v. 82, where it is also used of meals. Verse 94. M², P, L, V: ὀλίγοις; B: ὄγκοις.

COMMENTARY

Verses 76–79. Moderation (σωφροσύνη) was one of the cardinal virtues of Greek morality and a favorite theme of gnomic authors.[65] Evidence of its impact on biblical literature can be found in passages like Esth 3:13; Wis 8:7; 2 Macc 4:37; 4 Macc 1:3, 6, 18, 30–31, 5:23; 1 Tim 2:9, 15.[66] In philosophical circles, it was associated especially with the objectives of self-understanding and self-mastery, which in turn were understood to foster moral stability and decorum. In *Amat.* 138A, for example, Plato interprets the Delphic maxim, "know thyself," as an appeal "to practice moderation" (σωφροσύνην ἀσκεῖν).[67] The term's specific denotation for our author is provided by the second half of verse 76; moderation entails developing an ability to sense what is shameful, that is, to anticipate and avoid what may bring public disgrace (cf. v. 67).[68] Those who earn a good reputation among friends, family, and fellow citizens are by definition those who "refrain from shameful deeds" (αἰσχρῶν δὲ ἔργων ἀπεχόμενοι: Xenophon, *Hell.* 6.5.42).[69] As Johan Thom points out,

---

[65] For some examples of gnomic instruction on moderation, see Stobaeus, *Anth.* 3.5, 21 and Wilson, *Love Without Pretense*, 141 n. 85. Also cf. Aristotle, *Eth. nic.* 3.10.1–3.12.10; Iamblichus, *Vit. Pyth.* 31.187–213; Cicero, *Off.* 1.93–143.

[66] Cf. Titus 1:8, 2:2, 4–6, 12.

[67] Cf. Xenophon, *Cyr.* 8.1.30; Isocrates, *Nic.* 44: the author claims to be "more assiduous than anyone else in practicing moderation (ἤσκησα τὴν σωφροσύνην)," since it ranks among the truest and most abiding of the virtues. For the form of v. 76a, cf. also *Carm. aur.* 13; Herodotus, *Hist.* 1.96; Plato, *Resp.* 407A; *Let. Arist.* 168, 225, 255, 285; Ps.-Phoc. 123.

[68] D. L. Cairns, *Aidōs*, 55 (cf. 54–60): shame connotes both "the state which might arouse popular disapproval and the state resulting from popular disapproval." Greek authors often associate σωφροσύνη with the theme of shame with the purpose of encouraging self-inhibition and propriety and discouraging excess; see pp. 104, 168, 306, 314–15, 339, 373, 404.

[69] On the need to learn shame: Democritus, frg. 244, 264; *Gnom. Democr.* 84; Menander, *Mon.* 24 ("Neither do nor learn what is shameful."), 367, 833; *Carm. aur.* 11–12; cf. Dover, *Popular Morality*, 236–42; D. Cohen, *Law, Sexuality, and Society*, 58–59.

the language of shame is often found in conversations about moderation "as a description of unrestrained acts and their results."[70] Compare Isocrates, *Demon.* 21, where an appeal to practice self-restraint is similarly associated with the avoidance of shameful acts: "Practice self-control (ἐγκράτειαν ἄσκει) in all matters in which it is shameful (αἰσχρόν) for the soul to be controlled, namely, gain, anger, pleasure, and grief."

The injunction not to "imitate evil" (cf. 3 John 11: μὴ μιμοῦ τὸ κακόν) in v. 77 is probably best understood as advice not to retaliate when wronged, a common gnomic theme, for example, Rom 12:17 ("Do not return evil for evil.");[71] cf. Lev 19:18: "Your hand shall not seek revenge." Pseudo-Phocylides implores the readers not to seek retribution themselves but to leave evildoers to "justice." Here, as elsewhere in both Greek and Jewish sources, δίκη apparently is understood to function as a personification of divine vengeance.[72] In this case, the maxim assumes a scenario of God's punishment of injustice comparable to that of vv. 11, 17–18, or 52; cf. Sir 28:1: "The one who seeks vengeance shall find vengeance from the Lord." The repudiation of retribution, accompanied by an appeal to leave judgment to the deity, occurs with regularity in ancient Near Eastern wisdom texts, for example, *Instr. Any* 8.14 ("Don't rush to attack your attacker; leave him to the god.") and *Instr. Amenem.* 5.14–17 ("A storm that bursts like fire in straw, such is the heated man in his hour. Withdraw from him, leave him alone; the god knows how to answer him.").[73] In each case, an assertion is being made regarding both the proper bounds of human action and the need to trust in the certainty of divine justice.

Verse 78 gives the motivation for the foregoing line, indicating both positive and negative ramifications. The 25th Instruction of P.Insinger (entitled, "The teaching to guard against retaliation, lest a portion of it return to you.") includes a number of precepts approximating our v. 78b, for example, 33.8 ("Violent vengefulness against the god brings a violent death."), 33.19–20 ("He who violates a man by force, his offspring will soon be buried. He who does harm for harm, his old age will be harmed."), and 34.8: "When (retaliation) reaches a town, it leaves strife among its people." All of these lines affirm the same logic of cause and effect: those who initiate violence or vengeance will suffer in kind. P.Ins. 34.13 is of special interest for our interpretation of v. 78: "There is no counsel or thought in a wise man who is in the state of retaliation." For those bent on strife it is difficult to think or speak reasonably; as we heard in vv. 63–64, a certain destructive rage overcomes those consumed

---

[70] Thom, *Golden Verses*, 131; cf. North, *Sophrosyne*, s.v. aidōs.

[71] Cf. *Jos. Asen.* 28:4; Menander, *Mon.* 461 ("Imitate the revered, not the ways of the wicked."); Wilson, *Love Without Pretense*, 187–88 for further examples.

[72] Cf. 4 Macc 8:14, 22, 9:9, 32, 11:3, 12:12, 18:22; Philo, *Conf.* 118, *Spec.* 4.201, *Prob.* 89, *Flacc.* 104; Hesiod, *Op.* 256–262; Plato, *Leg.* 716A; *Orph. hymn.* 62. That *dikē* lies with God is asserted in Lev 26:25; Deut 32:41, 43; Wis 1:8–9. Cf. Spicq, *Lexicon*, 1:318–20.

[73] Cf. Rom 12:19, with Wilson, *Love Without Pretense*, 192–94.

with anger. The antidote is persuasion, πειθώ, which offers an "advantage" inasmuch as it can break the cycle of violence and retaliation. Philo, for instance, lauds those who use the power of persuasion to diffuse enmity and hostility.[74]

It was a rudiment of gnomic wisdom that people are easily deceived in matters of personal loyalty. Consequently, warnings not to commit one's trust too readily are easy to find. For Ps.-Phoc. 79a, compare Menander, *Mon.* 460 ("Do not always try to trust everyone in everything.") and Sir 6:7: "If you would gain a friend, put him to the test, and do not put your trust in him quickly (μὴ ταχὺ ἐμπιστεύσῃς)."[75] The second half of v. 79 seems to supply the meaning of "quickly" for our author: do not put your trust in others until you can "see the end," which probably means until you can discern clearly their true intent, when it comes to expression in action.[76] The damaging consequences of broken trust are elucidated by P.Ins. 11.23: "Do not trust one whom you do not know in your heart, lest he cheat you with cunning."[77]

Verses 80–82. Verses 77–78 identified the injurious effects of returning evil for evil. In v. 80 we encounter something of the reverse argument: a person ought to return one good for another, even seeking to outdo favors received. No explicit indication is given as to why one should aspire to such conduct, simply that it is "fitting."[78] In contrast, comparable gnomic formulations might supply a self-serving motive for the practice, for example, Sir 3:31 ("He that repays a favor is mindful of what will follow: in the time of his fall he will find a stay.") and Hesiod, *Op.* 349–351 ("Get good measure from your neighbor, and give good measure back, with the measure itself and better if you can, so that when in need another time you may find something to rely on.").[79] In his legal summary, Philo provides a negative motivation: anyone guilty of impiety towards a benefactor (as much as towards God or one's parents) is subject to the death penalty (*Hypoth.* 7.2).

---

[74] Philo, *Her.* 244, cf. *Fug.* 139, *Jos.* 34, 269, *Virt.* 217; *Let. Arist.* 266; Plato, *Leg.* 722B–C; Euripides, *Hec.* 814–820; Plutarch, *Conj. praec.* 138C–D; Diogenes Laertius, *Vit. phil.* 1.88 ("Make your point by persuasion not force."); Babrius, *Fab.* 18.16; Stafford, "Plutarch on Persuasion," 162–72. *Peithō* can even be elevated to divine status, e.g., Hesiod, *Op.* 73; Theognis, *El.* 349; Aeschylus, *Suppl.* 1039–1040.

[75] Cf. Sir 19:4; Mic 7:5; Hesiod, *Op.* 372; Theognis, *El.* 75–82, 831–832; Isocrates, *Demon.* 24–25; *Gnom. Democr.* 67; Ps.-Plutarch, *Lib. ed.* 12E; *Anec. Gr.* 1.58, 139; P.Ins. 12.6; *Instr. Ankh.* 16.22; Polycarp, *Phil.* 6:1 (μὴ ταχέως πιστεύοντες).

[76] Cf. Hesiod, *Op.* 293–294; Theognis, *El.* 593–594: "Neither make your heart too sick with evil things nor too quickly glad of good, until the final outcome is seen."

[77] Cf. Josephus, *Bell.* 3.538–542.

[78] Cf. Schlier, "καθήκω," 437–40.

[79] Cf. 1 Macc 10:27–28; Sir 30:6, 35:2.

It was a cultural convention that bestowing a favor created an obligation of reciprocity on the part of the recipient.[80] The social pressure that accompanied such anticipation nourished a spirit of competitiveness, so that terms like νικᾶν fit naturally in the argot of benefaction. As Isocrates writes, "it is shameful to be outdone (νικᾶσθαι) by one's friends in giving favors" (*Demon.* 26).[81] The expectation that each benefit should be greater than the one that elicited it creates a situation of perpetual indebtedness between the parties, which helps to sustain their relationship.[82]

Verse 80's maxim on requiting kindnesses leads naturally to a rule on hospitality, or *xenia*.[83] In the area of entertainment, simpleness (here λιτότης)[84] was for the sages a virtue, while elaborate indulgences were viewed with suspicion; see the critique of sumptuary vices in vv. 61, 68–69 above. This preference could take the form of "better" sayings like vv. 81–82, for example, Prov 15:17 ("Better is an entertainment of herbs with friendliness and kindness than a feast of calves with enmity.") and Sir 29:22 ("Better a pauper's life ... than delicacies in another man's home."), cf. 32:1. In the Hellenistic world, the Cynics in particular advertised their satisfaction with "the simplest food" as a sign of their freedom and self-sufficiency.[85] To the criterion of simplicity Pseudo-Phocylides adds that of celerity. Like any social event, a meal has its *kairos*, or appropriate "time" and measure; exceeding it could be an embarrassing faux pas for the host (see 3 Macc 5:15).[86] Consideration for the *kairos* would also be "better" for the diners themselves; as Democritus, frg. 235 explains, "those who take their pleasures from their belly, exceeding what is appropriate (ὑπερβεβληκότες τὸν καιρόν) in food and drink or sex," experience only momentary gratification.

---

[80] Fiore, "Friendship in Cicero," 66–68.

[81] Cf. Josephus, *Ant.* 2.262; Xenophon, *Mem.* 2.6.35, *Cyr.* 5.1.29.

[82] Cf. *Gnom. Democr.* 92 ("One should receive favors with the intention of giving greater ones in return."); Xenophon, *Mem.* 4.4.24; Anaximenes of Lampsacus, *Rhet. Alex.* 1421B (one of the unwritten laws); Ps.-Socratics, *Ep.* 29; Cicero, *Off.* 1.48; Seneca, *Ben.* 1.4.3, 2.18.5, 3.1, *Ep.* 81.8; Saller, *Personal Patronage,* 7–39.

[83] For the practice, see Herman, *Friendship,* 14–35 and passim; Roth, "Corrupted *Xenia,*" 1–17; Spicq, *Lexicon,* 2:555–60.

[84] Theognis, *El.* 511–522; Euripides, *El.* 394–395; Plato, *Resp.* 404B–E; Diogenes Laertius, *Vit. phil.* 8.13, 10.130–131; Plutarch, *Sept. sap. conv.* 150C–D, *Cupid. divit.* 525C, *Quaest. conv.* 668F; Athenaeus, *Deipn.* 191E–F; Cicero, *Fam.* 7.26.2; Philo, *Contempl.* 81–82; P.Ins. 28.1; Gowers, *Loaded Table,* 7, 11, 16–21, and passim.

[85] Ps.-Socrates, *Ep.* 6.2; cf. Ps.-Crates, *Ep.* 13; Ps.-Diogenes, *Ep.* 27, 46; Teles, frg. 4A.115–119; Epictetus, *Diatr.* 3.22.87; Diogenes Laertius, *Vit. phil.* 6.31; Malherbe, *Paul,* 14–15; Billerbeck, "The Ideal Cynic," 205–21.

[86] Cf. P.Ins. 3.21. For παρὰ καιρόν, cf. Phocylides, frg. 6. Also see below, on vv. 93, 121.

Verses 83–85. The obligation to treat the poor with justice figures prominently in vv. 10, 19, 22–23, 28–29. The precept in v. 83 is apparently derived from injunctions not to charge interest on loans to fellow Israelites who are poor in Exod 22:24 ("If you lend money to a poor brother who is near you, you shall not oppress him or exact interest from him.") and Lev 25:35–37.[87] As Sir 29:1–3 observes, lending to a neighbor in his time of need constitutes an act of mercy. Pseudo-Phocylides generalizes the biblical obligation, stating that one should never be a "bitter"[88] creditor to any poor man, without mentioning additional status indicators like "brother" or "neighbor."[89] In this regard, his recommendation agrees with the directions of *Instr. Amenem.* 16.5–7: "If you find a large debt against a poor man, make it into three parts; forgive two, let one stand."

The couplet that follows is a versification of Deut 22:6–7: "If you should happen upon a nest of chicks … you shall not take the mother with the young. You shall let the mother go and take the young for yourself, so that it shall be good for you and you may live long."[90] Both Philo (*Hypoth.* 7.9)[91] and Josephus (*C. Ap.* 2.213) include this command in their respective summaries of the law, making it likely that Pseudo-Phocylides found some reference to it in the source he shares with them. Josephus cites this as an illustration of the "gentleness and humanity" fostered by the law. Our author may have agreed (note the element of mercy in v. 83), though the motivating clause in v. 85b lends the injunction a more pragmatic dimension (cf. Deut 22:7b). While the line's animal subject matter is unexpected in the context of vv. 75ff., the basic principle at work here parallels that of v. 83, i.e., the importance of restraint when procuring something from a weaker party.

Verses 86–90. This is one of the few places in the poem where Pseudo-Phocylides' perspective may be said to betray a certain elitism; cf. vv. 95–96 below. These verses, in fact, would function quite well as a summary of Ben Sira's comparison of the vocations of the artisan and the scribe (38:24–39:11),[92] which in turn has affinities with a famous Egyptian composition alternatively known as "The Satire on the Trades" or "The Instruction of Duauf" (*ANET* 432–34). Ben Sira concedes that laborers like the farmer, carpenter, smith, and potter are essential to a community's welfare. Nev-

---

[87] Cf. Deut 15:1–4, 23:20–21; 4 Macc 2:8; Luke 6:34–36; Philo, *Spec.* 2.71–78, *Virt.* 82–87; Josephus, *C. Ap.* 2.208; Gerstenberger, *Leviticus*, 386–88.

[88] LSJ s.v. πικρός III: "bitter, relentless, vindictive;" cf. the "sour" creditor of *Syr. Men.* 181–188.

[89] Cf. Taubenschlag, *Law*, 341–49. For χρήστης, cf. Phocylides, frg. 6 ("Be not the debtor of a bad man.").

[90] As Nelson (*Deuteronomy*, 268) notes, the "inclination to include the nonhuman world in the circle of decent behavior" is evident at various points in Deuteronomy.

[91] Cf. Philo, *Virt.* 125–130, *Hypoth.* 7.7.

[92] Cf. Skehan and DiLella, *Ben Sira*, 445–53.

ertheless, "their desire is in the work of their craft (τέχνης)."[93] Conversely, whoever has *sophia* manages (κατευθυνεῖ) counsel and knowledge (Sir 39:7; cf. Prov 23:19), since he alone possesses the intelligence, training, and leisure to speak wisely and meditate on divine mysteries. It stands to reason, then, that common workers will not be tapped to serve as judges, since they can neither declare nor even understand a judgment (Sir 38:33, cf. 10:1–2). Neither will they participate in the interpretation of parables and other difficult teachings, since this is the domain of the sages, who devote themselves to studying the legacy of great thinkers (39:2–3).[94]

Pseudo-Phocylides likewise acknowledges that tradesmen are skilled in their crafts (v. 88b). It is the sage, however, who manages (εὐθύνει) *sophia*, in contrast to those who are untrained, uneducated, and unenlightened in "noble" matters (cf. vv. 65–66). They have no hope of serving as competent judges (cf. vv. 9–12) or grasping the intricacies of a weighty teaching. Such disparagement of the ἀπαίδευτος, or untaught person, is in fact a mainstay of biblical wisdom. Sir 6:20–21 observes that *paideia* is quite disagreeable to such individuals; it lies on them like a great stone, to be cast off before long.[95] Conversely, the abilities to comprehend (νοέω) and to learn (μανθάνω) were defining attributes of the sage.[96]

Verses 91–94. The language of flattery (κολακεία, etc.) is missing from the Septuagint (cf. Prov 28:23), though Philo, influenced by Greek moral traditions, draws on it extensively. One thing his analysis of the problem illustrates is how it often fell under the aegis of the friendship *topos*. No one, says Philo, would call a flatterer (κόλαξ) a friend (ἑταῖρος), since "flattery is friendship diseased" (*Leg. all.* 3.182).[97] His loathing for this vice becomes even more apparent in *Plant.* 104–106, where we hear that a sensible person will never befriend flatterers, since "they often conceal unspeakable hatred toward those whom they fawn, being in love with over-eating and gluttony, by which they are induced to court those who supply their boundless desires."

Given attitudes like this, it is hardly surprising that the flatterer became a stock figure of Greco-Roman comedy and satire.[98] Characterized by a willingness to per-

---

[93] Sir 38:34, cf. 9:17; Aristophanes, *Vesp.* 1431: "Let each one exercise the craft he knows."

[94] Cf. Plato, *Resp.* 495D; 4Q424 III, 1–3; also the 14th Instruction of P.Insinger, entitled "Do not let the inferior man rule, lest he make your name that of a fool."

[95] Cf. Prov 5:23, 8:5, 15:12, 14, 17:21, 27:20; Wis 17:1; Sir 8:4, 10:3, 20:19, 24, 22:3, 51:23; *Sib. Or.* 3.670; Xenophon, *Mem.* 4.1.3–4; Ps.-Heraclitus, *Ep.* 4; *Gnom. Democr.* 59: "Neither skill nor wisdom is attainable if one does not learn."

[96] E.g., Prov 1:5–6, 8:5, 16:23, 17:16, 19:25; Sir 8:8–9, 14:21, 16:24–25.

[97] Cf. Plato, *Gorg.* 464C–465C; Aristotle, *Rhet.* 1.11.18; Theophrastus, *Char.* 2.1–13; Diogenes Laertius, *Vit. phil.* 6.4; Sextus, *Sent.* 149; Stobaeus, *Anth.* 3.14; Glad, *Paul and Philodemus*, 23–30; Spicq, *Lexicon*, 2:319–21.

[98] See Damon, *Mask of the Parasite*; Nesselrath, *Lukians Parasitendialog*; Wilkins, *The Boastful Chef*, 71–86; and cf. below, on Ps.-Phoc. 156–157.

form even the most degrading tasks in the hope of a return, such individuals were lampooned as much for their obsequiousness as for their insatiable hunger. Many chastised them as purveyors of dissipation and debauchery, since they encouraged their hosts to live extravagantly. The greatest risk in associating with such people, however, "lay in one's exposure to unrestrained flattery and in believing that a parasite was a friend."[99] The flatterer, then, is despised for both his voracity and his guile; he exploits the one fawned in order to feed his own excessive appetites.[100] A discriminatory attitude was therefore in order, as the warning of Epictetus, *Gnom.* 42 implies: "As a wolf resembles a dog, so do a flatterer and an adulterer and a parasite resemble a friend" (cf. *Dict. Cat.* 3.4). Plutarch deemed the problem posed by such individuals serious enough to devote an entire essay to the theme (*Quomodo adulator ab amico internoscatur*), in which they emerge as pestilent agents of moral corruption.[101] This is due, in part, to their ability to agitate in their victims those parts of the soul that incline to immoderate emotions, such as malice, fear, wrath, envy, and erotic passion (61D–F).[102]

Pseudo-Phocylides' treatment of flattery is fully recognizable against this background, with vv. 92–94 motivating the appeal of v. 91 and fleshing out the meaning of the apparent neology, τραπεζόκορος. The reader is advised not to take on "table-clearing" flatterers as friends, since they are constantly ravenous and dissatisfied (cf. the parasite of Plautus, *Men.* 77–78 nicknamed "the Brush" for the way he cleans off dinner tables).[103] Verse 92 is a quotation of Theognis, *El.* 115–116 (cf. 109, 113, 641–644), which goes on to give some explanation as to why one should not befriend such fickle freeloaders: "Many, indeed, are friends of drinking and eating (πολλοί τοι πόσιος καὶ βρώσιός εἰσιν ἑταῖροι), but in a serious matter they are few." Compare Menander, *Mon.* 682 ("Many are friends of tables, not of their friends.") and P.Ins. 26.5 ("Do not flatter nor be insolent in any home because of love of your belly."). The embellishment that follows in vv. 93–94 recalls especially satires of Hellenistic banqueting, for example, Philo, *Contempl.* 48–56, where the "dining" concludes as follows:

> Then, while some tables are taken out, emptied by the gluttony of the company who gorge themselves like cormorants, so voraciously that they nibble even at the bones, other tables have their dishes mangled and torn and left half eaten. And when they are

---

[99] Damon, *Mask of the Parasite*, 35.

[100] Cf. Philo, *Leg. all.* 2.10, *Agr.* 164, *Conf.* 48, *Migr.* 111–112, *Abr.* 126, *Virt.* 173, *Prob.* 99.

[101] On this treatise, see Gallo and Pettine, *Plutarco*, 7–26; Sirinelli, *Plutarque*, 65–81.

[102] Cf. Ps.-Plutarch, *Lib. ed.* 5B, 13A–C; Aristotle, *Eth. nic.* 10.3.11; Maximus of Tyre, *Or.* 14.

[103] Cf. above, on Ps.-Phoc. 68–69, 81–82.

quite exhausted, their bellies crammed up to the gullets but their lust still ravenous, impotent for eating (they turn to drink).[104]

In his caricature of such gluttons, Pseudo-Phocylides predictably introduces the vice of ἀπληστία, insatiability, which was frequently condemned by both Jewish and Greek moralists.[105] Menander would not have been alone in identifying it as "the greatest evil among mortals" (*Mon.* 386). Cf. above, on vv. 68–69, 81–82.

Verses 95–96. Much like vv. 86–90, these verses reveal something of an aristocratic attitude on the writer's part, though given the section's preoccupation with propriety and moderation, this kind of advice is hardly unexpected.[106] The first line may be understood as an extension of the gnome about trust in v. 79 (also with μὴ πίστευε). Mobs tends to get "shifty (πολύτροπον), confused, and violent" (Philo, *Ebr.* 113), and thus are properly approached only with caution (Sir 26:5).[107] Pseudo-Phocylides drives home this point with images that dramatize the volatility attending a large crowd; compare Sir 16:6 ("In a gathering of sinners a fire will be kindled.") and Dio Chrysostom, *3 Regn.* 49: "a motley impulsive mob of all sorts … always kept in a state of confusion and anger … just as a wild rough sea is whipped this way and that."[108]

---

[104] Philo, *Contempl.* 55, cf. *Opif.* 159, *Post.* 98, *Ebr.* 4, 6, 22, *Somn.* 2.211, *Spec.* 2.197, 4.100. For censorious depictions of the *convivium*, see Edwards, *Politics of Immorality*, 186–90, 202.

[105] E.g., Prov 27:20; Sir 31:16–20, 37:27–31; *T. Reub.* 3:3; *T. Iss.* 4:5, 6:1; Theognis, *El.* 109; Philo, *Ebr.* 22; *Gnom. Vat.* 59; Ps.-Heraclitus, *Ep.* 2; P.Ins. 6.19, 7.10.

[106] Cf. the typically Cynic attitude of Ps.-Socratics, *Ep.* 24.1–2: "I hate to associate with the masses … I left the city as if it were a cage for animals;" cf. Malherbe, *Paul*, 17–18, 41.

[107] For πολύτροπος, cf. Homer, *Od.* 1.1 and LSJ s.v.

[108] Cf. Menander, *Mon.* 372 ("A mob is powerful, but lacks good sense."); Cicero, *Resp.* 1.65; Seneca, *Ira* 2.8.1–3, *Ep.* 99.17; Tacitus, *Hist.* 1.69; *Instr. Any* 8.16–18; Philo, *Flacc.* 33, *Legat.* 67: "A multitude is unstable in everything – intentions, words, and deeds."

V. Fortitude and Fortune (Verses 97–121)

Bibliography: Cavallin, *Life After Death.* Gauthier, *Magnanimité,* 144–64, 202–22. Kassel, *Konsolations-literatur.* Krause, *ΑΛΛΟΤΕ ΑΛΛΟΣ,* 81–90. Lattimore, *Epitaphs.* Spanneut, "Geduld," 243–94.

The maxims relating to fortitude in the *Sentences* are organized into two paragraphs, each beginning with an appeal against excessive grief (vv. 97–98, 118). The moral problem of how best to respond to life's varied forms and sources of distress generally belonged to the ancient discussion about courage (ἀνδρεία) and the related virtues of fortitude (καρτερία) and endurance (ὑπομονή).[1] In its plainest sense, courage refers to physical bravery, especially as exhibited on the battlefield. On the whole, moral philosophers found this meaning too restricted and expanded the term's meaning to embrace perseverance in facing uncertainties and difficulties of all sorts, for example, Diogenes Laertius, *Vit. phil.* 7.126: "Courage is concerned with the things that must be endured." This understanding had an impact on Hellenistic Judaism as well, for example, Eleazar's claim that the Mosaic law "trains us in courage, so that we endure any adversity willingly" (4 Macc 5:23). Two aspects of this discussion bear upon our analysis of Pseudo-Phocylides.

First, courage could be depicted as the capacity to face death and its consequences without anxiety. As Musonius Rufus puts it, the one who possesses ἀνδρεία exhibits "a firm conviction that death and hardships are not evils" (frg. 8.62.23–26). This appears to be Pseudo-Phocylides' focus in the first paragraph, vv. 97–115. According to the philosophical literature, the ability to remain undismayed by the fear of death stems from a correct understanding about the nature of life, death, and the afterlife, and about what should and should not be feared.[2] Hence the common

---

[1] Cf. Thom, *Golden Verses,* 140–46; as he notes on p. 141, "Bearing up under misfortune falls under the heading of fortitude (καρτερία) which is a species of moral courage (ἀνδρεία)." On καρτερία, ὑπομονή, and their relationship with courage, see Plato, *Alc.* 122C, *Lach.* 192B–194A; Ps.-Plato, *Def.* 412C; Ps.-Aristotle, *Virt. vit.* 4.4; Ps.-Aristotle, *Mag. mor.* 1.20.1–12; Philo, *Leg. all.* 1.65, 68, *Cher.* 78, *Deus immut.* 13, *Mut.* 153, 197, *Mos.* 2.184; Iamblichus, *Vit. Pyth.* 32.214–221; Cicero, *Off.* 1.61–92; Hauck, "μένω," 581–88; Spicq, *Lexicon,* 3:414–20; Spanneut, "Geduld," 245–60; Gauthier, *Magnanimité,* 144–64; J. Ferguson, *Moral Values,* 28–30, 40–42, 46–50, 159–78; Devereux, "Courage and Wisdom,"129–41.

[2] According to the Stoic view, e.g., courage is exercised especially when one remembers the death of a family member or confronts the inevitability of one's own death without succumbing to grief or fear; see Cullyer, "Paradoxical Andreia," 222–24.

notion that "courage is knowledge."[3] This perspective may account for the relatively large number of declarative sentences in this section of the poem, as the author reminds the reader of certain traditional beliefs (see below).

Second, courage was associated with the capacity to bear the twists and turns of fate with composure, a trait sometimes referred to as μακροθυμία or μεγαλοψυχία.[4] As Cicero observes, those counted among the courageous are very often not warriors, but those who exhibit a spirit superior to life's vicissitudes:

> When fortune smiles and the stream of life flows according to our wishes, let us diligently avoid all arrogance, haughtiness, and pride. For it is as much a sign of weakness to give way to one's feelings in success as it is in adversity. But it is a fine thing to keep an unruffled temper, an unchanging mien, and the same cast of countenance in every condition of life. (*Off.* 1.90)

Perseverance in the midst of life's unexpected reversals is the theme of the second paragraph, vv. 118–121. The challenge of facing the caprice of fortune was a theme that combined naturally in gnomic discourse with that of facing the realities of death, as part of its general reflection on the human condition, for example, *Carm. aur.* 15–18: "Know that death has been destined for all, and that property is wont to be acquired now, lost tomorrow. But whatever pains mortals suffer through the divine workings of fate, whatever lot you have, bear it and do not be angry."[5]

In terms of its teaching on these subjects, the first paragraph of our text poses special problems. As commentators often note, the author juxtaposes several distinct explanations of the afterlife, all of them traditional, but not all of them strictly compatible with one another.[6] Verses 103–104, for instance, express belief in a bodily resurrection, while vv. 107–108 assume the separation of the spirit from the body at death, the latter returning to the dust out of which it was originally made. Verse 104 describes the departed as "gods," while vv. 112–113 locate the deceased in Hades, which was ordinarily depicted as a dank and gloomy abode.

On one hand, this sort of incongruity reflects the situation in Second Temple Judaism generally, which tolerated a wide range of perspectives on post-mortem

---

[3] W. T. Schmid, *On Manly Courage*, 95: "True courage … consists in knowledge or wisdom, so that one stands above the world of good and bad fortune and never succumbs, through false understanding of things, to foolish hopes or fears." Cf. Plato, *Lach.* 190B–201C, *Prot.* 360C–D; Aristotle, *Eth. nic.* 3.6.1–12; Xenophon, *Mem.* 4.6.11; Philo, *Spec.* 4.145, *Virt.* 1–4; Cicero, *Off.* 1.81.

[4] Aristotle, *Eth. nic.* 4.3.1–34; Ps.-Aristotle, *Virt. vit.* 5.6–7 (cf. φιλοπονία in 4.4); Schmidt, *Die Ethik der alten Griechen*, 2:450–53; Gauthier, *Magnanimité*, 202–22; J. Ferguson, *Moral Values*, s.v. megalopsuchia; Horst, "μακροθυμία," 374–87.

[5] Cf. Thom, *Golden Verses*, 135–44; further, Sir 38:16–23; *Syr. Men.* 444–473; Isocrates, *Demon.* 42–43, *Nic.* 35–39; P.Ins. 20.7–13.

[6] Collins, *Jewish Wisdom*, 166.

existence.[7] This phenomenon, in turn, can be understood against the background of similar inconsistencies on the subject within the broader Hellenistic world.[8] By the same token, it is important to bear in mind that the particular medium in which our poem communicates its views is gnomic in nature. The point of the passage is not to develop for the readers a coherent thanatological doctrine, but to encourage them not to grieve excessively (vv. 97–98, 118). Toward this end, the author seems to have gathered whatever traditional tenets he can in an effort to help assuage their apprehensions. In the same vein, it is noteworthy that no mention is made of post-mortem judgment, a rather remarkable fact given the text's Jewish origins.[9] Again, the author's tactic seems straightforward enough: anxiety about death and the here-after is unwarranted since everyone will experience the same kind of fate.

Given this strong moral interest, it is not surprising that our passage shares a number of themes with the ancient consolation genre, which utilized traditional beliefs together with philosophical propositions to construct exhortatory discourses addressed to individuals grappling with the death of a loved one.[10] Among the stock themes encountered in this literature are the arguments that:

1. immoderate grief should be avoided, since it is worthless to the mourned and potentially harmful to the mourner (cf. Ps.-Phoc. 97–98);[11]
2. the dead are in a better state than the living (cf. Ps.-Phoc. 103–108, 115);[12]
3. death is the inevitable destiny of all people (cf. Ps.–Phoc. 112–114);[13]
4. since they are beyond human comprehension and control, life's misfortunes should be faced with equanimity (cf. Ps.-Phoc. 118–121).[14]

---

[7] Cf. Cavallin, *Life After Death*, 212: "In the same writings, and even the same passages, concepts and symbols from widely differing anthropologies are used in order to express the hope of personal survival of death: immortality of the soul or resurrection of the body. The writers intend to state that the *personality* survives." Cf. Fischer, *Eschatologie*, 257–58.

[8] Cumont, *After Life*, 1–43; Hopkins, *Death and Renewal*, 226–35; Lattimore, *Epitaphs*, 21–28. Cicero, *Tusc.* 1.18–22, 38, 52, etc. gives evidence for varied philosophical views of the soul and afterlife.

[9] Cf. Sandmel, *Philo*, 116–17.

[10] On consolation: Esteve-Forriol, *Die Trauer- und Trostgedichte*; Kassel, *Konsolationsliteratur*; Stork, *Nil Igitur Mors est ad Nos*, 9–22. Such exhortations were frequently put into verse, e.g., Ovid, *Pont.* 4.11; Ps.-Ovid, *Cons. Liv.*; Catullus, *Carm.* 96; Propertius, *El.* 4.11; Horace, *Carm.* 1.24.

[11] E.g., Plutarch, *Cons. ux.* 608B–C, 609A–B; Ps.-Plutarch, *Cons. Apoll.* 102C–D; Seneca, *Marc.* 3.4, 7.1, 11.1, *Polyb.* 2.1, 4.1, 3, 5.1–2, 18.6, *Helv.* 16.1, *Ep.* 63.1–2, 99.4, 6, 15–16, 27.

[12] E.g., Plutarch, *Cons. ux.* 611D–612A; Ps.-Plutarch, *Cons. Apoll.* 106C–108E; Seneca, *Marc.* 19.4–5, 20.6, 23.1–2, 24.5, 25.1, 3, 26.6, *Polyb.* 9.7–8; Ps.-Ovid, *Cons. Liv.* 329–340; Menander Rhetor, *Epid.* 2.414.

[13] E.g., Ps.–Plutarch, *Cons. Apoll.* 103F–104C; Seneca, *Marc.* 6.2, 10.5–6, 11.1, 15.4, *Polyb.* 9.9, 11.1, 3–4, 17.1, *Ep.* 63.15–16, 99.6–9; Ps.-Ovid, *Cons. Liv.* 357–360; Menander Rhetor, *Epid.* 3.414.

[14] E.g., Plutarch, *Cons. ux.* 610E; Ps.-Plutarch, *Cons. Apoll.* 102F–103A; Seneca, *Polyb.* 9.5, 11.5, *Ep.* 63.7–8, 99.9, *Marc.* 9.2, *Helv.* 5.1, 5; Ps.-Ovid, *Cons. Liv.* 51–52.

In keeping with the philosophical ethos described above, the overarching goal of these kinds of arguments was to instill fortitude in the recipient. Ps.-Socratics, *Ep.* 21.3, for example, sums up its message of consolation with the appeal, "Be of good courage," while Teles avers that both men and women ought to bear the loss of a loved one "in a manly and courageous manner" (frg. 7.108).[15] Compare Plutarch, *Tranq. an.* 476B ("He who reflects on the nature of the soul and the change it undergoes at death secures tranquility of mind for facing life – fearlessness toward death.") and Seneca, *Helv.* 15.4: "The harder these circumstances are, the more courage must you summon, and you must engage with fortune the more fiercely, as with an enemy well known and often conquered before."[16]

---

[15] Cf. Seneca, *Marc.* 1.1, 2.4, 5.5, 15.2, 16.3, *Polyb.* 5.4, 6.2, 11.3, 14.5, 17.2, 4, 18.5, *Helv.* 15.3–4, 16.5, 7, 19.4, 7, *Ep.* 99.14; Teles, frg. 7.38–63.

[16] For the martial imagery, cf. Seneca, *Marc.* 1.2, 5, 10.4, *Polyb.* 5.4, 6.1–2, *Helv.* 2.1, 3.1, 5.2; Plutarch, *Cons. ux.* 609F–610A.

A. Verses 97–115

97   Weaken not your dear heart sitting in vain by the fire.
98   Make moderate your lamentations, for moderation is best.
99   Reserve a share of earth for the unburied dead.
100   Do not dig up the grave of the deceased, nor reveal
101   what may not be seen to the sun and incite divine wrath.
102   It is not good to dismantle a human frame.
103   And we hope, too, that quickly from the earth to the light will come
104   the remains of the departed; and then they become gods.
105   For souls remain unscathed in the deceased.
106   For the spirit is a loan from God to mortals, and is God's image.
107   For we possess a body out of earth; and then, when into earth again
108   we are resolved, we are dust; but the air has received our spirit.
109   When you are wealthy do not be sparing; remember that you are a mortal.
110   It is impossible to carry wealth and goods with you into Hades.
111   All the dead are alike, and God rules over their souls.
112   Their shared, eternal home and fatherland is Hades,
113   a common place for all, both poor and kings.
114   We humans live no long time, but only briefly.
115   But the soul lives immortal and ageless forever.

TEXTUAL NOTES

Verse 97. For the phrase φίλον ἦτορ, cf. Homer, *Il.* 5.250, 13.84, 21.114, etc. Some mss., missing the allusion, replace φίλον (in M, B) with τεὸν (L, V) or τεὴν (P). Verse 98a. Following Bernays (*Gesammelte Abhandlungen*, 200–202), Diehl (*Anthologia*, 2.105) and van der Horst (*Sentences*, 95 n. 2, 180), who read γόοισι instead of θεοῖσι in the mss. Derron (*Sentences*, 9, 25–26) opts for the latter, translating: "mais honore modérément les dieux." Young (*Theognis*, 103) conjectures τεῦχ᾽ ἔθ᾽ ἑοῖσι, which he translates: "modum impone etiam tuis" (cf. Walter, *Poetische Schriften*, 206: "<rate auch den Deinen zur Mäßigung>"); but cf. West (*CR* 30 [1980]: 137) and Derron (*Sentences*, 25–26). Also cf. H. J. de Jonge in *NedTT* 33 (1979): 246: τεῦχ᾽ ἐθέεσσι. Verse 99. For this use of ἐπιμοιρᾶσθαι, cf. Philo, *Mos.* 2.283. Verse 100. ἀνορύσσω + τάφος (which can have the same meaning as τύμβος): Isocrates, *Big.* 26; Herodotus, *Hist.* 1.68, cf. 2.41. // P, L replace φθιμένων (in M, B, V) with νεκύων. The former in reference to the dead (also in v. 105) is Homeric; see LSJ s.v. φθίνω I.2.b; cf. Lattimore, *Epitaphs*, 56–57. The phrase τύμβον φθιμένων is familiar especially from the *Anthologia Graeca*, e.g., 7.426.1, 7.456.4, 7.615.2, 8.117.1,

8.215.3. Verse 101. For the phrase δαιμόνιον χόλον, cf. Dionysius of Halicarnassus, *Ant. rom.* 1.23.1, 3.5.1, 3.23.20, 8.52.3, 9.6.6. Verse 102. For ἁρμονία used "of the human frame," see LSJ s.v. I.4. // LSJ s.v. ἀναλύω II.3.b: "to resolve into its elements, undo, dissolve, loose." Verse 104a. λείψαν' ἀποιχομένων here refers to the physical remains of the dead; for the former, cf. Sophocles, *El.* 1113; *Sib. Or.* 3.646; and LSJ s.v. λείψανον 2; for the latter, cf. Pindar, *Pyth.* 1.93; and LSJ s.v. ἀποίχομαι 3. Verse 107. M, P, L, V: γάρ; B: μέν. // πρὸς αὖ γῆν is only in V; cf. P (– γῆ), L (πρὸς γῆν), B (καὶ πυρὸς αὐγήν; cf. v. 97), M², L²ʸᵖ (πρὸς αὐτήν). Verse 109. B, P, L, V: φείδου. M: γαυροῦ (cf. v. 53). Verse 110. οὐκ ἔνι εἰς is only in M²; cf. M, B, Lʸᵖ (οὐκὲν), P, L, V (οὐκ ἐς). // ἔνι = ἔνεστι, "it is possible," see LSJ s.v. ἔνειμι. Verse 111. M, B place this line after v. 112. Verse 112. For μέλαθρα δόμων, cf. Aeschylus, *Ag.* 851, 957. Verse 114. LSJ s.v. ἐπίκαιρος II: "for a time;" cf. Epictetus, *Gnom.* 8.

COMMENTARY

Verses 97–98. When Ben Sira offers instruction on proper burial and mourning in 38:16–23, he begins by urging the family to observe custom and provide the deceased a proper burial (v. 16). But after mourning for a day or two, the reader should begin to console himself, since "from grief comes death, and the heart's grief breaks one's strength" (v. 18). He goes on, saying: "do not give your heart to grief … you will do (the deceased) no good and hurt yourself" (vv. 20–21). In his treatment of the topic, Pseudo-Phocylides agrees in identifying three (presumably interrelated) priorities: to bury the dead, to be moderate in mourning, and to protect one's "heart" from excessive grief. The presence of similar themes in *Syr. Men.* 458–467 suggests a conventional pattern: a mourner should not vex himself with excessive sorrow, but should accompany the departed to the tomb for burial and "overcome his groaning."

The ancient psychology of grief often focused on the heart, for example, Homer, *Od.* 10.485–486 ("My comrades … make my dear heart waste away, as they sit about me mourning.") and P.Ins. 20.7 ("Do not worry your heart with the bitterness of one who is dying."), cf. 17.5–6. As Theognis, *El.* 361 observes, the heart "shrinks" (μινύθει) when faced with great trouble.[17] Warnings about the injury accompanying intemperate bereavement are commonplace, for example, Teles, frg. 7.84–86 ("But how is it not illogical, and futile as well, to sit weeping and grieving and even destroying oneself over the friend who has died?") and Ps.-Socratics, *Ep.* 21.1: "By grieving constantly you will harm both yourself and especially your children."

---

[17] Cf. "Do not eat your heart," one of the Pythagorean *akousmata*, which in Diogenes Laertius, *Vit. phil.* 8.17–18 is taken to mean, "Do not waste your life in troubles and cares."

Verse 98b essentially restates the rule of v. 69B, that "of all things moderation is best" (cf. also v. 59), applying it in this context to the expression of one's lamentations (γόοι).[18] If this refers principally to the weeping and wailing associated with mourning rites, then we may infer a different focus from v. 97, the former drawing attention to the problem of inner sorrow, the latter to visible demonstrations of grief. The pointless as well as destructive aspects of such demonstrations are asserted by Sophocles, *El.* 137–141: "But you will never raise up your father from the lake of Hades, to which all must come, by weeping (γόοισιν) or prayers. Rather, leaving moderation (μετρίων) aside and plunging into irresistible grief you ever lament, to your ruin." As Seneca contends, "There is such a thing as moderation even in grieving."[19]

Verses 99–102. Both Philo and Josephus mention burial rules in their summaries of the law. Josephus names as a general responsibility the duty "not to let anyone lie unburied" (*C. Ap.* 2.211). Philo lists the following among the "unwritten" customs of the Jews: "No one should debar the dead from burial, but should throw upon them as much earth as piety demands. No one should disturb in any way the graves or tombs of the dead" (*Hypoth.* 7.7). Pseudo-Phocylides echoes Philo in attaching an injunction against tomb violation (see vv. 100–102) to a command about interment (v. 99), indicating that he here follows the order of their common source. All three authors address what was widely felt by ancient people to be a time-honored and sacred duty, one upheld in part because of "the belief that denial of a proper burial ... angered the soul of the dead man and was productive of misfortunes for the living."[20] Jewish tradition was of course no exception in this regard;[21] Tobit, for example, counts burying the dead among acts of piety that protect the vulnerable, like almsgiving.[22] In the Greco-Roman world, this was one of the "unwritten laws" as well as one of the so-called Buzygian laws.[23]

It is noteworthy that the poet draws attention in vv. 100–102 not to the violation of the tomb itself, but to the disinterment of the corpse, in anticipation of vv.

---

[18] Cf. 3 Macc 1:18, 4:3, 6, 5:49; *Sib. Or.* 3.417; Homer, *Od.* 4.103, 758.

[19] Seneca, *Marc.* 3.4; cf. Isocrates, *Demon.* 42 ("Grieve in moderation over the evils that befall you."); Teles, frg. 7.111–112; Ps.-Charondas, *Prooem.* 2.62.8–11; Ps.-Plutarch, *Cons. Apoll.* 102D; Philo, *Abr.* 257–258; Cicero, *Leg.* 2.59–60.

[20] Dover, *Popular Morality*, 244.

[21] See Deut 21:23; Ps 78:2–3; Jer 16:4, 22:19; cf. Matt 8:21–22; Hengel, *Charismatic Leader*, 8–15; Str-B 1:487.

[22] Tob 1:16–18; cf. 2:7, 4:3–4, 8:12, 12:12–13, 14:9; *5 Ezra* 2:20–23.

[23] E.g., Sophocles, *Ant.* 450–470; Euripides, *Suppl.* 524–541; Isocrates, *Panath.* 169–170; Dio Chrysostom, *Consuet.* 5; Pausanias, *Descr.* 1.32.5; Horace, *Carm.* 1.28 (2); Virgil, *Aen.* 6.365; P.Ins. 2.9–13; Crouch, *Haustafel*, 40–45, 87; Hirzel, ΑΓΡΑΦΟΣ ΝΟΜΟΣ, 65–69; van der Horst, *Sentences*, 181.

103–104.[24] While neither the thought nor the language here are particularly biblical, we may compare Jer 8:1–3, where the remains of the Jerusalemites are removed from their graves and "spread before the sun" as a sign of divine punishment.[25] In Isocrates, *Big.* 26, digging up the tombs of an opponent's family is presented as an act of extreme animosity. Given the repulsion people felt toward such behavior, appropriate counter steps were often taken. Cicero, for instance, refers to a law of Solon about graves to the effect that "no one is to destroy them," with a penalty fixed "in case anyone violates, throws down, or breaks a burial mound ... or monument or column" (*Leg.* 2.64). That those guilty of such desecrations would incur not only human but also divine ire was a stock theme of sepulchral inscriptions, which evidence a widespread desire to safeguard burial sites as sacred places. Epitaphs intended to protect the tomb often conveyed imprecations on transgressors, for example, "Whoever does anything counter to the injunctions set forth above ... may he find the underground gods angry avengers."[26] Compare also this example from first-century c.e. Crete: "You who pass by, do not injure my sacred grave, lest you incur the sharp anger of Agesilaos and Persephone."[27]

Van der Horst conjectures that vv. 100–102 have to do with the exhumation of corpses for dissection. However, it is both "highly probable that dissection was practiced only in Alexandria" and questionable whether this practice continued in Roman times.[28] Given the gnomic ethos of the poem, with its tendency toward universalizing, such a localized meaning seems unlikely. Instead, corpse desecration of a more general nature seems to be in view here, a crime denounced also in the following inscriptional edict:[29]

> Ordinance of Caesar: It is my pleasure that graves and tombs ... remain unmolested in perpetuity. But if any person gives information that another either has destroyed (καταλελυκότα; cf. ἀναλυέμεν in Ps.-Phoc. 102) them, or has in any other way cast out the bodies which have been buried there, or with malicious deception has transferred them to other places ... in such a cases I command that a trial be instituted.

---

[24] Cf. Wedderburn, *Baptism and Resurrection*, 179–80.

[25] Cf. 4 Kgdms 23:16–18; Tob 2:4; Horace, *Epod.* 16.13–14 (exposing bones to the sun is hateful).

[26] *CIG* 3915, cited by Lattimore, *Epitaphs*, 116, cf. 106–25.

[27] van der Horst, *Epitaphs*, 55; for other defensive threats, see pp. 54–60. This is a regular theme in the *Anthologia Graeca* as well, e.g., 8.234 ("Avoid the wrath of the spirits who haunt me, for I contain nothing else; the tomb's sole riches are bones."), cf. 8.114–117, 213–217, 230–235.

[28] van der Horst, *Sentences*, 183–84, with further references, to which add Scarborough, *Roman Medicine*, 168–70.

[29] van der Horst, *Epitaphs*, 159–60: text and translation of *SEG* 8.13, a first- or second-century c.e. inscription, probably found in Nazareth.

In addition to such malevolent acts, Ps.-Phoc. 100–102 might also be taken to prohibit secondary burial, a custom known in Roman Judaea and elsewhere.[30]

Verses 103–104. This is one of the few sections of the poem that clearly reveals its Jewish origins. While tales of resuscitated corpses were not unknown in the Greco-Roman world,[31] belief in the physical resurrection of the dead was a distinctive tenet of Judaism and Christianity.[32] Of particular interest are texts that, like Pseudo-Phocylides, anticipate the exaltation of the resurrected, such as Dan 12:2–3 ("Many of those who sleep in the dust shall be raised, some to everlasting life … and the wise will shine as the brightness of the firmament, and many of the righteous as the stars forever.") and Luke 20:35–36 ("Those who are considered worthy of a place … in the resurrection from the dead … are like angels and are children of God."). In his survey of Jewish texts that treat the afterlife, Hans Cavallin identifies as a recurring motif descriptions that liken the risen righteous to "stars, angels, and other heavenly bodies or beings."[33] Given that such beings were generally understood to be divine in nature,[34] Pseudo-Phocylides' use of θεοί in this context is not altogether surprising, probably referring in the first place to the status the resurrected will enjoy as immortals; cf. vv. 105 (note the γάρ) and 115.[35] What is surprising is that, for our author, resurrection appears to have no judiciary function or aspect whatsoever, as it does in most all Jewish or Christian writings that express this hope. The text projects a scenario in which the remains of all people, not just the worthy, are deified.

Post-mortem deification was also a goal in certain Greco-Roman circles, as we learn from the conclusion to the *Carmen aureum*, which promises the obedient

---

[30] See Meyers, *Jewish Ossuaries*, 71–92; Finegan, *Archaeology*, 216–18; Figueras, *Decorated Jewish Ossuaries*, 1–23.

[31] Myths of people being resuscitated from the dead: Apollodorus, *Bibl.* 1.9.15, 3.3.1–2; Pliny, *Nat.* 29.1.3; Pausanias, *Descr.* 2.26.5, 2.27.4; Ovid, *Fast.* 6.733–762; cf. Plato, *Resp.* 614B; Aristotle, *De an.* 1.3; Xenophon, *Cyn.* 1.6. As Wedderburn (*Baptism and Resurrection*, 165) observes, a distinction can be made between resurrection as the means by which all people or a certain class of people enter their final state of being, and a raising which simply restores a particular individual temporarily to his/her previous mode of existence on earth, which still ends in death.

[32] *4 Ezra* 7:32; *1 En.* 51:1–5; *2 Bar.* 42:7–8, 50:2; *T. Benj.* 10:6–7; *Apoc. Mos.* 13:3; *L.A.B.* 3:10; etc. Collins, *Jewish Wisdom*, 165: the concept of physical resurrection is exceptional in Jewish literature written in Greek, though see 2 Macc 7:9–14, 12:44, 14:46; *Sib. Or.* 4.181–191.

[33] Cavallin, *Life After Death*, 203–205; cf. *4 Ezra* 7:97; *1 En.* 104:2–6; *2 Bar.* 51:5–12; 1QH XI, 19–23; 1Q28b III, 25–26; Matt 22:30.

[34] Cf. above, on vv. 71–75; also Philo, *Opif.* 55, 144, *Gig.* 8, *Migr.* 184, *Abr.* 159, *Spec.* 1.19, *Quaest. Gen.* 4.87; 1QM XVII, 7; 1QH XVIII, 8; Elior, "Mysticism, Magic, and Angelology," 3–53. Cf. Fletcher-Louis, *All the Glory of Adam*, xii: "the theology of ancient Judaism took for granted the belief that in its original, true, redeemed state humanity is divine (and/or angelic)."

[35] Cf. 4 Macc 18:3; Wis 5:5 (with Winston, *Wisdom*, 147); 4Q181 I, 3–4 (with Cavallin, *Life After Death*, 65).

that, "when you leave the body behind and go to the free ether, you will be immortal, an undying god, no longer mortal" (vv. 70–71).[36] In typically Greek fashion, though, becoming an immortal god presupposes not bodily resurrection but the soul's separation from the body (see below, on vv. 107–108). Compare Sallustius, *Deis mund.* 21: "Souls that have lived in accordance with virtue … purified from all body they are in union with the gods and share with them the government of the whole universe." Similar is Seneca's opinion that after death souls "find no joy lingering in the body," but rather "journey to the gods," flying back "to the source of their being" (*Marc.* 23.1–2).[37] A possible exception to the rule is provided by an interesting funerary inscription that associates the σῶμα of the deceased with her astral immortality: "Untouched and not concerned with a husband you made haste to join the immortals, purifying your body with the stars of heaven."[38]

Verses 105–108. The soul's immortality will be professed shortly, in v. 115. In v. 105 we have the closely related theme of the soul's incorruptibility. That it survives death "unharmed and undestroyed" was a thanatological principle advanced by philosophers like Plato,[39] as well as by philosophically inclined Jews.[40] In order to understand this maxim's place in its context, it is important to recognize that in vv. 105–106 ψυχή and πνεῦμα (cf. v. 108) are being used synonymously, a phenomenon with some precedent in Hellenistic Jewish anthropological reflection.[41] Thus the assertion of v. 106 is made in support of the preceding verse: the soul (i.e., spirit) survives bodily death because (γάρ) its origin and image are divine.

That human life is only a "loan" was a cliché of the consolation literature; eventually it must be returned.[42] The symbolism enjoyed a Platonic pedigree; according to *Tim.* 42E, when fashioning humankind the young gods, "imitating their own

---

[36] See Thom, *Golden Verses*, 226–27, who compares these lines with the Orphic Gold Leaves.

[37] Cf. Plutarch, *Suav. viv.* 1105E, *Rom.* 28.7–8; Lucian, *Hermot.* 7; Diogenes Laertius, *Vit. phil.* 8.68–69; Pausanias, *Descr.* 2.32.1; Cicero, *Tusc.* 1.75–76, *Amic.* 3.12, 4.13. Deification is also a common theme in funerary inscriptions, e.g., *IG* 12.7.123.5–6 ("Mother, do not weep for me … for I have become an evening star, among the gods."), *EG* 340.7 ("I have gone to the gods and I am among the immortals."), *SEG* 8.473–475 ("No longer, my daughter, shall I make sacrifice to you with lamentation, now that I know you have become divine."); see Lattimore, *Epitaphs*, 35, 49, 100–101, cf. 33–43.

[38] *SEG* 4.727, quoted by Lattimore, *Epitaphs*, 50, cf. 42. For affirmations of celestial immortality, cf. Aristophanes, *Pax* 832–841; Seneca, *Marc.* 25.3, *Polyb.* 9.8; Pliny, *Nat.* 2.26.95; Cassius Dio, *Hist.* 69.11.4; Cumont, *After Life*, 91–109.

[39] Plato, *Phaed.* 106E, cf. *Resp.* 608C–610A.

[40] Wis 3:1; Philo, *Quaest. Gen.* 1.16, 3.11; Josephus, *Bell.* 2.163; cf. Sextus, *Sent.* 397.

[41] E.g., Wis 16:14; *T. Abr.* (A) 16:15–17:3; Josephus, *Ant.* 3.260, 11.240; cf. BDAG s.v. πνεῦμα 3.a, ψυχή 2.f.

[42] E.g., Ps.-Plutarch, *Cons. Apoll.* 106F–107A; Seneca, *Polyb.* 10.4–5, *Marc.* 10.1–2; Ps.-Ovid, *Cons. Liv.* 369–370.

Maker, borrowed from the cosmos portions of fire, earth, water, and air, as if meaning to pay them back."[43] The same concept appears in Hellenistic Jewish literature, partly informed perhaps by reflection on Gen 6:3 ("My spirit shall not remain in mortals forever, because they are flesh."), cf. 2:7.[44] Faced with the loss of his wife, for example, Abraham countered his sorrow "with strength and courage," and strove for moderation of feeling (cf. Ps.-Phoc. 98), not resenting the fact "that nature should be paid the debt which is its due" (Philo, *Abr.* 256–257).

For his part, Pseudo-Phocylides augments the symbolism with "God's loan … and image," an obvious reference to Gen 1:26–27. Inasmuch as its subject is the human soul, though, and not the human creature as such, this line approximates Hellenized interpretations of the Genesis passage such as Philo, *Spec.* 1.171 ("The rational spirit … is shaped according to the archetypal form of the divine image.").[45] For Philo, the status of the rational or spiritual element of the human personality as the divine image served as an assurance of its immortality (e.g., *Plant.* 44), a connection made also by Wis 2:23: "God created humankind for immortality and made them in the image of his own proper being."[46]

Verses 107–108 build on the imagery of human life as a loan introduced in v. 106, specifying the nature of the repayment that takes place at death. Compare Wis 15:8: "These mortals who were made of earth a short time before after a little while go to the earth from which all mortals are taken, when the time comes to return the souls that were borrowed." It was a standard biblical teaching that the human body, composed of earth, dust, or ashes, eventually must revert to that out of which it was made, for example, Gen 3:19 ("You are earth and to earth you shall return.") and Qoh 3:20: "All were formed from dust and all will return to dust."[47] Later witnesses also express the idea that the human spirit separates from the body at death so as to return to its true home, for example, *4 Ezra* 7:78 ("The spirit leaves the body to return again to Him who gave it.") and Philo, *Abr.* 258 ("Death is not the extinction of the soul but its separation … from the body and its return to the place whence it came … from God.").[48]

---

[43] Cf. Plato, *Phaedr.* 248E; Ps.-Plato, *Ax.* 367B; Epictetus, *Diatr.* 1.1.32; Lucretius, *De rerum nat.* 3.970–971; Cicero, *Tusc.* 1.93; and Winston, *Wisdom*, 286–87 for more examples.

[44] Wis 15:8; Philo, *Cher.* 118, *Post.* 5, *Gig.* 13, *Her.* 104, *Spec.* 1.295; Josephus, *Bell.* 3.372, 374; *1 En.* 51:1; *L.A.B.* 3:10, 33:3; cf. Luke 12:20; Sextus, *Sent.* 21 ("Consider that your soul is a deposit from God.").

[45] Cf. Philo, *Her.* 57; Philo can also speak of the human soul or mind as the divine image, e.g., *Opif.* 69, *Somn.* 1.74, *Spec.* 1.81, 3.207; cf. Jervell, *Imago Dei*, 52–70.

[46] Cf. Merki, "Ebenbildlichkeit," 459–79.

[47] Cf. Gen 18:27; Ps 102:14; Job 10:9, 34:15; Sir 17:1, 40:11; 1 Cor 15:47–49; P.Ins. 30.6; *Apoc. Mos.* 41:2–3.

[48] Cf. Tob 3:6; Ps 103:29, 145:4; Qoh 12:7; Wis 2:3 ("The body will turn to ashes and the spirit will vanish as the empty air."); *Sib. Or.* 8.108–109; Philo, *Leg. all.* 1.105, 2.77, *Jos.* 264.

Such affirmations, including especially the motif of the spirit or soul leaving the body at death to return to the air, were characteristically Greek,[49] Euripides, *Suppl.* 531–536 being illustrative: "Let now the dead be hidden in the earth, and each part, whence it came forth to the light, thither return, the spirit to the air, and the body to the earth; for we hold it not in fee, but only to pass life therein; then she which fostered it must take it back." The formulation of the following Roman funerary inscription is particularly close to that of Ps.-Phoc. 107–108: "He has returned his soul to the air and his body to the earth" (τὴν ψυχὴν ἀπέδωκεν ἐς ἀέρα, σῶμα δὲ πρὸς γῆν.).[50] Ether could also be identified as the place or medium in which the detached soul enjoys immortality, for example, a fifth-century b.c.e. epigram for the Athenians slain at Potidaea proclaims: "the ether received their souls, the earth their bodies."[51] Since ether was the material out of which the soul was fashioned, it stood to reason that this would be its natural abode.[52] Josephus' (Hellenized) account of the Essenes reports the belief that although the body is corruptible the immortal soul emanates from the ether, being born aloft after death (*Bell.* 2.154–155).[53]

Verses 109–113. It is possible to interpret vv. 109–110 as an extension of the preceding argument in vv. 107–108: everything is lost in death except one's soul. Here the contemplation of human mortality is utilized to make a point about the vanity and transience of material wealth, a popular topic in antiquity.[54] As the Psalmist observes, the rich man "will take nothing when he dies; neither will his glory descend with him" (48:18).[55] The argument in vv. 109–110 coincides with thoughts

---

[49] Lattimore, *Epitaphs*, 28–43, e.g., *IG* 9.2.641.6 (cited on p. 32): "The soul given to the air and the body concealed in dust." Further: Epictetus, *Diatr.* 3.10.14, 3.22.34; *Orph. hymn.* 87.3; Plutarch, *Rom.* 28.6–7 (At death, the soul "flies from the body as lightning flashes from a cloud," returning to the gods, from whom it came.); Cicero, *Tusc.* 1.24 ("Souls, on their separation from the body, find their way to heaven as to their dwelling-place."); Marcus Aurelius, *Med.* 4.21; *Anth. Gr.* 7.337.7–8; Menander Rhetor, *Epid.* 2.414.

[50] *EG* 642, quoted by Lattimore, *Epitaphs*, 32.

[51] *EG* 21b, quoted by Lattimore, *Epitaphs*, 31.

[52] Lattimore, *Epitaphs*, 32–33: the ether was the "upper air about the stars and planets … imagined as the home of the gods and of those dead whose blessed and indestructible estate makes them virtually the equals of the gods." Examples are given on pp. 32–35, 40. Also cf. Euripides, *Hel.* 1014–1016; Ps.-Plato, *Ax.* 366A; *Carm. aur.* 70–71 (with Thom, *Golden Verses*, 224–26); Stobaeus, *Anth.* 1.49.46; Cicero, *Tusc.* 1.51; Waszink, "Aether," 150–58; Burkert, *Greek Religion*, 319–20.

[53] Cf. Neusner, *Death*, 167: "Philo sees rational souls as associated with the air, the heavens, and divinity. Human souls are of the same general substance as those who make up the ranks of the angels and the stars." E.g., *Opif.* 144, *Sacr.* 5, *Gig.* 9, *Somn.* 1.137–145.

[54] Cf. Pindar, *Nem.* 11.13–16: "But, if any man who has riches, excelling others in beauty of form, and is wont to display prowess by his courage in the games, let him remember that mortal are the limbs he robes, and that, in the end of all, he will be clad in a vesture of clay."

[55] Cf. Job 1:21; 1 Tim 6:7; Philo, *Spec.* 1.295; P.Ins. 18.12–13; Theognis, *El.* 725–726 ("No one takes all his exceeding riches with him to Hades."); Menander, *Mon.* 87 ("No mortal carries along wealth

expressed earlier in the poem about wealth, or ὄλβος, viz., that it is unstable (v. 27) and that taking pride in it is unwarranted since God alone is πολύολβος (vv. 53–54). Obviously, one cannot overcome life's limits by amassing possessions or riches. Although somewhat incongruous with the advice of v. 138, the basic point here seems clear enough: do not be preoccupied with the accumulation of possessions but put what wealth you have to good use. Such advice against illiberality had roots in the Jewish wisdom tradition. The formulation of vv. 109–110 approximates that of *Syr. Men.* 368–373 (cf. 380–381): "If you have goods, if you have possessions, live on your possessions as long as you are alive … For remember and see: one (can)not use (his) goods in Sheol, and riches do not accompany one into the grave." As Sir 14:3 explains, "wealth is unbecoming for a miser," since no one derives any benefit from it; a bit later the text continues:[56]

> According to what you have, treat yourself well … Before you die treat your friend well … Do not deprive yourself of a good day, and let not a portion of good desire pass you by. Will you leave your labors to another, and your earnings to be divided by lot? Give and take and charm your soul, for there is no pursuit of luxury in Hades.

In contrast to Ben Sira, who encourages the reader to enjoy his prosperity himself or use it to win friends, Pseudo-Phocylides advises that wealth be used to aid the poor; see v. 28.[57]

Verses 111–113 continue the thought, commenting on both the ubiquity and equality of death; note the emphatic position of κοινά and ξυνός (also ἴσον and ἄπασι). The final destiny of humanity is the same, and they all will experience that destiny in the same way, regardless of their previous stations in life. Although God is said to "rule" over the souls of the dead, no mention is made of post-mortem judgment or of any differentiation of human experience in the hereafter. Attention is drawn instead to the common "home" that all humankind will eventually share, where everyone will always be "alike." All of the author's comments here would have been in keeping with traditional assumptions about the afterlife. To begin with, we are presented with the idea that there is no favoritism in the administration of death, for example, Lucian, *Dial. mort.* 30.2: "In Hades there is equality (ἰσοτιμία) and all

---

when he departs."); Seneca, *Ep.* 102.25; Propertius, *El.* 3.5.13–18: "You will take no wealth to the waters of Acheron … Croesus of Lydia differs not from Irus of Dulichium: that death is best which comes when life has been first enjoyed."

[56] Sir 14:11–16; cf. Skehan and DiLella, *Ben Sira*, 257–61; also Qoh 5:12–19; Sir 11:18–19.

[57] Cf. Theognis, *El.* 905–909: "For if it were possible for us to see the end of our life, and know with how much accomplished we were to pass over into Hades, it would be reasonable that anyone who expected the lot of longer life should be more sparing (φείδεσθαι), so as to have something to live on." Also, Aeschylus, *Pers.* 840–842; Menander, *Dysk.* 805–812; Teles, frg. 4A.67–75; *Carm. aur.* 38; *Dict. Cat.* 3.9; P.Ins. 17.7–19; Gerhard, *Phoinix*, 57–62.

are alike (ὅμοιοι)." According to *Orph. hymn.* 87.1–8, death is "common" (κοινός) to all insofar as it guides the course of all mortals, executing upon each the same verdict.[58] The irrelevance of socio-economic distinctions in death is another commonplace (in this case building on the observations of vv. 109–110). As Job 3:13–19 explains, death is the final destiny for kings, the rich, the ungodly, and the weary: "the small and the great are there." Compare also *Sib. Or.* 8.107–108 ("Night is equal to all at once, to those who have wealth and to beggars.") and Horace, *Carm.* 1.4.13–14: "Pale Death with foot impartial knocks at the poor man's cottage and at princes' palaces."[59] For the motif of the "eternal home," *Syr. Men.* 127 ("All men go to the eternal house – they are mortal.") and *Gnom. Vat.* 31 ("When it comes to death, all people live in a city without walls.") are representative.[60] In keeping with the popular conception, our author images death here mythologically as a spatial and social phenomenon.[61] He assumes also its divine governance, though it is not Hades or Persephone who rules here, but rather the same θεός of vv. 1, 8, 11, 17, 29, 54, 106, and 125. The God who creates and judges humankind also determines its existence in the afterworld.

Verses 114–115. These lines exhibit a structure similar to that of vv. 107–108 and 111: a concession regarding an unhappy reality of human existence countered by an assertion based on beliefs about life in the hereafter. In v. 114, Pseudo-Phocylides registers a common complaint of both Jewish and Greco-Roman authors. As Job 10:20 puts it, the *chronos* of human life is short; cf. *Syr. Men.* 391–392 ("Short and limited is the space of life which God determines for men.").[62]

A distinctive feature of the paragraph in vv. 97–115 is the frequency with which the author includes himself in its observations (cf. vv. 103, 107–108); in v. 114 we learn that all people, even "the wisest of men" (v. 2), live but for a season.[63] The

---

58 Cf. Ps 88:49 ("What person is there who shall live and not see death? Who will deliver his soul from the hand of Hades?"); Qoh 3:20, 6:6; Wis 7:6; Homer, *Od.* 3.236–238; Menander, *Mon.* 110, frg. 538; Isocrates, *Demon.* 43 ("Death is the sentence fate has passed on all humanity."); *Carm. aur.* 15; *Instr. Ankh.* 8.8.

59 Cf. Lucian, *Dial. mort.* 1.4; Plautus, *Trin.* 493–494; Propertius, *El.* 3.5.13–17; Horace, *Carm.* 2.18.32–34; Seneca, *Marc.* 20.2, *Ep.* 91.16; *T. Abr.* (A) 8:9, 19:7.

60 Cf. Tob 3:6; Ps 48:12; Qoh 12:5; Diodorus Siculus, *Bibl.* 1.51.2; Cicero, *Nat. d.* 3.41; Stommel, "Domus aeterna," 109–28; Lattimore, *Epitaphs*, 165–67. For "the house of Hades," cf. Homer, *Il.* 22.52, 482, 23.19, 103, 179, *Od.* 4.834, 10.175, 491, 11.69, etc.; Euripides, *Alc.* 25, 73, 436, 626; Lattimore, *Epitaphs*, 53, 87.

61 On the Hades myth, see Burkert, *Greek Religion*, 194–99; Garland, *Greek Way of Death*, 48–76; Bremmer, "Hades," 382–83.

62 Cf. Ps 102:15; Job 14:1; Wis 2:1, 9:5; Isa 40:6; *2 Bar.* 48:12; Herodotus, *Hist.* 7.46; Ps.-Plutarch, *Lib. ed.* 13B; Seneca, *Marc.* 21.1–2, *Brev. vit.* 1.1–2, *Ep.* 99.7, 9–10; Marcus Aurelius, *Med.* 4.26; Lucretius, *De rerum nat.* 3.914–915; Catullus, *Carm.* 5.4–6; Stobaeus, *Anth.* 4.34.

63 Cf. the "self"-presentation of Solomon in Wis 7:1–6.

response to this in v. 115 builds on the claim made earlier in v. 105. Not only does the soul survive death, it continues "immortal and ageless" through time, invoking a Homeric expression.[64] For this pair of descriptors we may compare also the following funerary inscriptions: "Formerly I was mortal, now I am immortal and ageless (ἀθάνατος καὶ ἀγήρως);"[65] "Parthenis lies here. She is ageless and immortal (ἀγήρατος ἀθανάτη τε)."[66]

The Greek idea of the immortality of the soul[67] made an impression on a number of Second Temple Jewish texts written in Greek,[68] for example, Josephus, *Bell.* 3.372 ("All of us, it is true, have mortal bodies, composed of perishable matter, but the soul lives forever, immortal; it is a portion of the Deity housed in our bodies."), though even *1 Enoch* could write that "the spirits of those who die in righteousness shall live and rejoice; their spirits shall not perish" (103:4).[69] The author's assurance serves as an apt conclusion to a paragraph urging against excessive grief over death.

---

[64] Homer, *Il.* 8.539, *Od.* 5.218; cf. Homer, *Il.* 2.447, 12.323; Hesiod, *Theog.* 949.

[65] Lattimore, *Epitaphs*, 100. For assertions of immortality of the soul in Greco-Roman epitaphs: Lattimore, *Epitaphs*, 36, 48–55.

[66] *EG* 634, quoted by Lattimore, *Epitaphs*, 49.

[67] For arguments that the soul is immortal, see especially Plato's *Phaedo*, with Bostock, *Phaedo*, 21–41 and passim. Cf. Plato, *Tim.* 69C, *Phaedr.* 245C, *Resp.* 608D; Herodotus, *Hist.* 2.123; Ps.-Plutarch, *Cons. Apoll.* 120D; Cicero, *Tusc.* 1.31, 55; Seneca, *Marc.* 26.6, *Polyb.* 9.7–8; Lattimore, *Epitaphs*, 35–36, 44–65.

[68] 4 Macc 18:23; Philo, *Opif.* 154, *Conf.* 149, *Jos.* 264, *Quaest. Gen.* 1.16; Josephus, *Ant.* 18.14, 18, *Bell.* 1.650, 2.154; Wolfson, *Philo*, 1:395–413.

[69] Cf. Hengel, *Judaism and Hellenism*, 196–202.

B. Verses 118–121

118   Neither be distressed by evils nor overjoyed by success.
119   Often in life unbelievable suffering comes to the confident
120   and to the distressed a sudden release from evil.
121   Minister to the moment: do not blow against the winds.

TEXTUAL NOTES

[Verse 116.] "No one knows what is to be after tomorrow or after an hour." (οὐδεὶς
γινώσκει, τί μετ' αὔριον ἢ τί μεθ' ὥραν.) A spurious verse (only in V); see van der
Horst, *Sentences*, 195–96. [Verse 117.] "Obscure is the death of mortals; the future
is unclear." (ἄσκοπός ἐστι βροτῶν θάνατος, τὸ δὲ μέλλον ἄδηλον.) A spurious
verse (again only in V); see van der Horst, *Sentences*, 195–96. Verse 118. V omits
οὖν. Verse 120: M, B place this line after v. 121, breaking the connection with v.
119. // For the expression κακοῦ λύσις, cf. Herodotus, *Hist.* 6.139; Theognis, *El.*
1385; Diodorus Siculus, *Bibl.* 18.25.2; Pausanias, *Descr.* 2.29.7, 5.4.6; Josephus,
Ant. 9.70; for κακοῦ λύσις ἤλυθεν, cf. Phocylides, frg. 16 (ἐπερχομένου κακοῦ ...
ἐκλύσασθαι).

COMMENTARY

The section on fortitude opened with the topic of emotional moderation, specifically restraint in grieving (vv. 97–98). Here the theme is expanded with an appeal to
avoid the extremes of joy as well as grief (v. 118). Verses 119–120 give the reasoning behind this counsel (note the repetition of κακός and ἄχθομαι in vv. 118 and
120): overreacting to fortune, good or bad, is unwarranted, since circumstances can
change suddenly.

Greco-Roman philosophers often stressed the desirability of measure in respond-
ing to life's vicissitudes, so as to avoid the morally objectionable extremes of *hubris*,
on one hand, and despair, on the other.[70] One aim of philosophy was to train its
adherents "not to be overjoyed at success or over-distressed in misfortune" (Ps.-Plu-
tarch, *Lib. ed.* 7E). Similarly, in *Cher.* 29, Philo argues that the virtuous life entails

---

[70] The paragraph's contents are reminiscent also of the *praemeditatio malorum*. As Newman (*"Cotidie
meditare,"* 1482) observes: "Popular wisdom had always emphasized reflection on possible future evils
in order to lessen the surprise and distress when the event actually occurred." Such reflection typically
took the form of *sententiae* (pp. 1479, 1488–90). The aim of this practice was to rid one of the fear
of death and endure fortune's assaults with greater resolve.

"neither being uplifted to arrogance by prosperity ... nor abjectly giving up hope in the hour of unexpected misfortune." Compare Seneca, *Helv.* 5.5, which indicates how an individual's response to one extreme shapes his response to the other: "He who is not puffed up by happy fortune does not collapse when it is reversed. The man of long-tested constancy, when faced with either condition, keeps his mind unconquered." Gnomic authors weighed in on the subject as well, for example, Theognis, *El.* 657–664: "Don't be too vexed at heart in hard times or rejoice too much in good times, since it becomes a noble man to endure everything. ... Good comes from bad and bad from good; a poor man suddenly gets very rich, and he who has acquired a great deal suddenly loses it all in one night."[71]

As this last excerpt illustrates, such appeals for composure and perseverance were often grounded in reminders about the insecurity of the human situation; compare Isocrates, *Demon.* 42: "Consider that nothing in human life is stable; for then you will not exult overmuch in prosperity nor grieve overmuch in adversity."[72] That life by its nature is characterized by abrupt and unforeseen reversals is a sapiential cliché, for example, Qoh 9:11–12 and *Syr. Men.* 110–112 ("For neither riches are everlasting nor at all times is there poverty, for subject to change are all things."); also see above, on Ps.-Phoc. 27. Reversals of fortune are of special interest to Ben Sira: success can appear in the midst of evils, while a gain can turn quickly to a loss (20:9, 11, cf. 10:10, 11:5–6, 12–13, 21). The fact that current circumstances may not last long encourages contemplation about one's vulnerability to uncontrollable events: "remember the time of want in the time of plenty, poverty and need on the day of wealth; from morning 'til evening the times change, and everything is done quickly before the Lord" (18:25–26, cf. 11:25). Compare Seneca, *Marc.* 9.2: "So many rich men are stricken before our eyes with sudden poverty, yet it never occurs to us that our own wealth also rests on just as slippery a footing."

Advice on bearing turns of fortune with resignation was a special feature of the consolation literature. Besides the text just cited, mention may be made of *Cons. Apoll.* 116E, where "Plutarch" recommends several poetic selections on the subject (including *Carm. aur.* 17–18) for future contemplation:

> If, then, one keeps these in mind ... he will be able easily to adapt them to all the circumstances of life and to bear with such circumstances intelligently ... in whatever may befall him, not to go beyond the limit of propriety either in being elated to boastfulness or in being humbled and cast down to wailings

---

[71] Cf. Sir 2:4; Theognis, *El.* 591–594; Diogenes Laertius, *Vit. phil.* 1.93; Menander, *Mon.* 15; *Ceb. Tab.* 31; Cicero, *Off.* 1.90; *Dict. Cat.* 1.18.

[72] Hesiod, *Op.* 5–8; Solon, frg. 13.67–76; Euripides, *Phoen.* 555–558, frg. 1078; Demosthenes, *Or.* 20.162; Menander, frg. 94.5; Philemon, frg. 213; Diogenes Laertius, *Vit. phil.* 1.93; Seneca, *Marc.* 9.2; Dover, *Popular Morality*, 140–41; Krause, *ΑΛΛΟΤΕ ΑΛΛΟΣ*, 81–90 (on Phocylides and Theognis).

and lamentations, through weakness of spirit and the fear of death which is implanted in us as a result of our ignorance of what is wont to happen in life in accordance with the decree of necessity or destiny.

Allowing oneself to be emotionally overwhelmed by twists of fate is as much a sign of ignorance as it is of weakness, revealing an insufficient appreciation both for propriety and for one's place in the cosmic order.

Verse 121 summarizes the short paragraph with a pair of contrasting commands. The wind was a conventional trope for that which lies beyond human control,[73] including fortune.[74] In light of the realities outlined by vv. 119–120, it is futile to "blow against the winds," to resist the power of fate (v. 121b). The proper course, instead, is to "minister to the moment" (v. 121a), to make the necessary concessions to whatever the exigencies of one's situation demand.[75] The verse as a whole, including its imagery, accords with the advice of Teles:

> Therefore one should not try to change circumstances, but rather to prepare oneself for them as they are, just as sailors do. For they do not try to change the winds and the sea, but instead they prepare themselves to be able to cope with those things. There is fair weather, a calm sea: they propel the ship with oars. The wind is with the ship: they hoist the sails. It blows contrary: they furl the sails, they give the ship its way. And as for you, <regard> your present situation, use it. (frg. 2.65–73)

Here the Cynic philosopher promotes what we may call a spirit of accommodationism. This is not simply a resignation to life's eventualities, but a willingness to recognize and act on whatever possibilities current circumstances may afford. It was within the climate of this sort of reflection that the notion of "serving" καιρός became proverbial (usually with δουλεύειν or θεραπεύειν), referring to the need to wait upon opportunities as they presented themselves, even in a dire situation.[76] This, in turn, was a variation on the proverb, "καιρός is best in everything," for which see Hesiod, *Op.* 694 and Theognis, *El.* 401.[77]

---

[73] E.g., Prov 9:12, 11:29; Sir 5:9.

[74] E.g., Pindar, *Pyth.* 3.104–106; Lucian, *Tox.* 7; Polybius, *Hist.* 25.3.9; Propertius, *El.* 3.5.11; cf. Aeschylus, *Ag.* 187; Philo, *Jos.* 32–33; Josephus, *C. Ap.* 1.75; Seneca, *Marc.* 5.5, 6.3, *Polyb.* 9.6–7; Hermolochus, frg. 1: life is baffling and no one knows the future; a grim breeze blows (ἀντιπνεῖ) in the face of success.

[75] Cf. Cicero, *Fam.* 6.12.2, *Fin.* 3.73.

[76] E.g., Demosthenes, *Or.* 18.307; Polybius, *Hist.* 11.4.2; Dionysius of Halicarnassus, *Ant. rom.* 7.34.3, 11.18.4; *Anth. Gr.* 9.441.6; Plutarch, *Arat.* 43.2; Rom 12:11 v.l.

[77] Cf. Sophocles, *Oed. tyr.* 1516; Bacchylides, frg. 14.16–18; Pindar, *Pyth.* 9.78–79; Critias, frg. 7; Menander, *Mon.* 9, 382, 400; Delling, "καιρός," 455–62; also Ps.-Phoc. 82 and 93.

VI. Speech and Wisdom (Verses 122–131)

Bibliography: Betz, "De laude ipsius," 367–93. Glad, *Paul and Philodemus*, 107–24. Kröhling, *Die Priamel*, 63. McKane, "Functions of Language," 166–85. Wilckens and Fohrer, "σοφία," 465–528.

122	Do not revel in boastfulness and rage in your heart.
123	Practice speaking well, which will greatly benefit everyone.
124	Surely the word is for a man a weapon sharper than iron.
125	To each God has allotted a weapon: power to roam the air
126	to birds, to horses swiftness, strength to lions;
127	for bulls there are self-growing horns; stingers to bees
128	he's given as an inborn defense, but the word to people for protection.
130	Better than a strong man is one who is wise.
131	Wisdom steers the course of lands and states and ships.

TEXTUAL NOTES

Verse 122. Reading τρυφῶν with M, B, P, L, and printed by Young, *Theognis*, 105; Derron, *Sentences*, 11. Cf. Diehl, *Anthologia*, 2.107: φυσῶν ("puff up," cf. V's φυσσῶν). West (*CR* 30 [1980]: 137) suggests that τρυφῶν is in fact a corruption of τυφῶν ("smolder"). // The verb λυσσόω here is a *hapax*, based on the regular form λυσσάω ("to become mad, to rage;" cf. v. 214); for its combination with φρήν, cf. Sophocles, *Ant.* 492; Euripides, *Bacch.* 850–851. Verse 124. M², V: τομώτερόν; P, L: τομώτερός; B: στομώτερός ("harder"). Verse 125b. For the periphrastic use of φύσις, see LSJ s.v. II.5. // ἠερόφοιτον: Nonnus, *Dion.* 40.524; *Orph. hymn.* 82.4. Verse 126b. Mb, Pa: πώλοις; B, P: πολλοῖς; M², V: πολλήν; L: μὲν πολλὴν; M: πολλὺν. Verse 127a. Reading, with Bernays (*Gesammelte Abhandlungen*, 217 n. 2) and van der Horst (*Sentences*, 97 n. 3, 200), αὐτοφύτως; M, B have αὐτοχύτως ("self-flowing;" cf. P, L, V with αὐτοχύτοις). Young (*Theognis*, 105) prints ταύρους δ' αὐτοχύτως κέρα ἔσσεν (ἔννυμι: "to clothe"); Derron (*Sentences*, 11, 27 n. 3) has ταύροις δ' αὐτοχύτως κέρα ἐστίν ("chez les taureaux, les cornes viennent d'elles mêmes."). Given the regularity with which φύσις appears in this (v. 125, cf. ἔμφυτον in v. 128) and similar texts (see below; also Philo, *Opif.* 85), αὐτοφύτως seems more probable. Führer ("Pseudo-Phokylides Vers 127," 61) tries ταύροις δ' αὐτοφύτως κερατίσσαι (cf. Exod 21:28, 31, 32, 35). [Verse 129.] "The word of divinely inspired wisdom is best." (τῆς δὲ θεοπνεύστου σοφίης λόγος ἐστὶν ἄριστος.) A spurious verse (missing from M, B, as well as from the quotation of Ps.-Phoc. 125–130 in Stobaeus, *Anth.* 3.3.28); see van der Horst, *Sentences*, 201–202. Verse 131. For the metaphorical use of κυβερνάω, cf. Prov 1:5, 11:14, 12:5; Wis 10:4; Plato, *Euthyd.* 291D; also cf. Seneca, *Ep.* 16.3.

COMMENTARY

As most commentators observe, the final section of the *Sentences* organized according to the cardinal virtues constitutes a unified block of sayings on the topic of wisdom, or σοφία; see especially vv. 130–131.[1] Within this discussion, the center of attention is λόγος, which could refer in the first place to either speech or reason, but probably encompasses both meanings, i.e., speech informed by reason.[2] (For the sake of consistency, the term is translated as "the word" in vv. 124 and 128.) As such, it represents a special aspect or category of wisdom.[3] In the opinion of antiquity, speech represented one of the plainest ways in which one's intelligence could be tested for its true value in practical circumstances. Hence speaking both well and correctly were among the main attributes of the sage,[4] and eloquence itself could be elevated to a place among the primary virtues.[5]

Implicit throughout the paragraph is the idea that wisdom must be pragmatic and beneficial to the community; therefore it should not be reduced to merely theoretical or esoteric applications. In this regard our author participates in an ongoing critique of wisdom as a virtue among ancient moralists. Cicero, for example, contends that although the search for wisdom and truth possesses certain noble aspects, such pursuits should not detract from the active life or the fulfillment of one's moral duties to others. He complains that "some people devote too much industry and too deep study to matters that are obscure and difficult and useless as well."[6]

---

[1]   van der Horst, *Sentences*, 97, 198; Walter, *Poetische Schriften*, 208–209; Derron, *Sentences*, xxvii, 11; Thomas, *Der jüdische Phokylides*, 191–93. On σοφία and its role in virtue, see Wilckens and Fohrer, "σοφία," 465–509; Gooch, "Wisdom and Virtue," 153–59; Irwin, *Plato's Moral Theory*, 200–208; Sorabji, "Aristotle on the Role of Intellect," 201–19; Aristotle, *Eth. nic.* 6.1.1–6.13.8; Ps.-Aristotle, *Mag. mor.* 1.34.1–32; Iamblichus, *Vit. Pyth.* 29.157–166; Cicero, *Off.* 1.18–19.

[2]   Cf. van der Horst, *Sentences*, 201; Derron, *Sentences*, 27 n. 4; Bréhier, *Les Idées Philosophiques*, 83–111; Mack, *Logos und Sophia*, 97–102, 135–38, 141–54.

[3]   Cf. Ps.-Aristotle, *Virt. vit.* 4.1: one of the important components of wisdom is "to employ both *logos* and action shrewdly."

[4]   See, e.g., McKane, "Functions of Language," 166–85.

[5]   E.g., Euripides, frg. 282.23–28 (and Adkins, *Merit and Responsibility*, 191–92); Aeschines, *Ctes.* 168.

[6]   Cicero, *Off.* 1.19; cf. Ibscher, *Der Begriff des Sittlichen*, 106–12.

Formally, a coordinated introduction (vv. 122–123) and conclusion (vv. 130–131) frame the body of the passage. Each of these elements is constructed antithetically, contrasting real, as opposed to apparent, excellence in the area of speech and wisdom. The introduction contains two commands, the first warning against vain boastfulness, since it results in senseless rage,[7] the second urging the reader instead to develop his speaking ability on account of the benefits it confers on others. The conclusion, on the other hand, contrasts the wise sage, exercising his dynamic and useful wisdom, with the man whose strength is merely physical in nature. The former excels since the wisdom of which he partakes guides the course of vital human endeavors and institutions (v. 131). These elements flank the main body of the paragraph, a descriptive section that evaluates the *logos* of humankind by comparing it to the gifts allotted by God to other creatures (vv. 124–128). This comparative segment opens with a thesis statement (v. 124) connected to the main description in vv. 125–128 by catchword and *inclusio*.[8]

The nature of the descriptive section's design and argument is reminiscent of the priamel, a popular device in Greco-Roman literature, especially poetry.[9] Often, as here in vv. 125–128, a priamel will open with a general introductory statement that provides the theme, while the final item in the comparative catalogue is allotted special significance in one way or another. Such constructions were also employed on a regular basis in conjunction with gnomic forms, as Ovid, *Am.* 3.4.17–26 illustrates:[10]

> We ever strive for what is forbid, and ever covet what is denied;
> > so the sick man longingly hangs over forbidden water.
> A hundred eyes before, a hundred behind, had
> > Argus – and these Love alone did oft deceive;
> the chamber of Danae was eternally strong with iron and rock,
> > yet she who had been given a maid to its keeping became a mother.
> Penelope, although without a guard,
> > remained inviolate among so many youthful wooers.

---

[7] As van der Horst observes (*Sentences*, 198), v. 122 constitutes a warning against ὑπερηφανία, a common theme in Greek, Jewish, and Christian literature; cf. Bertram, "ὑπερήφανος," 525–29; Spicq, *Lexicon*, 3:390–95.

[8] ὅπλον in vv. 124 and 125; λόγος (v. 124) and λόγον (v. 128); ἀνδρί (v. 124) and ἀνθρώποισιν (v. 128). On the use of chiasm in these lines, see van der Horst, *Sentences*, 200.

[9] Kröhling (*Die Priamel*, 63) identifies vv. 125–128 of the *Sentences* as a priamel. See further van Otterlo, "Priamel," 145–76; U. Schmid, *Die Priamel*; Krischer, "Die logischen Formen der Priamel," 79–91; Race, *The Classical Priamel*.

[10] Additional examples: Theognis, *El.* 699–718; Plato, *Leg.* 660E–661C; Ovid, *Am.* 1.2.10–18, 2.17.14–24, 3.8.45–50, *Trist.* 1.2.4–12, 2.266–276, *Pont.* 1.5.35–42, 4.3.35–48; Propertius, *El.* 2.1.57–64.

Whatever is guarded we desire the more, and care itself
   invites the thief; few love what another concedes.

In this paragraph the maxims in vv. 17 and 25–26 flank the priamel itself (vv. 18–
24), which consists of a roster of four well-known examples illustrating the human
propensity to desire most things that are forbidden or closely guarded by others (vv.
18, 19–20, 21–22, 23–24). In addition to their structural role, the gnomic utterances that introduce and conclude the segment provide the poet with an opportunity to
elicit from the specific examples some general observations on human nature.

Verses 122–123. In v. 20, the reader was cautioned to be "mindful of your tongue."
Verse 122 opens a paragraph that explores the topic of speech further, bringing
into relief especially the tongue's manifold power: it can be used for defense or to
advance the common good, or it can be self-destructive.

Greek writers used τρυφάω to describe extravagant carousing and revelry (see
LSJ s.v. II, III), just the sort of conduct one would expect of an ἀλαζών or "brag-
gart," a stock character of Greek moral literature, detested for his imposture and
insolence.[11] The vices he embodies are condemned in Jewish and Christian writings
as well; also cf. above, on v. 53.[12] In the same vein, boasting (often καυχάομαι and
cognates), asserting oneself verbally at the expense of others, is roundly denounced
in both Greco-Roman and Jewish contexts.[13]

In v. 76, the reader was encouraged to "practice" moderation. In v. 123, he is
to practice εὐεπίη, "speaking well" or "good speech."[14] The term's meaning is clarified in the second half of the line: the most desirable words are those that "benefit
everyone," an expression reminiscent of Homer, *Il.* 8.36–37, 467–468, referring to
counsel that "benefits" by saving "all." As a rule, biblical sages were busy training in
eloquence, since "by speech wisdom shall be known" (Sir 4:24) or, as Prov 16:23
declares, "the sage wears knowledge on his lips."[15] Sayings like these attest to the

---

[11] E.g., Aristotle, *Eth. nic.* 2.7.12, 4.7.10–13; Aristophanes, *Ach.* 109, 135, 373; Theophrastus, *Char.* 23; Xenophon, *Mem.* 1.7.2; Plutarch, *Sera* 547E; Epictetus, *Diatr.* 2.19.19, 3.24.43, 4.8.27; Dio Chrysostom, *Hom. Socr.* 7, *1 Glor.* 25; Teles, frg. 4A.45; Sextus, *Sent.* 284; Glad, *Paul and Philodemus,* 107–24.

[12] E.g., Prov 21:24; Rom 1:30; 2 Tim 3:2; Jas 4:16; *Jos. Asen.* 2:1, 21:12, 16; Philo, *Virt.* 161–174.

[13] E.g., Theognis, *El.* 159–160; Menander, *Mon.* 778; Epictetus, *Ench.* 33.14, 48.13; P.Ins. 3.10–11. This is a *topos* of biblical wisdom, e.g., Prov 11:7, 20:9, 25:14, 27:1–2; Sir 10:26–27, 11:4, 32:12; Jas 3:5, 14; cf. *T. Reub.* 3:5; *T. Jud.* 13:2–3; *T. Job* 15:5–7; Sextus, *Sent.* 432; Bultmann, "καυχάομαι," 645–54; Spicq, *Lexicon,* 2:295–302.

[14] Cf. Philo, *Jos.* 269; Sophocles, *Oed. tyr.* 932; Menander, *Mon.* 94, 397 ("Strive both to speak and to learn the noblest things."), 648.

[15] Cf. Prov 10:20–21, 31–32, 12:6, 25, 16:21, 23–24, 22:11; Sir 4:23, 5:13, 6:5, 8:8–9, 21:7, 16; cf. Philo, *Spec.* 1.343.

fundamental connection understood to exist between wisdom and eloquence. This belief is often accompanied by the assumption that the true sage will use his words for the collective good. Moses, as Philo explains, had one essential aim, "to benefit (ὀνῆσαι) those he led ... in all he said or did."[16] In this regard, Plutarch's *De laude ipsius* is especially instructive for understanding the logic behind vv. 122–123.[17] The tractate's overarching theme is that those who indulge in μεγαληγορία lose control of themselves easily and often go too far, producing envy and disgust in their listeners.[18] Such boasting can even bring on a certain μανία, or madness (539C). Nevertheless, self-praise may still be morally acceptable, especially in circumstances where it is done for the benefit of others (539F, 545D–546A, 547F).

Verses 124–128. The perspective on the power of speech changes with these lines, which concentrate on speech as an instrument not for helping others but for safeguarding oneself. The poet does not specify precisely how it serves this purpose, though the concept of the first verse would have been a familiar one. Biblical texts frequently compare the effects of words and weapons, for example, Prov 14:7: "Wise lips are weapons (ὅπλα) of discretion."[19] The form of this maxim is also similar to Menander, *Mon.* 621: "The greatest weapon (ὅπλον) for people is the word (λόγος)."[20]

In v. 32, the author grudgingly allowed protection by means of the sword. In vv. 125–128, he presents speech as humankind's unique and God-given means of defense. Comparison with Philo's reflections on the same subject sheds some light on precisely how it is suppose to function in this capacity. "The word was bestowed on humanity by God as the best of gifts," he writes, "a weapon of defense (ὅπλον ἀμυντήριον) against those who threaten violence" (*Somn.* 1.103). Philo deems the imagery of speech as a defensive weapon appropriate inasmuch as it can provide a remedy to violence, an idea with which our author would have readily agreed; see v. 78. A little further on Philo continues: "For as neighing is peculiar to a horse and barking to a dog and lowing to a cow and roaring to a lion, so is for humanity speech (τὸ λέγειν) and reason (ὁ λόγος); since with this humanity, the dearest to God of all living creatures, has been bestowed, to be its particular defense (ἔρυμα), protec-

---

[16] Philo, *Mos.* 1.151; cf. Diogenes Laertius, *Vit. phil.* 1.92; Sir 21:17, 37:22–23 ("Someone is wise in his soul, and the fruits of his intelligence are trustworthy in his mouth; a wise man teaches his people, and the fruits of his intelligence are trustworthy.").

[17] See Betz, "De laude ipsius," 367–93.

[18] On μεγαληγορία, see Plutarch, *De laude* 540E, 541B, D, 544F, 545B; cf. Euripides, *Heracl.* 353–357.

[19] Cf. Ps 51:4, 56:5, 58:8, 63:4; Prov 10:13, 12:18, 25:18; cf. Josephus, *Bell.* 5.361; Demosthenes, *Or.* 12.17. For Philo (*Leg. all.* 3.155), *logos* is an especially useful weapon (ὅπλον) at banquets.

[20] Cf. Menander, *Mon.* 361; Diogenes Laertius, *Vit. phil.* 5.82 (Demetrius: "All that iron can achieve in war is won in politics by the word."); *Orph. hymn.* 28.10; Malherbe, *Paul,* 91–119.

tion, armor, and wall" (*Somn.* 1.108). For Philo, the defensive weapon with which humankind has been equipped is speech together with reason, which distinguishes the human species from all others. As suggested at the beginning of this chapter, *logos* in Ps.-Phoc. 124 and 128 appears to encompass both of these concepts as well. Like Philo, in portraying the origin of *logos*, Pseudo-Phocylides projects the image of God as the benefactor of creation, indicating as well a hierarchy of divine gifts, the best going to humankind.[21] Also like Philo, Pseudo-Phocylides mentions several animals by way of comparison, including horses and lions, though he focuses not on the peculiar "speech" of each creature (neighing, etc.), but on the most notable asset each possesses for protection, drawing on traditional characterizations.[22] In this regard, his composition is closer to the myth of Prometheus, who was instructed to allot (νεῖμαι) each species with its proper faculty for preservation: strength to some, speed to others, but wisdom (and fire) to people (cf. Ps.-Phoc. 130–131).[23] Here, as in other texts (e.g., Cicero, *Off.* 1.50), humankind's special gift is understood as a basis of civilization; compare Isocrates, *Nic.* 5–6:

> (Speech is) that power which of all the faculties that belong to human na-
> ture (φύσει; cf. φύσιν in Ps.-Phoc. 125) is the source of most of our blessings.
> For in the other powers we possess we are in no respect superior to other
> creatures. Rather, we are inferior to many in swiftness and in strength and
> in other resources; but, because there has been implanted in us the power
> to persuade each other ... we not only have escaped the life of wild beasts,
> but we have come together to found cities and make laws.

The importance of speech/reason in building community is likewise asserted in Pseudo-Phocylides' conclusion to the paragraph, which immediately follows.

Verses 130–131. The superiority of humankind is further implied by v. 130. God has allotted lions with strength (ἀλκή, in v. 126), but in the world of human activity this attribute is secondary to wisdom. The readers were warned about priding themselves on ἀλκή in v. 53. Here strength is assessed in what may be a versified rendition of Prov 24:5 ("Better a wise person than a strong one."), which in turn

---

[21] Humanity alone possesses *logos*, while the animal world is *alogos*; see below, on Ps.-Phoc. 188.

[22] Horses: Hab 1:8; Jer 4:13. Lions: Judg 14:18; 2 Kgdms 1:23; Prov 30:30. Bees: 4 Macc 14:19; and cf. Ps.-Phoc. 171–174.

[23] Plato, *Prot.* 320D–321D; cf. Maximus of Tyre, *Or.* 20.6 ("Just as nature gives different animals different forms of protection, adapted to the preservation of their own particular kind of life ... so too it has a gift for people, though in other respects they lag behind the other creatures ... what God gave them, to balance out the other creatures' abilities, was reason."), cf. 10.5, 31.4, 41.5; Plutarch, *Fort.* 98C–E; *Anacreont.* 24.1–7: "Nature gave horns to bull and hooves to horse, gave lions ravening jaws, gave hares swift course, made fish to swim, birds to fly, man to be wise."

belongs to a category of "better" sayings that compare wisdom favorably to physical force, for example, Qoh 9:16 ("Better wisdom than might.").[24] Ingredient to the logic of such platitudes is the idea that individuals are called upon to make choices about the respective roles of prudence and power in their lives. While everyone may possess *logos*, not everyone possess the wisdom to use it properly! Very often strength without wisdom "harms more then it helps" and "obscures the care of the soul" (Isocrates, *Demon.* 6).[25] The reasoning that supports this conclusion is supplied by v. 131, which is reminiscent of various self-proclamations uttered by *Sophia* in Jewish wisdom texts, such as Prov 8:15–16 ("By me rulers rule and the mighty decree justice. By me nobles become great and by me monarchs conquer the earth.") and Sir 24:6 ("In the waves of the sea and in all the earth and in every people and nation I have procured for myself."). Because Solomon has acquired wisdom he can declare, "I shall administer peoples, and nations shall be subject to me" (Wis 8:14); this is because "she reaches mightily from one end of the earth to the other, and she administers all things well" (8:1).[26] Texts like these emphasize both the power and the scope of wisdom, conceived as a practical force that guides the course of all human communities, encompassing the full range of human endeavors.[27] As "the wisest" (v. 2), Pseudo-Phocylides can also speak with authority on the subject.

---

[24] Cf. Qoh 4:13, 7:19, 9:18; Wis 7:8; also cf. Ps.-Phoc. 88.

[25] Cf. Herodotus, *Hist.* 3.127 ("Where wisdom is needed, force has no role."); Euripides, *Orest.* 709–716; Xenophanes, frg. 2; *Dict. Cat.* 4.12.

[26] Cf. Heraclitus, frg. 41: "The wise is one thing: to know the judgment that steers (ἐκυβέρνησε; cf. κυβερνᾷ in Ps.-Phoc. 131) all things through all things."

[27] Cf. Winston, *Wisdom*, 42–43.

VII. Enemies and Evildoers (Verses 132–152)

Bibliography: Berthelot, "Philo and Kindness Towards Animals," 48–65. Crouch, *Colossian Haustafel,* 48, 55–56, 60–61, 67–70, 81. Dickie, *Magic,* 79–95, 99–109, 117–23, 138–39, 164–68, 170. Hine, "Moral Evil," 93–106. Meeks, "Circle of Reference," 305–17. Praechter, *Hierokles,* 7–90.

132	It is not holy to conceal unconvicted a reckless man;
133	rather it is necessary to deter an evildoer with force.
134	Often those who go with the wicked perish with them.
135	Accept not into illegal deposit the thievery of criminals;
136	both are thieves, the one who accepts and the one who's stolen.
137	Render to all their due; equality is best in everything.
138	When beginning, use everything sparingly lest you end up in want.
139	Take not for yourself the daily food of a man's animal.
140	And if an enemy's animal falls along the way, help to lift it up.
141	Never censure an errant man or a transgressor.
142	It is better to make a gracious friend instead of an enemy.
143	Cut off the evil when it starts and heal the wound.
147	Eat no meat torn by wild beasts, but to swift-footed dogs
148	leave the remains: beasts feed on beasts.
149	Mix no potions; from books of magic keep away.
150	On tender children lay not a hand in violence.
151	Flee dissension and strife when a fight's approaching.
152	Do no good to an evil man; it's like sowing in the sea.

TEXTUAL NOTES

Verse 132. Before this line, B, P, L²ᵐᵍ repeat Ps.-Phoc. 21, expressing as it does an outlook compatible with that of vv. 132–136. // ἀνέλεγκτον (in P, V) gives good sense, though subsequent copyists appear to have found it difficult; B: ἀνάδεκτον ("admitted"); M: ἄδεκτον ("unacceptable"); L: διάδεκτον ("received"); L²ᵞᵖ: ἄτιτον ("unavenged"). Verse 133. For ἀνάγκη meaning "by force," cf. *Sib. Or.* 3.525; LSJ s.v. ἀνάγκη 1. Verse 135. δέχομαι (also in v. 136) is the usual word for accepting a deposit, e.g., Plato, *Resp.* 442E; Herodotus, *Hist.* 6.86; Isocrates, *Trapez.* 18. // For the translation, cf. van der Horst, *Sentences,* 204: "Accept not from thieves a stolen, unlawful deposit." Verse 137a. Reading πᾶσι in P, L, V, Young (*Theognis*, 106), and Derron (*Sentences*, 12), against παισὶ in M (cf. B), Brunck (*Gnomici Poetae Graeci*, 164), and Bergk (*Poetae Lyrici Graeci*, 99); cf. Walter, *Poetische Schriften*, 209: "Teile den Kindern ihre (Erb-)Anteile (gleichmäßig) zu." Cf. Ps.-Phoc. 150. Verse 138. For the adverbial use of τέρμα, see LSJ s.v. II.2. // Given the rarity of ἐπιδεύομαι in the active voice (see LSJ s.v.), ἐπιδεύης in M² is the *lect. diff.*, printed by Diehl (*Anthologia*, 2.108), Young (*Theognis*, 106), van der Horst (*Sentences*, 205), and Derron (*Sentences*, 12). Cf. Bergk's (*Poetae Lyrici Graeci*, 100) and Bernay's (*Gesammelte Abhandlungen*, 258) conjecture ἐπιδεύῃ. P, L, V have the adjective ἐπιδευής. Verse 141. In lieu of ἀλίτροπον (in M, B), P, L, V have ἀλήμονα ("wanderer"); presumably they replaced the *hapax* with a more recognizable synonym. // For the translation, cf. van der Horst, *Sentences*, 207–208: "Never expose a wandering man and a sinner;" Walter, *Poetische Schriften*, 210: "Einem verirrten und umhergetriebenen Menschen mache niemals Vorhaltungen;" Derron, *Sentences*, 12: "Tu ne repousseras jamais un homme errant et égaré." Verse 142. For φίλον εὐμενέοντα, cf. Euripides, *El.* 601, *Med.* 809; Philo, *Somn.* 1.110. Verse 143. For the phrase ἕλκος τ᾽ ἀκέσασθαι, cf. Homer, *Il.* 16.29, 523. [Verse 144.] "From a tiny spark a mighty forest burns." (ἐξ ὀλίγου σπινθῆρος ἀθέσφατος αἴθεται ὕλη.) A spurious verse (only in V); see van der Horst, *Sentences*, 209–10. [Verse 145.] "Have a steadfast heart and refrain from baneful thoughts as well." (ἐγκρατὲς ἦτορ ἔχειν, καὶ λωβητῶν δ᾽ ἀπέχεσθαι.) A spurious verse (only in V); see van der Horst, *Sentences*, 210. [Verse 146.] "Flee evil gossip; flee lawless people." (φεῦγε κακὴν φήμην, φεῦγ᾽ ἀνθρώπους ἀθεμίστους.) A spurious verse (again only in V); see van der Horst, *Sentences*, 211. Verse 147. For the phrase δαίσῃ κρέας, cf. Homer, *Od.* 9.162, 557, 10.477, 12.30; Josephus, *Ant.* 6.121. // M, B, P, L²ʸ, V have ἀργίποσιν, while L offers ἀρτίποσιν ("sound of foot;" cf. Homer, *Il.* 9.505, etc.). Verses 147b–148a. For the diction, cf. Homer, *Il.* 24.211; Euripides, frg. 469. Verse 149b. M, B, L, V have μαγικῶν; P exhibits metathesis: γαμικῶν ("marital"). Verse 150. νηπίαχος: Homer, *Il.* 2.338, 6.408, 16.262; cf. Apollonius of Rhodes, *Argon.* 4.136–137. // Reading ἀπαλοῖς μὴ μάρψῃ with Diehl (*Anthologia*, 2.109), supported by M², V. Cf. Bergk (*Poetae Lyrici Graeci*, 102) and Bernays (*Gesammelte Abhandlungen*, 259): ἀταλοὺς μὴ μάρψῃς (cf. M, B). Homer uses both ἀπαλός and ἀταλός (each meaning "soft, delicate") in connection with youth, e.g., *Il.* 11.115, 18.567, *Od.* 11.39. Also cf. Young (*Theognis*, 107), van der Horst (*Sentences*, 213–14), and Derron (*Sentences*, 12): ἀταλοῖς μὴ ἅψῃ (cf. P, L). // For μάρψῃ χεῖρα, cf. Euripides, *Hipp.* 1188. Verse 151. Cf. the Homeric expression, "flee from war:" *Il.* 7.118–119, 173–174, 11.590, 12.123, 18.307, *Od.* 3.192. // The pairing of ἔρις and πόλεμος is also Homeric: *Il.* 5.861, 891, 14.149, 389, 17.253. Verse 152. Omitted by M, B, perhaps on account of the incongruity with vv. 140–143.

COMMENTARY

The third and final major section of the *Sentences* is vv. 132–227. The organizing principle at work in this block of material is no longer the canon of cardinal virtues, as it was in vv. 9–131. Instead, the units have been arranged according to different areas or spheres of social life, with the topic of each successive unit addressing a more specific and more familiar domain of moral responsibility. From a material standpoint, the section may be viewed as a series of three concentric rings, each somewhat more restricted or focused in its point of reference than the last. Thus the first paragraph of sayings (vv. 132–152) discusses what we might call social "outsiders," that is, assorted referents on the periphery of moral life and conduct, with an emphasis on how one ought to deal with evil persons. The second paragraph (vv. 153–174) concentrates on how the reader ought to earn a living, treating a more specific topic as well as a more pertinent and common area of life than the preceding paragraph. The third and final unit offers advice on the most intimate referents and the most customary aspects of social life, namely, the reader's obligations to family members (vv. 175–227).

One place where we find exhortation structured according to the different relationships in which one lives is the Stoic lists of καθήκοντα, or duties. The *Epitome* of Hierocles, for instance, summarizes Stoic moral teaching in a format based upon such traditional lists. While reconstruction of the text remains tentative, it appears to have been sub-divided as follows:[1]

1	On Conduct Towards the Gods
2	On Conduct Towards One's Country
3	On Conduct Towards Parents
4	On Fraternal Love
5	On Conduct Towards Relatives
6	On Economics
7	On Marriage and Children

Although the *Sentences* contains no paragraphs with topics comparable to those of the first three chapters of Hierocles' *Epitome*, both the themes and ordering of chapters 4–7 show some basic similarities with those of vv. 132–227. Thus chapters 4 and 5 discuss, respectively, how to treat all people with consideration (including certain "outsiders") and how to conduct oneself towards relatives outside the immediate family. Chapter 6 then summarizes the types of labor that are appropriate for different members of the household. Finally, chapter 7 instructs the reader on

---

[1] Praechter, *Hierokles*, 14–90; Powell and Barber, *New Chapters*, 36–40; Crouch, *Colossian Haustafel*, 67–70; Malherbe, *Moral Exhortation*, 85–104.

the importance of marriage and on the responsibilities that parents have toward their children. The same general arrangement of topics is discernible in Ps.-Phoc. 132–227: first, a broadly defined group of "outsiders," then labor, marriage, and, finally, children. Thus the καθήκοντα scheme that modern critics have seen at work in vv. 175–227 may be extended to include vv. 132–174 as well. A literary format of this type would be comparable to treatments of moral duties found in other Hellenistic-Jewish gnomic sources. Sir 7:1–28, for example, opens with miscellaneous precepts against evil, injustice, and sinning (vv. 1–14), followed by counsel not to disdain manual labor (vv. 15–17), and then advice that touches upon obligations owed to different members of the household, including wives, slaves, children, and parents (vv. 18–28).[2]

Also of special interest are texts that in some manner connect exhortation organized according to the different relationships in which one lives with exhortation organized according to the cardinal virtues. Indeed, it appears that the merging of these two literary schemes represents something of a convention in moral philosophy. This can be discerned most clearly, perhaps, in the *De officiis*, where, as we saw above, Cicero organizes the first major section of his teaching about moral duties according to the canon of cardinal virtues.[3] Additionally, in the course of his analysis, Cicero is able to catalog some of the duties dictated by each virtue as it pertains to various referents, for example, in 1.53–58 and 1.122–125.[4] Cicero's association of the canon with his exploration of moral duties apparently evokes a fairly standard procedure in Stoic philosophy, as evidenced by some of the more substantial summaries of its moral teachings (e.g., Diogenes Laertius, *Vit. phil.* 7.84–131; Cicero, *Fin.* 3.15–76; Arius Didymus, *Epitome*) which employ the canon of virtues together with an evaluation of καθήκοντα (in collaboration with other literary schemes).[5]

Moral rudiments informed by this type of reasoning left their mark on Jewish reflections of the Second Temple period as well, as Philo's allegorical exegesis of the trees and rivers in the Garden of Eden illustrates. In *Leg. all.* 1.56–64, he develops a hierarchical framework that relates virtue as an absolute with both the canon of virtues and the καθήκοντα. Philo situates at the top of this hierarchy "generic virtue," which, he argues, is the source for the virtues of the Platonic tetrad. In turn,

---

[2]   Cf. Skehan and DiLella, *Ben Sira*, 197–206. Also cf. *Syr. Men.* 126–228, which is divided into three major units: (1) counsel regarding different "outsiders" and unjust behavior (enemies: vv. 126–132; public arguments: vv. 133–144; theft: vv. 145–147; bad men: vv. 148–153; bad servants: vv. 154–169; lascivious old men: vv. 170–172); (2) advice on dining at banquets and loaning money (vv. 181–188); (3) exhortation about the family (brothers and friends: vv. 189–193; sons and brothers: vv. 194–210; fathers: vv. 211–212; friends: vv. 213–226; and slaves: vv. 227–228).

[3]   See Introduction IV.

[4]   Cf. Seneca, *Ep.* 95.47–55.

[5]   Praechter (*Hierokles*, 7–14) also raises the possibility that the *Epitome* of Hierocles opened with a (now lost) analysis of the virtues, continuing with the exhortation on duties that survives.

each of these is manifested through various activities, identified as either moral accomplishments or moral duties. Finally, at the bottom of the hierarchy, he identifies noble deeds as the specific acts that constitute these accomplishments or duties.[6] In this manner, Philo demonstrates how one's obligations to different types of people, and the concrete actions associated with these obligations, correspond to the primary virtues as well as to virtue in its perfect, divine sense. This sort of hierarchy appears to drive the formation of other Philonic texts, such as *Virt.* 102ff., where he illustrates how the virtue of φιλανθρωπία applies to different categories of people and things. Thus one ought to demonstrate humanity in dealing with strangers (102–108), enemies (109–120), slaves (121–124), animals (125–147), and plants (148–160).[7]

Lastly, mention should be made of Josephus' summary of the law in *C. Ap.* 2.190–219, which, as we saw earlier, most likely utilizes a source known to Pseudo-Phocylides as well.[8] Of particular interest for the analysis of Ps.-Phoc. 132–227 is the literary structure of *C. Ap.* 2.199–213. The summary in its entirety can be outlined as follows:

190–198	I. On εὐσέβεια
190–192a	A. On the nature of God
192b–198	B. On the worship of God: the temple and its operation
199–213	II. On φιλανθρωπία
199–206	A. Conduct within the household
199–203	1. Laws regarding marriage and sex
204	2. On the upbringing of children
205	3. Obligations to the dead
206	4. Obligations to parents and elders
207–208	B. Conduct within the community
207a	1. On friendship
207b–208	2. Miscellaneous duties within the community
209–213	C. Conduct towards "outsiders"
209–210	1. On aliens
211–212	2. On foreigners and enemies
213	3. On animals
214–219	III. Rewards and punishments
214–217a	A. Penalties for disobedience
217b–219	B. Rewards for obedience

---

6   Jastram, "Generic Virtue," 327–30.
7   Cf. Crouch, *Colossian Haustafel*, 48, 55–56, 60–61, 81.
8   See Introduction III.

The first two sections (190–213) recount various obligations, whereas the concluding segment (214–219) stipulates rewards for those who honor them (217b–219) and punishment for those who do not (214–217a). The first section on obligations (190–198) addresses some significant aspects of the Jewish conception of God (190–192a) and the proper manner of worshipping God (192b–198). The second section, 199–213, which constitutes the heart of the summary, enumerates obligations in the domain of human relations. As Geza Vermes has observed, the main thrust of the text at this point is the idea that such relations ought to be governed by the virtue of φιλανθρωπία, explicitly mentioned in 213.[9] Thus it appears that Josephus has applied a schema familiar from the canon of two virtues as an organizational device in his presentation of the Torah's requirements.[10] Furthermore, he organizes the directives that are placed under this heading (section II) in a manner comparable to the approach detected in vv. 132–227 of our poem, though the order of analogous topical units is reversed.

To begin with, Josephus mentions rules that pertain to obligations within the household (199–206). This section incorporates counsel on responsibilities to one's spouse, especially in matters of sexual conduct (199–203; cf. Ps.-Phoc. 175–205), to children (204; cf. Ps.-Phoc. 207–217), and to parents and elders (206; cf. Ps.-Phoc. 220–222). The second paragraph (207–208) contains a miscellany of precepts that advise the reader on duties to different members of the community who are neither part of the household nor reckoned as "outsiders." With regard to the nature of its referents, then, the advice here occupies a sort of middle ground between the teaching in II.A and II.C. While a number of themes emerge in this section, some of its directives touch upon economic and monetary matters, which are also part of Pseudo-Phocylides' middle section in vv. 153–174. In drawing section II to a close, Josephus discusses the treatment of different social "outsiders" (209–213), a theme that is also central to Ps.-Phoc. 132–152. It follows that a number of the referents Josephus mentions in 209–213 match those in this part of our poem, particularly enemies and evildoers (211–212; cf. Ps.-Phoc. 132–136, 141–143, 151–152) and animals (213; cf. Ps.-Phoc. 139–140, 147–148). Most important to Josephus' presentation at this juncture is the obligation to show mercy (214), a concern that resonates throughout vv. 132–152 of the *Sentences* as well.

So in the matter of its literary composition, the section on φιλανθρωπία in Josephus' *Contra Apionem* manifests the same sort of three-part concentric ring structure observed in vv. 132–227 of our poem. We should bear in mind additionally that both authors in some manner link their καθήκοντα schemes with literary configurations informed by a canon of virtues. There are, of course, some important differences to be noted between the two texts as well. An obvious one is that

---

[9]   Vermes, "A Summary of the Law," 299.

[10] Cf. above, pp. 74–75.

Josephus begins his discussion at the center of the ring structure and works out-wards, whereas Pseudo-Phocylides moves in the opposite direction, starting at the periphery and moving inwards. Also, Josephus bases his summary of Torah obliga-tions on the canon of two virtues and allows exhortation organized according to the virtues and exhortation organized according to duties to overlap (like Cicero in the *De officiis*) whereas Pseudo-Phocylides avails himself of the Platonic-Stoic tetrad, separating the teaching structured around the cardinal virtues from that on duties in different areas of life.

The first unit in the section of the *Sentences* organized according to this schema, vv. 132–152, is in many respects the most miscellaneous of the poem. As mentioned above, the maxims here are affiliated insofar as they offer recommendations con-cerning referents who are social "outsiders."[11] Advice on how to evaluate and handle such types is a basic element of the gnomic style, as passages like P.Ins. 11.22–15.6[12] and Sir 8:1–19,[13] 11:29–12:18[14] attest. Although the range of referents that these texts take on is often considerable (enemies, fools, and evildoers being the most popular), emphasis is placed throughout upon the importance of exercising cau-tion and discrimination when interacting with such people, while at the same time displaying as humane an outlook as possible.[15]

A similar attempt at balance is evident in Ps.-Phoc. 132–152. The paragraph begins and ends with warnings to avoid evildoers and the havoc they wreak (vv. 132–136, 151–152; note the correspondence of terms with the κακ stem in vv. 133–134 and 152). In sum, one ought to do no good for the wicked. Offsetting this rather negative attitude are a number of sayings in the center section of the paragraph (vv. 137, 140–143) that convey a more optimistic approach to dealing with such individuals – it may even be possible to turn an enemy into friend! Most

---

[11] On "outsiders" as a reference group for moral exhortation, cf. Meeks, "Circle of Reference," 305–17.

[12] This passage embraces the 12th (entitled, "Do not trust one whom you do not know in your heart, lest he cheat you with cunning."), the 13th (entitled, "Do not trust a thief, lest you come to grief."), and the 14th (entitled, "Do not let the inferior man rule, lest he make your name that of a fool.") Instruc-tions; cf. Lichtheim, *Late Egyptian Wisdom*, 208–12.

[13] These verses contain advice on dealing prudently with a whole array of different types of people, including many "outsiders:" fools, sinners, evildoers, strangers, and so forth; cf. Skehan and DiLella, *Ben Sira*, 209–14.

[14] Here the author urges caution in choosing associates, with many observations pertinent to dealing with "outsiders," for example, slanderers, evildoers, the wicked, sinners, enemies, and the proud; cf. Skehan and DiLella, *Ben Sira*, 242–48.

[15] Also cf. *Gnom. Democr.* 87–97; *Ahiqar* 162–172; *Did.* 3:1–6 (with van de Sandt, "Didache 3.1–6," 21–41); Thomas, *Der jüdische Phokylides*, 171–79. For the Stoic notion that "there are some forms of virtue that by definition require evil men before they can be exercised," see Hine, "Moral Evil," 93–106 (quote from p. 103).

of the remaining verses of the paragraph deal with another kind of social "outsider," animals (vv. 139, 147–148, cf. v. 140).

Verses 132–136. The preceding paragraph had spoken about the need to develop skills that can benefit others, even "all" people (v. 123). This impulse, however, must be balanced by an awareness of the risks this can pose to one's self-preservation. As Sir 12:1 puts it, "when you do good, know for whom you do it." In its context, Ben Sira's warning introduces the argument that, while assisting the righteous is admirable, one ought not to help miscreants at all. Rather, they should be left to God's punishment (12:2–7; cf. Ps.-Phoc. 77). In fact, those who help the sinful not only work to no avail, they may also earn pain and shame for their efforts: "Who pities a snake charmer when he's bitten?" (12:13). Pseudo-Phocylides broaches this subject with a specific case: it is not "holy" to protect a wrongdoer from justice (cf. Deut 13:9).[16] Instead of sheltering criminals from conviction, the reader is admonished to deter (ἀποτρωπᾶσθαι) them. For Philo, the deterrence of evils (κακῶν ἀποτροπή) is a fundamental goal of the virtuous life, though by "evils" he means principally injustices one might personally commit or experience.[17] For Pseudo-Phocylides, in contrast, the act of deterrence focuses on the use of force against others who do wrong (cf. vv. 32–34).[18] The injunction in v. 133 is reminiscent of the Deuteronomic refrain, "You shall remove the evil one from among you" (Deut 13:6, 17:7, etc.), referring to the Israelites' responsibility to eradicate the perpetrators of transgressions understood to be contagions within the community. Sapiential texts like Prov 4:14–15 speak more of shunning evil than purging it: "Go not in the ways of the ungodly, nor covet the ways of wrongdoers … turn from them and pass by."[19]

The rationale for the commands of vv. 132–133 is provided in v. 134: those who consort with criminals frequently share their fate. The image of dying together with evildoers here may have been inspired by Num 16:26 ("Separate yourselves from the tents of these stubborn people … lest you perish with them in all their sin."), though non-Jewish authors make comparable observations, for example, P.Ins. 13.18 ("When a thief commits a theft, his companions get a beating.") and *Instr. Ankh.* 14.3: "Do not make a thief your companion, [lest] he cause you to

---

16 For the formula οὐχ ὅσιον, cf. Prov 17:26, 18:5; Josephus, *Vita* 171; Demosthenes, *Or.* 21.148: it is not ὅσιος to pardon a man guilty of *hubris*.

17 Philo, *Det.* 123, *Her.* 15, 172, *Fug.* 99, *Mos.* 2.5, *Spec.* 1.283, 3.171.

18 ἀτάσθαλος, common in Homer, is generally associated with *hubris*: *Il.* 11.695, 13.634, *Od.* 3.207, 16.86, 17.588, 20.170, 370, 24.282, 352; cf. Hesiod, *Op.* 134. For κακοεργός, cf. D. Cohen, *Law, Sexuality, and Society*, 111–13.

19 Cf. Prov 14:16; *Ahiqar* 163–164; *m. 'Abot* 1:7; *ARN* A 9.1.1–2; *Instr. Ankh.* 12.15; Theognis, *El.* 113–114, 1165; Euripides, *El.* 1355, *Suppl.* 226–228; Menander, *Mon.* 25, 66, 423, 856; *Anec. Gr.* 1.12, 158; Ps.-Charondas, *Prooem.* 2.60.20–21: those who assist the condemned should expect to be disgraced.

be killed." For a more dramatic example, compare Hesiod, *Op.* 240–243: "Often even a whole city suffers together for a wicked man who does wrong and contrives reckless deeds (ἀτάσθαλα; cf. Ps.-Phoc. 132, with ἀτάσθαλον)," so that "the people perish away."[20]

Verses 135–136 continue the line of thought from the preceding section: disassociate from evildoers and their offenses. Here another specific case of criminal collusion is raised: accepting stolen goods into deposit. As Pseudo-Phocylides sees it, the one who does this is as guilty as the one who robbed the goods in the first place. This judgment extends and qualifies the poem's earlier rules regarding deposits (v. 13) and stealing (vv. 5–6, cf. vv. 18, 154). While Exod 22:6–12 does discuss the theft of a deposit, the problem of accepting into deposit something known to be stolen is not addressed. Although no mention is made of deposits, partnership in thievery is censured in Prov 29:24 ("He that shares with a thief hates his own soul.") and Publilius Syrus, *Sent.* 677: "To help the guilty is to share his crime."[21]

Verses 137–138. In v. 69B, moderation was named the best of all things (cf. v. 98); here a similar designation applies to ἰσότης, a term that connotes equality, impartiality, or proportionality. In texts like *Pss. Sol.* 17.41 and *Let. Arist.* 263, it is understood as the opposite of insolent arrogance.[22] Menander, *Mon.* 362 also defines the concept in negative terms (cf. 358, 366): "Honor equality: never overreach." In light of the immediately preceding lines (vv. 132–136), observing the norm of equality in our text means not being greedy or grasping. By the same token, the first half of v. 137 also develops the theme by expressing a positive responsibility (cf. v. 30). According to Plato, *Leg.* 757A–C, the best form of equality involves giving due measure to everyone according to their nature.[23] Other thinkers joined Plato in using the criterion of "rendering to each his due" to encapsulate the essence of justice.[24] Among these was Philo, who even ranked the principle of equality among "the best of all things."[25] For Plutarch, such equality is worth pursuing since it constitutes the foundation of peace and concord.[26]

---

[20] Cf. Aeschylus, *Sept.* 597–608; Euripides, *Suppl.* 226–228; Babrius, *Fab.* 13.13–14, 94.9–10.

[21] Cf. Dio Chrysostom, *3 Regn.* 52.

[22] Cf. 2 Cor 8:13; Col 4:1.

[23] In Homeric contexts, "to render someone his due" means to give him his due share or portion, e.g., *Od.* 8.470, 15.140; cf. Josephus, *Ant.* 5.343.

[24] E.g., Plato, *Resp.* 331E; Cicero, *Off.* 1.15, 49, 59; Seneca, *Ep.* 81.7; Philo, *Mos.* 2.9: justice means "to honor equality and to render to each his due."

[25] Philo, *Spec.* 4.165, cf. *Sacr.* 27, *Conf.* 48, *Her.* 161, 191–193, *Mos.* 1.328, *Spec.* 4.166–167, 169, 230–231, *Contempl.* 17; Aristotle, *Eth. nic.* 5.1.8.

[26] Plutarch, *Frat. amor.* 484B; cf. Ps.-Aristotle, *Mund.* 5. Further, Stählin, "ἴσος," 343–55; Spicq, *Lexicon*, 2:223–32.

It is possible to take the next verse with the one that precedes it: thrift better enables one to render to others their due. It should come as no surprise that economy was a gnomic value. As Miriam Lichtheim points out, one of the emphases in P.Insinger, for example, is "the need to obtain a minimum for a livelihood, to make it last by living frugally, and not to hanker after wealth."[27] Among its relevant recommendations are 4.6–7 ("Do not squander the little you have if there is no storehouse behind you. Do not eat the profit of something before the fate has given it.") and 6.17 ("Poverty does not rule over him who controls himself in expenditure.").[28] Pseudo-Phocylides' particular interpretation of this value in v. 138 may represent a critique (and radicalization) of Hesiod, *Op.* 368–369: "At the start (ἀρχομένου) of a cask or the end of it, take your fill, in the middle be sparing (φείδεσθαι): parsimony at the bottom is mean." By contrast, our author recommends conservation from beginning to (apparently) end; compare Theognis, *El.* 931–932: "It is better to be sparing (φείδεσθαι), since not even after your death does anyone mourn, unless he sees possessions left behind" (cf. 903–930).

Verses 139–140. Verse 139 is best understood in conjunction with the rule in vv. 147–148 about not eating food meant for animal consumption (cf. vv. 156–157). The verse's assumed priorities also can be seen to cohere with those of the preceding material. Even beasts should receive their due (cf. v. 137), that is, their allotted measure of food (βορὴ κατὰ μέτρον; cf. v. 14).[29] It is important to be frugal with everything (v. 138), but this norm does not sanction depriving animals of their rations. Philo insists that the principles of decency embodied by the Mosaic law are such that they extend even to beasts (e.g., *Virt.* 81, 125, 140), an attitude reflected also in Prov 12:10: "A righteous man has pity for the lives of his animals."[30] Josephus makes the same case in his summary of the law: Moses "has taught us gentleness and humanity so effectively that he has not overlooked the care of brute beasts, by permitting only legal use of them" (*C. Ap.* 2.213; similarly, Philo, *Hypoth.* 7.7). This exemplifies the fairness that the law inculcates in its adherents (2.214; cf. Deut 25:4; *T. Zeb.* 5:1).

With this we may compare the rules for feeding livestock Hesiod provides in *Opera et dies*. During the threshing season, the farmer ought to "maintain a dog with sharp teeth, not sparing his food … and bring in hay and rubbish so that your oxen and mules may have enough to eat" (604–607). During winter, though, "oxen should have half, a man the greater part of his full ration" (559–560). By contrast,

---

[27] Lichtheim, *Late Egyptian Wisdom*, 153.

[28] Cf. *Gnom. Vat.* 43; Sextus, *Sent.* 252.

[29] For κατὰ μέτρον referring to the regular measure of something, cf. Lucian, *Nav.* 44.

[30] Cf. Berthelot, "Philo and Kindness Towards Animals," 48–65.

Pseudo-Phocylides seems to take the position that an animal's rations should never be cut, even in order to help feed oneself.[31]

The humane treatment of animals links vv. 139 and 140 thematically; note the parallelism of κτήνους θνητοῖο and κτῆνος ... ἐχθροῖο. The command in the latter verse is based on Exod 23:5: "If you see the beast of your enemy (ἐχθροῦ) fallen (πεπτωκός) under its burden, you shall not pass it by but help to lift (συνεγερεῖς) it with him" (cf. Deut 22:4). In his interpretation of this passage, Philo suggests that it teaches that people should not take pleasure in their enemies' misfortunes; instead, they should take steps to encourage reconciliation.[32] Similarly, 4 Macc 2:14 cites this ordinance as one of the ways in which "reason through the law can prevail over enmity." Whether Pseudo-Phocylides' concern is more with the plight of the animal or that of its owner is unclear, though the verses that follow concentrate on the latter (note ἐχθρός in vv. 140 and 142).

Verses 141–143. The subject of v. 141 is at first difficult to discern. The word ἀλίτροπος is a *hapax*, a fusion of ἀλιτρός and τρόπος, and so describing a person "of sinful ways." The line's first word, πλαζόμενον, refers literally to a wanderer (cf. vv. 40–41), though the term readily lent itself to figurative use, for example, *Sib. Or.* 3.9, where it describes someone who strays from the divine path.[33] The reader is called upon not to censure or reproach (ἐλέγχω) such individuals. In biblical wisdom, ἔλεγχος is ordinarily assigned positive value, since it is an obligatory element of moral instruction.[34] We do encounter, however, certain caveats regarding the administration of such correction that share the viewpoint of vv. 141–142, for example, Prov 9:7–8: "He that censures an ungodly person will disgrace himself; do not censure evil people, lest they should hate you." It seems that the effective correction of others is possible only if they are already predisposed to seek what is good. Reproving the unworthy is understood not only as wasted effort but even as counterproductive, insofar as it fosters resentment or animosity.[35]

The thought of doing what creates friendship and not enmity (cf. vv. 34, 46–47) continues in v. 142. Among Hellenistic Jewish authors Ben Sira speaks most intently about the value and responsibilities of friendship.[36] The goal is summed up in 6:1: "Do not become an enemy instead of a friend, for a bad name inherits shame and reproach." The importance of preserving friendship is a particular concern, es-

---

[31] Cf. the tale of the groom who sells his horse's barley in Babrius, *Fab.* 83.

[32] Philo, *Virt.* 116–118; cf. Josephus, *Ant.* 4.275.

[33] Cf. Philo, *Jos.* 147, *Decal.* 81, *Praem.* 98.

[34] Cf. Büchsel, "ἐλέγχω," 473–76; Link, "ἐλέγχω," 140–42.

[35] Cf. Lev 19:17; Prov 15:12; Sir 20:1, 31:31; *Jos. Asen.* 11:10; *Instr. Ankh.* 7.4–5; Democritus, frg. 192; *Gnom. Democr.* 60, 109. For the opposing view, cf. Plato, *Leg.* 917D; further, Glad, *Paul*, 69–98.

[36] See Corley, *Ben Sira's Teaching on Friendship*.

pecially when disputes arise that may jeopardize the relationship: see 19:13–17, 22:19–22; cf. *Syr. Men.* 213–214. *Let. Arist.* 227 indicates one possible motive for such efforts: "We must show liberal charity to our opponents so that in this manner we may convert them to what is proper and fitting for them."[37]

Verse 143 offers practical advice on achieving the objective identified by the preceding maxim: at the first sign of trouble one should act quickly and decisively (note the verb used here, κόπτω, "to strike, to chop off"). Verses 142–143 may have been composed in imitation of Theognis, *El.* 1133–1134: "With the friends (φίλοισι) we have let us put a stop to the beginning of evil (κακοῦ ... ἀρχήν) and seek a remedy for the wound (ἕλκει) before it grows." The sources of enmity need to be addressed promptly, lest they become uncontrollable (cf. vv. 57–58, 63–64); afterwards it is too late (cf. vv. 55–56).[38] Comparable advice can be found in philosophical instruction about avoiding the damage brought on by anger, for example, Plutarch, *Cohib. ira* 454E–F (cf. 455A): "The man who at the beginning gives heed to his temper ... need have no great concern about it. ... For he who gives no fuel to a fire puts it out, and likewise he who does not in the beginning nurse his wrath ... takes precautions against it and destroys it." Also see Seneca, *Ira* 1.7.4: "There are certain things whose beginnings are in our power, but which later carry us away by their force and leave us no way of turning back." Cf. Publilius Syrus, *Sent.* 87–88.

Verses 147–148. Biblical law strictly forbids human consumption of flesh torn by animals (θηριάλωτον); taking it renders one ritually unclean.[39] The source of these lines is one such rule, Exod 22:30: "You shall not eat meat taken from wild beasts; you shall throw it to the dog" (κρέας θηριάλωτον οὐκ ἔδεσθε, τῷ κυνὶ ἀπορρίψατε αὐτό.). Philo thinks advice like this makes sense both because such food may be unhealthy and because it is unfitting for human beings to share a meal with beasts (*Spec.* 4.119–120).[40] Pseudo-Phocylides similarly motivates the injunction with a culturally-grounded observation about the natural world: it is unacceptable for peo-

---

[37] Cf. Euripides, *Hec.* 848 ("changing to friends the bitterest of enemies"); Philo, *Virt.* 152; Diogenes Laertius, *Vit. phil.* 1.87, 91, 8.23 (Pythagoras bade his disciples "so to behave one to another as not to make friends into enemies, but to turn enemies into friends."); Cicero, *Off.* 1.34–40 (extending justice even to enemies); J. Ferguson, *Moral Values*, 53–75; Spicq, *Lexicon*, 3:448–51.

[38] Cf. *Gnom. Vat.* 66; Euripides, frg. 32; Babrius, *Fab.* 82.9–10; *T. Ash.* 1.6–7.

[39] Gen 31:39; Lev 5:2, 7:24, 17:15, 22:8; Ezek 4:14, 44:31.

[40] Cf. Diogenes Laertius, *Vit. phil.* 8.33 (Pythagoras: "Abstain from meat and the flesh of animals that have died."); Plutarch, *Def. orac.* 417C; Maximus of Tyre, *Or.* 36.2; Aratus, *Phaen.* 130–132; Ovid, *Metam.* 15.75–95; *Carm. aur.* 67–68, with Thom, *Golden Verses*, 215–22.

ple to take what properly belongs to animals; cf. v. 139.[41] Later he will make the additional point that the readers should procure their own food (vv. 156–157).

Verse 149. Although *pharmakon* can have a positive connotation (e.g., Sir 38:4), biblical authors usually associate it with sorcery and mischief.[42] The polemic against *pharmakeia* continued in Christian circles,[43] often in conjunction with denunciations of magic, for example, *Did.* 2:2: "You shall not practice magic, you shall not mix potions" (οὐ μαγεύσεις, οὐ φαρμακεύσεις).[44] Ancient moralists on the whole imputed venal motives to these kinds of activities. Philo, for instance, condemns those who use such devices to harm or kill others (*Spec.* 3.93–103).[45] For the wording of v. 149, compare Homer, *Od.* 10.290 (cf. 10.213, 316–317): "She will mix (τεύξει) for you a drug and put potions (φάρμακα) in the food." As this line exemplifies, women were stereotypically connected with magic and sorcery.[46]

Verse 150. Verse 57 counseled the reader, "Be not rash with your hands." This principle is here applied to the treatment of children (cf. v. 137 v.l.). Our author's cue may have come from the legal source he shares with Josephus and Philo; the later indicates that in Jewish communities, "if you do violence to a child (ἐὰν βιάσῃ παῖδα)," the prescribed penalty is death (*Hypoth.* 7.1).[47] The manner in which this line might expand upon v. 149 thematically is unclear, though it is noteworthy that certain biblical passages do link condemnations of magic with prohibitions of child sacrifice (Lev 20:4–6; Deut 18:10), while in Greco-Roman society boys "were believed to be killed for a variety of magical purposes."[48]

---

[41] Cf. Hesiod, *Op.* 276–280: "For this was the rule for men that Kronos' son laid down: whereas fish and beasts and flying birds would eat one another, because Right is not among them, to men he gave Right, which is much the best in practice."

[42] E.g., Exod 22:17; Deut 18:10; Wis 12:4; Mic 5:11; Nah 3:4; Mal 3:5; Isa 47:9; cf. *Sib. Or.* 3.225, 5.165.

[43] E.g., Gal 5:20; Rev 9:21, 18:23, 21:8, 22:15. For books of magic, see *Jub.* 10:10–14; Acts 19:19; *PGM* III.424, VII.249, XIII.3, 15, 16, etc.; Dickie, *Magic*, 117–23 and s.v. magical books.

[44] Cf. *Mart. Isa.* 2:5; *T. Reub.* 4:9; *Sib. Or.* 1.96; *L.A.B.* 34:1–5; *Did.* 5:1; *Barn.* 20:1; also cf. Euripides, *Orest.* 1497.

[45] Cf. Plato, *Resp.* 364C, *Leg.* 909B, 933C–D; Ps.-Heraclitus, *Ep.* 7.4; Philo, *Sacr.* 26; Josephus, *Ant.* 19.193, *Bell.* 1.596, 637.

[46] E.g., *1 En.* 7:1; *T. Reub.* 4:9; *T. Jos.* 5:1, 6:1; *m. 'Abot* 2:7; Tacitus, *Ann.* 2.74, 3.7, 12.65–66; Pliny, *Nat.* 25.10; Quintilian, *Inst.* 5.10.25; Theocritus, *Id.* 2; cf. Ilan, *Jewish Women*, 221–25; Dickie, *Magic*, 79–95, 99–109, 164–68; Edwards, *Politics of Immorality*, 51–52.

[47] Cf. Philo, *Spec.* 2.232: fathers have the right to beat, degrade, and bind their children.

[48] Dickie, *Magic*, 138, cf. 139, 170; e.g., Cicero, *Vat.* 14; Horace, *Epod.* 5; Cassius Dio, *Hist.* 74.16.5; Juvenal, *Sat.* 6.550–552.

The strict discipline of children, including physical punishment, is taken for granted as a parental responsibility in Jewish wisdom, reflecting ancient norms.[49] Regular physical punishment was understood to be in the best interest of both parents and children, as we learn in Sir 30:1–13, which likens a young boy to a colt that must be broken before it can be trained: "Beat his sides while he is still a child (νήπιος) lest he become stubborn and disobey you" (v. 12).[50] Against this background the view expressed by Pseudo-Phocylides seems remarkably restrained, though the main thought may be about the treatment of children who are not one's own.[51] At any rate, the principle affirmed here anticipates the counsel of vv. 207–209, which encourages the gentle treatment of one's own offspring.

Verses 151–152. Verse 151 contributes to the paragraph's message about wrongdoing with the advice to "flee" strife and quarrelling (cf. vv. 132–134).[52] In vv. 75 and 78, the author identified strife as a source of suffering and instability. While terms like διχοστασίη, ἔρις, and πόλεμος could be used with reference to major social upheavals or the activities of armies, they could describe private disputes as well, which seems to be the case here.[53] Thus we might compare Sir 28:8 ("Refrain from a fight, and you will diminish sins."), Syr. Men. 139–142 ("Do not pass through a market street in which there is a quarrel, lest … you badly suffer, and, if you part them, you be wounded and your garments be rent, and, if you stand there and watch, you be summoned to court to give evidence."), or Carm. aur. 59–60: "Strife (ἔρις) … one must not promote; but withdraw and flee (φεύγειν) from it."[54]

Instructions to do good for one's benefactors were given in v. 80. The need for selectivity in benefaction is addressed in the paragraph's final line, which picks up a theme of gnomic teaching we find in texts like Sir 12:1–7 and Isocrates, Demon. 29. The former cautions against giving alms to sinners, with v. 5 supplying the rationale: "Do not give to the ungodly; hold back your bread and give it not to him, lest he overpower you thereby; for you will receive twice as much evil for all the good you

---

[49] Cf. Dionysius of Halicarnassus, Ant. rom. 2.26.1–6; further: Wiedemann, Adults and Children, 25–32; Dixon, Roman Family, 116–19.

[50] Cf. Prov 13:24, 19:18, 22:15, 23:13, 29:17.

[51] Prov 1:32 may supply something of a biblical precedent, which says of those who reject wisdom, "Because they wronged children (ἠδίκουν νηπίους) they shall be killed." The meaning of νηπίους, however, is unclear; it could mean "the simple." Cf. Publilius Syrus, Sent. 123; and see the discussion of Ps.-Phoc. 207–209 below.

[52] For φεύγω in the sense of avoiding a vice, see BDAG s.v. 3; e.g., Sir 21:2; 1 Cor 6:18, 10:14; 1 Tim 6:11; 2 Tim 2:22.

[53] Paul can list both ἔρις and διχοστασίαι as community vices, alongside fornication, jealousy, etc.: Gal 5:20; cf. Rom 16:17; 1 Cor 3:3 v.l.; Jas 4:1; Philo, Gig. 51; T. Sim. 4:8; T. Gad 5:1; 1 Clem. 3:2; Epictetus, Diatr. 3.20.18.

[54] Cf. Thom, Golden Verses, 198–99; Solon, frg. 4.38–39 (διχοστασία + ἔρις); P.Ins. 3.24–4.3.

did him."[55] The latter sounds a similar warning: "If you do good to evil men, you will have the same reward as those who feed stray dogs; for these snarl alike at those who give them something and those who happen by; likewise evil men wrong alike those who help them and those who wrong them." Pseudo-Phocylides would seem to agree that charity ought not be squandered on the unworthy, thus creating a restriction on unconditional almsgiving (cf. vv. 22–30) and challenging the reader to make a moral assessment of the recipient of any "good" deed.[56] In contrast to Ben Sira and Isocrates, he concentrates not on the possible negative repercussions for those who try to help the reprobate, but on the futility of such actions. To sow on the water was proverbial for a wasted or foolish effort. Our author's source is most likely Theognis, El. 105–106: "Doing a good turn (εὖ ἔρδοντι) to the base is an utterly useless act of kindness; it is the same as sowing on the expanse of the white-capped sea (ἶσον καὶ σπείρειν πόντον ἁλὸς πολιῆς)."[57] In evaluating our author's appropriation of this text, it should be noted that the cynicism of v. 152 is balanced by the more optimistic perspective of vv. 140–143: there is hope of redeeming at least some sinners![58]

---

[55] Cf. Did. 1:6, with Niederwimmer, Didache, 83–86.

[56] Cf. Theognis, El. 955–956; Gnom. Democr. 93; Plato, Leg. 936B–C; Aristotle, Eth. nic. 4.1.22; Ps.-Charondas, Prooem. 2.61.23–27; Dict. Cat. pr. 17, 39; Cicero, Off. 2.54; Seneca, Vit. beat. 23.5.

[57] Cf. vv. 107–110 ("You cannot reap a tall crop by sowing the sea, and you cannot get anything good in return by doing good to the base. For the base have an insatiable desire; if you make one mistake, the friendship shown by all former acts is wasted."); also Sib. Or. 8.409; Philo, Post. 162–164, Spec. 3.32; Paroem. Gr. 1.70.55.

[58] Collins, Jewish Wisdom, 167.

VIII. Earning a Living (Verses 153–174)

Bibliography: Agrell, *Work*, 33–45. D'Arms, *Commerce and Social Standing*, 20–47, 149–71. Küchler, *Weisheitstraditionen*, 292–98. van Geytenbeek, *Musonius Rufus*, 129–34. West, *Works and Days*, 229–37. Wilkins, *The Boastful Chef*, 71–86.

153	Work with much labor so that you can live from your own means;
154	for every man who's idle lives off thieving hands.
156	You should not eat refuse from the meal of another's table,
157	but you should live life from your own means without disgrace.
158	And if someone does not know a trade, he should dig with a mattock.
159	There is in life all sorts of work, if you are willing to labor.
160	If as a mariner you are willing to sail, broad is the sea;
161	but if you want to pursue farming, quite large are the fields.
162	No work is wont to be without trouble (or) easy for men,
163	not even for the blessed ones themselves; but toil greatly strengthens virtue.
164	Ants, once they have left homes very deep underground,
165	come in need of food, whenever fields,
166	sheared of their crops, fill threshing floors with grain.
167	And they themselves have a newly threshed load of wheat
168	or barley – and bearer ever follows bearer –
169	from summer's harvest gathering their food for winter
170	untiringly. (This) tiny folk is quite hard-working.
171	And the air-roving and industrious bee labors,
172	either in the crevice of a hollow rock or in reeds,
173	or in the hollow of a primal oak, inside beehives,
174	in swarms building with wax at thousand-celled honeycombs.

TEXTUAL NOTES

[Verse 155.] "<For> a trade sustains a man, but hunger oppresses an idler." (τέχνη <γὰρ> τρέφει ἄνδρα, ἀεργὸν δ' ἵψατο λιμός.) A spurious verse (only in V); see van der Horst, *Sentences*, 217. Verse 156. σκυβάλισμα (a *hapax*) = σκύβαλον, for which see Spicq, *Lexicon*, 3:263–65 (e.g., Sir 27:4; Philo, *Sacr.* 109, 139; Strabo, *Geogr.* 14.1.37; *Anth. Gr.* 6.303.4). Verse 157. Reading βίοτον διάγοις ἀνύβριστος (cf.

P, L) with Diehl, *Anthologia*, 2.109; cf. Bernays, *Gesammelte Abhandlungen*, 259; Bergk, *Poetae Lyrici Graeci*, 102; for the phrase βίοτον διάγοις, cf. Aeschylus, *Pers.* 711; Sophocles, *Oed. col.* 1619; Aristophanes, *Nub.* 464; Plato, *Resp.* 579D; Philo, *Spec.* 3.166; 1 Tim 2:2. Derron, *Sentences*, 13: βιότων φαγέοις ἀνυβρίστως (cf. M, L²ᵞᵖ). Young, *Theognis*, 107: μισθῶν φαγέοις (cf. B); also van der Horst, *Sentences*, 218: "eat … from what you have earned yourself." Verse 158. For δάω + τέχνην, cf. Homer, *Od.* 6.233–234, 23.160–161. M, B, Pᵞᵖ, Lᵞᵖ have δικέλλῃ (a two-pronged fork or mattock; cf. Sophocles, *Ant.* 250; Menander, *Dysk.* 766–767; Josephus, *Ant.* 6.96); P, L go with a more familiar substitute, μακέλλῃ. Verse 159a. πᾶν: "all sorts;" see BDAG s.v. πᾶς 5. Verse 160. Cf. Derron, *Sentences*, 13: "Marin, si tu veux naviguer, la mer est vaste." Verse 163. Omitted by M, B, perhaps because of μακάρεσσι. Verse 164. LSJ s.v. μύχατος: the irr. superlative of μύχιος, "inward, inmost;" used of a house's inner room: Callimachus, *Hymn.* 3.68; Apollonius of Rhodes, *Argon.* 1.170. Verse 165a. LSJ s.v. χράω C (perf. with pres. sense, c. gen): "to be in need of, to desire, yearn after." Verse 166. M, B have πλήθωσιν, while P, V read βρίθουσιν (L: βρίθωσιν), perhaps echoing Homer, *Il.* 18.561, *Od.* 19.112. Verse 169. ποτί = πρός. Verse 170b. M², B, V¹: φῦλον; V: φύλων; L: φύλλον; M, P: φίλον. Verse 171. ἠεροφοῖτις (cf. ἠερόφοιτις in v. 125): for this usage, cf. *Orph. hymn.* 9.2, 81.1. Verse 172. ἠέ = ἤ. // The line's phrasing may be inspired by Homer, *Il.* 21.494–495, describing a dove that flies into "a hollow rock, a crevice (κοίλην … πέτρην, χηραμόν)," cf. 2.87–88, 12.167–169. Verse 173. For the expression δρυὸς ὠγυγίης, cf. Josephus, *Ant.* 1.186. Verse 174. For σμῆνος as a swarm of bees, cf. Hesiod, *Theog.* 594; Philo, *Hypoth.* 11.8; Josephus, *Ant.* 5.288. // P, V have μυριότρητα; M, B, L replace the *hapax* with μυριότητα ("myriad"). // κηροδομέω is also a *hapax*.

COMMENTARY

These verses represent a unified section on the importance and the nature of work,[1] a gnomic theme going back at least to Hesiod[2] and Phocylides of Miletus.[3] In terms of its overall design, this paragraph occupies a sort of middle ground between the advice concerning evildoers *et alii* in vv. 132–152 and the material on members of the household in vv. 175–227.[4] Overall, our author has marshaled a fair number of effective arguments for why one ought to esteem industriousness: it fosters virtue and self-sufficiency; it wards off crime and shame; there are always numerous op-

---

[1]   On this entire section, in addition to the commentaries, see Küchler, *Weisheitstraditionen*, 292–98; Thomas, *Der jüdische Phokylides*, 292–94, 326.

[2]   See especially Hesiod, *Op.* 286–319, with West, *Works and Days*, 229–37.

[3]   Phocylides, frg. 2, 7, 9.

[4]   See above, pp. 164–68.

portunities to pursue it; and in laboring one follows the example of (it seems) every living thing, from insects to the heavenly bodies.

The unit has two coordinated segments, distinguished by their function and argumentative stance. The first, which is prescriptive in nature, offers instruction on the necessity and value of hard work (vv. 153–163). It is comprised of two thematically distinct clusters of sayings, rounded off with a summarizing statement in vv. 162–163. The first cluster calls upon the reader to labor diligently (vv. 153–157), while the second argues that all sorts of employment are possible (vv. 158–161).

The second segment (vv. 164–174) supports the first with two illustrations that have animals as their subjects:[5] the first is about ants (vv. 164–170), the second about bees (vv. 171–174). Here we find one of the few places in the poem where some narrative element drives the ordering of the verses. To begin with, we learn how ants, a traditional symbol in antiquity for industry and methodicalness, diligently set out to gather food for themselves. In the second vignette, the author enumerates some of the various locations where bees may labor.

Together these sketches furnish models of the sort of conduct requested in the first segment. Additionally, it should be observed that each illustration relates on a more specific level to one of the two exhortatory clusters in vv. 153–161. Thus the depiction of the ants in vv. 164–170 highlights their hard won self-sufficiency, which is the main theme of vv. 153–157. Meanwhile, the illustration of the bees' toil in vv. 171–174 draws attention to how they busy themselves in all sorts of different places, an aspect of labor that figures in the argument of vv. 158–161, where the poet mentions different locales for plying one's trade.[6] All of this is reinforced by some fairly extensive lexical coordination between the prescriptive and descriptive segments; note μοχθέω (vv. 153, 159) and πολύμοχθος (v. 170); βιοτεύω (v. 153), βίος (v. 159), and βίοτος (vv. 157, 165); γεηπονίη (v. 161) and γαῖα (v. 164); γεηπονίη (v. 161), πόνος (v. 163), and ἀριστοπόνος (v. 171); κάματος (v. 162) and κάμνω (v. 171).

Verses 153–157. While Greco-Roman elites generally disdained manual labor as servile and humiliating,[7] a number of philosophers extolled physical work as a means of attaining freedom and self-sufficiency.[8] Jewish authors were also quick to promote the virtues of hard work. In *C. Ap.* 2.291, Josephus claims that obedience to the law renders people industrious and not idle, an argument made by Philo as

---

5   Cf. above, pp. 159–60.

6   For such interlocking structures that alternate precepts with the descriptive examples corroborating them, cf. *Syr. Men.* 99–112, where the description of old age in vv. 102–104 supplements prohibitions not to scorn the elderly in vv. 99–100, whereas the description of poverty and the reversal of fortune in vv. 105–112 augments an appeal not to despise the poor in v. 101. Cf. also P.Ins. 4.17–5.1.

7   E.g., Plato, *Resp.* 495D; Aristotle, *Pol.* 8.2.1, *Rhet.* 1.9.27; Cicero, *Off.* 1.42, 50; D'Arms, *Commerce and Social Standing*, 20–47, 149–71; Rosivach, "Athenian Presuppositions," 192.

8   E.g., Xenophon, *Mem.* 2.7.7–8; Ps.-Socratics, *Ep.* 12, 13; Musonius Rufus, frg. 11.

well.[9] The biblical wisdom writers spent a fair amount of time on the subject and, like v. 153, many of their proverbs underscore the benefits that accrue to the diligent, for example, Prov 16:26 ("A man in his labors labors for himself and drives off his own destruction.").[10] Work as a theme of Greek sentential literature goes back at least to Hesiod's *Opera et dies*, for example, 302–304: "Hunger goes always with an idle man (ἀεργῷ … ἀνδρί). Gods and men disapprove of that man who lives in idleness;" cf. 309–313, 381–382, 397–398.[11]

While v. 153 attests to the profit of hard work, v. 154 predicts the fate of those who avoid it, implicating idleness in theft, a crime condemned by vv. 6, 18, and 135–136. The idler (ἀεργός) was a subject of proverbial reflection: he goes hungry, his way is strewn with thorns, he is overcome by his cravings.[12] A similarly dismal picture is drawn of the sluggard (ὀκνηρός).[13] According to the moral logic of the sages, the indolence of such characters leads ultimately to poverty and hunger, which in turn lead to theft; see Prov 6:30, 30:8–9. This association of thievery with sloth is at work in the appeal of Eph 4:28 as well: "Thieves must give up stealing; rather let them labor and work honestly with their own hands." For a Greek perspective, we may turn again to Hesiod, for example, *Op.* 314–316: "Whatever your fortune, work is preferable, that is, if you turn your misguided heart from others' possessions to your work and tend to your livelihood."[14] Several of our author's concerns are present also in Xenophon, *Oec.* 20.15: "If a man will not farm (cf. Ps.-Phoc. 161) and knows no other profitable trade (cf. Ps.-Phoc. 158), he is clearly minded to live by stealing or robbery or begging (cf. Ps.-Phoc. 156–157)."

The section's opening lines make the case that hard work offers protection from situations where one might be tempted to steal. The argument extends in vv. 156–157 to eating the scraps left behind by others. As the poet sees things, since all sorts of work are available (see vv. 158–161), it is always possible to earn a living and avoid this humiliation.[15] Shame as a motivation for avoiding the remains of someone else's

---

9   Cf. Philo, *Opif.* 169, *Her.* 77, *Spec.* 2.60, *Prob.* 69; cf. Josephus, *C. Ap.* 2.228.

10   Further: Prov 18:9, 31:18; Sir 10:27, 11:20–21; cf. *Ahiqar* 127; *Syr. Men.* 412–413; 1 Thess 2:9, 4:11, 5:14; 2 Thess 3:6–13; *ARN* A 11.1.1–8; Agrell, *Work,* 33–45.

11   For additional examples, see Stobaeus, *Anth.* 3.29–30; also Menander, *Mon.* 317, 463 ("To labor is a necessity for those wishing to succeed."); *Instr. Ankh.* 23.17; cf. Hock, *Social Context,* 35–40.

12   Prov 13:4, 15:19, 19:15.

13   Prov 6:9–11, 11:16, 18:8, 20:4, 21:25, 22:13, 26:13–16; Sir 22:1–2, 37:11; cf. Qoh 10:18.

14   Cf. Hesiod, *Op.* 498: "The idle man (ἀεργὸς ἀνήρ), waiting on empty hope, lacking a livelihood, lays to heart many evils." Also P.Ins. 27.2–3: "Do not steal out of hunger, you will be found out. Better death in want than life in shamelessness." Cf. Isocrates, *Areop.* 44: "Poverty comes about through idleness, and wrongdoing through poverty."

15   For the disgrace of gathering scraps from another's table, cf. Judg 1:7; Mark 7:28; Luke 16:21; Str–B 3:641–42. For ἀνύβριστος ("without insolence or outrage"), cf. *Gnom. Democr.* 73; Philo, *Abr.* 98; Josephus, *Ant.* 1.208–209.

meal is also an element of Sir 40:28–30: "Do not live a life of begging, for it is better to die than to beg. A man who looks to another's table, his life is not reckoned a life … In the mouth of the shameless begging is sweet, but in his belly a fire will burn." We can infer that begging would be included in what vv. 156–157 proscribe as well, though the means of obtaining such refuse is not at issue.[16] Perhaps closer to the intended reader's social reality is one of the stock characters of Roman comedy and satire, the slothful, parasitic flatterer who must resort to eating the leftovers of his host's meal in order to feed himself (cf. above, on vv. 91–94).[17]

Verses 158–161. In v. 158, the poet acknowledges, albeit indirectly, the importance of learning a trade; the alternative is demeaning, back-breaking work.[18] In *C. Ap.* 2.283, Josephus boasts about the diligence of Jewish folk in their trades, a quality even gentiles are obliged to admire. The Mosaic law, he says, encourages people to take up either such trades or farming (τέχναις ἢ γεωργίαις, 2.294; cf. Ps.-Phoc. 161). Although Ben Sira accords the skilled professions secondary importance in relation to the vocation of the sage, he acknowledges that "without them no city can be inhabited" (Sir 38:32); cf. above, on v. 88.

The observation in v. 159 follows closely on the section's introduction in v. 153 (note ἐργ- and μοχθ- in both). The repetition of ἐθέλω in vv. 159 and 160 is notable; what is at issue here is the willingness, not the ability, to work (cf. Homer, *Od.* 17.321; 2 Thess 3:10). This claim is substantiated by two illustrations in vv. 160–161. Sailing may have been understood as a last resort for men who have not learned a craft (v. 158). As we hear in Wis 14:4, "Even someone without a trade (ἄνευ τέχνης) may put to sea."[19] The expansive opportunities offered by seafaring are evoked with the comment that "the sea is broad," perhaps in imitation of the Homeric tag, "the broad back of the sea" (εὐρέα νῶτα θαλάσσης); cf. Theognis, *El.* 179–180: "One should search over land and the broad-backed sea alike, Cyrnus, to find release from grievous poverty."[20] The inclusion of farming as an illustration of the possibilities for hard work is hardly unexpected. Both the difficulties and the rewards of this way of life were well-known.[21] The pairing is reminiscent also of

---

[16] Cf. Homer, *Od.* 19.27–28; Hesiod, *Op.* 393–395, 397–400; *Instr. Ankh.* 17.24; Küchler, *Weisheitstraditionen*, 295–96.

[17] E.g., Plautus, *Curc.* 321, 388, *Pers.* 77–79, 138, *Stic.* 231, 496; Juvenal, *Sat.* 11.142–144, 14.126–128; Martial, *Epig.* 7.20; cf. Horace, *Sat.* 1.3.80–83; Damon, *Mask of the Parasite*, 27–28; Wilkins, *The Boastful Chef*, 71–86.

[18] Cf. Aristophanes, *Av.* 1432.

[19] Cf. Hesiod, *Op.* 634; *T. Zeb.* 5:5–6:8; Stobaeus, *Anth.* 4.17.

[20] Homer, *Il.* 2.159, 8.511, and often; cf. *Sib. Or.* 3.615; also Ps 103:25; Job 11:9; *4 Ezra* 7:3.

[21] Besides Hesiod's *Opera et dies*, see especially Xenophon, *Oec.* 5.1–17 and Musonius Rufus, frg. 11 (with van Geytenbeek, *Musonius Rufus*, 129–34); also Prov 12:11, 28:19; Sir 7:15; *Instr. Ankh.* 9.14, 17.23; *Instr. Amenem.* 8.17–20; *Ahiqar* 127; *T. Iss.* 5:3–5; Philo, *Opif.* 80, *Sacr.* 38, *Spec.* 2.213,

Hesiod's *Opera et dies*, where instruction on the principles of farming (383–617) is accompanied by a section on sailing (618–694), the two being representative of the basic endeavors of the industrious man.[22] It is interesting that Pseudo-Phocylides recommends these occupations despite having already acknowledged the uncertainties that attend them (vv. 25 and 41, cf. v. 131).

Verses 162–163. For the unlikely possibility that v. 162 quotes a line from the so-called Branchidae oracle, see van der Horst, *Sentences*, 220–21. It is more probable that this is an aphorism of ultimately unknown origin on the pervasiveness of trouble, or κάματος, in human work, a popular subject.[23] Philo expresses a common opinion when he says in *Sacr.* 38 that any worthwhile endeavor entails "much trouble," giving farming as an example.[24]

Verse 163a may be a reference to the movements or "work" of the celestial bodies, in which case they are being held up as a model for imitation as in vv. 71–75; cf. μακάρεσσιν in v. 75. Of the sun, moon, and heavens, Philo points to the seasonal changes as clear proof of their κάματος (*Cher.* 88–89).[25] Compare also Hesiod, *Theog.* 881, which refers to the toil (πόνος) of the blessed gods (μάκαρες θεοί).

In v. 66, Pseudo-Phocylides identified the advantages associated with "toiling" at good deeds. In v. 163b, the specific benefit of toil is said to be ἀρετή, an observation that would recommend itself to various ancient moralists, especially Philo, who championed πόνος with declarations like *Sacr.* 35: "God has appointed toil as the beginning of every goodness and every virtue."[26] Josephus emphasizes the *ponoi* Torah imposes on its adherents (*C. Ap.* 2.228), teaching them to be hard-working and self-dependent (2.291). Such statements contributed to the larger commendation of φιλοπονία, or industriousness: "That the good things of life, above all manliness and the capacity to earn respect by achievement, can be won only by exertion is one of the commonest

---

Praem. 128–129; Phocylides, frg. 7; Ps.-Aristotle, *Oec.* 1.2.2–3; Maximus of Tyre, *Or.* 24; Cicero, *Off.* 1.150–151; Virgil, *Georg.* 2.513–540; Cato, *Agr.* pr. 4; Columella, *Rust.* pr. 10–11; Stobaeus, *Anth.* 4.15. On romantic notions of farming life cherished by Roman elites, see W. Fitzgerald, "Labor and Laborer," 389–418; Shelton, *As the Romans Did*, 149–50, 160–62.

22   Cf. Solon, frg. 13.43–46; *Anth. Gr.* 9.23.

23   E.g., Hesiod, *Op.* 303–306 (cf. 42–44); Heraclitus, frg. 84b, 111; Theognis, *El.* 925; Sophocles, *Oed. col.* 1231; Pindar, *Pyth.* 12.28 (cf. *Ol.* 5.16, *Nem.* 8.50); *L.A.E.* 24:1–3 (cf. Gen 3:17–19).

24   Cf. *Opif.* 80, 167, *Sacr.* 38, 113.

25   On the labor of the heavenly bodies, cf. Mimnermus, frg. 8; Dio Chrysostom, *3 Regn.* 73–75; Varro, *Sat.* frg. 231; Cicero, *Tusc.* 1.92; Virgil, *Georg.* 2.478, *Aen.* 1.742.

26   Cf. Philo, *Sacr.* 37, 40–41, 112–114, *Det.* 27, *Post.* 154, *Ebr.* 94, *Sobr.* 65, *Congr.* 161–167, *Spec.* 4.124, *Prob.* 69; Xenophon, *Oec.* 5.12; Phocylides, frg. 9: "Seek a living, and when you have a living, virtue." Further, Spicq, *Lexicon*, 3:139–40.

Greek maxims."[27] See, for example, Menander, *Mon.* 221, 252, 256 ("Be industrious in deeds not just words."), and 811: "Be industrious and you'll gain a good life."

Verses 164–174. The source for these two models of industriousness is Prov 6:6–8.

(6) Go to the ant, you sluggard, and emulate his ways, and become wiser than him. (7) For although he has no agriculture, nor anyone compelling him, and is under no master, (8) still he provides food for himself during the summer harvest, and in the harvest he creates a large store. (8a) Or go to the bee, and learn how industrious she is, and how nobly she does her work. (8b) Her toils kings and commoners take for their health, and she is desired and respected by all. (8c) Although weak in bodily strength, she is advanced by honoring wisdom.

Like Proverbs 6, Pseudo-Phocylides begins with ants, describing how they gather a large supply of food from the summer harvest (note θέρος in Prov 6:8 and v. 169). He also draws attention to how the ants do this work on their own (note αὐτοί in v. 167 and σφέτερος in v. 169; cf. Prov 6:7). The poet departs from his source by adding a number of vivid details, drawing from epic diction (cf. Homer, *Il.* 5.499–501, 11.68–69, 558–560, 23.599, *Od.* 7.118, 9.233, 19.112). He describes how ants leave their subterranean dwellings for the threshing floors, which are filled with the fruits of the land,[28] wheat and barley.[29] Despite their small size, because they work untiringly,[30] they are able to store what food they need for the winter.[31]

Pseudo-Phocylides takes even greater liberties with his source in describing the activity of the bee, detailing the various locales for her work, while Proverbs 6 emphasizes the desirability of her product. Our author does pick up on the excellent "toil" exemplified by the bee in v. 171 (cf. πόνοι in Prov 6:8b, also ἐργάτις in 6:8a). In their original context, these illustrations contribute to an exhortation against laziness, which is said to cause poverty (Prov 6:9–11a). Prov 6:11a gives the main point in the form of a promise: "If you are diligent, then your harvest will arrive as a fountain." Pseudo-Phocylides' application is comparable, yet while Proverbs sees the animals' industriousness as proof of their wisdom (8:6, 8c), here the association

---

[27] Dover, *Popular Morality*, 163; e.g., Democritus, frg. 179, 182, 240–241; Isocrates, *Demon.* 40; Sophocles, *El.* 945; Euripides, frg. 233, 236–238; Xenophon, *Mem.* 2.1.28; Diogenes Laertius, *Vit. phil.* 6.2, 7.168–170; Musonius Rufus, frg. 7; Arius Didymus, *Epit.* 11k; Horace, *Sat.* 1.9.59–60.

[28] For "fruits of the land," cf. Ps.-Phoc. 38. For the imagery of threshing floors filled with grain, cf. Num 15:20; Job 5:26.

[29] For the combination of wheat and barley, see Deut 8:8; Ruth 2:23; 2 Kgdms 17:28; Philo, *Sacr.* 109, *Spec.* 4.29; Homer, *Il.* 11.69, *Od.* 9.110, 19.112; Herodotus, *Hist.* 2.36.2.

[30] For this use of ἄτρυτοι, cf. Philo, *Opif.* 80, 167.

[31] On the ant: Horace, *Sat.* 1.1.32–38; Rech, "Ameise," 375–77.

seems to be with virtue (see v. 163b).[32] For the combination of ant and bee, compare Aristotle, *Hist. an.* 8.38, Ovid, *Ars* 1.93–96, and Marcus Aurelius, *Med.* 5.1: "Consider each tiny plant, each little bird, the ant, the spider, the bee, how they go about their own work and do each his part for the building up of an orderly universe. Do you then refuse to do the work of a man?"[33]

---

[32] On the bee: Hesiod, *Theog.* 594–599; Phocylides, frg. 2; Aelian, *Nat. an.* 5.12; Horace, *Carm.* 4.2.27–32; Virgil, *Aen.* 1.430–435; Koep, "Biene," 274–82.

[33] The combination of ant and bee in LXX Proverbs 6 itself probably reflects Hellenistic influence, the latter not being mentioned in the Hebrew.

IX. Sex and the Household (Verses 175–227)

Bibliography: Balch, "Household Codes," 25–50. Edwards, *Politics of Immorality.* Feldmann, *Birth Control.* Foucault, *History of Sexuality,* 2:38–93, 3:147–227. Gardner, *Women in Roman Law.* Gielen, *Haustafelethik,* 24–67. Licht, *Sexual Life.* Richlin, "Not Before Homosexuality," 523–73. Saller, "Corporal Punishment," 144–65. Treggiari, *Roman Marriage,* 60–80, 95–100, 215–24, 245–53, 323–64.

The last major section of the poem, vv. 175–227, has attracted a fair amount of scholarly attention on account of its parallels with the so-called *Haustafeln* literature.[1] Although representative examples vary, one influential version of this form (see, e.g., Aristotle, *Pol.* 1.2.1–2; Eph 5:21–6:9; Col 3:18–4:1) will: 1) outline relationships among three pairs of social classes, 2) relate the classes reciprocally, and 3) depict one class in each pair as being governed by the other. Although Pseudo-Phocylides does employ the scheme of the "Household Code" as a general framework, he has also given the material its own stamp.[2] To begin with, the section's introductory paragraph, vv. 175–194, focuses on matters of sex and reproduction, consisting largely of precepts that circumscribe the conduct of the male head of the household (vv. 175–176, 179–183, 186–191, 193), as well as women who are presumably under his control (vv. 177–178, 184–185, 192).[3] The ethos of the section is grounded to no small extent in Leviticus 18–19, as this chart of likely parallels shows:[4]

Ps.-Phoc.	177	179	182	183	188	189	191
Leviticus	19:29	18:8	18:9	18:16	18:23	18:19 (?)	18:22

---

[1] For reviews of relevant literature see P. Fiedler, "Haustafel," 1063–73; Balch, "Household Codes," 25–50; Gielen, *Haustafelethik,* 24–67; cf. van der Horst, "Pseudo-Phocylides and the New Testament," 196–200.

[2] Cf. Thomas, *Der jüdische Phokylides,* 57–59, 326–27, 378–91.

[3] The exhortation consists largely of negative prohibitions, with every line beginning with μη- except vv. 176, 178, 191, and 194. The paragraph is also unified by the repeated use of words that contain the λοχ or λεχ (λεκ) stem: vv. 176, 177, 178, 179, 181, 183, 186, 188, 189, and 192.

[4] Cf. Josephus, *Ant.* 3.274–275; Thomas, *Der jüdische Phokylides,* 57–89, 425–28; Niebuhr, *Gesetz und Paränese,* 26–31.

The second paragraph (vv. 195–227), while organized according to the topics marriage, children, and slaves, also exhibits some distinctive features.[5] First, in keeping with the bent of the opening paragraph, the advice on children (vv. 207–217) concentrates on the parents' responsibilities to protect them from unwanted sexual advances (vv. 210–217). No mention is made of the children's reciprocal obligations. Similarly, the cluster of maxims on slaves (vv. 223–227) names only the slaveowners' responsibilities. Consequently, the idea of the subordination of weaker parties in the household is not as prominent in the *Sentences* as it is in comparable codes. In keeping with this, the section on marriage (vv. 195–206) highlights not the wife's obedience, but the couple's mutual love (vv. 195–197).[6] Second, between the paragraphs on children and slaves there are precepts urging respect to kinfolk (v. 219, cf. v. 206) and the elderly (vv. 220–222), enlarging the scope of social obligations beyond the traditional three pairs. Finally, we should bear in mind that the entire unit belongs to a larger structural and conceptual framework, vv. 132–227. In this regard, the importance assigned in the immediately preceding section to work and self-sufficiency (vv. 153–174) is noteworthy, inasmuch as it parallels discussions about acquiring wealth and managing financial affairs in some *Haustafeln* (again, cf. Aristotle, *Pol.* 1.2.1–2).[7] Comparison with similar schemes in Hellenistic-Jewish literature, especially Josephus, *C. Ap.* 2.199–206, reveals both similarities and differences with respect to the content and mode of organization; see above, pp. 166–68.

---

[5]   The second paragraph parallels the first in beginning with precepts on marriage (vv. 195–206, cf. vv. 175–178).

[6]   Passages like Josephus, *C. Ap.* 2.201 and 1 Pet 2:18 are noticeably absent from the *Sentences*.

[7]   Cf. Balch, *Wives*, 39, 42, 56; idem, "Household Codes," 45; Wood and Wood, *Class Ideology*, 233–37; Miller, "Naturalism," 321–43.

A. Verses 175–194

175   Remain not unmarried, lest you perish nameless.

176   And give something to nature yourself: beget in turn as you were begotten.

177   Do not prostitute your wife, defiling your children;

178   for an adulterous bed does not produce similar offspring.

179   Touch not your stepmother, since she is your father's second wife;

180   but honor as mother the one following your mother's footsteps.

181   Have no sort of sexual relations with your father's mistresses.

182   Approach not your sister's bed, (which is) abhorrent.

183   Do not go to bed with your brothers' wives.

184   A woman should not destroy an unborn babe in the womb,

185   nor after bearing it should she cast it out as prey for dogs and vultures.

186   Lay not a hand on your wife while she is pregnant.

187   Do not cut the male procreative nature of a youth.

188   Do not engage in sexual mating with senseless animals.

189   Do not outrage a woman with shameful acts of sex.

190   Go not beyond natural sexual unions for illicit passion;

191   unions between males are not pleasing even to beasts.

192   Let not women mimic the sexual role of men at all.

193   Be not inclined to utterly unrestrained lust for a woman.

194   For *Erōs* is no god, but a passion destructive of all.

TEXTUAL NOTES

Verse 175. For μή πως, see LSJ s.v. μήπως: "lest in any way." // For the expression, "perish nameless," cf. Homer, *Il.* 12.70, 13.227, 14.70, *Od.* 1.222; Hesiod, *Op.* 153–154; Euripides, *Iph. taur.* 502. Verse 176a. M¹, L: τι; M, B, P, V: τῇ. // Cf. van der Horst, *Sentences*: "Give nature her due." Verse 178. For μοιχικὰ λέκτρα, cf. *Anth. Gr.* 5.302.7. Verse 179. Following Bergk's (*Poetae Lyrici Graeci*, 104) conjecture μὴ ψαῦ', ἅτε. Young (*Theognis*, 109) and Derron (*Sentences*, 14, 29 n. 4) print μὴ ψαῦε τὰ (with Mᶜ). Or we could adopt the latter and place a raised stop after ψαῦε, as van der Horst (*Sentences*, 229–30) suggests. // In v. 178, λέκτρον has its usually meaning ("couch, bed"); here it is a circumlocution for "wife," an apparently unique though not idiosyncratic usage, since it can sometimes refer to marriage; see LSJ s.v. Verse 180. For ἴχνια βᾶσαν, cf. the Homeric expression ἴχνια βαῖνε: *Od.* 2.406, 3.30, 5.193, 7.38; cf. Philo, *Gig.* 39. Verses 181–182. Only Rᶜ has this order; the major mss. invert the lines, disrupting the apparent organization of vv. 179–183 (see the commentary). Verse 181. B: μηδέ τι; M, P, L, V: μὴ δ' ἐπὶ. //

LSJ s.v. μείγνυμι B.4: the term is used frequently of sexual intercourse in Homer, Hesiod, etc.; cf. *Sib. Or.* 3.596, 5.390; Ps.-Phoc. 198. // For λέχος (cf. Ps.-Phoc. 188–189, 192) referring to sexual relations: Josephus, *C. Ap.* 2.202; Pindar, *Pyth.* 9.37, 11.24; Aeschylus, *Pers.* 895; Sophocles, *Aj.* 491, *Trach.* 360, 514; Euripides, *Hipp.* 1003. Verse 182. For εὐνή (cf. Ps.-Phoc. 190–191) referring to sexual acts: Homer, *Il.* 3.445, 9.133, 14.336, *Od.* 1.433, 10.297; *Sib. Or.* 3.595, 764; Philo, *Spec.* 3.14, 63, *Virt.* 112, 223. // For the translation, cf. van der Horst, *Sentences*, 231: "Approach not the bed of your sister, a bed to turn away from." Verse 183. Only R^c has the line here; the major mss. place it after v. 194, where it ill fits the context. // For ἐπὶ δέμνια βαίνειν used of sexual relations, cf. Homer, *Od.* 8.296, 314; Hesiod, *Op.* 328 (quoted below). Verse 185. For the verse's diction, cf. Homer, *Il.* 1.4–5; Sophocles, *Aj.* 830; Aeschylus, *Suppl.* 800. // For the combination of dogs and vultures, cf. Homer, *Il.* 18.271, 22.42; *Sib. Or.* 5.279. Verse 187. P, V: τέμνειν φύσιν ἄρσενα κούρου; M, B, L: ποτὲ τέμνειν ἄρσενα κοῦρον. Verse 188. LSJ Sup s.v. βατήριος (a *hapax*): "of or connected with (animal) copulation." // For the expression ἐς λέχος ἐλθεῖν, cf. Hesiod, *Theog.* 912; Pindar, *Pyth.* 3.99. Verse 189. αἰσχυντός is a *hapax*. Verse 191. Only P^b has the line here; the major mss. place it between vv. 186 and 187 (perhaps because of ἄρσενα in the latter), missing the connection with vv. 190 and 192 (for which see the commentary). Verse 192. For the form θηλύτεραι, see LSJ s.v. θῆλυς. Verse 193. For ἔρωτα … ἀκάθεκτον, cf. Philo, *Spec.* 2.9 ("raging lusts or unrestrained desires," λελυττηκότες ἔρωτες ἢ ἐπιθυμίαι ἀκάθεκτοι), also *Jos.* 153, *Spec.* 2.193, 4.82.

COMMENTARY

Verses 175–176. Jewish sources frequently stress both the obligation to wed and the disgrace attending failure to marry and have children.[8] On the desirability of marriage see below, on vv. 195–197. In early Judaism, as in all traditional societies, children were a barometer of success, for example, Sir 11:28 ("Judge no one blessed before his death: for a man shall be known in his children.").[9] A strong need was felt to produce sons who would perpetuate the family name (ὄνομα), for example, Gen 48:16; Deut 25:5–10; Ruth 4:5, 10; Sir 40:19. Greek and Roman authors often (though not always) expressed a preference for marriage and children as well.[10]

---

[8]   The biblical creation account, e.g., emphasizes that human beings were made for marriage (Gen 2:24) and reproduction (1:28); cf. 4 Macc 16:9; Josephus, *Ant.* 4.244; Epstein, *Sex Laws*, 14–15, 141–43; Feldman, *Birth Control*, 46–59. Philo insists on sex for procreation only, e.g., *Det.* 102, *Abr.* 248–249, 253, *Jos.* 43, *Mos.* 1.28, *Spec.* 1.112, 2.133, 3.113, *Virt.* 207.

[9]   Cf. Prov 17:6, 31:28.

[10] E.g., Hesiod, *Op.* 376–380; Diogenes Laertius, *Vit. phil.* 7.121; Epictetus, *Diatr.* 3.7.25–26; Arius Didymus, *Epit.* 11b, m; Stobaeus, *Anth.* 4.22 (part 1), 24 (part 1); Cassius Dio, *Hist.* 56.3; Catul-

In this vein, vv. 175–176 announce not only the section's major theme but also its fundamental criterion, φύσις. Marriage and procreation are what, in the eyes of our author, "nature" requires. Activity exceeding or frustrating this end is consistently rejected, with v. 181 indirectly allowing one exception. While the term itself will surface only twice more (see vv. 187, 190), many of the rules laid down in this section were defended by ancients with rhetoric about nature and its "laws." Indeed, it was customary to substantiate one's moral views by depicting them, not as the culturally specific mores that they in fact were, but as predicated upon observations about the inherent constitution of the *kosmos*.[11] Foundational to much of this conversation was the idea that desire for the opposite sex "pays tribute to the laws of nature" (Philo, *Contempl.* 59) and that it is "in accordance with nature" that men and women join to procreate (Aristotle, *Eth. nic.* 8.12.7).[12] Like all the participants in this conversation, Pseudo-Phocylides' assumptions about nature advance a certain construal of social order, one in which the adult free male occupies the center.[13] For the overall perspective of this section we may compare Ps.-Charondas, *Prooem.* 2.62.30–33: "Let every man love (στεργέτω; cf. Ps.-Phoc. 195) his lawful wife and beget children by her. But let none shed the seed due his children into any other person, and let him not disgrace that which is honorable to both nature (φύσει) and law. For nature produced the seed for the sake of producing children and not for the sake of lust." The direct source for vv. 175–176 may be the summary of the law Pseudo-Phocylides shares with Philo and Josephus. The latter, much like our author, opens a section on marital issues by rejecting all sexual relations "except union with a woman in accordance with nature (κατὰ φύσιν), and that only for the sake of having children" (*C. Ap.* 2.199).

---

lus, *Carm.* 61.204–208; Musonius Rufus, frg. 13A–B, 14 (with van Geytenbeek, *Musonius Rufus,* 62–71). Mention may also be made of the *lex Iulia de maritandis ordinibus*, which discouraged childlessness through a graduated series of rewards and penalties; see Treggiari, *Roman Marriage,* 60–80; McGinn, *Prostitution,* 70–139. At the same time, of course, dissenting views were also voiced, e.g., 1 Cor 7:8, 11 (μενέτω ἄγαμος; cf. Ps.-Phoc. 175a), 26–27, 38; Philo, *Hypoth.* 11.14, 16–17; Josephus, *Bell.* 2.120–121; Democritus, frg. 276–277; Epictetus, *Diatr.* 1.23, 3.7.19; Ps.-Diogenes, *Ep.* 47; Plutarch, *Sol.* 7.3, *Quaest. conv.* 654C; Diogenes Laertius, *Vit. phil.* 6.29, 10.118–119; Stobaeus, *Anth.* 4.22 (part 2), 24 (part 2). For the debate, see Yarbrough, *Not Like the Gentiles,* 31–46; Deming, *Paul on Marriage,* 50–107.

[11] On the role of nature in ancient discourse about sexual behavior, see Foucault, *History of Sexuality,* 3:150–57, 193–227; cf. Horsley, "Law of Nature," 35–59; Koester, "ΝΟΜΟΣ ΦΥΣΕΩΣ," 521–41; Striker, *Essays,* 209–80; Najman, "Law of Nature," 55–73; and below, on Ps.-Phoc. 190–192.

[12] Cf. Aristotle, *Pol.* 1.1.4, *De an.* 2.4; Ps.-Aristotle, *Oec.* 1.3.1; Democritus, frg. 278; Diodorus Siculus, *Bibl.* 32.10.4, 9; Dio Chrysostom, *Ven.* 134–136; Philo, *Praem.* 108; Cicero, *Off.* 1.54, *Fin.* 3.20.68; Seneca, *Ep.* 9.17–18.

[13] As Winkler (*Constraints of Desire,* 21, cf. 20–23, 36–37, 114–18) puts it, acting contrary to nature, especially in the case of sex, means "going AWOL from one's assigned place in the social hierarchy."

Verses 177–178. The theme of procreation, introduced in the preceding lines, continues here. Philo's summary of the law indicates that it is a crime for Jews to prostitute themselves (*Hypoth.* 7.1). Lev 19:29 provides a somewhat better parallel for v. 177, relating an injunction not to prostitute a female relative, though there the subject is one's daughter, not one's wife: "You shall not profane your daughter to prostitute her."[14] This dictum is consistent with Levitical categorizations of prostitution as a polluting act (21:7, 9, 14). In this connection, it is noteworthy that the verb μιαίνω ("to defile") in v. 177b is employed regularly in Leviticus of sexual sins (e.g., 18:24–25, 27–28, 30).[15] For Pseudo-Phocylides, it is not the prostitute who is defiled, though, but her children. The notion that such adulterous relations[16] in some way taint any resulting children also informs Sir 23:22–27, which depicts the public examination of an adulteress and her illegitimate offspring: "She shall be brought out to the assembly and inquiry shall be made into her children; they will not take root and her branches will bear no fruit. She shall leave her memory to be cursed" (cf. Deut 23:3; Wis 4:6). This apparently refers to the ostracization of the children, who will not be allowed to "take root" in their community. In our text, the repercussions of extramarital sex for the resulting children, including the sense in which they are understood to be "defiled," are clarified by v. 178. The reader is told that his wife's children are "not similar," presumably referring to their physical dissimilarity from the reader himself as well as perhaps to their dissimilarity from one another.[17] The scenario envisioned here is comparable to that of *Decal.* 121–131, where Philo condemns unchaste wives because they deprive their husbands of all hope of legitimate heirs. However, it is the children in his estimation who are most unfortunate, since they will not be recognized as full members of either the adulteress' or the adulterer's respective families. Consequently, "they form an alien brood," whose true lineage and loyalty are always in doubt.[18]

Pseudo-Phocylides' stand here would have resonated with Roman sensibilities as well. Under the Julian law on adultery, for instance, pandering became a criminal offence; if a husband knew of his wife's adultery but did not divorce and prosecute

---

[14] Cf. Epstein, *Sex Laws*, 152–78.

[15] Cf. Milgrom, *Leviticus*, 1571–84.

[16] For prostitution as a species of adultery, cf. Philo, *Spec.* 3.31. For adultery see above, on Ps.-Phoc. 3. For the condemnation of μοιχεία, etc.: Exod 20:13; Lev 20:10; Deut 5:17; Prov 6:32, 18:22, 30:20; Sir 23:23, 25:2; Hauck, "μοιχεύω," 729–35; Epstein, *Sex Laws*, 194–215; Berger, *Gesetzesauslegung*, 312–26.

[17] Cf. Hesiod, *Op.* 182, 235; Aeschines, *Ctes.* 111; Ps.-Phintys, *Mul. mod.* 2.153.12–15; Theocritus, *Id.* 17.40–44; Macrobius, *Sat.* 5.11.17, 7.16.13; Horace, *Carm.* 4.5.23; Martial, *Epig.* 6.27, 39; Catullus, *Carm.* 61.214–223.

[18] Cf. Philo, *Jos.* 44–45, *Spec.* 1.326, 332, 3.11; Josephus, *Ant.* 3.274; S. J. D. Cohen, *Beginnings of Jewishness*, 274–82.

her, he could be charged.[19] Tacitus records a senate resolution prohibiting prostitution for any woman whose father, grandfather, or husband is of equestrian rank (*Ann.* 2.85). Complaints about the prevalence (especially among elites) of married women prostituting themselves, conniving husbands, and illegitimate children were a stock-in-trade of contemporary moralists and satirists, who pointed to such indiscretions as evidence for the decline of traditional family values.[20]

Verses 179–181. The precepts of this sub-section forbid sex with the partners of one's father. The Pentateuch includes several commands concerning sexual relations with one's stepmother, for example, Lev 18:8 ("You shall not uncover the nakedness of your father's wife; it is your father's nakedness."); cf. Lev 20:11; Deut 23:1, 27:20.[21] Here, as elsewhere, the onus of the crime is with the violation of paternal privilege. By contrast, Pseudo-Phocylides introduces an obligation to honor the stepmother as well as the father. In this respect v. 180 extends the circle of reference implicated by the command to honor (τιμᾶν) parents in v. 8. Honoring one's stepmother as fully as one's mother is important to Philo as well (*Virt.* 225). He reasons that a man is forbidden to wed his stepmother in part "because the names stepmother and mother (μητρυιᾶς καὶ μητρός) are closely akin."[22] The structure of vv. 179–180 also draws attention to this similarity, with μητρυιῆς and μητέρα occupying the first position in their respective lines. The reader is warned not to "touch" his stepmother, utilizing a common euphemism for sexual contact.[23]

Verse 181 extends the prohibition of vv. 179–180 to another of the father's sexual partners, his mistress or concubine. Roman law recognized living in an avowed monogamous relationship with a slave as an alternative to marriage, an option that was especially attractive to widowers: "to take a *concubina* rather than a second wife allowed him to avoid introducing a stepmother into the family and so confusing existing arrangements for distribution of property."[24] Although no biblical text parallels v. 181, the scandal of Reuben's affair with Bilhah, his father's concubine,

---

[19] Edwards, *Politics of Immorality*, 38–39; cf. Treggiari, *Roman Marriage*, 288; Gardner, *Women in Roman Law*, 131–32; Tracy, "The Lenomaritus," 62–64; also Demosthenes, *Or.* 59.41–42.

[20] E.g., Lysias, *Or.* 1.33–34; Horace, *Sat.* 2.3.237–238; Juvenal, *Sat.* 1.55–57, 6.76–81; Seneca, *Ben.* 1.9.3; Martial, *Epig.* 8.31; cf. Edwards, *Politics of Immorality*, 49–50, 61.

[21] Further, Ezek 22:10; 1 Cor 5:1–2; Josephus, *Ant.* 3.274; Cicero, *Clu.* 14–15; Gaius, *Inst.* 1.63; Str-B 3:349–50; Gardner, *Women in Roman Law*, 155.

[22] Philo, *Spec.* 3.20–21, cf. 3.11–19.

[23] Cf. Gen 20:6; Prov 6:29; 1 Cor 7:1; Philo, *Spec.* 3.32; Josephus, *Ant.* 1.163, 2.57; *T. Reub.* 3:15; Plato, *Leg.* 840A.

[24] W. Fitzgerald, *Slavery*, 52; cf. Treggiari, *Roman Marriage*, 51–52; Gardner, *Women in Roman Law*, 56–60; Gardner and Wiedemann, *Roman Household*, 61–62.

became a paradigmatic sin in Jewish circles.[25] The interpretation given the story by *Jubilees* 33 is of special interest, since it characterizes the incident as an infraction of biblical rules against incest with the wife of one's father.[26] Pseudo-Phocylides may share this judgment, which would help explain why v. 181 is positioned with vv. 179–180. From Greek literature we have the tale of Phoenix in *Iliad* 9, who earns his father's curse after sleeping with his concubine (παλλακίδι προμιγῆναι, 9.452; cf. *Anth. Gr.* 3.3).

Verses 182–183. These lines continue the list of forbidden sexual relations, this time with reference to sisters and sisters-in-law (note the parallelism of μηδὲ κασιγνήτης and μηδὲ κασιγνήτων). The foregoing unit drew on Lev 18:8, this one on Lev 18:9 and 16. The former verse condemns relations even with one's half-sister, or with a sister or half-sister who does not reside in one's household: "The nakedness of your sister by your father or your mother, born at home or abroad: you shall not uncover her nakedness."[27] In *Spec.* 3.22–25, Philo contrasts this law favorably with the customs of the Greeks and the Egyptians, who permit (respectively) marriage with half sisters and sisters.[28] Plato calls the prohibition of sex with a sibling one of the unwritten laws (*Leg.* 838A–B).[29]

Lev 18:16 bans sex with one's sister-in-law as a violation of the brother's privilege: "You shall not uncover the nakedness of your brother's wife; it is your brother's nakedness."[30] For his part, our author makes no mention of such privilege; the acts of vv. 182–183 are simply judged ἀπότροπος ("grim, direful"). Despite its biblical foundation, the thought and diction of this line are familiar especially from Hesiod, *Op.* 328–329, where divine punishment is forecast for anyone who "goes to the bed of his own brother for clandestine sexual relations with his wife" (ὅς τε κασιγνήτοιο ἑοῦ ἀνὰ δέμνια βαίνῃ κρυπταδίης εὐνῆς ἀλόχου).

---

[25] Gen 35:22, 49:4; 1 Chr 5:1; *T. Reub.* 3:11–15 (with Kugel, "Reuben's Sin," 525–54); cf. 2 Kgdms 3:7, 16:21.

[26] Milgrom (*Leviticus*, 1538) suggests that the prohibition of Lev 18:8 itself may have included concubines, "in order to prevent a son from usurping his father's position." Cf. Lysias, *Or.* 1.30–31, which interprets a statute regarding wives to include concubines.

[27] Cf. Lev 20:17; Deut 27:22; 2 Kgdms 13:1–22.

[28] Pomeroy, *Families*, 194: marriage between half-siblings was permitted in Athens and Sparta, and presumably elsewhere in the Greek world; cf. Hopkins, "Brother-Sister Marriage," 303–54. Foxhall, "Foreign Powers," 143: in contrast to Greek custom, "Roman law was far less accommodating of endogamous marriages, drawing the limits of incest much more firmly ... All marriages between ascendants ... were forbidden, as were marriages between collaterals closer than second cousin."

[29] Cf. Euripides, *Andr.* 173–175; Plutarch, *Cic.* 29.4–5; Cicero, *Pis.* 28, *Mil.* 73.

[30] Cf. Lev 20:21; Mark 6:18; Philo, *Spec.* 3.26. Presumably our author joins Leviticus in rejecting the practice of Levirite marriage; see Deut 25:5–10; Milgrom, *Leviticus*, 1545.

Verses 184–186. These verses support the directive of vv. 175–176 to beget children. In his summary of the law, Josephus states that a woman is forbidden to induce an abortion or destroy a newborn after its birth (*C. Ap.* 2.202; cf. Philo, *Hypoth.* 7.7). Pseudo-Phocylides, probably drawing on a shared source, in vv. 184–185 similarly focuses on the mother's actions, reflecting typical male anxieties about feminine disdain for reproduction; compare Plutarch's invective against "licentious women who employ drugs and instruments to produce abortions for the sake of the enjoyment of conceiving again" (*Tu. san.* 134F).[31]

The general prohibition of abortion and post-partem infanticide was a distinctive trait of Jewish and Christian morality.[32] This tradition's roots are in Exod 21:22–23, which prescribes penalties for an unintentional miscarriage resulting from an altercation: "If two men are fighting and one strikes a woman having (a child) in her womb and her child is born imperfectly formed, he shall be forced to pay a penalty … but if it be perfectly formed, he shall give life for life."[33] Commenting on the ordinance, Philo explains that it carries with it the prohibition of infanticide, that is, of leaving newborns for wild beasts and carnivorous birds to devour (*Spec.* 3.108–119, cf. *Mos.* 1.10–11, *Virt.* 131–133). Both practices, he says, contravene nature's laws.[34]

"Despite the urgings of a few philosophers that it was better to rear many children, Roman moral and legal views of abandonment appear to have been quite indulgent."[35] Nevertheless, we do hear Greco-Roman authors speaking out occasionally against both abortion and exposure. Aristotle, for one, draws a distinction between "lawful" and "unlawful" abortions and shows an awareness of local customs that hinder exposure (*Pol.* 7.14.10). Parental love is natural, says Epictetus: even sheep and wolves do not abandon their offspring (*Diatr.* 1.23).[36]

---

[31] Edwards, *Politics of Immorality*, 84: women's lack of interest in reproduction was a favorite object of moralists' concern; cf. Plato, *Theaet.* 149D; Ps.-Heraclitus, *Ep.* 7.5; Cicero, *Clu.* 32–34; Seneca, *Helv.* 16.3–4; Wiedemann, *Adults and Children*, 35.

[32] E.g., *1 En.* 99:5; *Sib. Or.* 2.281–282, 3.765–766; *Did.* 2:2; *Apoc. Pet.* 8; cf. Diodorus Siculus, *Bibl.* 40.3.8; Tacitus, *Ann.* 5.5.

[33] Cf. Feldman, *Birth Control*, 251–67.

[34] That abortion contravenes the course of nature: Plutarch, *Am. prol.* 497D; Pliny, *Nat.* 10.83.172.

[35] Boswell, *Kindness of Strangers*, 91, cf. 53–179; on p. 87 he quotes Hierocles (ap. Stobaeus, *Anth.* 4.24.14): "the rearing of all or at least most children born to one is in accord with nature and proper respect for marriage. But the majority of people appear to ignore this advice for a reason which is not particularly laudable: out of love of wealth and the conviction that poverty is the greatest evil."

[36] Cf. Isocrates, *Panath.* 122; Hippocrates, *Jusj.* 20–21; *SIG* 3.985.20–21; Musonius Rufus, frg. 15 (with van Geytenbeek, *Musonius Rufus*, 78–89); Seneca, *Contr.* 9.3.11; Ovid, *Fast.* 1.621–624, *Her.* 11.37–44, 83–118, *Am.* 2.13–14; Juvenal, *Sat.* 6.595–597; Martial, *Epig.* 9.7; Dionysius of Halicarnassus, *Ant. rom.* 9.22; Tacitus, *Germ.* 19.5; further: Eyben, "Family Planning," 5–82; Riddle, *Contraception*, 7–23, 62–65; Harris, "Child-Exposure," 1–22; Patterson, "Not Worth the Rearing," 103–23.

Verse 186 is probably best taken with vv. 184–185,[37] and so alludes to the scenario of a man striking a pregnant woman in Exod 21:22–23. To "lay a hand" ([ἐπι]βάλλειν + χεῖρ) on a person could mean to strike with the hand or to seize someone with the intent of doing harm.[38] In contrast to the biblical case, Pseudo-Phocylides' rule seems to point to an intentional rather than inadvertent act.

Verse 187. This line picks up the thought of vv. 175–176, which identified procreation as an obligation to *phusis*. Here the reader is instructed not to violate a boy's procreative *phusis*,[39] an obvious reference to castration.[40] In his summary of the Torah (*Hypoth.* 7.7), Philo includes the prohibition of severing the male generative power (μὴ γονὴν ἀνδρῶν ἐκτέμνοντας) among the unwritten laws, a likely allusion to Deut 23:2, which names genital impairment as cause for exclusion from "the Lord's assembly."[41] Josephus' reflections on this same passage lead to the following mandate: "Shun eunuchs and flee all dealings with those who have deprived themselves of their virility and of those fruits of generation which God has given to men for the increase of our race ... For plainly it is by reason of the effeminacy of the soul that they have changed the sex of their body" (*Ant.* 4.290–291). At another point he goes so far as to rank castration as a capital crime (*C. Ap.* 2.270–271). Although eunuchs seem to have been ubiquitous in the Hellenistic world, some people did condemn the practice of castrating slave boys (e.g., Herodotus, *Hist.* 8.105), one author branding it "a sacrilege against *phusis*" (Ps.-Lucian, *Am.* 21).[42] Eventually, it was prohibited by imperial edict (Suetonius, *Dom.* 7.1; cf. Martial, *Epig.* 2.60, 6.2, 9.5, 7).

Verse 188. This line continues the assault on sexual practices inconducive to the goals laid out in vv. 175–176. The author appears to return to Leviticus 18 again, this time verse 23, which bars men and women from lying with animals.[43] According to Philo (*Spec.* 3.43–50), people should be kept apart from beasts sexually be-

---

[37] Alternatively, the line could refer to sex with a pregnant woman, for which see Josephus, *C. Ap.* 2.202, *Bell.* 2.161; Feldman, *Birth Control*, 180–87.

[38] E.g., *Jos. Asen.* 11:16; *T. Levi* 4:4, 14:1–2; Philo, *Somn.* 1.195; and BDAG s.v. ἐπιβάλλω 1.b. Cf. Homer, *Il.* 19.261.

[39] Referring to genitalia: BDAG s.v. φύσις 2; Winkler, *Constraints of Desire*, 217–20; cf. LSJ s.v. παιδογόνος I.

[40] Cf. Licht, *Sexual Life*, 507 ff.; Epstein, *Sex Laws*, 138–41; Str-B 1:807.

[41] For the admission law, see Nelson, *Deuteronomy*, 278.

[42] Cf. Seneca, *Contr.* 10.4.17; Seneca, *Nat.* 7.31.3; Dio Chrysostom, *De lege* 14, *Invid.* 36; Hopfner, *Sexualleben*, 382–435; Nock, "Eunuchs," 7–15; Bradley, *Slaves*, 115–16, 128–29; Hopkins, *Conquerors and Slaves*, 172–96; Guyot, *Eunuchen*.

[43] Cf. Exod 22:18; Lev 20:15–16; Deut 27:21; *T. Levi* 17:11; *Sib. Or.* 5.393; *Der. Er. Rab.* 1.12–13; Epstein, *Sex Laws*, 132–34; Str-B 3:73–74.

cause it is unseemly for a rational being to have passion for a creature that is ἄλογος, lacking reason or sense.[44] Predictably, he says, such unions do not produce normal offspring, but bizarre monsters like the minotaur. Accordingly, Moses provided against such abominations with rules that assure conformity with nature.[45]

Plutarch appeals to the same criterion in *Brut. an.* 990F: "men do such deeds as wantonly outrage nature, upset her order, and confuse her distinctions. For they have, in fact, attempted to consort with goats and sows and mares, and women have gone mad with lust for male beasts." In his summary of the law, Josephus also makes mention of "irrational animals," though only to say that they should be used strictly in accordance with the law (*C. Ap.* 2.213, cf. 2.271).

Verse 189. This line could also be translated: "Do not outrage a woman on shameful couches." Compare *Sib. Or.* 12.219–220: ἐν λεχέεσσιν αἰσχρὸς ἀβουλεύτοις, "shameful on ill-advised couches," (referring to Commodus' incest). In Greek society, a man who was "shameless, importunate and headstrong" in the satisfaction of his sexual desires was liable to be branded a ὑβριστής, and ὑβρίζω could be used of a man's sexual assault of a woman.[46] Philo may have such situations in mind when he criticizes individuals whose natural need for pleasure (ἡ κατὰ φύσιν ἡδονή) becomes immoderate, deteriorating into lustful and lascivious passion for their wives.[47] Comparison may also be made with Seneca, *Matr.* 85, which is representative of the "austere norms of sexual morality" advocated by the Stoic school: "Nothing is more shameful than to love your wife as if she were your mistress."[48] Viewed against this backdrop, it is probable that v. 189 is a variation on the theme of v. 67, namely, that the love of passion earns shame (cf. v. 76).

Given the extensive parallels between Ps.-Phoc. 179–194 and Leviticus 18, another possibility for interpretation is that this line refers specifically to intercourse during menstruation, which is forbidden by Lev 18:19.[49] Also compare Josephus, *C. Ap.* 2.201, part of his summary of the law: "Let a wife obey her husband, but not for *hubris*."

---

[44] For this designation, cf. 4 Macc 14:14, 18; Wis 11:15; 2 Pet 2:12; Jude 10; Democritus, frg. 164; Plato, *Prot.* 321C; Xenophon, *Hier.* 7.3; BDAG s.v. ἄλογος 1.

[45] Milgrom (*Leviticus*, 1570) notes that during the rabbinic period, "the belief was prevalent that bestiality was practiced by pagans," referring to *m. 'Abod. Zar.* 2:1.

[46] Dover, *Greek Homosexuality*, 34–39; D. Cohen, *Law, Sexuality, and Society*, 177; Fisher, "Hybris and Dishonour," 183, 186–87; Fisher, *Hybris*, s.v. heterosexual offences; cf. Isocrates, *Nic.* 36; Demosthenes, *Or.* 17.3, 23.141; Euripides, *Hipp.* 1073; Dio Chrysostom, *3 Regn.* 98; Josephus, *C. Ap.* 2.270, *Ant.* 1.164.

[47] Philo, *Spec.* 3.9, cf. 3.79, 113; further, Feldman, *Birth Control*, 155–63.

[48] Edwards, *Politics of Immorality*, 57; cf. Treggiari, *Roman Marriage*, 215–24.

[49] Cf. Lev 20:18; Ezek 18:6; Philo, *Spec.* 3.32; Josephus, *Ant.* 3.275; *Pss. Sol.* 8.12; CD 5.6–7; *ARN* A 2.1.1–5; Ilan, *Jewish Women*, 100–105.

Verses 190–192. For the third time in the section, *phusis* appears as an explicit norm for human sexuality (cf. vv. 176, 187). Here the appeal is to observe εὐναὶ φύσεως, sexual relations ordered by nature. Anything that violates this criterion constitutes "illicit" passion.[50] Presumably, our author is working with the assumption that *phusis* has set limits on sexual desire and the means by which it should be satisfied. By the same token, we should bear in mind that what generally earns the label "unnatural" from an ancient moralist is not behavior that in fact defies some "cosmic principle of physical and generational order," but behavior deemed "self-indulgent, luxurious, and exceedingly appealing" by that individual's standards.[51]

Given the connection between v. 190 and v. 191 (note the repetition of εὐνή), the former most likely refers in the first instance to male-male sex, thus reintroducing the subject of homosexual passion (κύπρις) from the opening summary of the Decalogue (v. 3). At the same time, we should bear in mind that a Jewish author like Pseudo-Phocylides would probably include a great many sexual acts as violations of nature. For instance, in his survey of legislation relating to the commandment against adultery (*Spec.* 3.8–82), Philo designates as "unnatural" any union with menstruating (32) and sterile women (36), bestiality (48), prostitution (51), as well as adultery itself (52). As we have seen, in vv. 175–176, our author establishes the norm of nature in terms of marriage and procreation. Presumably anything that departs from that norm would be "unnatural." Consequently, it may be best to understand v. 190 as both a summarizing statement, referring potentially to the whole range of proscribed activities in vv. 177ff. as well as an anticipation of v. 191.[52]

In classifying male couplings as an aberration of nature, Pseudo-Phocylides may be drawing from the source he shares with Josephus and Philo. The former writes: "The law recognizes no sexual relations except union with a woman in accordance with nature (κατὰ φύσιν) … It abhors male-with-male relations, and punishes anyone guilty of the infraction with death" (*C. Ap.* 2.199; cf. Philo, *Hypoth.* 7.1).[53] Our author makes no mention of capital punishment, though v. 194 will indicate the destructive effect erotic passion can have. Precedent for the appeal to *phusis* in casting aspersions on same-sex unions comes from a host of philosophical sources, for example, Plato, *Leg.* 636C: "when male unites with female for procreation, the pleasure experienced is held to be due to nature, but contrary to nature when male

---

[50] For this use of ἄθεσμος, cf. *Sib. Or.* 5.166, 430; Philo, *Spec.* 2.50; 2 Pet 2:7, 3:17; Iamblichus, *Vit. Pyth.* 17.78.

[51] Winkler, *Constraints of Desire*, 22; cf. Dio Chrysostom, *Ven.* 81–103; Cicero, *Fin.* 5.35–36; Seneca, *Ep.* 122.5–9.

[52] Also note that while *kupris* in v. 3 pertains to homosexual passion, in v. 67 it can refer to passion more generally.

[53] Cf. Josephus, *C. Ap.* 2.215, 273–275; Philo, *Abr.* 135, *Spec.* 2.50, 3.37–39, *Contempl.* 59; *T. Naph.* 3:4; *Let. Arist.* 152; Scroggs, *Homosexuality*, 66–98.

mates with male or female with female."[54] As Bruce Thornton observes, in various sources of the time "passive homosexuality … is seen as unnatural and shameful, the worst in a continuum of appetitive excess that delivers a man to the destructive forces of the irrational."[55]

The point of departure for v. 191 must be Lev 18:22 (cf. 20:13), which prohibits all couplings between males;[56] cf. above, on v. 3, and below, on vv. 213–214. The basis and means of the author's critique, however, are Greco-Roman in their pedigree. In formulating a perspective on the "natural" order of human sexuality, Hellenistic moralists were inclined to turn to animal models. Of course such strategies teach us more about prevailing cultural norms than anything about actual animal behavior.[57] Plutarch, for example, believes that it is wholly in accord with *phusis* that "the desires of beasts have encompassed no homosexual mating" (*Brut. an.* 990D); compare Ps.-Lucian, *Am.* 22 (cf. 20): "If each man abided by the ordinances prescribed for us by Providence, we should be satisfied with intercourse with women and life would be uncorrupted by anything shameful. Certainly, among animals … the laws of nature are preserved undefiled."[58]

Similar arguments could be made regarding female couplings, for example, Ovid, *Metam.* 9.733–734 (cf. 9.758): "Among all the animals no female is seized by desire for a female." The LXX has nothing on the subject, though Pseudo-Phocylides' extension of Lev 18:22 and 20:13 to include females is mirrored in Rom 1:26–27, where Paul's condemnation of same-sex couplings is similarly grounded in assumptions about passion and *phusis*: "Their women exchanged natural intercourse for unnatural (τὴν φυσικὴν χρῆσιν εἰς τὴν παρὰ φύσιν); likewise men also, giving up natural intercourse (τὴν φυσικὴν χρῆσιν) with women, were consumed with passion for one another." That female-female sex contravenes the laws of nature could be asserted by Greco-Roman authors as well.[59] What appears to be particularly "unnatural" about such acts for our author is that the participants try to imitate (μιμέομαι) sexual roles that are properly male. This manner of characterization in

---

54   Cf. Plato, *Symp.* 192B, *Leg.* 836E, 841D; Aristotle, *Eth. nic.* 7.5.3; Aeschines, *Tim.* 185; Musonius Rufus, frg. 12.86.8–10; Dio Chrysostom, *Ven.* 149–152; Scroggs, *Homosexuality*, s.v. *Phusis*; Ward, "Why Unnatural?" 263–84.

55   Thornton, *Eros*, 114, cf. 99–120; Xenophon, *Lac.* 2.12–14; Epictetus, *Diatr.* 2.10.17; Sextus Empiricus, *Pyr.* 1.152; Juvenal, *Sat.* 2.132–170. On the *lex Scantinia* (which may have penalized free men who allowed themselves to be sexually penetrated), see Richlin, "Not Before Homosexuality," 523–73; as she notes, "mainstream Roman culture was severely homophobic, at least where passives were concerned" (p. 530).

56   Cf. Milgrom, *Leviticus*, 1565–70.

57   Cf. Boswell, *Christianity*, 137–43, 152–56; C. Williams, *Roman Homosexuality*, 232–34.

58   See also Plato, *Leg.* 836C; Philo, *Anim.* 49. For the contrasting view regarding same-sex couplings among animals, see Aristotle, *Hist. an.* 6.2; Pliny, *Nat.* 10.166; Aelian, *Nat. an.* 15.11.

59   E.g., Lucian, *Dial. meretr.* 5.289; Vettius Valens, *Anth.* 2.17.66–68; Ovid, *Metam.* 9.745–759; cf. Brooten, *Love Between Women*, 41–54 and passim.

turn reflects prevailing tendencies to conceptualize female sex, including sex between women, in male terms. Hellenistic men were appalled by women who "have
intercourse with each other just as men do" (Ps.-Lucian, *Am.* 28), presumably because such acts fail to inscribe traditional, hierarchical arrangements of power.[60]

Verses 193–194. The last two lines of the paragraph summarize the author's critique
of ἔρως (cf. vv. 61, 67, 214); note the parallelism of ἔρωτα and ἔρως. In an important respect it functions as a counter-norm to *phusis* (see above, on vv. 175–176),
undermining as it does the quest for stability and discretion in one's sexual behavior.
Our author's comments need to be read against the widespread opinion among Hellenistic elites that a man, especially a man in authority, must exercise control over
his sexual appetites. Failure to do so not only leads to moral turpitude and shame,
it also undermines his capacity to exercise control more generally.[61] This view helps
explain the role of vv. 193–194 (and the preceding directives it summarizes) in
the author's household code. As Craig Williams explains, it was a prime directive
of Greco-Roman morality that a man "must exercise dominion over his own body
and his own desires as well as the bodies and desires of those under his jurisdiction
– his wife, children, and slaves."[62] In order to properly rule the household, he must
first rule his sexual drive. In this vein, Catharine Edwards notes that the Greco-Roman critique of erotic gratification applied to sex even with one's wife, since such
conjugality could distract a man from his moral responsibilities; this expressed "the
commonly held view that excessive indulgence in sex diminished a man's potency in
other respects."[63] Philo's corpus provides us with some particularly good illustrations
of this discourse. In *Spec.* 3.79–82, for example, he castigates men who manifest a
certain "madness" for women, acting impulsively on their promiscuous and unbri-
dled desires; ultimately, they will be stripped of their matrimonial prerogatives. The
pleasure-lovers (φιλήδονοι) of *Spec.* 3.113 even lose their semblance of humanity,
joining with their wives not to procreate, "but like pigs and goats in quest of the
enjoyment such intercourse gives."

---

[60] What "the ancient Greeks and Romans found disturbing was not sexual contact among woman as
such, but rather a woman's playing an assertive masculine role, deviating from usual gender categories." Nussbaum and Sihvola, "Introduction," 17; cf. Lucian, *Dial. meretr.* 5.289–292 (male-faced
women who have sex as if they were men); Vettius Valens, *Anth.* 2.17.66–68; Martial, *Epig.* 1.90,
7.67.1–3, 7.70; Feldman, *Birth Control*, 125; Licht, *Sexual Life*, 316–28; Hallett, "Female Homoeroticism," 209–27; Szesnat, "Philo and Female Homoeroticism," 140–47.

[61] Foucault, *History of Sexuality*, 2:38–93; Stowers, *Romans*, 42–65; Winkler, *Constraints of Desire*, 45–
70.

[62] C. Williams, *Roman Homosexuality*, 141, cf. 125–59.

[63] Edwards, *Politics of Immorality*, 86, cf. 81–97, 195–98. On "the principle of moderate conduct in a
married man" manifested "above all in showing a certain respect for one's wife," see Foucault, *History
of Sexuality*, 3:147–85 (quotes from pp. 148–49).

In v. 59, Pseudo-Phocylides identified the need to moderate one's πάθη. Here one of the passions is singled out for special condemnation.[64] To be sure, Greek mythology depicted *Erōs* as the "most handsome among the immortal gods" (Hesiod, *Theog.* 120) and a primeval force of generation.[65] At the same time, the erotophobia expressed here would have resonated with poets like Apollonius of Rhodes: "Ruthless *Erōs*, great bane, great curse to humankind, from thee come deadly strifes and lamentations and groans, and countless pains as well have their stormy birth from thee" (*Argon.* 4.445–447). The totality of the sway exercised by this passion (note Pseudo-Phocylides' ἁπάντων) is magnified even further in Sophocles, frg. 684: "For *Erōs* comes not only upon men and women, but troubles the souls even of the gods above and moves over the sea; not even the all-powerful Zeus can keep him off, but he too yields and willingly gives way."[66]

---

[64] Cf. Nussbaum, "*Erōs* and Ethical Norms," 55–94.

[65] Thornton, *Eros*, 124–27; cf. Plato, *Symp.* 178A–C, 186A–B; Xenophon, *Symp.* 8.1; Aristophanes, *Av.* 693–702, *Nub.* 1080–1082; Euripides, frg. 269; Menander, frg. 235; Plutarch, *Lyc.* 31; Cicero, *Tusc.* 4.68; Seneca, *Phaed.* 177–185.

[66] Cf. Euripides, *Hipp.* 538–544 (*Erōs* "ruins mortals and launches them among every kind of disaster."), 1274–1280, frg. 161; Menander, frg. 798; Athenaeus, *Deipn.* 562A–563F; Philo, *Jos.* 56, *Decal.* 151–152, *Spec.* 4.85; Clement of Alexandria, *Strom.* 2.107.3; Stobaeus, *Anth.* 4.20 (part 2); Thornton, *Eros*, 11–47.

B. Verses 195–227

195	Love your wife: for what is sweeter and better
196	than when a wife is lovingly disposed to her husband into old age
197	and husband to his wife, and strife does not split them asunder?
198	Let no one have sex with maidens forcibly (or) without honorable wooing.
199	Bring not into your house an evil, wealthy woman;
200	you will be your wife's hireling, all for a wretched dowry.
201	We seek well-bred horses and ploughers of earth –
202	strong-necked bulls – and of dogs the best of all.
203	But foolishly we do not contend to marry a good woman;
204	nor does a woman reject a wicked man if he's wealthy.
205	You should not add marriage to marriage, misery to misery.
206	Engage not in strife over possessions with your kinfolk.
207	Be not severe with your children, but be gentle.
208	If a child sins against you, let the mother judge her son,
209	or else the elders of the family or the chiefs of the people.
210	Do not grow locks in the hair of a male child.
211	Braid not his crown or the cross-knots on the top of his head.
212	For men to wear long hair is not seemly, just for sensual women.
213	Protect the youthful beauty of a handsome boy;
214	for many rage with lust for sex with a male.
215	Guard a virgin in closely shut chambers,
216	and let her not be seen before the house until her nuptials.
217	The beauty of children is hard for parents to protect.
219	Bestow on your kinfolk love and genuine harmony.
220	Respect those with gray hair on the temples, and yield to the aged
221	a seat and all privileges. To an elder equal in descent
222	and of like age with your father show the same honors.
223	Grant a servant the share he needs for his stomach.
224	Apportion to a slave what is prescribed, so that he will be to your liking.
225	Make no marks on a servant, disgracing him.
226	Do not harm a slave by speaking ill of him to his master.
227	Even accept counsel from a household slave who's prudent.

TEXTUAL NOTES

Verse 195a. M, P, L^γρ, V have στέργε τεὴν, while L has στέργε τέκνων ("love [your] children," cf. vv. 207–217). Verse 196. For the expression φρονέῃ φίλα, cf. Homer,

Il. 4.219, 5.116, *Od.* 1.307, 6.313, 7.15, 42, 75; Ps.-Phoc. 227. // γήραος ἄχρις: cf. v. 230. Verses 197–198. Omitted by M, B. Verse 197b. P, L: ἄνδιχα, V: ἄνδρα. Verse 198. For the expression κούρῃσι μιγείη, cf. Hesiod, *Theog.* 979–980. Verse 200. εἵνεκα: Ionic for ἕνεκα. Verses 201–202. For the sequence horse-bull-dog, cf. Xenophon, *Cyr.* 7.5.62. Verse 201. In lieu of ἵππους (in P, L, V), M, B have κάπρους ("boars"), missing the allusion to Theognis, *El.* 183–184 (see the commentary); cf. Sophocles, *El.* 25. Verse 202. M, L, V have ὑψιτένοντας; other mss. replace the *hapax* with ὑψιταίνοντας (P) or ὑψιτέοντας (B). // ἀτάρ ("but, yet") usually marks a transition, though cf. Denniston, *Greek Particles*, 53. Verse 204. Reading οὐδὲ, following van der Horst's (*Sentences*, 245) suggestion; Derron (*Sentences*, 16) has οὐ δὲ. Verse 205. For the use of ἄγω here, cf. v. 199. Verse 206. Omitted by M, B. L puts the line before v. 205, perhaps to continue the focus on wealth in vv. 199–204. Verse 208b. Reading κρινάτω with V and Diehl, *Anthologia*, 2.113; cf. Bergk's (*Poetae Lyrici Graeci*, 107) conjecture κολουέτω (κολούω: "to cut short, put down"), followed by Young (*Theognis*, 111), van der Horst (*Sentences*, 248–49), and Derron (*Sentences*, 16), but in no mss. Verse 209. For δημογέροντες, cf. Homer, *Il.* 3.149, 11.372; Aristotle, *Eth. nic.* 2.9.6; Philo, *Mos.* 1.86. Verse 210. μέν = μήν ("truly, surely"): Denniston, *Greek Particles*, 362. // For the language of τρέφειν πλοκάμους ἐπὶ χαίτης, cf. Homer, *Il.* 14.175–176; Euripides, *Bacch.* 494, *El.* 527–528, *Phoen.* 309–310. Verse 211. P, Lʸᵖ, V have ἄμματα, while M, B, L have θαύματα ("wonders, oddities"). // For the translation, cf. van der Horst, *Sentences*, 249–50: "Braid not his crown nor make cross-knots at the top of his head;" Walter, *Poetische Schriften*, 215: "nicht sollst du das Scheitel(haar) flechten oder Zöpfe zu Haarknoten (winden)." Verse 212b. For χλιδαναῖς, cf. Euripides, *Cycl.* 500; Plutarch, *Alc.* 23.5. Verse 213. For εὔμορφος, cf. 4 Macc 8:10, where Antiochus admires the youth and "handsome appearance" (εὐμορφία) of the seven brothers; also Ps.-Lucian, *Am.* 10. // For ὥρη meaning "youthful beauty," see LSJ s.v. ὥρα B.II. Verse 214. λυσσάω of sexual frenzy: Plato, *Resp.* 586C; Philo, *Jos.* 40. // μεῖξις describes male-male sex in Plato, *Leg.* 836C; *T. Levi* 14:6; cf. μεῖγνυμι in vv. 181, 198. Verse 215. παρθενική is poetic for παρθένος, e.g., Homer, *Il.* 18.567, *Od.* 11.39; Hesiod, *Op.* 699. // πολύκλειστος is a *hapax*. Verse 216. γάμων: for the plural used of a single wedding, see LSJ s.v. γάμος I; BDAG s.v. γάμος. // δόμων: the plural is often used of a single house, see LSJ s.v. δόμος 1. Verse 217. For κάλλος to describe a child, cf. Plato, *Phaed.* 251C; Josephus, *Ant.* 15.25. [Verse 218.] "Love your friends till death, for faithfulness is better." (στέργε φίλους ἄχρις θανάτου· πίστις γὰρ ἀμείνων.) A spurious verse (only in V); see van der Horst, *Sentences*, 252–53. Verse 222. τιμαῖσι γέραιρε: cf. Xenophon, *Cyr.* 8.1.39, 8.8.4. Verses 223–227. The different terms for slave (θεράπων, δοῦλος, οἰκέτης) overlap in meaning, though the translation tries to reflect the variation. Verse 223. For the expression γαστρὸς ὀφειλόμενον δασμόν, cf. Ps.-Lucian, *Am.* 45. Verse 224a. For the expression δούλῳ ... νέμοις, cf. Plato, *Leg.* 848B. Verse 225. ἐπονειδίζω is a *hapax*; see LSJ Sup. s.v. Verse 226. B, P, V: κακηγορέων (cf. Plato, *Leg.* 934E; Aristotle, *Eth. nic.* 5.1.14); M: κατηγορέων ("accusing"). Verse 227. Cf. van der Horst, *Sentences*, 257: "Accept advice also from a kindly disposed slave."

Commentary

Verses 195–197. In vv. 175–176, Pseudo-Phocylides extolled marriage in connection with the obligation to procreate. Here it is praised in its own right, the rhetorical question of vv. 195b–197 deriving from Homer, *Od.* 6.182–184: "For nothing is greater and better than when husband and wife dwell in a home in one accord" (οὐ μὲν γὰρ τοῦ γε κρεῖσσον καὶ ἄρειον, ἢ ὅθ᾿ ὁμοφρονέοντε νοήμασιν οἶκον ἔχητον ἀνὴρ ἠδὲ γυνή.).

This unit introduces a counterpart to the unrestrained, destructive *erōs* of vv. 193–194: note in particular how Pseudo-Phocylides' adaptation of the Homeric passage emphasizes both the presence of mutual and abiding love in marriage and the absence of strife this fosters. Indeed, it appears that it is in its contribution to familial stability that spousal devotion is ranked "better" than anything else, and thus to be cultivated by the reader.[67] In this, our passage resembles other ancient appropriations of *Od.* 6.182–184, which also tend to emphasize the desirability of marital harmony, or *homonoia*.[68] This in turn reflects the widespread opinion that concord was the key to a successful marriage.[69] Ben Sira lists among the seemly things in life "a man and wife who agree with one another" (25:1); the benefits of such a relationship extend into old age: "Blessed is the man with a good wife, for the number of his days will be double … he shall fulfill his years in peace" (26:1–2). This ideal informed a broad tradition of marital advice in the ancient world, for example, *Instr. Ankh.* 25.14 ("May the heart of the wife be the heart of her husband, that they may be far from strife.").[70] With the perspective advanced by Pseudo-Phocylides in these lines (cf. vv. 193–194) we may compare Plutarch's advice on love and marriage, which is sometimes taken as evidence for "a domestication of *erōs*" taking place at this time "through the valorization of the marital bond and a shift in the concept

---

[67] Cf. Hesiod, *Op.* 702–705 ("For a man wins nothing better than a good wife, and, again, nothing worse than a bad one, a greedy soul who roasts her man without fire, strong though he may be, and brings him to a raw old age."); Theognis, *El.* 1225; Euripides, *Andr.* 179–180.

[68] Cf. Plutarch, *Amat.* 770A; Delling, "Eheleben," 691–97.

[69] E.g., Philo, *Spec.* 1.138; Isocrates, *Nic.* 41; Dio Chrysostom, *Nicom.* 15; Plutarch, *Conj. praec.* 142E–143A, 144B–C; Martial, *Epig.* 4.13; cf. Dixon, "The Sentimental Ideal of the Roman Family," 99–113; Treggiari, *Roman Marriage*, 245–53; Patterson, "Plutarch's Advice," 129–32; Thornton, *Eros*, 161–92.

[70] Cf. 3 Macc 4:6; Prov 5:18, 12:4, 18:22, 31:10–31; Qoh 9:9; Sir 7:19, 25:8, 26:3–4, 13–18, 36:24–25, 40:23; *Der. Er. Rab.* 2.16; Isocrates, *Nic.* 40; Euripides, *Med.* 14–15; Musonius Rufus, frg. 13A, 14; *Dict. Cat.* pr. 20.

of self-control." According to this view *"erōs* is not only a passion, but a unifier and cause of affection, and male limitation of pleasure is seen as desirable."[71]

Verse 198. Behind this admonition may lie an interpretation of Exod 22:15, which dictates the obligations of a man guilty of seducing an unengaged girl: "If anyone deceives an unbetrothed virgin (παρθένον ἀμνήστευτον) and lies with her, he shall pay the bride-price for her and make her his wife."[72] For the element of force, however, we must turn to a different passage, Deut 22:28–29, which states that any man who lies forcibly (βιασάμενος) with a virgin who is not betrothed (οὐ μεμνήστευται) must pay a fine to the girl's father and marry her (cf. 22:25). Both rape and sexual relations apart from betrothal are in view here, as well as the "penalty" of marriage for both the culprit and his victim. Philo expounds on both of these texts in *Spec.* 3.65–71, arguing that a man who desires a virgin ought not to attempt any shameless treachery with her but approach her parents with a marriage proposal. Like his compatriot, it seems that our author has transformed biblical penalties for taking advantage of a virgin into an appeal not to do such a thing in the first place, linking the appeal with a discussion of appropriate courtship protocol.[73]

The same problem is addressed by Josephus in *C. Ap.* 2.200 (cf. 2.201, 215): "The law commands us, when we marry, not to have regard for the dowry, nor to take a woman by force, nor to persuade her with guile and deceit."[74] Pseudo-Phocylides also joins the themes of rape/seduction and marrying for a dowry (cf. vv. 199–200), suggesting that he may be following the source he shares with Philo and Josephus at this juncture (cf. Philo, *Hypoth.* 7.1). Also like Josephus (and all the texts discussed here), betrothal and marriage provide the larger context of the discussion.[75] In this case, we can understand this line as the first of several recommendations in vv. 198–205 about obtaining a wife.[76] There may even be a narrative principle at work in the ordering of these lines, as the topics proceed from courtship (v. 198), to bringing a wife home (v. 199), to marriage per se (vv. 200–204), and finally to remarriage and inheritances (vv. 205–206).

---

[71] Stadter, "Subject to the Erotic," 221–36 (quotes from p. 222); cf. Foucault, *History of Sexuality*, 3:147–210.

[72] The only other prior usage of ἀμνήστευτος is Euripides, frg. 818.

[73] In the biblical texts it is principally the father who is the injured party (on account of the depreciated value of the bride-price); in contrast, Pseudo-Phocylides makes no mention of him, drawing more attention to the daughter herself.

[74] Cf. *Sib. Or.* 2.280–281; Ps.-Heraclitus, *Ep.* 7.5; Epstein, *Sex Laws*, 179–93.

[75] Also note the reference to dowry in Exod 22:15 and Ps.-Phoc. 199–200.

[76] *Pace* van der Horst, *Sentences*, 243, who thinks the verse is "oddly situated."

Verses 199–204. According to *C. Ap.* 2.200, the law commands men not to have regard for the dowry when marrying. What text (if any) Josephus has in mind here is unclear, since the Pentateuch gives no particular instructions regarding the administration of a dowry (usually προίξ or φερνή), though it does provide evidence that the practice was generally observed in ancient Judaism.[77] That in selecting his spouse a man should look to her morals and not her money was, however, stock advice in philosophical and gnomic writings of the Greco-Roman world, for example, Menander, *Mon.* 148, 154 ("Wed the wife, not the dowry."), and 296: "When marrying, put disposition before wealth."[78]

In this regard, a bride who brought a dowry of substantial value posed a special problem. If the husband was not wealthy himself, he was for all intents and purposes bound to his wife, since the marriage portion would have to be returned in the event of divorce.[79] The prevailing sentiment is summarized by Euripides, *Andr.* 1279–1282: "Shall not a man then take a wife from a noble family and give his daughter in marriage to the great and good, if he has sense? Shall he not avoid desiring an ignoble wife even if she brings a rich dowry to the house?" A woman with a large dowry was thought to invert the natural household order (Aristotle, *Eth. nic.* 8.10.5); therefore smaller dowries could be prescribed, so as to curtail feminine *hubris* (Plato, *Leg.* 774C–E). Such scenarios even became something of a comic cliché, viz., the poor man who becomes his rich wife's "servant," dependent on her for his survival and subject to her control by the threat to leave and take the dowry with her.[80] As Pseudo-Plutarch warns, "Those who wed women far above themselves (i.e., in birth or wealth) unwittingly become not the husbands of their wives, but the slaves of their wives' dowries" (*Lib. ed.* 13F).

Verses 201–204 have been composed in imitation of Theognis, *El.* 183–188: "We seek out rams and asses and horses that are well-bred ... but a noble man does not mind marrying the base daughter of a base father if the latter gives him a lot of money, and a woman does not refuse to be the wife of a base man who is rich." The important verbal similarities may be charted as follows:

Theognis	*Pseudo-Phocylides*
183: διζήμεθα	201: διζήμεθα
183–184: ἵππους εὐγενέας	201: ἵππους εὐγενέας
185: γῆμαι ... μελεδαίνει	203: γῆμαι ... ἐριδαίνομεν

---

[77] E.g., Gen 34:12; Exod 22:15–16; cf. Josh 16:10; 2 Macc 1:14; Str-B 2:385–87.

[78] Cf. Sir 7:19; Musonius Rufus, frg. 13B; Plutarch, *Sol.* 20.1–5; Ps.-Kallikratidas, *Dom. felic.* 4.106.14–107.11; Stobaeus, *Anth.* 4.22 (part 6); *Dict. Cat.* 3.12.

[79] Cf. Treggiari, *Roman Marriage*, 95–100, 323–64; Westbrook, *Property*, 142–64; Gardner, *Women in Roman Law*, 97–116.

[80] Juvenal, *Sat.* 6.136–141; Menander, *Epitr.* 134–135; Plautus, *Asin.* 84–87, *Aul.* 498–504, 532–535; cf. Plutarch, *Amat.* 752E–F, 754A–B; Rosivach, "Athenian Presuppositions," 193.

187: οὐδὲ γυνὴ κακοῦ ἀνδρὸς   204: οὐδὲ γυνὴ κακὸν ἄνδρ᾽
    ἀναίνεται   ἀπαναίνεται

Also note the antithesis of κακός verses ἀγαθός throughout the Theognidean passage and in Ps.-Phoc. 203–204. Pseudo-Phocylides may have been anticipating this passage as early as v. 199 with πολυχρήματον; cf. χρήματα in Theognis, *El.* 186, 189. In both texts the underlying argument is in the form *a minore ad maius*; if it is necessary for a man to select good farm animals, then it is all the more important for him to exercise good judgment in selecting a wife. It is noteworthy that in v. 204, our author follows Theognis in representing the woman as a moral subject, equal to the man in her responsibility to choose a mate wisely and in her failure to do so.[81] The use of the first-person plural lends the advice an aura of even broader applicability: even the wisest of men (v. 2) is a fool when it comes to finding a wife!

Verses 205–206. The prohibition of multiple marriages in v. 205 refers in the first instance to remarriage, though there is no reason bigamy could not also be in view.[82] Biblical texts make little attempt to curtail these practices, though Philo castigates men who remarry, arguing that they not only neglect their former families but show themselves to be in the grip of uncontrollable passion.[83] Elsewhere, he censures a woman who remarries her first husband after being another man's wife (*Spec.* 3.30–31; cf. Deut 24:1–4). According to our text, marrying more than once amounts to adding "misery to misery." For the paronomasia πήματι πῆμα, compare Herodotus, *Hist.* 1.67–68; Sophocles, *Ant.* 595; Euripides, *Orest.* 1257; also cf. Ps.-Phoc. 45, 120. Although remarriage would have been fairly routine,[84] those who took wedding vows a second or third time could expect to be the subject of some ridicule, for example, *Anth. Gr.* 9.133: "If one who has been married once seeks another wife, he is like a shipwrecked sailor who sets sail again on the dreadful deep." Another text focuses more on the trouble remarriage can cause the children: "Let him who on his offspring a second mother foists be held without esteem nor count among his countrymen for aught, since it's a bane that he has brought from an alien source upon

---

[81] Ilan, *Jewish Women*, 80–83: rabbinic literature gives examples of women who choose husbands without parental mediation. For the *topos* that it is better to marry a man than money, see Treggiari, *Roman Marriage*, 97. The parallelism of vv. 203 and 204 is reinforced by the lines' similar endings: ἀφρονέοντες and ἀφνεὸν ὄντα.

[82] The later is prohibited by CD 4.20–5.2; 11Q19 LVII, 17–18. Cf. Vermes, "Matrimonial Halakhah," 197–202; Ilan, *Jewish Women*, 85–88; Pomeroy, *Families*, 194, 201–202; Gardner, *Women in Roman Law*, 91–93; Kötting and Hopfner, "Bigamie," 282–86.

[83] *Spec.* 2.135; cf. Lev 21:7, 13–14; Ezek 44:22; Josephus, *Ant.* 17.349–352; Feldman, *Birth Control*, 37–41.

[84] Treggiari, *Roman Marriage*, 501–502. Levirite marriage: Ilan, *Jewish Women*, 152–57.

his own affairs" (Diodorus Siculus, *Bibl.* 12.14.1).[85] Conversely, being married only once was idealized. Numerous sepulchral inscriptions, for example, commemorate "a surviving spouse by noting that he or she was married only once, thereby suggesting the virtue of extraordinary fidelity."[86] For the theme, see Tacitus, *Ann.* 2.73, *Germ.* 19.4; Propertius, *El.* 4.11.36; Diodorus Siculus, *Bibl.* 1.80.3; Ps.-Charondas, *Prooem.* 2.63.1–2.[87]

The discussion of greed as a baneful force in marriage (vv. 199–204) ushers in a line regarding the familial strife caused by disputes over possessions, v. 206. The subject matter here harks back to v. 47, where the love of money was identified as a root of familial conflict; see the discussion there. The importance attached to avoiding *eris* here contributes to a guiding theme of the section; cf. also vv. 75, 78, 151. Given the line's location, the possessions in mind here are probably inheritances.[88] As Plutarch notes, the task of dividing the father's estate usually precipitates "implacable enmity and strife" among siblings (*Frat. amor.* 483D).

Verses 207–209. Verse 207 introduces a section on parental responsibilities that extends through v. 217 (note forms of παῖς in vv. 207, 208, 210, 213, 217).[89] The first line essentially recasts the prohibition of v. 150 in positive terms, though the reference to "your" children, as well as the general context, indicates a shift in focus from children per se to children within one's own household. Various sources assume that fathers ought to treat their children in a manner guided by care and devotion.[90] It is also noteworthy that fatherly affection serves as a standard of gentleness in the Homeric epics, for example, *Il.* 24.770, *Od.* 2.47, 234, 5.12, 15.152.

Verses 208–209 proceed with a specific rule about parental discipline, illustrating how the principle of gentleness can be put into action. As Philo notes in his summary of the law, "(both) parents must have power over their children to keep them safe (cf. Ps.-Phoc. 213) and tend them carefully" (*Hypoth.* 7.3). The protocol prescribed by our author for the correction of a male child draws on Deut 21:18–21, which

---

[85] Cf. Martial, *Epig.* 6.7; Publilius Syrus, *Sent.* 260 ("Frequent re-marriage gives room for the evil tongue.") and 381: "The woman who marries many is disliked by many."

[86] BDAG s.v. εἷς 2.b, referring to *CIL* VI: 723, 1527, 3604, 12405, 14404, 31670, 37053, etc.; cf. Stählin, "χήρα," 442.

[87] Cf. Gardner, *Women in Roman Law*, 50–51. Marital status is advanced as a domestic virtue in the Pastoral Epistles; among the qualifications for ecclesial office listed there are that a man should be "husband of one wife" (1 Tim 3:2, 12; Titus 1:6; cf. 1 Tim 5:9). Other NT texts also frown upon remarriage: Matt 5:32, 19:9; Mark 10:11–12; Luke 16:18; 1 Cor 7:10–11; and Kötting, "Digamus," 1016–24.

[88] van der Horst, *Sentences*, 247.

[89] Cf. Riaud, "Quelques observations," 86–90.

[90] Cf. Menander, *Mon.* 635; Stobaeus, *Anth.* 4.26; Ps 102:13; Eph 6:4; Col 3:21; Philo, *Mos.* 1.328; Iamblichus, *Vit. Pyth.* 31.198; Menander, frg. 808 ("A better son is found in a father's affection."); Dio Chrysostom, *3 Regn.* 5; Ps.-Plutarch, *Lib. ed.* 7E.

instructs parents to take a recalcitrant son to the city's council of elders for judgment and stoning.[91] Philo approves of this law, interpreting it as giving parents the right to punish their children even with death, so long as they agree about the course of action.[92] Although Pseudo-Phocylides also promotes the practice of delegating the discipline of sons to certain "elders" (compare δημογέρων in v. 209 with γερουσία τῆς πόλεως in Deut 21:19),[93] in tone and intent v. 208 is closer to the affirmation of maternal authority in Sir 3:2: "the Lord ... has confirmed a mother's judgment (κρίσιν) over her sons." Even in comparison with this affirmation, however, Pseudo-Phocylides' advice is striking in its reticence about the father's role in punishment; his "gentleness" requires that he relinquish a basic paternal right.

That family members other than the father could exercise the prerogative of corporal punishment, however, was not altogether unknown. Cicero, for instance, stipulates that misbehaving boys can expect to be corrected by their mothers (*Tusc.* 3.64), while the elder Seneca notes the propriety of a grandfather doing likewise (*Contr.* 9.5.7). Such steps toward moderation in paternal discipline need to be interpreted as part of a broader conversation taking place about the role of physical violence in the ancient family. As Richard Saller points out, one of the primary distinctions between the condition of a free person and a slave in the Roman mind was the vulnerability of the latter to corporal punishment. Within the household it was the *paterfamilias* who wielded legal authority to inflict punishment on both children and slaves. But "because beating was such a potent symbol in the antithesis between *libertas* and servility, its infliction on free children was discouraged."[94] See, for example, Ps.-Plutarch, *Lib. ed.* 8F: "Children ought to be led to honorable practices by means of encouragement and reasoning, and most certainly not by blows nor by ill treatment; for it is surely agreed that these are fitting rather for slaves than for the freeborn." Compare Menander, frg. 730: "One ought not always correct a child with grief, but also with persuasion." It is noteworthy that Pseudo-Phocylides, for all the forbearance encouraged here, says nothing about the physical abuse of slaves when addressing their treatment in vv. 223–227.

---

[91] "This law is one of several in which Deuteronomy introduces local elders into family affairs. Intergenerational conflict is to be resolved in the public arena, where the influence of the elders can modify an unrestrained paternal authority that might lead either to excessive harshness or to inappropriate laxity." Nelson, *Deuteronomy*, 261; cf. Willis, *Elders of the City*, 163–85.

[92] Philo, *Spec.* 2.232, cf. *Ebr.* 14; Josephus, *C. Ap.* 2.206.

[93] Also cf. below, on vv. 221–222. For πρεσβύτατοι γενεῆς in v. 209, cf. πρεσβύτεροι τοῦ οἴκου (Gen 50:7; 2 Kgdms 12:17), πρεσβύτεροι τοῦ λαοῦ (Exod 17:5, 19:7; Num 11:16, 24).

[94] Saller, "Corporal Punishment," 158, cf. 144–65; Seneca, *Clem.* 1.15.1, *Ira* 2.26.6; Pliny, *Ep.* 9.12.1–2; Quintilian, *Inst.* 1.3.13; Dionysius of Halicarnassus, *Ant. rom.* 20.13; *Gnom. Vat.* 62; Publilius Syrus, *Sent.* 514: "A parent enraged is most cruel to himself."

Verses 210–217. These eight lines constitute a unit on protecting children from sexual exploitation; the sub-unit in vv. 210–214 (note ἄρσην in vv. 210, 212, 214) continues the discussion of the parenting of sons from vv. 208–209.

There were a number of ancient venues in which long hair (often κόμη or χαίτη) on men met with approval. Spartan men were famous for their long hair, a style that Cynic philosophers could also adopt, as a sign of freedom.[95] In Judaism, the Nazirite is to cherish his long hair (Num 6:5). Discouragement of the practice in Jewish circles originated partly as a response to Hellenism, where a long or elaborate hairstyle could be interpreted as a sign of sexual availability. Greek vase-paintings, for example, routinely picture male youths who are the object of "homosexual courting or pursuit" with long hair.[96] Philo, trading in an ancient caricature, observes how pederasts themselves typically "braid and adorn their hair conspicuously." This, together with the application of cosmetics and perfumes, is tantamount, he thinks, to "the transformation of the male nature to the female."[97] That long hair is indecent for men is well-known from 1 Cor 11:14–15, a lesson that Paul says "nature itself" teaches.[98] Elaborate hairstyles could be rejected as immodest for women as well, for example, *T. Reub.* 5:5: "flee sexual promiscuity, and order your wives and daughters not to adorn their heads and their appearances so as to deceive men's sound minds."[99] Such personal presentation was generally associated with feminine wiles and lasciviousness, as we hear in Philo's description of the prostitute in *Sacr.* 21: her gait has been bred by "luxury" (χλιδή; cf. χλιδανός in Ps.-Phoc. 212), she assumes a stature nature has not given her, her hair is dressed in elaborate plaits, and so on.[100] Pseudo-Phocylides frowns on males, especially boys, adopting such an appearance; cf. Musonius Rufus, frg. 21. As Bernadette Brooten observes, the logic of this passage in the *Sentences* is "based on strict gender differentiation in dress and sexual role."[101]

Verses 213–214 give the point and rationale for vv. 210–212. Parents are encouraged to prohibit such coiffure as part of an effort to protect their sons from ped-

---

[95] E.g., Herodotus, *Hist.* 1.82.8; Aristotle, *Rhet.* 1.9.26; Epictetus, *Diatr.* 4.8.34; Ps.-Crates, *Ep.* 23; Apollonius of Tyana, *Ep.* 8; Julian, *Or.* 6.201A.

[96] Dover, *Popular Morality*, 78–79; cf. Aristophanes, *Vesp.* 1069–1070; Plutarch, *Mulier. virt.* 261F; Horace, *Epod.* 11.27–28; Juvenal, *Sat.* 2.96; Martial, *Epig.* 10.65; Seneca, *Contr.* 1 pr. 8 ("Look at our young men … Libidinous delight in song and dance transfixes these effeminates. Braiding the hair, refining the voice till it is as caressing as a woman's, competing in bodily softness with women, beautifying themselves with filthy fineries – this is the pattern our youths set themselves."); also cf. Plutarch, *Quaest. rom.* 267B; Dio Chrysostom, *Ven.* 117.

[97] Philo, *Spec.* 3.37, cf. *Mos.* 1.54.

[98] Cf. Str-B 3:440–42; Thiselton, *First Epistle to the Corinthians*, 844–46.

[99] Cf. 1 Tim 2:9; 1 Pet 3:3; Ps.-Periktione, *Mul. harm.* 1.143.23; Ilan, *Jewish Women*, 130.

[100] Cf. *Sib. Or.* 3.356–359; Juvenal, *Sat.* 6.486–511.

[101] Brooten, *Love Between Women*, 63.

erastic overtures. Pederasty is vigorously condemned in Judaism, a position which can be interpreted as part of its critical response to Hellenic culture.[102] Philo mentions it as a crime in his summary of the law (*Hypoth.* 7.1) and elsewhere.[103] For the basic parental obligation identified here, we may compare *Syr. Men.* 49 ("Keep your son away from fornication."). The Roman response was similarly disapproving: "The Greek tradition of pederasty, whereby citizen males might openly engage in romantic and sexual relationships with free-born adolescent males who would one day be citizens, in Roman terms was *stuprum*; it was disgraceful, illicit behavior."[104] Affairs with boys were often classified by both Greek and Roman moralists as illustrations of decadent self-indulgence.[105]

In antiquity the sexuality of an unwed daughter was understood as something that her father had an obligation to control. A sexually-active daughter "would violate social norms and would render the father dishonored before his friends and colleagues."[106] Understood as her father's property, there would have been an economic incentive for the daughter to remain inviolate as well (cf. Deut 22:20–21). The solution to the problem, of course, was to keep the young woman sequestered. Ben Sira, representative of his time, sees an adolescent daughter as a necessarily sexual and untrustworthy being, with little self-control. Sir 42:9–11 in particular sheds light on the provisions called for in Ps.-Phoc. 215–216. An unwed daughter is for her father "a wakeful care," his principal fear being that she should lose her virginity while still living under his roof. The author's advice in response to this anxiety is to "keep a sure watch (στερέωσον φυλακήν) over your shameless daughter."[107] Sir 26:10–12 elaborates, instructing the father to guard (φύλαξαι) his daughter's "shameless eye," since she is likely to stray: "She will open her mouth … and drink from every nearby water; she will sit by every peg and open her quiver to every arrow" (cf. 7:24–25).[108] In contrast, Pseudo-Phocylides emphasizes not the daughter's promiscuous drives but the obligation of both parents to protect her (v. 217). His

---

[102] On Greek pederastic traditions, see Dover, *Greek Homosexuality*; D. Cohen, *Law, Sexuality, and Society*, 171–202; Percy, *Pederasty and Pedagogy*, 1–11, 185–92; Thornton, *Eros*, 193–212.

[103] Cf. Philo, *Decal.* 168, *Spec.* 2.50, 3.37–42, 4.89, *Contempl.* 61; *T. Levi* 17:11; *Sib. Or.* 5.166, 430; *Did.* 2:2.

[104] C. Williams, *Roman Homosexuality*, 62, cf. 63–72.

[105] Swain, "Plutarch's Moral Program," 89: among Hellenistic elites one notes a "particular imperative to moralize sexual conduct, especially the accent on sexual relations within marriage as the means of promoting family values and disapprobation of pederastic homosexual relations." For the critique of men who spend vast sums on beautiful slave boys, see Isocrates, *Nic.* 39; Juvenal, *Sat.* 5.56–59, 11.147–148; Martial, *Epig.* 1.58, 3.62.1, 9.21, 12.16, 12.33; Polybius, *Hist.* 31.25.4–5; cf. Xenophon, *Lac.* 2.12–13, *Symp.* 8.34; Plutarch, *Amat.* 752A–C, *Marc.* 2.3–4.

[106] Berquist, "Controlling Daughter's Bodies," 99; cf. S. J. D. Cohen, *Jewish Family*, 105–106; D. Cohen, *Law, Sexuality, and Society*, 103; Epstein, *Sex Laws*, 68–75.

[107] For the language of "guarding" a daughter, cf. Herodotus, *Hist.* 5.6; Josephus, *Ant.* 7.163.

[108] Cf. Trenchard, *Ben Sira's View of Women*, 129–65.

solution to the problem, though, is the same. He shares the general opinion that public places are inappropriate for unmarried girls, who should not venture even beyond the inner doors of their homes.[109] Verse 217 concludes and summarizes the section in vv. 210–217 with a thought that would have resonated with Plautus, *Epid.* 404–405 ("No one can be too careful to preserve his daughter's modesty.") and Juvenal, *Sat.* 10.295–298 (cf. 299–328): "A handsome son keeps his parents in constant fear and misery; so rarely do modesty and good looks go together" (cf. Democritus, frg. 275). Preserving a child's innocence would have been a matter of honor for the entire family.[110]

Verse 219. Love and concord, earlier extolled as marital values (vv. 195–197), are here extended to the entire household (cf. v. 206). Familial harmony is highly prized in a range of Jewish writings of the Hellenistic era. In 4 Macc 13:23–26, *homonoia* is presented as one manifestation of the seven brothers' love (φιλαδελφία) for one another. Among the things that are seemly to both God and humanity according to Sir 25:1 is "the harmony (ὁμόνοια) of siblings and the love (φιλία) of neighbors." And *T. Jos.* 17:3 claims that "God is delighted by harmony (ὁμονοίᾳ) among brothers and the intent of a heart well-pleased by love (ἀγάπην)." As these illustrations suggest, the pairing of harmony and love was conventional: bonds strengthened by love are a prerequisite for familial concord.[111]

Verses 220–222. The need to respect one's elders and seek out their wisdom is a refrain of most all traditional societies, early Judaism being no exception.[112] The source for these lines appears to be Lev 19:32: "You shall rise up before a gray (πολιοῦ) head and honor (τιμήσεις) the face of an elder (πρεσβυτέρου)."[113] Philo interprets this text as a provision of the Decalogue's fifth commandment. The final proof of filial piety, he says, is the courtesy shown to persons who share the seniority of one's parents: "one who pays respect to an elder man or woman who is not of his kin may be regarded as having remembrance of his father and mother" (*Spec.* 2.237). In his summary of the law, Josephus also links the rules to honor parents and elders (*C. Ap.* 2.206; cf. Philo, *Hypoth.* 7.13; *Syr. Men.* 9–14). From the Greek legal tradition, we have Plato, *Leg.* 879C: "Let everyone respect (αἰδείσθω) his elder

---

[109] See Philo, *Spec.* 3.169, cf. 3.171, *Flacc.* 89; 2 Macc 3:19; 3 Macc 1:18; 4 Macc 18:7.

[110] Cf. Richlin, "Not Before Homosexuality," 537–38, 546–48.

[111] Cf. Tob 4:13; *Sib. Or.* 3.373–376; *Syr. Men.* 189; Philo, *Mut.* 200, *Spec.* 1.295, *Praem.* 92, 154; *Let. Arist.* 241–242; Aristotle, *Eth. nic.* 8.1.4, *Eth. eud.* 7.7.3–8; Demosthenes, *Or.* 25.88; Diogenes Laertius, *Vit. phil.* 6.6; Babrius, *Fab.* 47.15–16; Menander, frg. 809: "Sweet is the love of harmony among brothers."

[112] E.g., Prov 16:31; Sir 8:6, 9; *Syr. Men., Epit.* 3; Philo, *Post.* 181, *Decal.* 167.

[113] "The young man was to rise before the elderly man, a reference to the place where men met in the city gate, or to assemblies of the congregation or common meals." Gerstenberger, *Leviticus,* 279.

(πρεσβύτερον) in both deed and word," regarding members of the previous generation "as a father or a mother." For evidence that the practice recommended in vv.
220b–221a may have been considered exceptional, see Herodotus, *Hist.* 2.80.1:
"There is a custom, too, which no Greeks except the Lacedaemonians have in common with the Egyptians: younger men, encountering their elders (πρεσβυτέροισι),
yield (εἴκουσι) the way and stand aside, and rise from their seats (ἕδρης) for them
when they approach." As Cicero notes, yielding one's seat to an elder would have
been interpreted as a sign of deference (*Sen.* 18.63).[114]

Earlier in the poem, Pseudo-Phocylides had spoken about the reader's obligation
to respect a woman who is "like" his mother (v. 180). Verses 221b–222 provide the
counterpart to this, communicating the reader's obligation to honor a man who is
"like" his father in age and ancestry. In light of the texts discussed above, this advice
can also be understood as an extension of the command to honor parents in v. 8.

Verses 223–227. The Greco-Roman world was essentially a slave economy, and
slaves were legally considered the movable property of their masters, who could
dispose of them as they wished. As a class, they were generally viewed as crimi-
nous, disloyal, and lazy.[115] The available evidence suggests that practices of slave
ownership among Jews of the period did not differ substantially from those of the
pagan host culture.[116] The Pentateuch places few restrictions on the institution,
though penalties for striking or killing a slave are set in Exod 21:20–21, 26–27.[117]
Ben Sira usually advocates hard work and discipline for slaves, though he reveals a
more compassionate side (albeit one motivated by self-interest) in 33:32–33: "If
you own a slave, treat him like a brother, for you need him as you need your soul. If
you ill-treat him and he runs away, which way will you go searching for him?" (cf.
7:20–21). In his summary of the law, Philo indicates that it is an outrage for Jews
to bind, kidnap, or sell slaves (*Hypoth.* 7.2). Elsewhere, he champions *philanthrōpia*
as a standard for slave treatment.[118] Such statements are consistent with a proclivity
among Hellenistic elites "to found the domination of the masters not only on the
use of violence, but also on the consent of those dominated: to replace enforced

---

[114] Cf. Tyrtaeus, frg. 12.41–42; Plato, *Resp.* 425B; Xenophon, *Mem.* 2.3.16, *Cyr.* 8.7.10; Ps.-Plutarch,
Lib. ed. 7E; Diogenes Laertius, *Vit. phil.* 8.22; *Dict. Cat.* pr. 10; *Instr. Any* 6.11–12; Gardner and
Wiedemann, *Roman Household*, 90–91.

[115] Bradley, *Slaves and Masters*, 26–45.

[116] D. B. Martin, "Slavery," 113–29.

[117] Cf. Lev 25:43, 53; Philo, *Spec.* 3.137–143; Josephus, *C. Ap.* 2.215.

[118] Philo, *Virt.* 121–124, cf. *Decal.* 167, *Spec.* 2.69, 79–85, 3.184, *Contempl.* 70; Demosthenes, *Or.*
21.49.

obedience with spontaneous obedience and thus to reduce the sources of tension within the social organism."[119]

For his part, Pseudo-Phocylides specifies five obligations for slave-owners (note that the projected reader is assumed to own slaves), all of which evidence this sort of perspective. For the sentiment of the first of these (v. 223), Epictetus, *Gnom.* 24 ("It is best if … while feasting, you share with those who serve you the things which are before you.") is comparable, though for the basic rule *Instr. Ankh.* 14.19 ("Do not let your servant lack his food and clothing.") is a better parallel.[120] As Ps.-Aristotle, *Oec.* 1.5.3 points out, when slaves are compelled to work without adequate food, "such treatment is oppressive, and saps their strength."

In v. 224, τακτά (things which have been ordered or prescribed) presumably refer to the kind and amount of work imposed on a slave. The line vaguely implies that there would have been some generally accepted limit to this. The slave-owner is to observe this limit so that the slave will end up καταθύμιος, compliant to the owner's will, and hence satisfactory. Philo seems to be making the same point in *Spec.* 2.90–91, where he urges masters not to treat their slaves harshly, but to observe moderation in their orders (ἐπιτάγματα) so that they will work both more efficiently and more obediently; cf. Col 4:1: "Grant (παρέχεσθε; cf. παρέχειν in Ps.-Phoc. 223) your slaves what is just and fair."[121]

Lev 19:28 stipulates that "you shall not make on yourselves any inscribed marks (γράμματα στικτά)." In v. 225, Pseudo-Phocylides attempts to dissuade the reader from marking any of his slaves with στίγματα, which he believes is a mark of disgrace.[122] C. P. Jones' extensive survey of the use of this term yields the following conclusion: "'Stigmata' are almost always tatoo- and not brand-marks; the branding of animals is virtually never designated by *stigma* but by a word denoting a burn or a stamp; the branding of humans was exceptional, and is designated by the word *stigma* only rarely and at a comparatively late date."[123] Among the texts examined is a fragmentary legal code of the third century B.C.E., stating that masters may "not sell slaves for export, nor tatoo (στίζειν) them." Later the same text gives the exception to this rule: any slave convicted of a crime is to be whipped and given a tatoo

---

[119] Garlan, *Slavery*, 149; cf. Shelton, *As the Romans Did*, 180–85; Harris, *Restraining Rage*, 317–36; Plato, *Leg.* 777D–E; Aristotle, *Eth. nic.* 8.11.7–8; Ps.-Plutarch, *Lib. ed.* 17E; Seneca, *Ep.* 47, *Clem.* 1.18: "It is praiseworthy to use authority over slaves with moderation. Even in the case of a human chattel you should consider not how much he can be made to suffer without retaliating, but how much you are permitted to inflict by the principles of equity and right, which require that mercy should be shown even to captives and purchased slaves."

[120] Cf. Matt 24:45; Luke 12:42; Diodorus Siculus, *Bibl.* 34.2.2; Theophrastus, *Char.* 30.11; Xenophon, *Cyr.* 8.1.43–44, *Oec.* 13.9; Juvenal, *Sat.* 14.126–127; Seneca, *Ben.* 3.22.3.

[121] Cf. *Did.* 4:10; Ps.-Aristotle, *Oec.* 1.5.3.

[122] Cf. Seneca, *Ben.* 4.37.3–5; Diodorus Siculus, *Bibl.* 34.2.1.

[123] Jones, "Stigma," 140–41.

on his forehead.[124] Indeed, the punitive tattooing of slaves, especially runaways, appears to have been fairly commonplace.[125]

The ultimate source for v. 226 may be the Hebrew text of Prov 30:10: "Do not slander a slave to his master or he will curse you and you will be held guilty." It is possible that Pseudo-Phocylides had access to a different, more literal translation of this saying than our Septuagintal version, which has: "Do not deliver a servant into the hands of his master, lest he curse you and you be destroyed."[126] Despite their differences, the texts agree that is it unwise to interfere in the master-slave relations of another household. While Prov 30:10 draws attention to the damage incurred by the slanderer, our author focuses on the harm done to the slave; cf. Eph 6:9.

In the last verse of the section, the author suggests that the reader consult with a slave, provided that he is prudent. With this we may compare *Her.* 5–6, where Philo identifies the conditions under which a slave may speak freely to his master: if he has not wronged his master, and if his words may bring him some benefit. Seneca agrees that slaves should be allowed to converse with their masters and even concedes that under certain circumstances the former can confer a benefit on the latter.[127] The thought finds gnomic expression elsewhere in *Dict. Cat.* 3.10: "Sound counsel from your slave do not despise: spurn no one's view at all, if it is wise." Social status, then, does not necessarily determine intelligence. On a more cynical note, Columella's farming manual advises a master to include slaves in his deliberations, since they will be more enthusiastic about their work if they think their opinions actually carry some weight (*Rust.* 1.8.9, 15, 11.1.21, 12.1.6; cf. Varro, *Rust.* 1.17.5–7).

The *Sentences* concludes in vv. 228–30 with an epilogue that has been coordinated with the poem's prologue (vv. 1–2). For discussion, see above, Chapter I.

---

[124] Jones, "Stigma," 148, referring to P.Lille 29.1.13–14, 2.33–36.

[125] E.g., Herodotus, *Hist.* 2.113; Plato, *Leg.* 854D; Aristophanes, *Av.* 760–761; Menander, *Sam.* 323; Diodorus Siculus, *Bibl.* 34.2.1.

[126] Cf. Deut 23:16–17; *Instr. Ankh.* 16.6: "Do not cast a slave into the hands of his master."

[127] Seneca, *Ep.* 47.4, 13, 16, *Ben.* 3.18–28.

APPENDIX

The Greek Text of the *Sentences*

ΦΩΚΥΛΙΔΟΥ ΓΝΩΜΑΙ

1 ταῦτα δίκησ᾽ ὁσίῃσι θεοῦ βουλεύματα φαίνει
2 Φωκυλίδης ἀνδρῶν ὁ σοφώτατος ὄλβια δῶρα.
3 μήτε γαμοκλοπέειν μήτ᾽ ἄρσενα κύπριν ὀρίνειν.
4 μήτε δόλους ῥάπτειν μήθ᾽ αἵματι χεῖρα μιαίνειν.
5 μὴ πλουτεῖν ἀδίκως, ἀλλ᾽ ἐξ ὁσίων βιοτεύειν.
6 ἀρκεῖσθαι παρεοῦσι καὶ ἀλλοτρίων ἀπέχεσθαι.
7 ψεύδεα μὴ βάζειν, τὰ δ᾽ ἐτήτυμα πάντ᾽ ἀγορεύειν.
8 πρῶτα θεὸν τιμᾶν, μετέπειτα δὲ σεῖο γονῆας.
9 πάντα δίκαια νέμειν, μὴ δὲ κρίσιν ἐς χάριν ἕλκειν.
10 μὴ θλίψῃς πενίην ἀδίκως, μὴ κρῖνε πρόσωπον·
11 ἢν σὺ κακῶς δικάσῃς, σὲ θεὸς μετέπειτα δικάσσει.
12 μαρτυρίην ψευδῆ φεύγειν· τὰ δίκαια βραβεύειν.
13 παρθεσίην τηρεῖν, πίστιν δ᾽ ἐν πᾶσι φυλάσσειν.
14 μέτρα νέμειν τὰ δίκαια, καλὸν δ᾽ ἐπὶ μέτρον ἅπασι.
15 σταθμὸν μὴ κρούειν ἑτερόζυγον, ἀλλ᾽ ἴσον ἕλκειν.
16 μὴ δ᾽ ἐπιορκήσῃς μήτ᾽ ἀγνὼς μήτε ἑκοντί·
17 ψεύδορκον στυγέει θεὸς ἄμβροτος ὅστις ὀμόσσῃ.
18 σπέρματα μὴ κλέπτειν· ἐπαράσιμος ὅστις ἕληται.
19 μισθὸν μοχθήσαντι δίδου, μὴ θλῖβε πένητα.
20 γλώσσῃ νοῦν ἐχέμεν, κρυπτὸν λόγον ἐν φρεσὶν ἴσχειν.
21 μήτ᾽ ἀδικεῖν ἐθέλῃς μήτ᾽ οὖν ἀδικοῦντα ἐάσῃς.
22 πτωχῷ δ᾽ εὐθὺ δίδου μὴ δ᾽ αὔριον ἐλθέμεν εἴπῃς·
23 πληρώσει σέο χεῖρ᾽· ἔλεον χρήζοντι παράσχου.
24 ἄστεγον εἰς οἶκον δέξαι καὶ τυφλὸν ὀδήγει.
25 ναυηγοὺς οἴκτειρον, ἐπεὶ πλόος ἐστὶν ἄδηλος.
26 χεῖρα πεσόντι δίδου, σῶσον δ᾽ ἀπερίστατον ἄνδρα.
27 κοινὰ πάθη πάντων· ὁ βίος τροχός· ἄστατος ὄλβος.
28 πλοῦτον ἔχων σὴν χεῖρα πενητεύουσιν ὄρεξον·
29 ὧν σοι ἔδωκε θεός, τούτων χρήζουσι παράσχου.
30 ἔστω κοινὸς ἅπας ὁ βίος καὶ ὁμόφρονα πάντα.
32 τὸ ξίφος ἀμφιβαλοῦ μὴ πρὸς φόνον, ἀλλ᾽ ἐς ἄμυναν.
33 εἴθε δὲ μὴ χρήζοις μήτ᾽ ἔκνομα μήτε δικαίως·
34 ἢν γὰρ ἀποκτείνῃς ἐχθρόν, σέο χεῖρα μιαίνεις.
35 ἀγροῦ γειτονέοντος ἀπόσχεο, μὴ δ᾽ ἄρ᾽ ὑπερβῇς.

38   μηδέ τιν' αὐξόμενον καρπὸν λωβήσῃ ἀρούρης.
39   ἔστωσαν δ' ὁμότιμοι ἐπήλυδες ἐν πολιήταις·
40   πάντες γὰρ πενίης πειρώμεθα τῆς πολυπλάγκτου,
41   χώρης δ' οὔ τι βέβαιον ἔχει πέδον ἀνθρώποισιν.
42   ἡ φιλοχρημοσύνη μήτηρ κακότητος ἁπάσης.
43   χρυσὸς ἀεὶ δόλος ἐστὶ καὶ ἄργυρος ἀνθρώποισιν.
44   χρυσέ, κακῶν ἀρχηγέ, βιοφθόρε, πάντα χαλέπτων,
45   εἴθε σε μὴ θνητοῖσι γενέσθαι πῆμα ποθεινόν·
46   σεῦ γὰρ ἕκητι μάχαι τε λεηλασίαι τε φόνοι τε,
47   ἐχθρὰ δὲ τέκνα γονεῦσιν ἀδελφειοί τε συναίμοις.
48   μὴ δ' ἕτερον κεύθῃς κραδίῃ νόον ἄλλ' ἀγορεύων,
49   μηδ' ὡς πετροφυὴς πολύπους κατὰ χῶρον ἀμείβου.
50   πᾶσιν δ' ἁπλόος ἴσθι, τὰ δ' ἐκ ψυχῆς ἀγόρευε.
51   ὅστις ἑκὼν ἀδικεῖ, κακὸς ἀνήρ· ἢν δ' ὑπ' ἀνάγκης,
52   οὐκ ἐρέω τὸ τέλος· βουλὴ δ' εὐθύνεθ' ἑκάστου.
53   μὴ γαυροῦ σοφίῃ μήτ' ἀλκῇ μήτ' ἐνὶ πλούτῳ·
54   εἷς θεός ἐστι σοφὸς δυνατός θ' ἅμα καὶ πολύολβος.
55   μὴ δὲ παροιχομένοισι κακοῖς τρύχου τεὸν ἧπαρ·
56   οὐκέτι γὰρ δύναται τὸ τετυγμένον εἶναι ἄτυκτον.
57   μὴ προπετὴς ἐς χεῖρα, χαλίνου δ' ἄγριον ὀργήν·
58   πολλάκι γὰρ πλήξας ἀέκων φόνον ἐξετέλεσσεν.
59   ἔστω κοινὰ πάθη· μηδὲν μέγα μηδ' ὑπέροπλον.
60   οὐκ ἀγαθὸν πλεονάζον ἔφυ θνητοῖσιν ὄνειαρ·
61   ἡ πολλὴ δὲ τρυφὴ πρὸς ἀσέμνους ἕλκετ' ἔρωτας·
62   ὑψαυχεῖ δ' ὁ πολὺς πλοῦτος καὶ ἐς ὕβριν ἀέξει.
63   θυμὸς ὑπερχόμενος μανίην ὀλοόφρονα τεύχει.
64   ὀργή δ' ἐστὶν ὄρεξις, ὑπερβαίνουσα δὲ μῆνις.
65   ζῆλος τῶν ἀγαθῶν ἐσθλός, φαύλων δ' ὑπέρογκος.
66   τόλμα κακῶν ὀλοή, μέγ' ὀφέλλει δ' ἐσθλὰ πονεῦντα.
67   σεμνὸς ἔρως ἀρετῆς, ὁ δὲ κύπριδος αἶσχος ὀφέλλει.
68   ἡδὺς ἄγαν ἄφρων κικλήσκεται ἐν πολίταις.
69   μέτρῳ ἔδειν, μέτρῳ δὲ πιεῖν καὶ μυθολογεύειν.
69Β   πάντων μέτρον ἄριστον, ὑπερβασίαι δ' ἀλεγειναί.
70   μὴ φθονέοις ἀγαθῶν ἑτάροις, μὴ μῶμον ἀνάψῃς.
71   ἄφθονοι οὐρανίδαι καὶ ἐν ἀλλήλοις τελέθουσιν.
72   οὐ φθονέει μήνη πολὺ κρείσσοσιν ἠλίου αὐγαῖς,
73   οὐ χθὼν οὐρανίοισ' ὑψώμασι νέρθεν ἐοῦσα,
74   οὐ ποταμοὶ πελάγεσσιν· ἀεὶ δ' ὁμόνοιαν ἔχουσιν·
75   εἰ γὰρ ἔρις μακάρεσσιν ἔην, οὐκ ἂν πόλος ἔστη.
76   σωφροσύνην ἀσκεῖν, αἰσχρῶν δ' ἔργων ἀπέχεσθαι.
77   μὴ μιμοῦ κακότητα, δίκῃ δ' ἀπόλειψον ἄμυναν.
78   πειθὼ μὲν γὰρ ὄνειαρ, ἔρις δ' ἔριν ἀντιφυτεύει.

79 μὴ πίστευε τάχιστα, πρὶν ἀτρεκέως πέρας ὄψει.
80 νικᾶν εὖ ἔρδοντας ἐπὶ πλεόνεσσι καθήκει.
81 καλὸν ξεινίζειν ταχέως λιταῖσι τραπέζαις
82 ἢ πλείσταις θαλίαισι βραδυνούσαις παρὰ καιρόν.
83 μηδέποτε χρήστης πικρὸς γένῃ ἀνδρὶ πένητι.
84 μηδέ τις ὄρνιθας καλιῆς ἅμα πάντας ἑλέσθω,
85 μητέρα δ' ἐκπρολίποις, ἵν' ἔχῃς πάλι τῆσδε νεοσσούς.
86 μηδέποτε κρίνειν ἀδαήμονας ἄνδρας ἐάσῃς.
88 τὴν σοφίην σοφὸς εὐθύνει, τέχνας δ' ὁμότεχνος.
89 οὐ χωρεῖ μεγάλην διδαχὴν ἀδίδακτος ἀκοή·
90 οὐ γὰρ δὴ νοέουσ' οἱ μηδέποτ' ἐσθλὰ μαθόντες.
91 μὴ δὲ τραπεζοκόρους κόλακας ποιεῖσθαι ἑταίρους·
92 πολλοὶ γὰρ πόσιος καὶ βρώσιός εἰσιν ἑταῖροι
93 καιρὸν θωπεύοντες, ἐπὴν κορέσασθαι ἔχωσιν,
94 ἀχθόμενοι δ' ὀλίγοις καὶ πολλοῖς πάντες ἄπληστοι.
95 λαῷ μὴ πίστευε, πολύτροπός ἐστιν ὅμιλος·
96 λαὸς γὰρ καὶ ὕδωρ καὶ πῦρ ἀκατάσχετα πάντα.
97 μὴ δὲ μάτην ἐπὶ πῦρ καθίσας μινύθῃς φίλον ἦτορ·
98 μέτρα δὲ τεῦχε γόοισι· τὸ γὰρ μέτρον ἐστὶν ἄριστον.
99 γαῖαν ἐπιμοιρᾶσθαι ἀταρχύτοις νεκύεσσιν.
100 μὴ τύμβον φθιμένων ἀνορύξῃς μηδ' ἀθέατα
101 δείξῃς ἠελίῳ καὶ δαιμόνιον χόλον ὄρσῃς.
102 οὐ καλὸν ἁρμονίην ἀναλυέμεν ἀνθρώποιο·
103 καὶ τάχα δ' ἐκ γαίης ἐλπίζομεν ἐς φάος ἐλθεῖν
104 λείψαν' ἀποιχομένων· ὀπίσω δὲ θεοὶ τελέθοντα·
105 ψυχαὶ γὰρ μίμνουσιν ἀκήριοι ἐν φθιμένοισιν·
106 πνεῦμα γάρ ἐστι θεοῦ χρῆσις θνητοῖσι καὶ εἰκών·
107 σῶμα γὰρ ἐκ γαίης ἔχομεν κἄπειτα πρὸς αὖ γῆν
108 λυόμενοι κόνις ἐσμέν· ἀὴρ δ' ἀνὰ πνεῦμα δέδεκται.
109 πλουτῶν μὴ φείδου· μέμνησ' ὅτι θνητὸς ὑπάρχεις·
110 οὐκ ἔνι εἰς Ἅιδην ὄλβον καὶ χρήματ' ἄγεσθαι.
111 πάντες ἴσον νέκυες, ψυχῶν δὲ θεὸς βασιλεύει.
112 κοινὰ μέλαθρα δόμων αἰώνια καὶ πατρὶς Ἅιδης,
113 ξυνὸς χῶρος ἅπασι, πένησί τε καὶ βασιλεῦσιν.
114 οὐ πολὺν ἄνθρωποι ζῶμεν χρόνον, ἀλλ' ἐπίκαιρον·
115 ψυχὴ δ' ἀθάνατος καὶ ἀγήρως ζῇ διὰ παντός.
118 μήτε κακοῖσ' ἄχθου μήτ' οὖν ἐπαγάλλεο χάρμῃ·
119 πολλάκις ἐν βιότῳ καὶ θαρσαλέοισιν ἄπιστον
120 πῆμα καὶ ἀχθομένοισι κακοῦ λύσις ἤλυθεν ἄφνω.
121 καιρῷ λατρεύειν, μὴ δ' ἀντιπνέειν ἀνέμοισιν.
122 μὴ μεγαληγορίῃ τρυφῶν φρένα λυσσωθείης.
123 εὐεπίην ἀσκεῖν, ἥτις μάλα πάντας ὀνήσει.

124 ὅπλον τοι λόγος ἀνδρὶ τομώτερόν ἐστι σιδήρου·
125 ὅπλον ἑκάστῳ νεῖμε θεός, φύσιν ἠερόφοιτον
126 ὄρνισιν, πώλοις ταχυτῆτ', ἀλκήν τε λέουσιν,
127 ταύροις δ' αὐτοφύτως κέρα ἐστίν, κέντρα μελίσσαις
128 ἔμφυτον ἄλκαρ ἔδωκε, λόγον δ' ἔρυμ' ἀνθρώποισιν.
130 βέλτερος ἀλκήεντος ἔφυ σεσοφισμένος ἀνήρ·
131 ἀγροὺς καὶ πόλιας σοφίῃ καὶ νῆα κυβερνᾷ.
132 οὐχ ὅσιον κρύπτειν τὸν ἀτάσθαλον ἄνδρ' ἀνέλεγκτον,
133 ἀλλὰ χρὴ κακοεργὸν ἀποτρωπᾶσθαι ἀνάγκῃ·
134 πολλάκι συνθνήσκουσι κακοῖσ' οἱ συμπαρεόντες.
135 φωρῶν μὴ δέξῃ κλοπίμην ἄδικον παραθήκην·
136 ἀμφότεροι κλῶπες, καὶ ὁ δεξάμενος καὶ ὁ κλέψας.
137 μοίρας πᾶσι νέμειν, ἰσότης δ' ἐν πᾶσιν ἄριστον.
138 ἀρχόμενος φείδου πάντων, μὴ τέρμ' ἐπιδεύῃς.
139 μὴ κτήνους θνητοῖο βορὴν κατὰ μέτρον ἕλῃαι.
140 κτῆνος δ' ἢν ἐχθροῖο πέσῃ καθ' ὁδόν, συνέγειρε.
141 πλαζόμενον δὲ βροτὸν καὶ ἀλίτροπον οὔποτ' ἐλέγξεις.
142 βέλτερον ἀντ' ἐχθροῦ τεύχειν φίλον εὐμενέοντα.
143 ἀρχόμενον τὸ κακὸν κόπτειν ἕλκος τ' ἀκέσασθαι.
147 μὴ δέ τι θηρόβορον δαίσῃ κρέας, ἀργίποσιν δέ
148 λείψανα λεῖπε κυσίν· θηρῶν ἄπο θῆρες ἔδονται.
149 φάρμακα μὴ τεύχειν, μαγικῶν βίβλων ἀπέχεσθαι.
150 νηπιάχοις ἁπαλοῖς μὴ μάρψῃ χεῖρα βιαίως.
151 φεῦγε διχοστασίην καὶ ἔριν πολέμου προσιόντος.
152 μὴ κακὸν εὖ ἔρξῃς· σπείρειν ἴσον ἔστ' ἐνὶ πόντῳ.
153 ἐργάζευ μοχθῶν, ὡς ἐξ ἰδίων βιοτεύσῃς·
154 πᾶς γὰρ ἀεργὸς ἀνὴρ ζώει κλοπίμων ἀπὸ χειρῶν.
156 μὴ δ' ἄλλου παρὰ δαιτὸς ἔδοις σκυβάλισμα τραπέζης,
157 ἀλλ' ἀπὸ τῶν ἰδίων βίοτον διάγοις ἀνύβριστος.
158 εἰ δέ τις οὐ δεδάηκε τέχνης, σκάπτοιτο δικέλλῃ.
159 ἔστι βίῳ πᾶν ἔργον, ἐπὴν μοχθεῖν ἐθέλησθα.
160 ναυτίλος εἰ πλώειν ἐθέλεις, εὐρεῖα θάλασσα·
161 εἰ δὲ γεηπονίην μεθέπειν, μακραί τοι ἄρουραι.
162 οὐδὲν ἄνευ καμάτου πέλει ἀνδράσιν εὐπετὲς ἔργον
163 οὐδ' αὐτοῖς μακάρεσσι· πόνος δ' ἀρετὴν μέγ' ὀφέλλει.
164 μύρμηκες γαίης μυχάτους προλελοιπότες οἴκους
165 ἔρχονται βιότου κεχρημένοι, ὁππότ' ἄρουραι
166 λήϊα κειράμεναι καρπῶν πλήθωσιν ἁλωάς.
167 οἱ δ' αὐτοὶ πυροῖο νεοτριβὲς ἄχθος ἔχουσιν
168 ἢ κριθῶν, αἰεὶ δὲ φέρων φορέοντα διώκει,
169 ἐκ θέρεος ποτὶ χεῖμα βορὴν σφετέρην ἐπάγοντες

170 ἄτρυτοι· φῦλον δ' ὀλίγον τελέθει πολύμοχθον.
171 κάμνει δ' ἠεροφοῖτις ἀριστοπόνος τε μέλισσα
172 ἠὲ πέτρης κοίλης κατὰ χηραμὸν ἢ δονάκεσσιν
173 ἢ δρυὸς ὠγυγίης κατὰ κοιλάδος ἔνδοθι σίμβλων
174 σμήνεσι μυριότρητα κατ' ἄγγεα κηροδομοῦσα.
175 μὴ μείνῃς ἄγαμος, μή πως νώνυμνος ὄληαι·
176 δός τι φύσει καὐτός, τέκε δ' ἔμπαλιν, ὡς ἐλοχεύθης.
177 μὴ προαγωγεύσῃς ἄλοχον σέο τέκνα μιαίνων·
178 οὐ γὰρ τίκτει παῖδας ὁμοίους μοιχικὰ λέκτρα.
179 μητρυιῆς μὴ ψαῦ', ἅτε δεύτερα λέκτρα γονῆος·
180 μητέρα δ' ὡς τίμα τὴν μητέρος ἴχνια βᾶσαν.
181 μηδέ τι παλλακίσιν πατρὸς λεχέεσσι μιγείης.
182 μηδὲ κασιγνήτης ἐς ἀπότροπον ἐλθέμεν εὐνήν.
183 μηδὲ κασιγνήτων ἀλόχων ἐπὶ δέμνια βαίνειν.
184 μηδὲ γυνὴ φθείρῃ βρέφος ἔμβρυον ἔνδοθι γαστρός,
185 μηδὲ τεκοῦσα κυσὶν ῥίψῃ καὶ γυψὶν ἕλωρα.
186 μηδ' ἐπὶ σῇ ἀλόχῳ ἐγκύμονι χεῖρα βάλῃαι.
187 μηδ' αὖ παιδογόνον τέμνειν φύσιν ἄρσενα κούρου.
188 μηδ' ἀλόγοις ζῴοισι βατήριον ἐς λέχος ἐλθεῖν.
189 μηδ' ὕβριζε γυναῖκα ἐπ' αἰσχυντοῖς λεχέεσσιν.
190 μὴ παραβῇς εὐνὰς φύσεως ἐς κύπριν ἄθεσμον·
191 οὐδ' αὐτοῖς θήρεσσι συνεύαδον ἄρσενες εὐναί.
192 μηδέ τι θηλύτεραι λέχος ἀνδρῶν μιμήσαιντο.
193 μηδ' ἐς ἔρωτα γυναικὸς ἅπας ῥεύσῃς ἀκάθεκτον·
194 οὐ γὰρ ἔρως θεός ἐστι, πάθος δ' ἀΐδηλον ἁπάντων.
195 στέργε τεὴν ἄλοχον· τί γὰρ ἡδύτερον καὶ ἄρειον,
196 ἢ ὅταν ἀνδρὶ γυνὴ φρονέῃ φίλα γήραος ἄχρις
197 καὶ πόσις ᾗ ἀλόχῳ, μηδ' ἐμπέσῃ ἄνδιχα νεῖκος;
198 μὴ δέ τις ἀμνήστευτα βίῃ κούρῃσι μιγείη.
199 μὴ δὲ γυναῖκα κακὴν πολυχρήματον οἴκαδ' ἄγεσθαι·
200 λατρεύσεις ἀλόχῳ λυγρῆς χάριν εἵνεκα φερνῆς.
201 ἵππους εὐγενέας διζήμεθα γειαρότας τε
202 ταύρους ὑψιτένοντας, ἀτὰρ σκυλάκων πανάριστον·
203 γῆμαι δ' οὐκ ἀγαθὴν ἐριδαίνομεν ἀφρονέοντες·
204 οὐδὲ γυνὴ κακὸν ἄνδρ' ἀπαναίνεται ἀφνεὸν ὄντα.
205 μηδὲ γάμῳ γάμον ἄλλον ἄγοις ἔπι, πήματι πῆμα.
206 μηδ' ἀμφὶ κτεάνων συνομαίμοσιν εἰς ἔριν ἔλθῃς.
207 παισὶν μὴ χαλέπαινε τεοῖς', ἀλλ' ἤπιος εἴης.
208 ἢν δέ τι παῖς ἀλίτῃ σε, κρινάτω υἱέα μήτηρ
209 ἢ καὶ πρεσβύτατοι γενεῆς ἢ δημογέροντες.
210 μὴ μὲν ἐπ' ἄρσενι παιδὶ τρέφειν πλοκάμους ἐπὶ χαίτης·
211 μὴ κορυφὴν πλέξῃς μήθ' ἄμματα λοξὰ κορύμβων·

212   ἄρσεσιν οὐκ ἐπέοικε κομᾶν, χλιδαναῖς δὲ γυναιξίν.
213   παιδὸς δ' εὐμόρφου φρουρεῖν νεοτήσιον ὥρην·
214   πολλοὶ γὰρ λυσσῶσι πρὸς ἄρσενα μεῖξιν ἔρωτος.
215   παρθενικὴν δὲ φύλασσε πολυκλείστοις θαλάμοισιν,
216   μὴ δέ μιν ἄχρι γάμων πρὸ δόμων ὀφθῆμεν ἐάσῃς.
217   κάλλος δυστήρητον ἔφυ παίδων τοκέεσσιν.
219   συγγενέσιν φιλότητα νέμοις ὁσίην θ' ὁμόνοιαν.
220   αἰδεῖσθαι πολιοκροτάφους, εἴκειν δὲ γέρουσιν
221   ἕδρης καὶ γεράων πάντων· γενεῇ δ' ἀτάλαντον
222   πρέσβυν ὁμήλικα πατρὸς ἴσαις τιμαῖσι γέραιρε.
223   γαστρὸς ὀφειλόμενον δασμὸν παρέχειν θεράποντι.
224   δούλῳ τακτὰ νέμοις, ἵνα τοι καταθύμιος εἴη.
225   στίγματα μὴ γράψῃς ἐπονειδίζων θεράποντα.
226   δοῦλον μὴ βλάψῃς τι κακηγορέων παρ' ἄνακτι.
227   λάμβανε καὶ βουλὴν παρὰ οἰκέτου εὖ φρονέοντος.
228   ἄγν' εἴη ψυχῆς οὗ σώματός εἰσι καθαρμοί.
229   ταῦτα δικαιοσύνης μυστήρια, τοῖα βιεῦντες
230   ζωὴν ἐκτελέοιτ' ἀγαθὴν μέχρι γήραος οὐδοῦ.

Index of References

1. Bible

3. Dead Sea Scrolls and Related Texts

4. Apostolic Fathers and New Testament Apocrypha and Pseudepigrapha

5. Rabbinic Literature

6. Classical and Ancient Jewish and Christian Writers and Works

7. Ancient Egyptian Writings

8. Papyri, Inscriptions

Index of Subjects

Index of Modern Authors